CAMBRIDGE
UNIVERSITY PRESS

Sociology

for Cambridge IGCSE™ and O Level

COURSEBOOK

Jonathan Blundell & Katherine Roberts

Shaftesbury Road, Cambridge CB2 8EA, United Kingdom

One Liberty Plaza, 20th Floor, New York, NY 10006, USA

477 Williamstown Road, Port Melbourne, VIC 3207, Australia

314–321, 3rd Floor, Plot 3, Splendor Forum, Jasola District Centre, New Delhi – 110025, India

103 Penang Road, #05–06/07, Visioncrest Commercial, Singapore 238467

Cambridge University Press & Assessment is a department of the University of Cambridge.

We share the University's mission to contribute to society through the pursuit of education, learning and research at the highest international levels of excellence.

www.cambridge.org
Information on this title: www.cambridge.org/9781009282963

© Cambridge University Press & Assessment 2023

First published 2014
Second edition 2023

20 19 18 17 16 15 14 13 12 11 10 9 8 7 6

Printed in Malaysia by Vivar Printing

A catalogue record for this publication is available from the British Library

ISBN 978-1-009-28296-3 Coursebook with digital access
ISBN 978-1-009-28295-6 Digital coursebook

....

....

2022 CAMBRIDGE DEDICATED TEACHER AWARDS

Teachers play an important part in shaping futures. Our Dedicated Teacher Awards recognise the hard work that teachers put in every day.

Thank you to everyone who nominated this year; we have been inspired and moved by all of your stories. Well done to all of our nominees for your dedication to learning and for inspiring the next generation of thinkers, leaders and innovators.

Congratulations to our incredible winners!

WINNER

Regional Winner
Australia, New Zealand & South-East Asia

Mohd Al Khalifa Bin Mohd Affnan
Keningau Vocational College, Malaysia

Regional Winner
Europe

Dr. Mary Shiny Ponparambil Paul
Little Flower English School, Italy

Regional Winner
North & South America

Noemi Falcon
Zora Neale Hurston Elementary School, United States

Regional Winner
Central & Southern Africa

Temitope Adewuyi
Fountain Heights Secondary School, Nigeria

Regional Winner
Middle East & North Africa

Uroosa Imran
Beaconhouse School System KG-1 branch, Pakistan

Regional Winner
East & South Asia

Jeenath Akther
Chittagong Grammar School, Bangladesh

For more information about our dedicated teachers and their stories, go to
dedicatedteacher.cambridge.org

CAMBRIDGE UNIVERSITY PRESS

Brighter Thinking
Better Learning

Building Brighter Futures **Together**

› Contents

> How to use this series

This suite of resources supports learners and teachers following the Cambridge IGCSE™ and O Level Sociology syllabuses (0495, 2251). The components in the series are designed to work together and help learners build sociological knowledge and develop research skills. With clear language and style, they are designed for international learners.

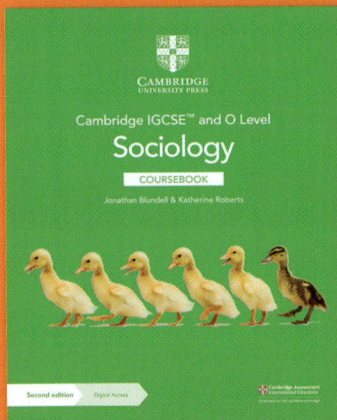

The Coursebook is designed for learners to use in class with guidance from the teacher. It offers complete coverage of the Cambridge IGCSE™ and O Level Sociology syllabuses. Each chapter contains in-depth explanation of sociological concepts, definitions of key terms and a variety of activities and case studies to engage learners, help them make real-world connections and develop their sociological skills.

The Teacher's Resource is the foundation of this series because it offers inspiring ideas about how to teach the course. It contains teaching ideas, suggestions for differentiation, formative assessment, language support, answers and extra materials including topic and language worksheets and editable PowerPoint™ slides for each chapter.

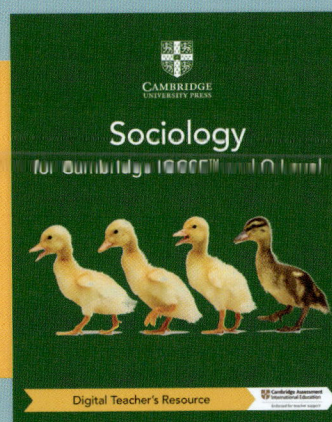

> How to use this book

LEARNING INTENTIONS

These set the scene for each unit, help with navigation through the Coursebook and indicate the important concepts in each topic.

THINK LIKE A SOCIOLOGIST

This feature provides the opportunity for you to use the sociological skills and concepts you have learned about and how they can be applied to real-world scenarios. Sometimes the content in this feature may extend beyond the scope of the syllabus.

KEY TERM

Key vocabulary is highlighted in the text when it is first introduced, and definitions are given in boxes near the vocabulary. You will also find definitions of these words in the Glossary at the back of this book.

KEY POINTS

- Throughout the unit you will see a short series of statements after topics which summarise the key points you have just learnt about.

TIP

Throughout this book, you will study the ways in which these different research approaches or perspectives have been applied to different topics in sociology (families, education, crime and so on). When writing about research methods, you can bring in relevant examples from any of the topic areas.

STRETCH AND CHALLENGE

These are short activities that challenge you to think hard about what you have learned and test the boundaries of your understanding. Sometimes the content in this feature may extend beyond the scope of the syllabus.

ACTIVITIES

There are three types of activities throughout this Coursebook: discussion activities, written activities and research activities. These will help you to develop different learning styles and offer opportunities to produce your own work either individually, or in pairs or groups.

REFLECTION

These activities ask you to reflect on your approach to or performance in other activities and how you might improve this in the future.

CASE STUDY

The case studies and the accompanying questions allow you to actively explore real global sociological issues. You are provided with opportunities to produce your own work either as an individual, in pairs or in groups.

CHECK YOUR UNDERSTANDING

Appearing throughout the units, these questions give you a chance to check how well you have understood the topic you have just covered.

MAKING CONNECTIONS

This feature encourages you to make links between different sociological topics and perspectives and help you to understand how they are connected.

SUMMARY

- This feature contains a series of statements which summarise the key learning points you will have covered in the unit.

KEY SKILLS EXERCISES

These are activities that help you to develop essential sociological skills such as knowledge, analysis and evaluation.

SELF-EVALUATION CHECKLIST

At the end of each unit, you will find a series of statements outlining the content that you should now understand. You might find it helpful to rate how confident you are for each of these statements when you are revising. You should revisit any topics that you rated 'Needs more work' or 'Almost there'.

You should be able to:	Needs more work	Almost there	Ready to move on

PRACTICE QUESTIONS

At the end of each unit, you will find a set of more challenging questions. To answer some of these, you may need to apply what you have learnt in previous units as well as the current unit you are studying.

IMPROVE THIS ANSWER

This is your opportunity to evaluate a sample answer written by the authors and then challenge yourself to write a better one based on the guidance given.

> Introduction

Who is this book for?

This book has been specifically written for the revised Cambridge IGCSE™ and O Level Sociology syllabuses 0495/2251. Its global and international scope also makes it ideal for introducing sociology to young people studying similar courses.

The book is written in language carefully designed to be clear and accessible to 14- to 16-year-olds. Sociology involves the use of many specialist terms; such terms are explained where they first occur in the book and they are also defined in the Glossary.

What makes this book different?

The book shares with the syllabus the aim of making this exciting subject accessible to young people around the world. It brings together the knowledge gained from classic studies in the development of the subject and more recent research findings. It uses examples and case studies from around the world and reflects contemporary developments such as globalisation and the growth of new media. Learners are encouraged to reflect on their learning and to apply their sociological understanding to their own country and social situation.

Introducing Sociology

Humans are social. We cooperate to create and maintain the societies in which we live. We all belong to different groups, some made up of people around us (such as our family or community) and others that link us to people we do not know (such as gender, ethnic group or nationality). To live in a society, we need to learn how to behave in ways that other people will accept. Sociologists study how people live together and how there can be disagreement and conflict.

Sociology is a particular way of looking at what happens in society and the ways in which the people and institutions that make up societies work. Not all sociologists, however, look at the same aspects of society in the same way. In this book, you will learn about some of the different perspectives sociologists have, such as functionalism, Marxism and feminism.

Sociology and the social sciences

Sociology is one of the social sciences. Other social sciences include human geography, economics, political science, international relations and psychology. This group of subjects is different from the natural sciences – which include biology, chemistry and physics – as well as arts and humanities subjects such as history, literature and language.

Social sciences are about people. All the social sciences overlap to some extent; for example, sociologists often draw on ideas from economics and political science. However, they each have a slightly different focus. The focus of sociology is how people live together in societies.

Sociology as a way of thinking

Sociologists are always asking questions. As sociologists, we want to understand why people behave in the ways that they do. To find answers to sociological questions, we have to collect and analyse a range of evidence and examples. We also have to challenge existing ideas that might be wrong or misleading. Sociologists have to be critical thinkers.

For example, a sociologist might ask the following questions about information published on a website:

* Who owns the website?

* Who wrote the content? What experience or qualifications do they have?

* Could they be biased?

* What is the purpose of the website?

* Does it say where the information or ideas are from?

Applying sociology to what is around you

Many people who study sociology find that it becomes more than just another subject that they study. They say it begins to affect how they see things – they notice more and ask more questions. A lot of the time, people accept what is going on around them because it is what they have always known and are familiar with. For example: if in your society, older people (your grandparents' generation) live with their children and grandchildren, you might find it strange that in other societies older people live in homes with other older people to whom they are not related.

As you study sociology, you will come across people and societies whose ways of life, behaviour and values may seem strange to you, perhaps even confusing. As far as possible, try to understand and see life from their point of view. It is likely that your study of sociology will allow you to think more critically about your own society and your own life; this can be uncomfortable, but it is part of learning about the social world around us.

The origins of sociology

Sociology as we know it today grew out of the changes caused by industrialisation in Europe in the 18th century. A Frenchman called Auguste Comte (1798–1857) is often identified as the first sociologist. However, people have always been interested in the things sociologists study and there are people who lived earlier who could also be described as sociologists. For example, Ibn Khaldun (1332–1406), who was born in what is now Tunisia, wrote about the way of life in different societies. At the time, the main distinction was between societies where people had settled in one place, and those whose way of life involved moving around (nomads).

After Comte, sociology gradually became established as an academic discipline, studied in universities in Europe and North America. The origins of sociology are important because they have shaped what the subject is like today. Sociology developed in societies where, at the time, women and minority ethnic groups were usually treated as inferior and had few opportunities to study. This is why the figures who have had the most notable influence on the study of sociology today – the so-called founding fathers: Marx, Durkheim and Weber – were all white men. However, other important thinkers (usually those unable to go to university) who contributed to sociological thought are gradually being given more attention. They include Mary Wollstonecraft (1759–1797), a British woman who wrote about the position of women in society, and W.E.B. Du Bois (1868–1963), an African American who wrote about racism in the USA.

Traditional and modern societies

In the past, it was common for sociologists to assume that there were two basic types of society. Societies that had existed for centuries, or longer, were thought of as 'traditional societies'. In these societies, people lived in small communities, supporting themselves by hunting and farming. Over time, some of these societies began to change, evolving into so-called 'modern industrial societies'. In these, many people lived in cities and worked in industries and people moved around much more. These changes were thought to affect many areas of social life; for example, people began living in nuclear families rather than extended families (see Unit 4) and adopted different values (for example, often becoming less religious). Some people assumed that eventually the whole world would be 'modern', leading to the disappearance of traditional societies.

The differences between these two types of society seemed so clear that two different subjects developed. Sociologists focused on modern industrial societies, while anthropologists studied traditional societies. Both sociologists and anthropologists were mainly from Europe and North America. Some early anthropologists thought of the traditional societies they studied as 'primitive' and saw their beliefs as 'superstitions'; they assumed that their own society was more advanced and superior. Other anthropologists, however, became deeply involved in the lives of the people they studied, seeing things from their point of view and finding much to admire. The anthropological method of living with the people under study, trying to see things through their eyes, developed into participant observation in sociology (see Unit 1).

Seeing things as either one thing or another (known as a dichotomy) is almost always misleading in sociology. Sociologists now recognise that social life is more complicated than 'traditional vs modern'. There are many aspects of 'modern' societies that are traditional; for example, traditional festivals are celebrated and extended families are important. Equally, supposedly traditional societies – when examined more closely – often have features we associate with modern societies. Sociologists today try to avoid seeing things in a dichotomous or simplistic way. Societies are constantly changing in a variety of ways and for a variety of reasons, and the job of the sociologist is to observe and understand these changes, without making assumptions.

The sociology of WEIRD people

It is, perhaps, natural for people to be most interested in their own experiences and in people like themselves. Sociology as a subject, studied first in universities and later in schools, evolved in Europe and North America. As a result, most sociological research has focused on these regions: sociologists of the past focused on understanding the societies in which they lived and the issues facing those societies and their populations.

This Western focus also applies to other subjects, such as psychology. The psychologist Joseph Henrich has argued that psychological research tends to focus on WEIRD people. The term does not contain any moral judgement; rather, it stands for:

- Western
- Educated
- Industrialised
- Rich
- Democratic.

The same is true of sociological research: it tends to focus on particular people and societies that are different in some ways from most of the world's population. (Henrich, J., 2021)

Sociology goes global

All of this means that many of the research findings and the theories in this book are about Henrich's 'weird' people. This is inevitable, as most research has been conducted with 'weird' people and by 'weird' people. So far, little sociological research has been performed in societies that are not Western, educated, industrialised, rich or democratic.

Now that most countries have universities, however, people are studying sociology all over the world – and they are turning their attention to their own societies. Sociology is becoming a truly global subject (the International Sociological Association, for example, brings together sociologists from around the world to share ideas and knowledge) and we have tried to include in this book ideas and examples from different parts of the globe. The fact that you are studying Cambridge IGCSE™ Sociology, wherever you are, is also a small step towards making sociology as global and inclusive as possible.

How will you be assessed in Cambridge IGCSE™ Sociology?

The information in this section is based on the Cambridge International syllabus. You should always refer to the appropriate syllabus document for the year of examination to confirm the details and for more information. The syllabus document is available on the Cambridge International website at www.cambridgeinternational.org.

The Cambridge IGCSE™ and O Level syllabuses are examined by two papers. On the first paper, three topics will be assessed:

Research methods; Identity: self and society; Social stratification and inequality

These three topics are covered in the first three chapters of this book. Together, these topics will provide learners with the basic sociological skills and knowledge needed for studying other topic areas.

The second paper contains three more topics:

Family; Education; Crime, deviance and social control

In the assessment, learners only need to answer questions on two of these three topics. These topics are covered in the second three chapters of this book.

The final chapter focuses on the skills learners will need to prepare for assessment. In both papers, learners are assessed against three assessment objectives:

1   **AO1 Knowledge and understanding**

    Demonstrate knowledge and understanding of sociological concepts, theories, evidence, views and research methods.

2   **AO2 Interpretation and application**

    a   Apply relevant sociological concepts, theories, evidence, views and research methods to support points or develop arguments.

    b   Explain how sociological concepts, theories, evidence, views and research methods apply to a particular issue or question.

3   **AO3 Analysis and evaluation**

    Analyse and evaluate sociological theories, evidence, views and research methods:

    a   Explain the strengths and limitations of sociological theories, views and research methods.

    b   Construct, develop and discuss sociological arguments.

    c   Reach conclusions and make judgements based on a reasoned consideration of available evidence.

Getting started

You are almost ready! Hopefully, you now feel confident about starting to learn about sociology.

Sociology is an exciting and relevant subject. During this course, and especially learning from this book, you will have many opportunities to 'think like a sociologist' and apply your learning to the world around you. Studying sociology will change the way you think about your life and understand your society. We hope you enjoy it!

Command words

Questions have content words and command words or phrases. Look at this example question:

*Explain **three** aspects of the feminist view of socialisation.*

In this example, 'explain' is the command word and 'the feminist view of socialisation' is the content phrase. Content words and phrases tell you what to write about, while command words tell you *how* to write about them. Command words are associated with the assessment objectives, so they help you to work out what skills you should demonstrate in your answer.

The assessment objectives may be associated with the following command words:

- AO1 Knowledge and understanding: define, give

- AO2 Interpretation of evidence: describe, outline

- AO3 Analysis and evaluation: evaluate, discuss

Different questions have different numbers of marks for each AO. You do not need to worry about this: the questions will be worded to show the skills that are required. It is important, however, to do exactly what the question says.

Usually, questions using an AO3 command word will also cover AO1. This is because you can only analyse and evaluate the sociological knowledge you present. It is particularly important to recognise when AO3 skills are required: for these questions, you must show that you can analyse and evaluate the information you present.

The command words and definitions in the following table are taken from the Cambridge IGCSE™ and O Level syllabuses 0495/2251 for first examination in 2025. Always refer to the appropriate syllabus document for the year of your examination to confirm the details and for more information. The syllabuses documents are available on the Cambridge International website at www.cambridgeinternational.org. The guidance in this table has been written by the authors.

Command word	Definition	Guidance	How to approach these questions
Assess	Make an informed judgment	Compare the advantages and disadvantages of a particular issue and come to a supported conclusion.	Make an overall judgement or decision; e.g. on whether strengths outweigh limitations.
Define	Give precise meaning	The terms to be defined are likely to be key terms included in the Glossary.	Show clearly that you understand the term; you do not need to use the exact wording from the Coursebook. In your definition, do not repeat words that are part of the term you are asked to define.
Describe	State the points of a topic/give characteristics and main features	Expand on a topic or point.	Describing involves giving the key points about something, to show understanding of its overall nature.

Command word	Definition	Guidance	How to approach these questions
Develop	Take forward to a more advanced stage or build upon given information	Go a step further than identifying or giving a point.	Develop your answer to a 'define' or 'identify' question.
Discuss	Write about issue(s) or topic(s) in depth in a structured way	Give a number of points about an issue or topic.	Approach this in a critical way: you are not asked to evaluate but you can show, for example, how ideas are linked.
Evaluate	Judge or calculate the quality, importance, amount, or value of something	Examine the issue or topic thoroughly and reach a judgement based on this.	Include a balanced judgement or conclusion at the end of your answer.
Explain	Set out purposes or reasons/ make the relationships between things clear/say why and/or how and support with relevant evidence	Give more detail than for a 'define' or 'identify' question; for example, say more or give an example.	Give reasons and evidence to develop your answer to a 'define' or 'identify' question.
Give	Produce an answer from a given source or recall/memory	Identify a point; a word or phrase may be sufficient.	Make sure the point you identify is clearly relevant to the question.
Identify	Name/select/recognise	Identify a point; a word or phrase may be sufficient.	Make sure the point you identify is clearly relevant to the question.
Justify	Support a case with evidence/argument	Come to a conclusion and support this with evidence.	Reach a conclusion and support this with developed evaluative comments.
Outline	Set out the main points	As with 'discuss', give a number of points about an issue or topic.	Develop each point by giving some additional information.
State	Express in clear terms	Identify a point as clearly as possible.	Make sure that the point you identify is clearly relevant to the question.
Suggest	Apply knowledge and understanding to situations where there is a range of valid responses in order to make proposals/put forward considerations	Put forward answers that are plausible, with sufficient detail (if asked for) to explain why they are appropriate.	The nature of sociology means that there are not always 'correct' answers. This word allows you to use your sociological imagination to put forward an explanation or interpretation.
Summarise	Select and present the main points, without detail	Decide on the most important points to include in your summary.	There is no need to add detail or examples: you are being asked for a summary only.

› Unit 1
Research methods

LEARNING INTENTIONS

In this unit you will learn how to:

- Understand the differences between the positivist approach and the interpretivist approach to researching society

- Evaluate different research choices using ideas including validity, reliability, representativeness and generalisability

- Describe and evaluate the types of data and evidence that sociologists use, including primary and secondary data and qualitative and quantitative data

- Understand differences in the ways that primary and secondary data can be interpreted and analysed

- Describe and understand the different stages in research design

- Understand the sampling process, including different sampling techniques and their strengths and weaknesses

- Understand some of the main research methods for collecting primary data and their strengths and limitations

- Consider theoretical, practical and ethical issues affecting research.

Introduction

This unit looks at how sociologists approach the study of society and the types of information and data they use. Different sociologists use approaches that are based on very different ideas about the relationship between people and societies; as a result, the methods they use are also very different from each other. In this unit, you will learn about the important features of different research methods.

1.1 How do sociologists approach the study of society?

In all sciences, including social sciences, the methods used to carry out research are important. Sociologists use a range of different methods. They choose methods that are appropriate for what is being studied and for what they want to find out. If the methods are appropriate and implemented well, other researchers – and society in general – are more likely to accept that the research findings add to our knowledge. If the method is not chosen or carried out well, the research will be criticised by other researchers and the findings may be rejected.

Positivism

There are two main approaches or **perspectives** in sociology: **positivism** and interpretivism. Positivist approaches focus on large-scale (**macro**) social structures and institutions, rather than on individuals.

The positivist approach concentrates on producing **quantitative data**, usually in the form of statistics. Positivism is based on the belief that, as far as possible, sociology should use the same research methods as the natural sciences such as physics, chemistry and biology.

This approach in sociology goes back to the 19th and early 20th centuries and sociologists such as Auguste Comte and Emile Durkheim, who saw the growing ability of the natural sciences to understand and predict the workings of the natural world. They believed that there were laws of social behaviour that could be discovered using similar methods, and so they advocated the use of **scientific method** in sociology.

A key part of the scientific method is **reliability**. This refers to the extent to which the research findings can be confirmed if the study is repeated (replicated). Science experiments can be carried out again in exactly the same way and in the same conditions, because they follow standardised procedures. If the experiment is reliable, the same results should be obtained each time. Positivists value reliability in their research and so they use standardised methods which can be reproduced as accurately as possible, to allow the confirmation of results.

Scientists try to be **objective**. They try to be neutral, to avoid **bias** and to discover the truth, rather than being guided by their values and by what they would *like* to be true. If a researcher can be objective, the results will be unbiased, giving an accurate account of what really happened. Critics have pointed out that this is probably impossible. For example, scientists' research is influenced by their values from the very beginning, because they *choose* to research something they think is important. The positivist view is that sociologists should aim to be as objective as possible – even though scientists cannot be completely objective.

KEY TERMS

perspectives: ways of viewing society and social life

positivism: an approach to sociology which takes a macro (large-scale) view of society and is based on studying society in a scientific manner, using quantitative methods

macro approaches: approaches that take a large-scale view of whole societies

quantitative data/research: information and facts that take a numerical form. Quantitative research generates this kind of data

scientific method: the way in which scientists work, by observing, formulating and testing hypotheses, analysing the results and drawing conclusions

reliability: when research can be repeated to produce similar responses

objectivity: being open-minded and avoiding bias

bias: when a researcher is not neutral in carrying out their research

Positivists favour experiments, using standard methods (based on ones used in the natural sciences) to produce quantitative data. However, it is often difficult to carry out experiments in sociology. As a result, positivists tend to use official statistics, social surveys and questionnaires instead, since they also produce quantitative data.

When analysing quantitative data, positivists look for **patterns** and **trends**. Patterns are links between variables: for example, data might show that people from certain age groups are more likely to commit crime, or that women are more likely to do a certain job than men. Trends are changes over time. Quantitative data in the form of statistics is often produced annually, or every few years, so positivists can look for trends in the data – such as whether the number of marriages in the population is increasing, or whether the number of crimes committed is going down.

A well-known example of a positivist approach is the work of Emile Durkheim on suicide, published over 100 years ago. Durkheim argued that behaviour is governed by **social facts** – laws, values, customs and other social rules over which we have no control. He also discussed social forces: the pressures on us and our behaviour which come from our relationships with others and the expectations of society. We may think of suicide as an individual act, motivated by private troubles. However, Durkheim wanted to show that it is linked to social facts and social forces and, specifically, to the way societies are organised.

Durkheim noticed that suicide rates (the proportion of a population who committed suicide each year) in a country did not change much – there were no obvious trends. However, there were significant differences in suicide rates between countries, so there were patterns within suicide statistics. Durkheim tried to show that social forces affected individual actions (such as suicide) and led to the different suicide rates. An example of a social force is the connection between individuals and support networks, such as families and religious organisations. In societies with strong connections – such as high rates of religious belief or strong family values – there were lower suicide rates. However, there were higher suicide rates in countries with weaker levels of religious control. Thus, according to Durkheim (and other positivists), suicide rates show us something about the nature of a society – not about individuals.

Durkheim used a scientific method. Like other positivists, he took a large-scale view and looked for **correlation** and **causation** between variables. Correlation is when two or more variables change at the same time, which suggests that the changes are related to each other. Causation is

Figure 1.1: Emile Durkheim.

when one variable has a direct effect on another, bringing about a change. In the case of suicide, Durkheim found a correlation between the type of religion in a country and that country's suicide rate. Where the religion brought people together with a strong sense of belonging and community, the suicide rate was low. Where the religion played a lesser role and people behaved more as individuals, the suicide rate was higher.

KEY TERMS

patterns: links between different variables, for example gender, ethnicity or age

trends: changes over time in a particular direction

social facts: laws, values, customs and other social rules over which individuals have no control

correlation: when two variables change at the same time, suggesting they are connected

causation: when a change in one variable has a direct effect on another variable

Interpretivism

Interpretivists take a different view from positivists. They argue that there are key differences between the subject matter of sociology and natural science. Humans are active, conscious beings who make choices about how to behave. Their behaviour cannot easily be predicted. This means that people's behaviour cannot be studied in the same way as scientists study things like cells, chemicals and forces in the natural world.

An interpretivist approach focuses on the individual rather than society, and on the **micro** scale rather than the macro scale. Focusing on small-scale interactions often means studying individuals and small groups rather than whole societies. Interpretivists believe individuals are in control: people make the societies they live in and change them through their actions. We are born into particular societies but, although we learn the norms and values of the society we grow up in, we do not have to accept them. Instead, these norms and values change continuously over time as people's ideas change. Interpretivists are interested in how individuals make sense of society and of social actions – the things they do, their meanings and motivations.

Interpretivists say that social reality does not exist separately from human actions; rather, it is embedded in these actions. Sociologists need to understand how people make sense of the social reality around them before they can understand their actions. Interpretivists argue that if we want to understand an individual's actions, we first have to understand the motivations behind them and their meanings from the individual's point of view. This way of understanding society is sometimes called **verstehen**, a word used by the German sociologist Max Weber, meaning to see things from the point of view of others.

According to interpretivists, the subject of sociology is so different from the natural sciences that sociologists need to use different methods. Positivists may be able to *describe* the social world using quantitative data, but interpretivists think it is more important to *understand* why people behave as they do. Where positivists prefer experiments and surveys, interpretivists prefer to use methods that produce **qualitative data**, such as unstructured interviews and participant observation, which are more helpful in uncovering why people behave as they do.

For example, a positivist may be able to say how many people commit different types of crime, while an interpretivist will want to find out *why* those people commit crimes.

While interpretivists are not very concerned about reliability – since they do not take a scientific approach – they do value **validity** in their research. Validity refers to the extent to which the research findings accurately reflect reality and give a true picture. An interpretivist would see the findings of in-depth research methods (such as unstructured interviews) as more valid than the findings of a questionnaire, because the in-depth methods allow the researcher to develop a detailed understanding of the respondents and how they actually feel about the issue being researched.

Interpretivists are less concerned about objectivity than positivists. Rather than trying to be neutral (which they argue may not be possible), they feel that sociologists should be open about who they are and why they are doing the research. **Subjectivity** – the particular viewpoint of the researcher – can be more important than trying to be objective.

KEY TERMS

interpretivism: approaches that start at the level of the individual, focusing on small-scale interactions and usually favouring qualitative methods

micro approaches: approaches that take a small-scale view of social interaction between individuals and groups in society

verstehen: a German word used to mean identifying with another person or group and seeing things from their point of view

qualitative data/research: information (such as attitudes or kinds of actions) that cannot be presented in numerical form; qualitative research generates this kind of data

validity: the extent to which research findings reflect reality and give a true picture

subjectivity: allowing a personal point of view to influence understanding and interpretation

Approaches that combine different research methods and evidence

Triangulation

Triangulation is when a researcher decides to use a variety of research methods, usually including both qualitative and quantitative data. This has many advantages and is common in sociology. For example, a study may be conducted based on both observation and structured interviews, or on both closed questionnaires and diaries.

KEY TERM

triangulation: use of two or more methods in the same research project

Strengths and limitations of triangulation

Strengths:

- It can allow the researcher to support quantitative data with qualitative examples, giving a study both reliability and validity.
- It can be used to check the validity of the research.
- It can be used to check the reliability of the research using different sources.

- It can be used to cross-reference the researcher's interpretations of other data collected, to check for accuracy.
- It can provide balance between methods, where one may be weaker than another in a particular area of research.

Limitations:

- Using several methods is time-consuming and expensive.
- The researcher needs to be skilled in several research methods.
- Positivist and interpretivist approaches are based on very different ideas, so it may be difficult to combine them in one piece of research.

Longitudinal studies

Longitudinal studies are carried out at intervals, over a period of time, rather than as a one-off piece of research. Longitudinal research is often used by government-funded research organisations to study basic questions about changing lifestyle, health, illnesses, education and employment and find out about changes over time. The census, carried out by governments in many countries every ten years, can be seen as a type of longitudinal study.

In most longitudinal studies, the same **sample** is used each time. The group of people or households being studied is called the panel or the panel sample. Panel members are interviewed or complete questionnaires on a regular basis, with a period of months or years between interviews. The key requirement of panel studies is that, as far as possible, the respondents are the same people throughout the study. This is also one of the main disadvantages of longitudinal studies, because respondents in the original sample may drop out of the research at a later stage.

KEY TERMS

longitudinal study: research taking place at intervals over a long period of time

sample: the group of people on whom research is carried out, used to represent the target population

this affects the **representativeness**. However, a strength of longitudinal studies is that they do not rely on people's memory or provide a 'snapshot' of people's opinions. Instead, they allow researchers to find out how people's lives, views and actions change over time.

KEY TERM

representativeness: the degree to which research findings about one group can be applied to a larger group or similar groups

ACTIVITY: RESEARCH 1.1

The Centre for Longitudinal Studies in London runs four longitudinal studies. Search online for the CLS website and view the homepage.

Working with three other learners, each choose one of the four projects. Click on it to find out more, then write a short summary to share with the others in your group.

CASE STUDY 1.1

The *Up* series – a television longitudinal study which went global

The *Up* series is a longitudinal study in the form of a television documentary which began in the UK in 1956. In *7-up*, a group of 7-year-old children were interviewed about their lives, their families and their future ambitions. Then they were revisited every seven years by the same documentary makers. Clips from what they had said in previous years were put together with updates and new interviews. This television series proved very popular, giving viewers an insight into how the lives of people from various social backgrounds developed and changed over the decades. The series is still being made – with many of the original participants still taking part – and the most recent version, *63-up*, was shown in the UK in 2019. A new UK version was started in 2000, with another set of 7-year olds.

This longitudinal research-based documentary series has also been copied in other countries. In the USA, they started with *Aged 7 in America* in 1991, and similar programmes have been made in Japan, South Africa, Russia, Sweden, France, Denmark and Australia.

Figure 1.2: 7-up children.

Task

1   In what ways does the data gathered in longitudinal research differ from information gathered in a one-off interview or questionnaire?

2   How might the individuals involved in a longitudinal study such as the *Up* series be affected by taking part in this research?

In Activity: Research 1.1, did you and the others in your group include the same kinds of information in your summaries, or did you focus on different things?

How did you decide which information to include in your summary and what to leave out?

Having heard the summaries from other members of your group, is there anything you would change about yours?

Strengths and limitations of longitudinal research

Strengths:

- One of the standard criticisms of a lot of research is that it only gives us a 'snapshot' view of society – what things are like at one moment in time. A study based on questionnaires or interviews may tell us how some people think or behave in specific respects. But longitudinal research can show us how people's lives change over time. This is a great advantage of this type of research.

- It becomes possible to see what factors may have caused changes in people's lives over time.

- Because the respondents have to be committed to the research, there is a good chance that they will provide valid data.

Limitations:

- This kind of research requires a considerable commitment of time and funding over a long period.

- There are, inevitably, people who stop participating in the research. This is known as sample attrition. It happens because individuals die, move away or decide they do not want to take part anymore. One way of dealing with this problem is by following individuals wherever they go and also by including new household members to 'top up' the original sample (for example, when a child becomes an adult and marries, their partner will be invited to join the study). This keeps the total numbers roughly the same, but there is some movement of individuals into and out of the study at each wave.

- Being part of research like this may change the participants. Sociologists call this the Hawthorne Effect.

Someone taking part in this kind of research may start to think more carefully about aspects of their lives they are questioned about; this may lead them to act differently or even make different choices.

The analysis and evaluation of research choices

Bias

Bias may come from the researcher's values, such as their political views. Positivists argue that researchers should be neutral and objective, so the findings would be the same regardless of who carries out the research and analyses the findings. Interpretivists argue that because sociology is about people, it is not possible to be completely unbiased. Researcher or **interviewer bias** – which may include the ways in which the interviewer asks questions or interprets answers – will inevitably have an effect on the research findings.

interviewer bias: ways in which the interviewer asks questions or interprets answers that have an effect on the findings

Even deciding what to research is likely to be influenced by the researcher's values. Thus, researchers should be completely open about any bias so that readers can make their own decisions about the validity and reliability of the findings. This approach has been adopted by many feminist researchers, who tend to take an interpretivist approach.

The ways in which researchers can influence the findings is called researcher imposition; that is, the problem of the researcher imposing themselves or their values on the research. This can happen because the social characteristics of the researcher (gender, age and so on) influence the answers given or the behaviour observed, or because the researcher words questions or analyses data in particular ways. The findings of sociological research need to be interpreted; we cannot assume that the meaning is clear to everyone. When interpreting research, we need to be aware of any bias that may have influenced it.

Interviewer effect

Since any interview involves at least two people, the respondent and the interviewer, the responses may be affected by **interviewer effect**. This is when the answers are affected by, for example, the interviewer's sex, age or ethnicity or their reaction to the answers received. People being interviewed may adjust their answers to give the interviewer a particular impression of themselves. For example, the interviewee may not want to offend the interviewer or give an answer they think the interviewer will disapprove of.

Hawthorne effect or observer effect

While the interviewer effect is an issue for interviews, the **Hawthorne or observer effect** is an issue in research that involves observing people. It refers to the ways people change their behaviour when they know they are being watched. As with the interviewer effect, this can be because they want to give the observer a particular impression of themselves, or simply because they are more aware of their actions due to being observed.

KEY TERMS

interviewer effect: ways in which an interviewer may influence participants' responses, for example through their characteristics, appearance or verbal cues, such as facial expressions and tone of voice

Hawthorne or observer effect: the unintended effects of the researcher's presence on the behaviour or responses of the people being studied

The name Hawthorne comes from an American factory where this effect was observed. Researchers wanted to find out how to increase productivity – the amount of work the workers did – so they changed a number of variables, such as the temperature and lighting in the

factory, to see what effect the changes had. They found that whatever variable they changed, the workers worked harder. The researchers realised that this was not because of the changes to variables, but because the workers knew they were being observed and their productivity was being recorded.

You may have noticed a similar effect in your school or college. When a visitor is in a classroom, both the learners and the teacher may behave differently.

Figure 1.3: The Hawthorne or observer effect.

Validity

As mentioned earlier, validity refers to the extent to which the research findings accurately reflect reality. The findings of participant observation and unstructured interviews are usually said to be valid because they are detailed and give an in-depth understanding of how the respondents feel about the research topic and how they actually behave, rather than just how they say they behave in a questionnaire. In these situations, it is more difficult for the respondents to mislead the researcher or provide false information. However, while these methods produce valid findings, their reliability is not as strong. These methods are favoured by interpretivists, who see validity as more important than reliability.

Reliability

As we have seen, reliability refers to the extent to which research findings can be confirmed by repeating the study.

Although it is difficult to replicate sociological research exactly, research which uses standardised procedures and can be repeated with a similarly representative sample should produce broadly similar results (allowing for individual differences within a sample). Questionnaires and structured interviews are more reliable than participant observation and unstructured interviews, because they have a standardised set of questions and so can be carried out many times with no variation in the procedures. However, these methods tend to be less valid, because standardised, closed questions do not allow respondents to expand on their answers or go into any detail about how they really feel. Such inflexible methods may not give a true picture of how the respondent really feels or behaves, and why.

TIP

Many learners think that reliability and validity are similar or confuse them with each other. It is important to understand how they differ and use them in the right way. Reliability tends to link with the structured, quantitative methods associated with positivism, whereas validity is associated with qualitative, in-depth research favoured by interpretivists.

Representativeness and generalisability

Most research is not carried out on the whole population being studied – the **target population**. Instead, it will focus on a smaller sample of people used to represent this target population. The sample used for the research must be representative of the target population. This means it must be, in effect, a smaller version of the population being studied, with the same proportions of people of different genders, ages and so on (according to what is relevant to the research). The researcher can then claim that the findings of the research apply not only to the sample but to the target population as a whole. If findings can be applied to a larger group of people than those who actually took part in the research, this is called **generalisability**.

Samples do not include the whole target population, so there are always differences between the results for a sample and the results for the target population. This is called sampling error. Researchers reduce sampling error by having a large random sample or using a representative **sampling method** to select their sample. The different types of sampling method – techniques to select a sample – are explained in section 1.2.

KEY TERMS

target population: the whole group that the research relates to and to whom the findings of the research will be applied

generalisability: when the findings about a sample can be said to apply to a larger group of people sharing the same characteristics

sampling methods/techniques: the different ways in which samples can be chosen

---

CHECK YOUR UNDERSTANDING 1.1

Work with another learner. One of you choose the positivist approach, the other the interpretivist approach. Without reading from your notes, explain the main points about your approach to your partner in one minute. Your partner should then ask you to say more about any points that were not clear. Then check the book and your notes to make sure what you said was correct.

You will now have a clearer understanding of both approaches. Draw a poster for display, showing the main points about the approach you chose.

ACTIVITY: DISCUSSION 1.1

Work in a group with three or four other learners. For each of the following, discuss whether a positivist approach or an interpretist approach would be better.

a   Researching why boys and girls tend to choose different school subject options

b   Researching which family members learners in your school or college live with

c   Researching what activities young people take part in in their free time.

REFLECTION

To what extent were members of your group able to agree? Did you find that your opinions changed as the discussion went on?

KEY POINTS

- Sociologists use two broad approaches to study society.

- The **positivist approach** argues that sociology should be as scientific as possible. This involves:

  - taking a macro view

  - studying social facts

  - producing quantitative data

  - looking for causation and correlation, patterns and trends

  - objectivity

  - reliability.

- The **interpretivist approach** argues that sociology cannot be scientific and should instead involve:

  - taking a micro view

  - studying meanings and motivations

  - producing qualitative data

  - trying to achieve verstehen

  - subjectivity

  - validity.

1.2 What types of data and evidence do sociologists use?

Differences between primary and secondary sources of data

Primary data are collected by the researcher using methods such as questionnaires, interviews or observations. **Secondary data** are data that already exist, having previously been gathered by an earlier researcher

or organisation (at which time they were primary data). In most research projects, the researcher first studies all the published research on the topic under investigation (secondary data). Then they carry out research that produces new primary data, adding to knowledge on the topic and supporting or questioning the secondary data.

Sociologists use four main types of secondary data:

- official statistics produced by government or official organisations

- research by other sociologists, journalists and the government

- the media (television, radio, internet, newspapers and magazines)

- other sources, mainly of qualitative data, such as diaries, letters and photographs.

KEY TERMS

primary data: information collected by the sociologist using methods such as questionnaires, interviews or observations

secondary data: information collected earlier by researchers or other organisations and used later by a sociologist

Strengths and limitations of primary data

Strengths:

- As the researcher carried out the research themselves, they know how valid and reliable it is. They also know of any flaws or problems with the sources.

- The research will have been designed to focus on the researcher's exact purpose and questions. The researcher will not need to adjust data collected by a different researcher for a slightly different purpose.

- The data are likely to be up to date.

Limitations:

- The data may be affected by interviewer bias and researcher imposition.

- Carrying out the research is likely to be more costly and time-consuming than finding secondary sources.

Strengths and limitations of secondary data

Strengths:

- Secondary sources are easily accessible; vast amounts of information are available on the internet and there is often no cost to access this.

- Secondary sources contain the accumulated knowledge on a topic. It is important for the researcher to be familiar with this before starting their own research.

- When researching certain topics – such as crime – it may be difficult to conduct primary research due to access issues or ethical issues. In these cases, secondary data are a valuable source of information.

Limitations:

- Older secondary data may be out of date.

- When there is a lot of secondary data on a topic, it can be difficult to decide what is the most relevant and useful.

- The details that are needed to assess a secondary source of data (such as information about sample sizes) may not be available.

- Secondary data have usually been interpreted and explained by others, so the researcher's view of the data may be influenced by this.

- Secondary data have often been collected for a specific purpose and may be biased.

THINK LIKE A SOCIOLOGIST

If you wanted to complete some research about the amount of employment in different types of industry in your country or local area, would it be better to use secondary data or primary data? Explain why.

Differences between qualitative and quantitative data

Both primary and secondary data can be either quantitative or qualitative. Qualitative data are descriptive, rather than numerical, and are in written or visual form. They are usually in the form of words describing phenomena. Secondary qualitative data include historical and personal documents, diaries and media content. Primary qualitative data may include detailed information from unstructured interviews or participant observation, for example.

Quantitative data are produced as numbers that can be used for statistics. Secondary quantitative data include numerical data from official statistics. Primary quantitative data may come from multiple-choice questions in structured questionnaires or interviews. Quantitative data can be displayed in diagrams, charts and graphs.

Positivists tend to prefer quantitative data, while interpretivists prefer qualitative data.

Strengths and limitations of qualitative data

Strengths:

- More in-depth.

- Provides an understanding of the meanings and motivations behind respondents' actions.

- More valid due to greater depth and detail.

- More led by the respondent, so the researcher is less likely to impose their own perspective.

Limitations:

- Less reliable because research is difficult to replicate.

- Difficult to generalise from, as samples are usually small and may not be representative.

- More time-consuming to gather and process the data than most methods producing quantitative data.

- Difficult to make comparisons or to identify patterns and trends.

Strengths and limitations of quantitative data

Strengths:

- More reliable because the research can be replicated and should produce the same or similar results due to standardised procedures.

- More objective because the researcher will not have much contact with the respondent and can remain unbiased.

- Can have large samples, which make generalisation possible.

- Can be presented in visual forms that help understanding, such as graphs and tables.

- Can make comparisons and identify patterns and trends.

Limitations:

- Lacking in validity; respondents in surveys cannot explain their answers fully to give a true picture.

- Difficult to gain an understanding of the meanings behind the data, so it does not achieve verstehen.

- The terms of the research are usually imposed by the researcher, such as standardised questions in a survey, which could lead to biased results.

Secondary data in more detail

Quantitative secondary data: official statistics

Official statistics are the main source of secondary quantitative data for sociologists and are widely used. They consist of numerical data produced by national and local governments and official bodies. It is useful to make a distinction between hard and soft statistics.

> ### KEY TERM
>
> **official statistics:** statistical data produced by government and official agencies

Hard statistics are those that should be complete accurate, apart from any errors or incompleteness. For example, in most countries, records are kept of all births, marriages and deaths. The number of people found guilty of a particular crime is also a hard statistic, since it simply involves counting the total number of guilty verdicts.

Soft statistics, on the other hand, depend on people making decisions about what to record and how. These decisions may lead to different statistics and there may be changes over time in what is recorded. Soft statistics include unemployment statistics and statistics showing how many crimes have taken place, because decisions are made about what to include and how to compile the statistics.

Figure 1.4: Official statistics are an important source of secondary quantitative data.

Strengths and limitations of official statistics

Strengths:

- They are readily available, often free of charge and on the internet, so they are cheap and easy to use. Governments have spent more time and resources collecting these statistics than a sociologist would be able to.

- They are usually produced by research that is well-planned and well organised, using large samples. They are likely to be reliable and representative, so they can be used to identify patterns.

- They are often repeated every year or every few years, so they show changes over time (for example, in crime, unemployment and divorce rates). This makes it possible to identify trends.

- They allow researchers to make comparisons, such as between men and women or between different areas of a country.

- They are widely used to help governments and other organisations plan ahead. They provide information that is useful to policymakers as well as sociologists.

- They have already been produced and are publicly available, so there are unlikely to be any ethical issues when using them.

Limitations:

- They lack validity, reducing everything to numbers and not showing any detail or reasons behind the data. This means they do not necessarily give a true picture.

- Interpretivists argue that statistics are socially constructed, not objective facts. Official statistics do not always mean what they seem to mean. For example, statistics showing an increase in speeding offences may not really mean there has been an increase in such offences. They may simply mean that the police have been spending more time and resources on detecting speeding, so more offences are being recorded. This further reduces the validity of official statistics.

- Statistics are rarely as complete or accurate as they appear or claim to be. For example, it is thought that the 2010 US census missed out more than a million people.

- Official statistics have been produced by others and are unlikely to contain exactly what a sociologist would like to know. For example, sociologists might want to know how many marriages break down, but official statistics will only count divorces and not separations.

- Official statistics are funded by a government, which means that politics can affect the statistics. Statistics may be biased in favour of the government and presented to show things in the best light. When statistics would be embarrassing for the government, they may not be published or they may never be collected in the first place.

- A researcher can only make comparisons over time if the same phenomenon has been measured in the same way at every stage. For example, if a government passes a new law making a certain activity illegal, the crime rate will go up even if people's behaviour has not changed.

As well as official statistics, sociologists can use other widely available **non-official statistics**. These include data from research commissioned by organisations such as religious groups, charities and policy institutes (often called 'think-tanks' in the media).

ACTIVITY: WRITTEN 1.1

1   List as many examples as you can think of for:

a   hard statistics

b   soft statistics

2   Use a government or news website to find some official statistics relating to your country.

3   Write a paragraph about the statistics you have found, including:

- who the statistics were produced by

- what the statistics show

- whether they are hard or soft statistics

- how a sociologist might use them in their research.

MAKING CONNECTIONS

Most countries produce official statistics related to education. (You will study the topic of education in Unit 4.) What types of educational statistics are gathered in your country?

Historical and personal documents

Historical and personal documents are a source of qualitative secondary data sometimes used by sociologists in their research. **Historical documents** will have been produced in the past and so may be useful to investigate how societies have changed over time.

KEY TERMS

non-official statistics: statistical data produced by other organisations, such as charities and think-tanks

historical documents: written sources from the past used as sources of information by sociologists

Historical documents include first-person accounts, such as letters and diaries, referred to as **personal documents**. The researcher will need to be aware that personal accounts may not be representative. For example, famous people (including politicians and leaders) may write letters and diaries with the intention that they will be published at some time in the future. It is likely that – deliberately or otherwise – they will give a favourable view of themselves and their actions. The researcher will need to check the validity of their accounts against other sources.

Other letters and diaries are written without the intention that they should be read by anyone else. These documents will be less easy for the researcher to obtain, since the writer or their family may feel that they are private, and may not make them available or even let others know that they exist. However, if such documents can be used, they have greater validity than letters and diaries written for publication. One famous example is the diary of Anne Frank, a Jewish child who, during the Second World War, went into hiding from the Nazis with her family in a house in Amsterdam.

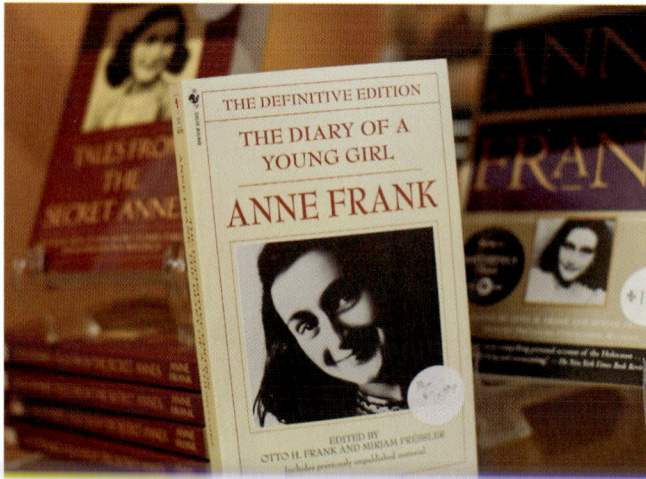

Figure 1.5: *The Diary of a Young Girl* by Anne Frank.

KEY TERM

personal documents: documents such as letters and diaries produced by individuals for their own purposes

ACTIVITY: RESEARCH 1.2

Use the internet to find out more about the diary of Anne Frank.

Consider the validity of this diary as a qualitative secondary source of data. Does it give a true picture of what life was like for a Jewish girl during the Nazi occupation of the Netherlands?

Sociologists may also make use of autobiographies – people's published accounts of their lives. As with diaries and letters intended for publication, these sources need to be treated with caution: the writer may have wanted to give their own version of events and present themselves in a favourable light, rather than writing an accurate account. In many cases, autobiographies are written many years after the events they describe, so the author might not remember everything accurately. The validity of autobiographies is therefore questionable.

Today, many people use social media sites to document their lives. As such, their posts on social media or blogs can be seen as a new form of diary or autobiography. In the future, it is likely that sociologists will use these sources for research.

Governments and other official organisations produce documents of many types. Some of these are immediately available to the public but others are made available only to particular researchers – and some are kept secret for many years, covered by official secrecy laws. In the UK, census returns (the actual forms filled in by the public, not the statistical summaries compiled from them) are only available after 100 years. Most documents are eventually made public, when they are no longer seen as confidential or sensitive.

Other types of documents can be useful in sociological research, such as household accounts, wills and even shopping lists. Documents are not necessarily written: photographs and home videos can also be useful sources. Some documents such as school reports may also contain quantitative data (such as exam or test grades). Some research has even used notes written by learners in class and passed around when the teacher was not looking! Sociologists are always curious about social life and use whatever sources of information are available.

Sometimes researchers ask people to keep diaries, which can then be used alongside data from interviews or questionnaires. One of the best known examples of this was the Mass Observation research in the UK in the 1930s in which large numbers of people were asked to keep diaries, providing a rich source of information about life at the time. During the Mass Observation, these diaries were primary data; when used by later researchers, they became secondary data.

Strengths and limitations of historical and personal documents

Strengths:

- They may be highly valid, providing a picture of reality at the time they were produced.

- They offer first-hand accounts from the people involved.

- They provide descriptive detail and insight which is missing in statistical sources.

Limitations:

- They may be unrepresentative.

- They need to be checked against other sources.

- They may be biased, intentionally or otherwise, and may reflect the emotional state of the writer at the time.

Digital sources

In the 21st century, people mostly access information through **digital sources**. Digital sources include webpages, blogs, vlogs, forums, apps and social media platforms, such as Instagram. People's use of social media is an interesting topic which sociologists are starting to study. However, digital sources can also be used as a form of secondary data – either as a type of personal document in the case of social media posts, or more widely as a source of information about things which are happening in society and the world. For example, the internet makes it much easier for a sociologist to find out about other countries if they want to make comparisons in their research.

Strengths and limitations of digital sources

Strengths:

- Digital sources make a vast range of information available, usually at very low cost and with easy access.

- Digital sources are global, making it much easier to get information about different parts of the world.

Limitations:

- All digital sources must be treated with caution as some are misleading, biased or have incorrect information.

- It can be difficult to assess the validity of digital sources because important context (such as who owns a website, or who wrote something) may be missing.

- In some countries, access to digital sources is controlled by the government.

Figure 1.6: Fake news vs facts.

KEY TERM

digital sources: the internet and other online sources

THINK LIKE A SOCIOLOGIST

Think of any websites that you use to find out the news. Have you ever seen anything on those sites that might be untrue (or that you know to be false)? How do you decide how much to trust a website?

Media content

Traditional media (such as newspapers, magazines, television, film and recorded music) provide a vast amount of material which is of interest to sociologists. **Media content**, such as advertisements and television shows, is consumed by many people. As a result, the ways in which certain groups (such as women or young people) are represented in the media are of interest to sociologists because they can affect people's views and attitudes. For example, feminist sociologists have studied the ways in which women are represented in magazines and advertisements. They have used this analysis to argue that the media reinforces stereotypes of men's and women's gender roles.

KEY TERM

media content: the content of newspapers, magazines, film, television and radio programmes and other forms of media

---

The media can also be a source of information about a specific topic. For example, a sociologist may use a relevant documentary television programme as part of their literature review at the start of a research project, together with printed material, to find out what is already known about a topic. The researcher needs to be aware of possible bias and selectivity in the content of the programme. Many parts of the media are inaccurate, so need to be used with caution.

Media such as novels and films explore themes of interest to sociologists. Sometimes, they are intended to be accurate representations of life in a particular time and place and they can bring that experience to life in a way that factual writing cannot. It can however, be difficult for the sociologist to separate the elements based on reality from those that come from a writer's imagination.

Strengths and limitations of media content

Strengths:

- Readily available and a source of information on many topics.

- Can be a useful starting point for other research.

- Can be studied; for example, counting and analysing the number of times something is referred to in newspapers may show how important

it was considered to be. This kind of analysis can be replicated and so can be seen as reliable.

Limitations:

- Difficult to assess the validity of media content.

- May be subjective and biased, so it is important to know some context (for example, who produced the content, in what circumstances and for what purpose).

- Quantitative analysis of media content (for example, counting the appearance of certain words or representations) might miss the wider context or message behind the portrayal, and so lack validity.

Analysis, interpretation and evaluation of data from qualitative and quantitative sources

Interpreting and evaluating evidence from qualitative sources

A sociologist using qualitative secondary sources needs to be able to interpret and evaluate the sources. These are some of the questions they might ask to help them do this:

- Who produced the source? For historical sources, we need to evaluate whose point of view is promoted and take into account groups whose points of view are not available. Many sources are written by people from the middle and upper classes, so the points of view of people lower down the social scale (who are more likely to be unable to write) may be missing.

- Why was the source produced? For example, was it intended to be read by others or not?

- Was the author in a position to know about the things they describe? (For example, is it a first-hand account of an event?)

- Does the source seem to be biased?

- Is it likely that the author's account is representative? For example, are they likely to have the same views as other similar people at that time?

- Are there other sources that corroborate or contradict the source?

- Is it clear how the author meant the document to be interpreted?

Summaries of studies

A common secondary source for sociologists is a summary of the research and knowledge on a particular area of study. A research article will usually start with a summary of knowledge on the topic – descriptions of and comments about research findings from other studies. These summaries are based on a literature review (a review of the previous studies that have been published on the topic). These summaries can be very helpful but they are not always comprehensive. They should also be checked against primary sources for accuracy.

Interpreting and evaluating evidence from quantitative sources

Statistics and quantitative data can be presented in a number of formats. Researchers have to choose the most appropriate format to present their data and make their findings accessible to their readers. Sociological researchers use various types of diagram, table, chart and graph. Sociology students need to be able to interpret these formats accurately and extract information; if you carry out your own research, you may also need to construct them. The studies below show examples of some of the most common ways of presenting statistical data. Answer the questions to see whether you can interpret the data.

CASE STUDY 1.2

Diagrams

Figure 1.7 shows the homicide rate in different regions of the world.

1   In which region of the world were the homicide rates for males and females most similar?

2   Which region had the highest homicide rate for females?

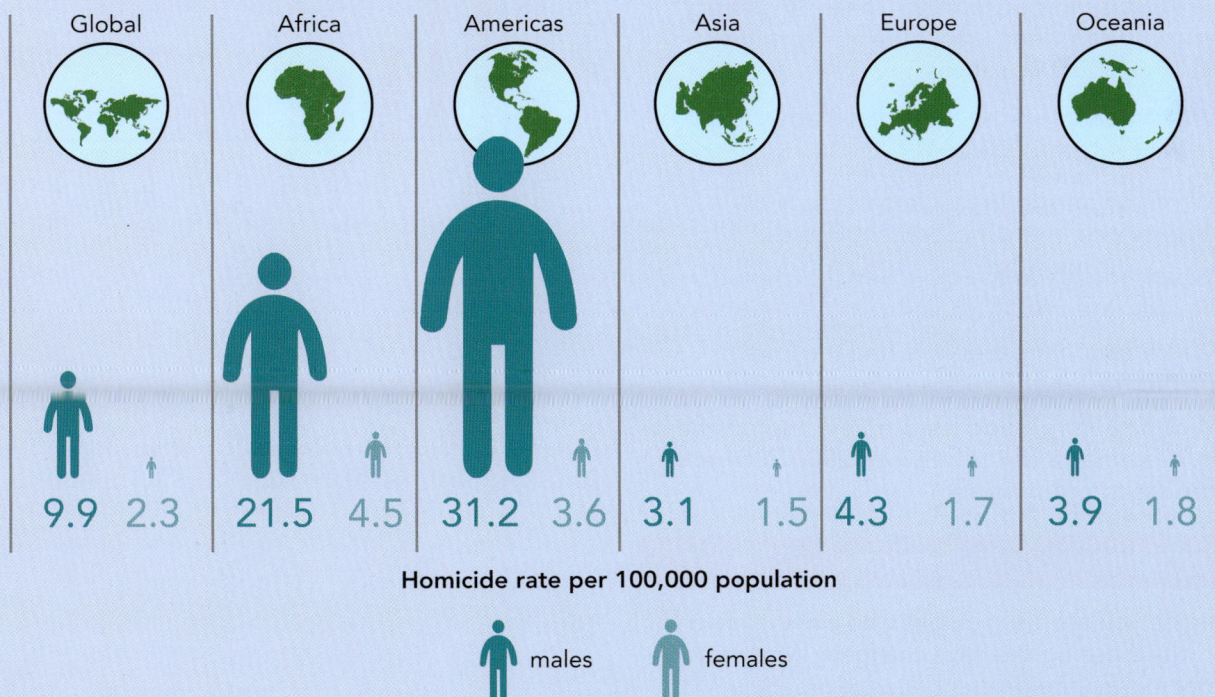

Global	Africa	Americas	Asia	Europe	Oceania
9.9 2.3	21.5 4.5	31.2 3.6	3.1 1.5	4.3 1.7	3.9 1.8

Homicide rate per 100,000 population

males   females

Figure 1.7: Homicide rates by region in 2017; dark blue figures indicate homicides by males and light blue figures indicate homicides by females [UNODC].

CONTINUED

Tables

Table 1.1 shows information about literacy rates in different countries.

Country	Literacy rate	
	2000/2001	Most recent figure
Mauritius	84	91 (2018)
Sri Lanka	91	92 (2019)
Bangladesh	47	75 (2020)
Singapore	93	97 (2019)
Italy	98	99 (2018)
The Gambia	37	51 (2015)
China	91	97 (2018)
Saudi Arabia	79	98 (2020)

Table 1.1: Literacy rates among adults [The World Bank].

Note: Data shows adult (15+) literacy rates (%). The total is the percentage of the population aged 15 and above who can, with understanding, read and write a short, simple statement. Generally, 'literacy' also encompasses 'numeracy' (the ability to make simple arithmetic calculations).

1   Which country in the table had the highest literacy rate in 2000/2001?

2   Which country in the table had the highest literacy rate in the most recent figures?

3   Which country in the table had the lowest literacy rate in 2000/2001?

4   Which country in the table had the lowest literacy rate in the most recent figures?

5   Which country made the greatest improvement in percentage points between 2000/2001 and the most recent figures?

STRETCH AND CHALLENGE

Imagine you are a sociologist who wants to find out why these figures have changed. What factors might explain the different rates of progress towards full adult literacy in different countries? How could you investigate which factors apply?

Charts

Figure 1.8 shows information about the source countries of refugees.

1   From which country did the highest number of displaced people come?

2   Which country had the highest percentage increase in displaced people?

3   From which three countries were there fewer displaced people than before?

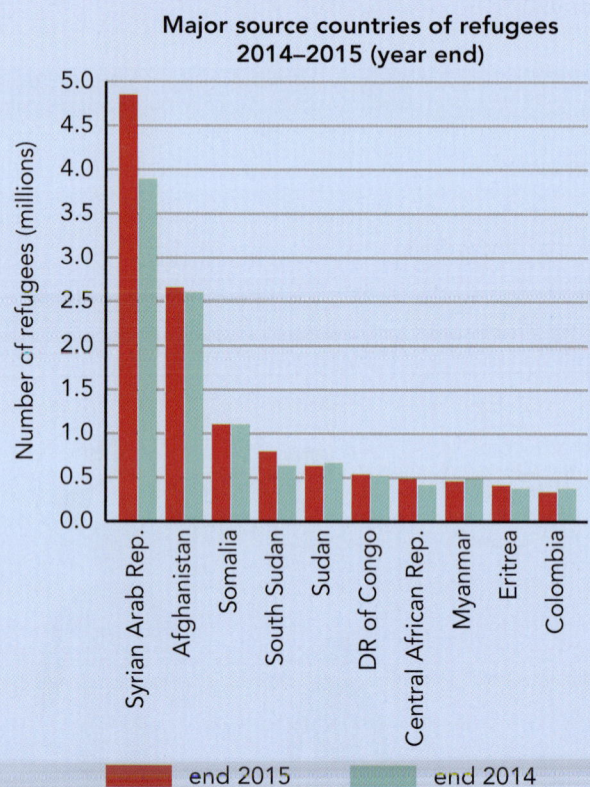

Figure 1.8: Major source countries of refugees 2014–2015 (year end) [UNHCR].

CONTINUED

Graphs

Figure 1.9 shows information about average life expectancy at birth for people living in different countries.

1   Of the countries shown, which had the highest life expectancy in 2015?

2   Of the countries shown, which had the lowest life expectancy in 2015?

3   In which three countries was life expectancy higher than the global average in 2015?

4   The overall trend shows considerable increases in life expectancy. There are, however, some countries where life expectancy falls for a while. What factors can you think of that could explain these falls?

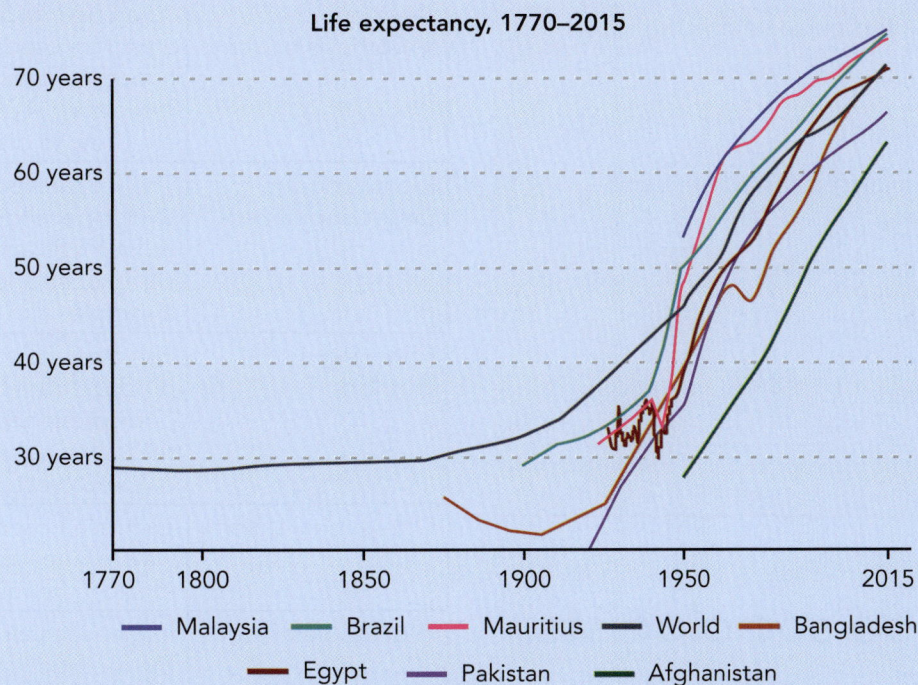

Figure 1.9: Life expectancy at birth, total (years) for selected countries [Our World in Data].

CHECK YOUR UNDERSTANDING 1.2

1   Give two examples of personal documents that sociologists use.

2   With a partner, discuss reasons why sociologists need to be careful about using news stories on the internet as a source of information.

3   In a small group, make a list of the main differences between qualitative and quantitative data.

a   Which type of data is likely to be more valid?

b   Which type of data is likely to be more reliable?

Make sure you can explain your answers to the others in your group.

- Sociologists use primary and secondary sources of data.

- Sociologists use qualitative and quantitative data.

- Different types of data have different strengths and limitations.

- Secondary data include:

  - official statistics

  - historical and personal documents

  - digital sources

  - media content.

- Data can be analysed, interpreted and evaluated using:

  - summaries of studies

  - diagrams

  - tables

  - charts

  - graphs.

1.3 How do sociologists investigate society?

TIP

The best way to learn about research methods is to try them out. The following guidelines for good questionnaires and interviews and on the types of question to ask should be helpful if you try these methods for yourself.

The stages in research design

Research stage	Potential problem
Identifying a topic for research	There may be practical problems such as finding respondents. It may also be difficult to get funding.
Reviewing existing evidence	It may be difficult to find existing evidence; the researcher may have to check many possible sources.
Developing a hypothesis or aim	It can be difficult to write a well-focused aim or hypothesis, especially if the researcher is unsure what they are likely to discover.
Identifying the target population	The researcher will need to decide who the findings will refer to and how they will choose and access a sample.
Choosing a method	The method chosen may not produce data that can confirm or disprove the hypothesis, or that does not meet the aims of the project.
Operationalisation	The researcher has to find ways of measuring the key ideas in the research.
Pilot studies	In many research projects, the method is tested with a small sample before the main research is carried out. If the pilot study shows significant issues (for example, with the questions asked), the researcher may have to start over again.
Implementing the research method	Possible problems with each method are explained in the sections on individual methods. The problems can be classified as practical, ethical or theoretical.

Table 1.2: Stages of research and potential problems.

Selection of topic

Sociological research starts with the identification of a problem. The best research often involves problems that are also puzzles: not just a lack of information, but also a lack of understanding. A researcher might ask, for example, why girls do better than boys at school in some countries. Research projects do not stand alone; they are always related to, or even arise directly from earlier research.

When deciding what to research, sociologists may be influenced by factors such as:

- their personal interests, experiences and observations

- what is already known about the topic and what is not yet known

- social changes and developments – there may be something new that we know little about

- whether funding is available; this may depend on the perceived importance of the topic to sources of funding

- how practical it will be to do the research; for example, will it be possible to identify and contact respondents?

- what ethical issues are raised by the topic.

It can be expensive to conduct research, so it is important to obtain funding. The costs include travel and materials (such as paper) and also the time spent on the research. Most research is carried out by sociologists employed by universities and other educational or research bodies, though the money may come from the government, businesses or charitable organisations. Before they can start any research, the sociologist may have to convince the funding bodies that their project is worthwhile by writing a proposal including estimates of what the study will cost.

Aims and hypotheses

Having identified the problem or puzzle, the next stage is to review the available evidence (in books and academic journals) to find out what is already known. Who else has identified the problem and how have they investigated it? This stage is often called the literature review. By drawing on the ideas of other researchers,

Figure 1.10: Investigating society.

Having collected their data, the sociologist has to analyse them and decide what they mean for the research question. This is often difficult; most research raises further questions because it is not clear what the findings mean or how they can be applied, and data can often be interpreted in different ways. The researcher then has to report their findings so they can be read and used by others researching the same or related areas. Findings of sociological research are usually published in academic journals or in books.

We will now look at the main stages in the research process in more detail.

the sociologist will be able to clarify the issues and decide how to proceed. They can then identify the specific **aims** of their research – what they intend to find out.

The next stage is to turn the ideas into a clear **hypothesis** that can be investigated. A hypothesis is a prediction or statement that the research will attempt to find evidence to support or disprove; it is a sort of educated guess, often about how two or more variables are connected. The hypothesis might suggest a cause-and-effect relationship, but sometimes research is only able to establish a correlation. While a research investigation using a positivist approach will probably have a hypothesis, a more interpretivist approach may have looser and broader aims, such as to find out what a group of people think about something.

Target population

Next, the sociologist has to identify their target population. This is the whole group of people the research is about – the people to whom the findings of the research will be applied. The target population may be quite broad, such as all the people in a particular country. Alternatively, it may be more specific, such as all women over 50 in the country or all people in a particular town. For practical reasons, research is unlikely to be carried out on the entire target population, even if the target population is quite specific. Instead, a sample of people will be selected to represent the target population, and the research will focus on this sample.

For research about a school or college, the target population might be all the learners in that school or college. The research itself would be carried out with a sample – a smaller selection – of those learners, but the results would be applied to all the learners, including those not in the sample. The methods of selecting a sample are covered in more detail later in this section.

Methods

Many different research methods are available, including different types of interview and observation. The sociologist has to choose from the methods; their choices will be influenced by practical, ethical and theoretical issues. The method or methods chosen must be able to produce data that will provide evidence supporting or disproving the hypothesis or achieving the aim. The methods available, and their strengths and limitations, are discussed later in this section.

Operationalisation

The aim or hypothesis will contain or refer to some sociological key terms or concepts. These ideas are often abstract so, to carry out the research, the sociologist needs to find ways ask questions about them, or to measure or observe them. This is known as **operationalisation**. A researcher will identify indicators which they will use to measure the concept more accurately.

For example, the term 'social class' is commonly used in sociology and will come up in all the topics you study on this course. But social class is an abstract idea which means different things to different people. To operationalise the concept, a researcher will probably use indicators such as people's occupation and income, because these indicators are fairly easy to measure and to ask questions about. The researcher will then use their findings about these indicators to decide what class each respondent belongs to.

The same considerations apply to terms that may seem more straightforward than 'social class'. For example, if a researcher wanted to compare the educational achievement of girls and boys, they would need to operationalise 'educational achievement' by identifying indicators that demonstrate educational achievement. They might decide to use IGCSE exam results, but they could also use results from other exams or tests, or whether learners go on to study at a higher level, such as university, as indicators.

Pilot studies

Whatever method is chosen, it is sensible to test it before beginning the main research. This is likely to involve a **pilot study**, in which the research methods are tested with a small number of respondents, or in a limited way,

---

> **KEY TERMS**

aims: what a researcher sets out to achieve through their research, for example to find out why something happens

hypothesis: a prediction or statement that research is designed to test

operationalisation: finding ways to ask questions about, or to measure and observe, abstract concepts so that research can be carried out

pilot study: a small-scale test of a research method before the main research is carried out to see if there are any problems in the design or whether the research plan can be improved. For example, a pilot questionnaire might be given to a small number of people to see if they understand all the questions, and whether the answers available cover the responses they want to give. The questionnaire can then be revised to make it better, based on feedback from these respondents. Resolving problems at an early stage saves money, time and effort later.

Sampling frames and sampling techniques

It is usually expensive and impractical to include the entire target population in research. Instead, the researcher will select a limited number of respondents to represent the target population. This is the research sample. A list of all (or most) of the people in the target population is called a **sampling frame**. Commonly used sampling frames include:

- register of electors (also called the electoral roll or electoral register): This is a list of everyone registered to vote in elections, often with their addresses. Many countries have one. The electoral register will include most adults living in a country, though it will not include anyone who is not registered to vote or who is not allowed to vote. If your target population is all adults in your country, then the electoral roll is a good sampling frame to use.

- school registers: Schools keep lists of their learners, including information such as their gender. However, these lists are available only to genuine researchers and the researcher will need to seek permission from someone in authority, such as the head teacher. If your target population is all learners in a particular school, or all children of particular ages in an area, then a school register might be a useful sampling frame.

It can be difficult to find a suitable sampling frame and for some target populations there may not be a sampling frame. For example, if your target population is people in your town who have brown hair, there is unlikely to be a list of these people. If there is no sampling frame, this will limit the methods you can use to select your sample.

Samples are usually chosen so that they are representative – that is, so the researcher can claim that the results apply to the whole target population. To be representative, the sample has to be a cross-section of the target population.

For example, if there are equal numbers of males and females in the target population, there should be equal numbers of males and females in the sample.

> **TIP**
>
> When you are writing about sampling, always make links with representativeness and generalisability (see section 1.1). Most sociologists will try to make their sample as representative of the target population as possible, so their findings are generalisable. However, this is more important to positivists, who value large-scale research, than it is to interpretivists, who focus on individuals.

Samples can be chosen in several different ways. Some of the most common sampling methods or techniques are described here.

1 **Random sampling**. This is when everyone in the sampling frame has an equal chance of being chosen. One way of doing this is to put names or numbers on small pieces of paper, mix them up in a bucket (or something similar) and then pick out the number required. This method is used in making draws for sports competitions and for lotteries, because it is fair. You would be annoyed if you chose a number in a lottery and found out later that it was less likely to be chosen than others. Random samples are not always representative; for example, even if a sampling frame contains equal numbers of boys and girls, random selection might produce a sample that is mostly boys or mostly girls. The researcher has no control over the selection.

2 **Systematic sampling**. This is when there is a regular pattern to the choice; for example, every tenth name in the sampling frame is chosen.

> **KEY TERMS**
>
> **sampling frame:** a list of all (or most) members of a target population from which the sample is chosen
>
> **random sampling:** when each person has an equal chance of being selected
>
> **systematic sampling:** when there is a regular pattern in selecting from the sampling frame, for example, every tenth name on a list

Like a random sample, a systematic sample does not suffer from selection bias: the researcher has no influence over which names are chosen. However, a systematic sample may not be representative of the target population, because the system used will not guarantee the appropriate proportions of genders, ages and so on.

3   **Stratified sampling.** To overcome the problem that random samples are not always representative, the sampling frame can be divided into sections or 'strata' (for example, into boys and girls) and a sample is then selected from each section. This ensures that the right proportions of each type of person are chosen. Samples can be stratified by gender, age, ethnic group or any other characteristic. In draws for sports competitions, seeding is a way of stratifying the sampling frame and making sure the top players or clubs do not face each other in the early stages of the competition. If the sampling frame is stratified and then a random sample taken, this is called a stratified random sample. This is likely to be representative of the target population.

4   **Snowball sampling.** This is a way of contacting people when other sampling methods will not work, usually because your target population is a very specific type of person and there is no sampling frame.

It involves finding one respondent and asking them to put you in touch with others. It has been used, for example, in interviewing criminals associated with organised crime – for whom there is no sampling frame. Because the members of the sample are all connected, it is not likely to give a representative sample; however, this method does allow access to groups who are more difficult to reach.

5   **Quota sampling.** This is when a researcher is sent out with instructions to find people with certain characteristics, for example, 10 learners aged 16 taking IGCSE Sociology. This is often used in market research.

KEY TERMS

stratified sampling: when the sampling frame is divided, for example by gender or age

snowball sampling: when one respondent puts the researcher in contact with others

quota sampling: when the researcher decides in advance how many people with certain characteristics to involve in the research and then identifies them

---

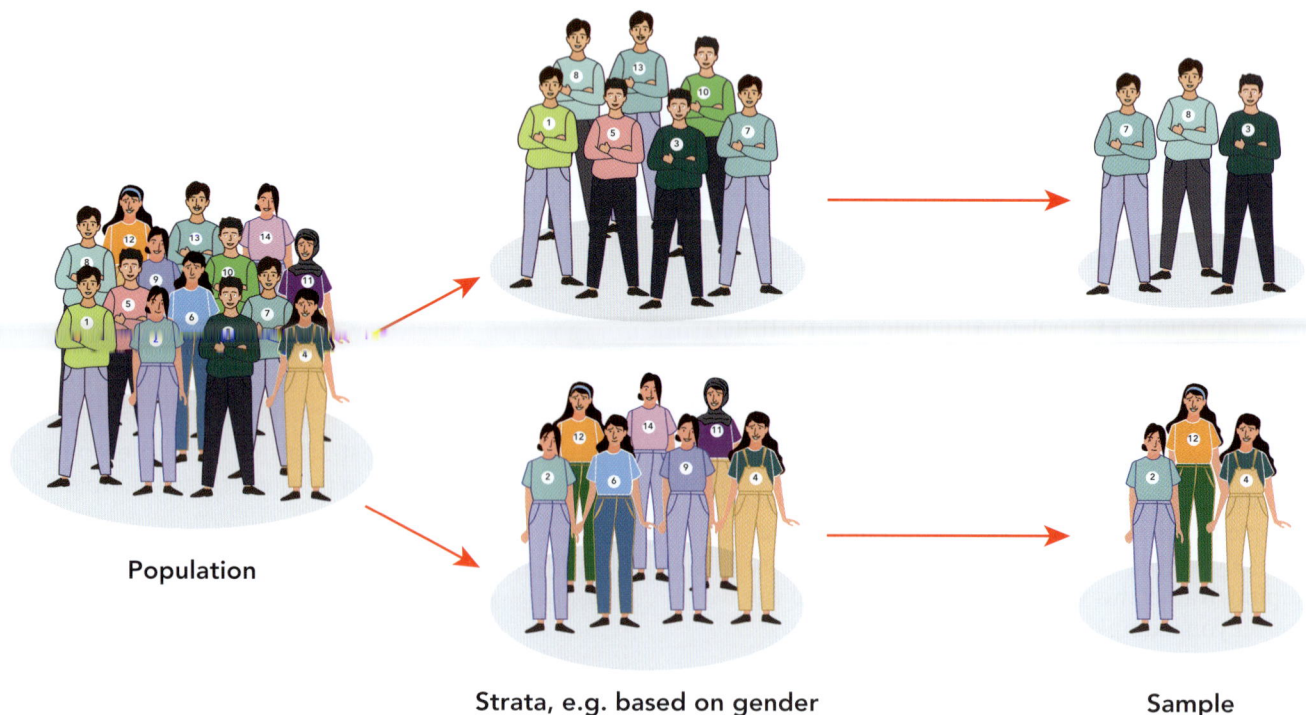

Figure 1.11: Stratified sampling.

Population   Strata, e.g. based on gender   Sample

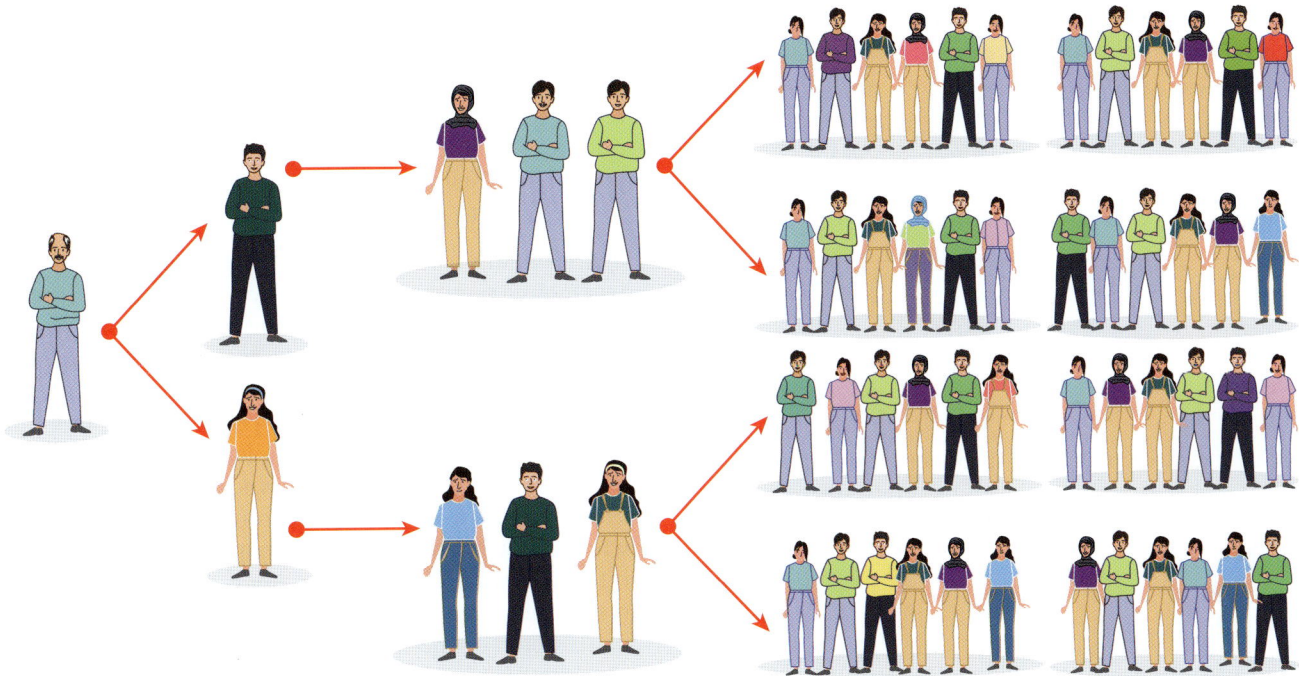

Figure 1.12: Snowball sampling.

If you are stopped in the street by someone asking questions, they may be trying to find out whether you are a suitable person for their survey. Quota sampling is fairly representative and is useful when there is no available sampling frame. Using a quota can ensure that you select appropriate numbers of different types of people, such as genders or age groups, to represent the target population. However, a quota sample may suffer from selection bias: the researcher will need to approach people to fill their quota and they might unconsciously choose those who look more friendly or less busy, for example.

Notice that snowball sampling and quota sampling do not require a sampling frame.

ACTIVITY: WRITTEN 1.2

You have been asked to carry out research to find out how teenagers in your town or local area spend their free time.

1 Write 2–3 paragraphs explaining how you will select your sample. Make sure you include the following:

- What is the target population for your research?

- What sampling frame will you use to select your sample from? (If you do not think there is a sampling frame, explain why.)

- Which sampling technique will you use, and how exactly will you apply it?

- Will there be any limitations related to your sample? For example, will it be difficult or time-consuming to create your sample? Will your sample be representative? Will there be any selection bias?

2 Swap your paragraphs with a partner and read each other's work. Did you write similar things? Did you choose the same sampling technique?

MAKING CONNECTIONS

Look back at Written Activity 1.2. Which sociological perspective would see representativeness of the sample and generalisability of the findings as more important – positivism or interpretivism?

Quantitative and qualitative primary research methods

Primary research methods – those carried out by the researcher themselves – can be referred to as quantitative or qualitative, depending on the type of data they gather.

Surveys

Survey techniques, which include questionnaires and structured interviews, tend to be carried out on a large scale, including many respondents. They usually generate quantitative data. These methods are favoured by positivists. Interpretivists prefer research methods which obtain qualitative data, including semi-structured and unstructured interviews and observations. Each of these research methods has strengths and weaknesses.

Questionnaires

Figure 1.13: A questionnaire.

Questionnaires are also known as self-completion questionnaires. Respondents answer the questions with no additional guidance from the researcher, who is not present. The most common type of self-completion questionnaire is sent to respondents by post – a postal questionnaire – although online questionnaires (distributed via websites and pop-ups) are becoming more common. Questionnaires can also be handed out for respondents to fill in. In a school, for example, you might distribute questionnaires by asking teachers to give them to their classes.

Questionnaires sent by post or via the internet can reach large numbers of people, so you can have a large sample which should be representative, allowing you to generalise your findings to your entire target population. However, the **response rate** for questionnaires is often very low – typically less than 50 per cent – and this can make the final sample who complete the questionnaire less representative. The people who return the questionnaire might be different in some way from those who do not; for example, they may have a particular interest in what the questionnaire is about. Because the researcher is not present, some questions might be left unanswered or the respondents might give inappropriate answers, perhaps because they did not understand what was being asked.

KEY TERMS

surveys: large-scale pieces of research which tend to generate quantitative data through methods such as questionnaires or structured interviews

questionnaire: a standardised list of questions used in social surveys

response rate: the proportion of people in the original sample who actually take part in the research, for example, by completing and returning the questionnaire

Researchers may try to improve the response rate by:

- sending a letter explaining the research in some detail; this ensures informed consent and also makes it more likely that the participant will answer

- sending an envelope in which the completed questionnaire can be returned, or calling to collect it

- reminding those who do not respond with a further letter about the questionnaire

- making the questionnaire as short and easy to complete as possible

- giving clear instructions and having questions that are likely to be relevant or of interest to participants

- using people's names in a letter (rather than 'Dear Sir or Madam') to make the participants feel more personally involved; the researcher could also sign each letter

- offering the participant an incentive of money or the chance of being entered into a prize draw if the questionnaire is returned.

Guidelines for good questionnaire design

- Make the questionnaire as short as possible, with a clear layout that is easy to follow.

- Ensure instructions for completing the questionnaire are easily understood.

- Ensure the questionnaire is easy to follow and complete.

- Start with short questions that need simple answers and are likely to interest participants.

- Include just enough answer options to allow participants to express their views and to provide the information required.

- Avoid leading questions that suggest to the participant that a particular answer is expected or correct.

- Avoid words that might not be understood by everyone, including sociological terms.

- Only ask questions about things participants are likely to know and be able to give meaningful answers to.

- Do not ask for personal information (such as the participants' name and age) until the end.

Strengths and limitations of questionnaires

Strengths:

- Can be used with large samples.

- Can be sent to participants (via post or the internet) who may not be near to the researchers.

- The researcher is not present, so cannot influence the answers given.

- Convenient for participants, who can complete the questionnaire when they choose.

Limitations:

- Response rate is low compared to interviews, affecting representativeness.

- Questions may be misunderstood and if a participant does not understand a question, there is no one present to explain it.

- The researcher cannot be sure who answered the questions and whether it was completed by the person it was sent to on their own.

- Participants often leave some questions unanswered.

ACTIVITY: WRITTEN 1.3

You have been asked to carry out an investigation into the future plans and ambitions of learners in your school/college.

1   Write a questionnaire containing 5–8 questions which will help you to find out about this topic. Use the guidelines for good questionnaire design given earlier in this section to help you.

2   Give your questionnaire to one of your fellow learners and ask them to complete it; this is a small pilot study, testing your questionnaire.

3   Ask them whether they think the questions are clear and easily understood. Consider the answers they gave to your questions: did they give you the information you were looking for?

4   Change any questions which they said were unclear or which did not give you the right type of information.

CASE STUDY 1.3

A large-scale survey using questionnaires: census in The Gambia

Figure 1.14: People in The Gambia.

Like many countries, The Gambia in West Africa holds a regular census to gather statistical information about everyone living there. The census has been carried out every ten years since 1963 and is administered by the Gambia Bureau of

Statistics. The most recent census was in 2013. Every household had to answer many pages of questions on a range of subjects, from the number and ages of people living there, to their ethnic group and religion, to what work people do.

To view the questionnaire used in 2013, search online for 'IHSN Gambia Population and Housing Census 2013 Form A Household Questionnaire – Part 1'.

Task

1   Download *Form A Household Questionnaire Part 1*. Make a list of the information that the questionnaire asks for on the first four pages.

2   How would this information help the government of The Gambia to prepare future policies?

3   What strengths and limitations of self-completion questionnaires does the census show?

Interviews

An interview involves a researcher asking questions directly to interviewees. They are usually conducted face-to-face, though they can also take place over the telephone or remotely online. Some interviews are quantitative and some are qualitative, depending on the structure of the interview and the types of questions asked. The main types of interviews are **structured interviews**, **semi-structured interviews**, **unstructured interviews** and **group interviews**.

Structured interviews

A structured interview is an alternative way of using a questionnaire. This type of interview usually involves closed questions with a limited range of answers and so creates quantitative data. The researcher reads out the questions – including the answer options allowed for closed questions – and records the participants' responses. This can be done by telephone or face-to-face. If the interviews are face-to-face, the location where they are held (administered) is very important.

Ideally, the time and place for the interview should have been agreed in advance and the interviewee should be made to feel at ease.

KEY TERMS

structured interview: an interview in which the questions are standardised (the same questions are asked in the same order) and the responses organised to produce quantitative data

semi-structured interview: an interview with some standardised questions, but allowing the researcher some flexibility on what is asked and in what order

unstructured interview: an interview without set questions that usually involves exploration of emotions and attitudes, leading to qualitative data

group interview: any interview in which several people are interviewed together at the same time

---

Figure 1.15: A structured interview.

For a structured interview, the questions need to be standardised (that is, the same questions are asked in the same order). Structured interviews normally have a higher response rate than self-completion questionnaires because the interviewer can explain the purpose of the research and reassure the participants if they have any questions or concerns. The interviewer may also be able to give the interviewee prompts or explain a question that the interviewee does not understand. However, interviews take up much more of the researcher's time than self-completion questionnaires do and are more expensive as a result. The researcher may employ assistants to carry out the interviews, which makes it possible to have a larger sample. In this case, the assistants will need clear and detailed instructions to ensure they all conduct the interviews in the same way.

Strengths and limitations of structured interviews

Strengths:

- If the participant does not understand a question, the interviewer can explain it.

- Have a higher response rate than self-completion questionnaires.

- Produce reliable data, since the questions are standardised and so the interviews can be repeated and the data can be checked.

- If several assistant interviewers are used, a large number of people can be interviewed.

Limitations:

- The interviewer may influence the answers given, either through their own social characteristics (such as their age, gender, ethnic group and so on) or by interaction with the participant.

- More time-consuming – and therefore more expensive – than self-completion questionnaires.

- Participants may give socially desirable answers (that is, the answers they think are the right ones, or which give the interviewer an impression the participant wants to create).

- If several assistant interviewers are used, they may approach their work in different ways.

Unstructured interviews

In unstructured interviews, the interviewer only has a brief set of prompts or themes to cover. The aim is to get the interviewee to talk freely, so the interviewer will avoid saying much except to encourage the interviewee or ask them to explain an answer in more detail. Unstructured interviews often last for more than an hour and take place in a relaxed setting so the interviewee feels relaxed enough to talk in detail about their thoughts, opinions and experiences. Any questions asked will be open, so unstructured interviews produce qualitative data. For this reason, unstructured interviews are favoured by interpretivists, who wish to gain a detailed understanding (or verstehen) and obtain valid data.

Figure 1.16: An unstructured interview.

Strengths and limitations of unstructured interviews

Strengths:

- Provide detailed and valid data on the point of view of the interviewees, who are able to say what they really think, in their own words.

- Interviewers will build up a good relationship with interviewees and can gain verstehen – an understanding of each interviewee's point of view.

- The flexibility of the interview allows the interviewer to explore some issues in more detail.

- Questions are not fixed beforehand, so interviewees may raise points which the researcher had not previously considered. This means that unstructured interviews might uncover unexpected information which can then be researched further.

Limitations:

- Time-consuming to carry out, transcribe (write out what was said) and analyse.

- Usually only carried out on very small, unrepresentative, samples (because they are so time-consuming), so their findings are not generalisable.

- It can be difficult to make generalisations because standardised questions are not used.

- Less reliable than structured interviews because they are difficult to replicate, since each interview includes different questions and ideas.

- Interviewers need to be highly skilled, able to establish a relationship and get interviewees to talk freely.

- Responses may be affected by interviewer bias (the intentional or unintentional effects of the way the interviewer asks questions or interprets answers).

- Responses may be affected by interviewer effect; for example, the interviewer's sex, age or ethnicity might lead respondents to give particular answers.

Semi-structured interviews

Semi-structured interviews aim to combine the best features of both structured and unstructured interviews. In semi-structured interviews, the interviewer has an interview guide rather than a standardised list of questions. This guide contains a set of questions or specific topics to be covered. The interviewer can change the order of questions, miss out questions which have already been covered and even ask follow-up questions that are not in the guide. Most semi-structured interviews contain open questions and so produce qualitative data, but some quantitative data may also be created.

Strengths and limitations of semi-structured interviews

Strengths:

- More flexible than structured interviews.

- The interviewer can ask additional questions, gaining more in-depth information, or avoid questions that are not relevant to the participant.

- Provide more valid data than structured interviews, since they usually involve open questions and interviewees are more likely to give detailed responses.

- More reliable than unstructured interviews, since they do have some structure and the same questions will be asked to most interviewees, making them easier to repeat than unstructured interviews.

Limitations:

- Less flexible than unstructured interviews, which may reduce the validity of the data.

- More time-consuming than structured interviews and so cannot be completed on such large samples, affecting representativeness.

- Less reliable than structured interviews because they are less standardised; the questions asked and their order will be different in each interview, so they cannot be repeated as easily as structured interviews.

Group interviews

Some group interviews simply involve a number of interviewees who are interviewed together – often to save time and money. These interviews are usually structured, with all respondents being asked the same questions in turn. Other group interviews take a more unstructured approach, focusing on one particular topic and using only a few, if any, set questions. This encourages the interviewees to respond to each other's answers and have a discussion.

Figure 1.17: A group interview.

Group interviews were first used in market research and are now used more often in sociology. The researcher will have an interview guide with different types of question.

Group interviews enable researchers to find out what individuals say as members of a group, and how they respond to the views of others. This may give a more realistic impression than individual interviews because, in real social life, people's opinions are influenced by the views of others and formed through discussion with others.

Individual members of the group bring out the issues they think are important and their views may be challenged by others in the group. The researchers need to decide how much they will be involved. If the group is allowed to discuss freely, they will decide what is important to them; however, this may lead to a lot of irrelevant discussion, so the researcher may intervene to keep discussion on track. The researcher will also need to decide how to deal with silences and with reluctant speakers, as well as with those who speak too much. It is much more difficult to record and transcribe group interviews than individual interviews; people often talk over each other and it can be difficult to work out who said what.

Guidelines for good interviews

Interviewing is a skill. Good interviewers have to be flexible and good listeners, knowing when to intervene and when not to. They need to create a rapport – a good relationship – with the interviewee, which will lead to rich, detailed and valid responses. They are likely to try to do the following things:

- Make the interviewee feel comfortable with the research situation, explaining the purpose of the interview and reassuring them that their anonymity and confidentiality will be preserved.

- Create a certain amount of order, so the questions flow well. (This order can be altered in the interview, unless it is structured.)

- Use language that is understandable and relevant.

- Avoid leading questions or questions that make assumptions.

- Keep a fact sheet record, including the interviewee's name, age and gender.

- Make sure the interview takes place in a quiet and private setting so the interviewee feels at ease and able to talk freely, and so they can be heard (including on a recording).

- Use a good-quality recording machine and microphone. It is sensible to record and transcribe interviews whenever possible because this allows the interviewer to examine thoroughly what the

interviewee said. It also means the data can be looked at again and used by others. However, recording and transcribing are time-consuming – transcribing usually takes about 5–6 times as long as the interview itself.

In unstructured and semi-structured interviews, an interviewer may use some or all of these open questioning techniques:

- Introductory questions such as, 'Can you tell me about…? Have you ever…?'

- Follow-up questions to encourage the interviewee to say more, such as, 'What do you mean by…? You mentioned…?'

- Probing questions, such as, 'Could you say a bit more about…?'

- Specifying questions, asking for detail, such as, 'What did you do then?'

- Indirect questions; for example, 'Why do many people feel that…?' is an indirect way of asking, 'Do you feel that…?'

- Silence, so interviewees can reflect on and perhaps add to an answer.

- Interpreting and checking responses, such as, 'Do you mean that…?'

THINK LIKE A SOCIOLOGIST

Research methods such as questionnaires and interviews are used beyond sociology. Have you ever filled in a questionnaire or been interviewed? If so, what was it about? What kinds of work or occupation can you think of where questionnaires or interviews are used?

Observations

Participant observation

Participant observation is used to develop an understanding of the world from the point of view of the research subjects. Researchers put themselves in the same position

KEY TERM

participant observation: when a researcher studies a group by joining them and living as they do

as the people they are studying. The idea is to get inside the subjects' heads, to see the world as they do and learn how they make sense of it. It involves joining a group of people and living as they do.

The stages of participant observation can be summed up in terms of getting in, staying in and getting out of the group concerned.

1 **Getting in.** Joining a group raises many questions about the researcher's role. A researcher may adopt an overt role, where they tell the group exactly who they are and what they are doing. Alternatively, they may adopt a covert role (concealing their identity) or produce a cover story (explaining that they are a researcher, but concealing elements of their role). To participate successfully, particularly in a covert role, the researcher needs to share some of the personal characteristics of the group, such as their age, gender or ethnicity.

   After deciding what role to play, the researcher needs to gain access to the group. They will need to explain their presence as a stranger. This may involve making friends with key individuals, known as gatekeepers.

2 **Staying in.** The observer has to gain the trust and cooperation of the group, so they can continue to participate and observe. At first this will involve learning, listening and getting a sense of what is going on. Problems during this stage may include the need to take notes (which may disrupt the natural behaviour of the group) and deciding how far to be involved, without losing either the trust of the group or objectivity as a researcher. To maintain the group's trust, researchers may be expected to participate in acts that they do not agree with.

3 **Getting out.** When they have finished their observation, the researcher needs to leave the group without damaging relationships. They must also become detached enough to write an impartial and accurate account, making sure members of the group cannot be identified.

Strengths and limitations of participant observations

Strengths:

- Usually highly valid, because the normal behaviour of the group is observed in its natural setting over a significant period of time.

- The researcher can gain a deep understanding by seeing things from the point of view of those involved.

Limitations:

- The presence of the participant observer may affect the behaviour of the group, but the researcher will not know how or how much this is happening.

- Reliability is low because the research is very difficult to repeat or check.

- It is unlikely that generalisations can be made about other groups.

- There are problems throughout the research in gaining access to the group, winning acceptance, recording information, leaving the group and analysing the data.

- The researcher needs to have social characteristics (such as age, gender, ethnicity) that will allow them to join the group and be accepted by it.

- Researchers may lose their objectivity if they come to identify strongly with the group and see things from its point of view. They may become too much of a participant and not enough of an observer.

Non-participant observation

Some sociological research is carried out by observation alone; the researcher does not participate. This is called **non-participant observation**. This method aims to reduce or eliminate the risk that people will be affected by the presence of a researcher or a new member of their social group. It may also be used when groups are unwilling to cooperate in the research, though this raises ethical issues. It is often used to produce quantitative data; for example, the observer might count the number of times something happens.

KEY TERM

non-participant observation: when a researcher studies a group but does not take part in what the group is doing

---

Non-participant observation allows sociologists to observe people in their normal social situations, avoiding the Hawthorne effect. This is only possible when the observation is carried out without the knowledge of the people being observed – for example, from a distance, by blending into the background, through one-way glass or by using video cameras. If the observer is visibly present – even if they are not participating – there is a risk that their presence will influence what is happening.

A problem with this method is that the research cannot investigate the meanings people attach to the observed behaviour because, as a non-participant, they will not usually ask any questions. The data produced may simply reflect the assumptions and interpretations of the researcher, reducing its validity. However, this is not always the case; a non-participant observer in a classroom (for example, someone observing a teacher's lesson) may ask the learners questions during or after the lesson to find out how well they understand what they are being taught.

Strengths and limitations of non-participant observation

Strengths:

- The researcher is less likely to affect how people behave.

- Allows the researcher to observe people in normal social situations.

Limitations:

- Observing without telling the group could be unethical, because the group cannot give informed consent.

- If the group are aware of being observed, their behaviour may change.

- It is not always possible to find out the reasons for people's behaviour.

Covert observation

In covert observation, the group being observed does not know that research is taking place. Covert observation can be participant or non-participant. The group may assume that a participant observer is a new member of their group. This involves the researcher deceiving the group by concealing the truth about what they are doing.

There are advantages to adopting a covert role in participant observation. It is most likely to be used when criminal or deviant activities are involved. It limits the risk of changing the behaviour of the group under study, because they do not know they are being studied. However, to maintain a covert role, the researcher must become a full participant in the group; the research may be ruined if the researcher's real identity and purpose are discovered. As a result, the participant may become involved in illegal or unpleasant activities. It is also difficult to ask questions and take notes without arousing suspicion. A covert participant observer will have to work hard to pass as a member of the group and ensure

the group does not discover the research is taking place. There are ethical concerns about deceiving people in this way. It is also unethical to observe and report on people's activities without obtaining their consent, although the published research is likely to protect their anonymity.

Strengths and limitations of covert observation

Strengths:

- People are more likely to behave as they normally would, because they do not know they are being observed. This makes the findings more likely to be valid.

- The researcher does not have to ask permission to enter and observe the group.

Limitations:

- The researcher must spend a lot of their time and energy maintaining their cover, rather than gaining information.

- Research may be unethical because the group are being deceived and have not given informed consent.

- To maintain cover, the participant observer may have to do things they do not want to do.

- It is difficult to make notes about what is observed, so it may be some time before observations are written down; this can affect the validity of the data, since it will rely on the researcher's memory.

- It is difficult to combine with other research methods; for example, asking interview-style questions is likely to raise suspicion.

Overt observation

If the researcher takes an overt role, the group will be aware that research is taking place. Overt observation can be participant or non-participant. An overt observer may introduce themselves, explain the purpose of the research and obtain the group's informed consent.

> ### KEY TERMS
>
> covert observation: when the group being studied is unaware of the research; covert means 'hidden'
>
> overt observation: when the group being studied is aware that research is taking place and know who the researcher is

During overt participant observation, the researcher can ask questions or interview people and avoid participating in illegal or immoral behaviour. It is ethically and morally right for the researcher to tell people they are being studied. However, adopting an overt role does have problems. The group being studied may change their behaviour, perhaps trying to make a particular impression on the observer. This raises questions over the validity of the research.

Strengths and limitations of overt research

Strengths:

- More ethical than covert research, since the participants can give their consent to being studied and are not deceived. These ethical considerations are often very important to the researcher, so this is a major advantage of overt research.

- The researcher does not have to spend time maintaining their cover.

- It is easier to make notes.

- Other methods can be used more easily during the observation, such as asking interview-style questions.

Limitations:

- People may behave differently when they know they are being observed, reducing validity.

- In some groups and settings, a researcher would not be accepted, so overt research is not possible.

The distinction between covert and overt research is not always clear. For example, one member of a group (usually the gatekeeper who has made it possible for the researcher to join) may be aware of the research, while other members of the group are not.

CASE STUDY 1.4

Participant observation: *Gang Leader for a Day* by Sudhir Venkatesh

Figure 1.18: Sudhir Venkatesh.

As a young sociology student in Chicago, USA, Sudhir Venkatesh decided to research the lives of people living in a poor area of the city. The area had many social problems, including high rates of crime and poor quality high-rise housing. Most of the people who lived in the neighbourhood were African Americans and living in poverty. People at his university thought that Venkatesh was either brave or foolish even to visit the area, which they considered dangerous.

Almost by chance, Venkatesh was able to win the support of J.T., the leader of the Black Kings gang. J. T. acted as a gatekeeper, taking Venkatesh around with him and showing him how the gang and social life in the area were organised.

Venkatesh found that the reality was very different from media accounts and accounts from outsiders. The gang played an important part in the life of the area, providing support to some of the most needy people and punishing people whose actions harmed others in the community. Venkatesh attended some violent incidents and even became involved at times. For several years, he spent most of his time in the neighbourhood.

Task

1 In what ways does this research show some of the strengths and limitations of participant observation?

2 This research was largely overt. People knew Venkatesh did not belong in the area, although not everyone knew he was doing research. What issues would the covert researcher encounter in an area like this?

ACTIVITY: DISCUSSION 1.2

1   In a small group, list the differences between participant and non-participant observation, referring to practical, ethical and theoretical issues. (These are covered in more detail later in this section.) You may find it helpful to think of a particular research setting, such as a classroom in a school.

2   Create a poster to display your findings and ask others to comment on it.

STRETCH AND CHALLENGE

In which research methods do the researcher's personal characteristics (sex, age and so on) make the most difference? Are there any methods where these features are not important? Explain your answers and compare your findings with those of other learners.

MAKING CONNECTIONS

In Cambridge IGCSE™ and O Level Sociology, you will study some of the following topics: Identity: self and society; Social stratification and inequality; Family; Education; Crime, deviance and social control. Which research methods do you think would be most useful in studying each of these topics?

Types of question

Questionnaires and interviews use different types of question. It is important to choose the right type of question for the information you want to collect; this will make it easier to analyse your data. The main types of question are open and closed but there are also specific types of closed question, including multiple-choice questions and scaled questions.

Open questions

Open questions are used to explore in detail why people believe or do particular things. An open question allows the respondent to explain or expand on their answer, rather than giving them a limited range of responses to choose from.

Open questions often start or end with words or phrases such as 'why…', 'give reasons for your answer' or 'explain how…'. The answers to open questions create qualitative data. It is unusual to include many open questions in a questionnaire. This is partly because people are less likely to write lengthy answers, and also because most questionnaires are designed to obtain quantitative data. The same applies to structured interviews, which are unlikely to contain many open questions. However, semi-structured and unstructured interviews are usually based on open questions and generate a lot of qualitative data.

Closed questions

Closed or fixed-response questions invite a limited range of answers (such as 'yes' or 'no') or ask the respondent to choose one or more answers from a list provided. Each answer is coded – given a number or value that is then used to analyse the data. The advantage of this is that it makes it easy to analyse the results and produce statistical tables. The disadvantage is that some respondents may want to give answers that are not allowed by the options provided. To avoid this problem, the researcher might include an 'Other (please specify)' option. Closed questions are most common in survey techniques such as questionnaires or structured interviews. They generate quantitative data.

Multiple-choice questions

Multiple-choice questions are a type of closed question. They have a stem (an opening statement) and several alternative answers from which the respondent has to choose. There is one correct answer, known as the key. Multiple-choice questions are often used in assessments in education.

KEY TERMS

open questions: questions to which the respondent can reply freely in their own words

closed questions: questions which allow limited or set answers

multiple-choice questions: closed questions with a number of answers from which the respondent has to choose the correct option

Scaled questions

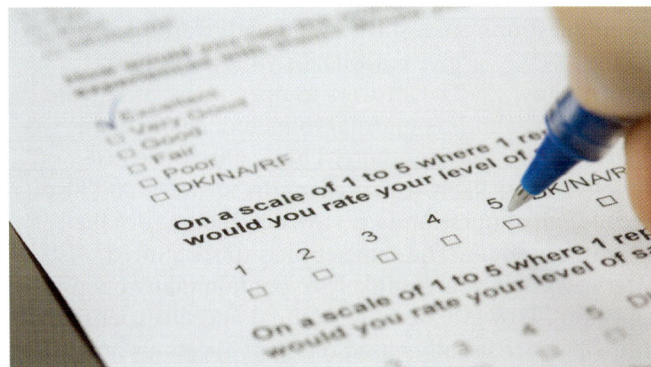

Figure 1.19: Scaled questions.

Scaled questions are a type of closed question with a range of possible answers, such as:

- strongly agree

- agree

- neither agree nor disagree

- disagree

- strongly disagree.

There is a debate about whether it is better to have an odd or even number of possible responses. If you have an odd number of responses – say, five options – most respondents are likely to choose the middle one (in this example, this would be 'neither agree nor disagree') because this avoids making a decision. If you have an even number of responses, with no middle option, you push your respondents to make a decision. This helps to produce data that seem to prove something but there is a risk that people will agree (or disagree) when they really do not have a preference.

Theoretical and practical issues affecting research

When you are choosing the method to use in your research, and when you are evaluating a research method, you must consider three types of issue: practical, ethical and theoretical.

- Practical issues involve, for example, the resources, time and money the project needs, the response rates and the difficulties of transcribing long interviews.

- **Ethical issues** involve anonymity, confidentiality, informed consent and potential risks and harm (considered later in this section).

- Theoretical issues include the research approach – positivist or interpretivist – and also validity, reliability, representativeness and bias. As we have seen, some methods may be higher in reliability and some may be higher in validity.

Researcher perspective

This is a theoretical issue affecting research. The researcher will have a particular perspective which will influence the research they choose to do and the methods they use. A positivist, for example, will favour more objective methods that produce quantitative data, such as questionnaires and structured interviews. An interpretivist will favour methods that will allow them to uncover the meanings behind actions and that produce qualitative data, such as participant observation and unstructured interviews.

Research is also influenced by the researcher's values – what they see as important and worth studying. For example, a Marxist sociologist might choose to research issues of social class, while a feminist might focus on gender-based topics.

Access to sample

This is a practical issue affecting research. Sometimes it is difficult or impossible to gain access to a sample of the target population. For example, to gain access to a sample of school learners, a sociologist may need to obtain permission from the head teacher (to be in the school) and from teachers (to be in their classrooms). They will also need to gain informed consent from the learners themselves and from their parents or guardians. For a sociologist hoping to study criminal behaviour, accessing a sample may be difficult or even dangerous.

Response rate

This is a practical issue that raises theoretical issues because it can affect the representativeness of the findings. Response rates to questionnaires are often very low; for example, many postal questionnaires are not completed or returned. This makes it difficult to be sure that the responses received are representative of the sample and therefore of the target population.

Funding/cost

Funding is a practical issue which raises theoretical issues. All research requires funding. To carry out a research project, a researcher will need a source of funding, such as a research grant from a government body. It is usually easier to get funding for research which produces quantitative data because funding bodies prefer findings that identify trends and patterns, or causes and correlations. Qualitative data can be seen as less useful to large-scale organisations or governments because the findings are small-scale and lack generalisability. Researchers often carry out surveys not because they think they are the best method, but because they quickly produce the sorts of results required by funding bodies. Many researchers work at universities and may be able to fund their research through the university. However, they still need to justify the research and prove it is a worthwhile use of their time and the university's funds.

Funding is limited, so all researchers need to control costs. This will affect the research design; for example, it may not be possible to use as large a sample as initially intended, or to employ assistants to help with interviews.

Time

Time is a practical issue closely related to funding and costs. Some types of research take more time than others, and the sample size also affects the time taken.

- Qualitative research is usually more time-consuming; participant observation, for example, can take months or even years – even before the data are written up and analysed. This raises the possibility that the research will be out of date before it is published.
- Quantitative research, such as surveys, is generally less time-consuming, despite involving more respondents.
- Longitudinal studies are very time-consuming, since they involve revisiting members of the sample at regular intervals, sometimes years apart. For this reason, it is difficult to get funding for this type of research.
- For large-scale surveys such as censuses, it can be years before the full findings are analysed and published.

Ethical issues affecting research

Sociological research involves people, so it raises issues about the welfare of both the researchers and the respondents. Ethical issues involve decisions about values – what is right and wrong. If a researcher makes the wrong decisions, their research might harm people or damage the reputation of the university or organisation they work for, or of sociology as a discipline. For this reason, the main professional associations in sociology have codes of conduct to guide researchers through these difficult areas.

Some of the main ethical guidelines that almost all researchers follow are:

1. The participants must not be harmed – either physically or psychologically.
2. The participants must give their informed consent.
3. The researcher should not invade the participants' privacy.
4. Participants should not be deceived.

The researcher must also ensure that, as far as possible and whenever appropriate, the research is:

- anonymous – for example, the participant's name (or any other information that might identify them) does not appear on the questionnaire. This is not always done if it might be necessary to contact someone again for more information.
- confidential – it is not possible to identify an individual's answers from the published findings.

TIP

Remember that anonymity and confidentiality are not the same, they are different. When someone completes a census form, for example, they are asked to give their name, so their information is not anonymous. It is, however, confidential because the findings of the census are published as statistics: it is impossible to find out what answers were given by any individual. Make sure you make this distinction in your answers.

Lots of different countries and regions of the world have their own sociological associations, which professional sociologists will be members of. These include the American Sociological Association, the British Sociological Association and the International Sociological Association. These associations publish ethical guidelines which help their members to plan research. These are guidelines, rather than rules. This is partly because there are disagreements over what is and is not ethically acceptable; there are also some situations in which breaking the guidelines might be justified. The guidelines exist to help researchers make the right decisions, not to tell them what to do in every situation.

Informed consent

The respondents must agree to take part, having fully understood what is involved. Informed consent includes explaining the purpose of the research, when and where the findings will be available and what they might be used for. People have the right to refuse to take part in research or to refuse to answer particular questions; the researcher should not try to persuade them to do anything they do not want to do. It is not always necessary or possible to get informed consent from everyone involved in research; for example, if observing a large number of people. However, the rule of obtaining informed consent means that covert observation is not an ethical research method. There is some debate about how much information the participants need in order to give informed consent. Explaining everything is time-consuming and probably not necessary. In fact,

researchers probably break this guideline frequently, in minor ways. For example, they might underestimate how long an interview will take when telling a participant.

Privacy/confidentiality

The researcher must respect the participants' privacy, even when they have given their informed consent. The participant might have agreed to be interviewed, but they can still refuse to answer particular questions that they see as invading their privacy – for example, ones that ask about their earnings or their religious beliefs.

Deception

A researcher may disguise the true purpose of their research. This can involve lying or giving incomplete information, to try to get the participants to respond more naturally. For example, a researcher observing in a classroom may tell the learners that they are helping the teacher, when they are actually researching the children's behaviour. This is deception.

Prevention of harm

It is wrong to harm participants in a study, but it is not easy to decide what harm means or to know in advance whether harm will be caused. Harm does not have to be physical. It might include making participants feel angry or upset, referred to as psychological harm. This could happen if they are asked about something that disturbs them; this can be difficult to avoid because researchers cannot know what might upset a particular person.

Confidentiality can protect participants from harm when the research findings are published. For example, research reports do not use participants' real names or include any information that might make it possible to identify a respondent. Even names of places, such as schools or towns, are changed.

Legality

Research must not break laws or encourage or condone the breaking of laws. Laws vary between countries and even areas within countries, so the researcher will need to check the legality of what they intend to do. For example, Sudhir Venkatesh (Case study 1.4) gained information about criminal offences committed by members of the gang he studied, and even witnessed and participated in violent behaviour. In some countries, it would be an offence not to give this information to the police. Other legal concerns in some countries include avoiding discrimination and protecting information.

ACTIVITY: DISCUSSION 1.3

There may be questions about whose consent is needed for research.

1   In a group, consider the following questions.

   a   For a group of school-aged children, should respondents get informed consent from the children, their parents (and which parent) or both?

   b   If the study takes place in a classroom, should the teacher and other staff also be asked to give informed consent?

2   Share your findings with other groups. Can you agree about what age a child must be to give fully informed consent?

ACTIVITY: DISCUSSION 1.4

You decide to observe a class in a primary school to see whether the teacher treats boys and girls differently. In a small group, discuss what ethical issues you would have to consider and how you would ensure you follow ethical guidelines. Make a list of ethical points to refer to when carrying out the research.

REFLECTION

How did you decide on your list of points? Which members of your group made the best case for including their ideas and how did they do this? Were anyone's views left out? Could you organise the discussion differently to make sure everyone had a fair say?

ACTIVITY: RESEARCH 1.3

Choose any of the case studies about research methods in this unit and use the internet to find out more about the research. Assess how valid, reliable and representative the findings are likely to have been. Make sure you understand these three terms and how they are different from each other.

CHECK YOUR UNDERSTANDING 1.3

1   Name four ways of obtaining a sample. With a partner, decide which of these sampling techniques is most likely to produce a representative sample and why. Put them into order from most to least representative.

2   Working with a partner, take it in turns to explain the following to each other:
  • the difference between an unstructured interview and a structured interview
  • the difference between open and closed questions
  • the difference between overt and covert participant observation
  • the difference between reliability and validity.

KEY POINTS

• Designing research involves a series of stages.

• Sociologists use sampling frames and sampling techniques.

• The main primary research methods are:
  • surveys and questionnaires
  • interviews (structured, semi-structured, unstructured, group)
  • observations (participant, non-participant, covert, overt).

• These methods have their own strengths and limitations.

• Types of question are:
  • open
  • closed
  • multiple choice
  • scaled.

• Theoretical and practical issues affecting research are:
  • researcher perspective
  • access to sample
  • response rate
  • funding/cost
  • time.

• Ethical issues affecting research are:
  • informed consent
  • privacy/confidentiality
  • deception
  • prevention of harm
  • legality.

SUMMARY

- Positivists and interpretivists have different approaches to carrying out research.

- Each stage of the research process involves choices and decisions relating to a range of practical, ethical and theoretical issues.

- Sociologists use different types of primary research method, including surveys, questionnaires, interviews and observations.

- Sociologists use a range of secondary data, including official and non-official statistics, documents such as diaries and letters, media content, digital sources and published sources.

- Research can produce quantitative or qualitative data.

- Sociological methods and their findings can be evaluated in terms of their validity, reliability, representativeness and generalisability.

KEY SKILLS EXERCISES

1 Knowledge and understanding

Without using this book or your notes, see if you can list the **four** types of interview. Check your answer. Then give **two** strengths and **two** limitations for each type.

2 Presenting data

These data would be better presented visually. Convert them into a graph, chart or table.

The number of undernourished people in the world went down from 883 million in 2001 to 663 million in 2017. In Asia, the number of undernourished people went down during these years from 565 to 378 million. In South America, the number of undernourished people went down from 38 million to 22 million. In Africa, the number of undernourished people increased from 198 to 231 million. [Ourworldindata.org]

3 Analysis and evaluation

Write up to 500 words to answer the question: 'To what extent is participant observation a useful method in sociology?' In your essay, try to use these terms (and any others you think are relevant): qualitative data, validity, verstehen, meanings and motivations. Make sure you cover both the strengths and limitations of participant observation.

IMPROVE THIS ANSWER

Research methods, identity and inequality

Evaluate the view that objectivity is essential in sociological research. Your answer should include:

- at least two arguments for and two arguments against the approach

- a conclusion.

Objectivity means that the researcher is unbiased, being neutral and not influencing the results. One reason this is essential is because it means that the results are more likely to be accurate and reliable; the research can be repeated by another researcher, and the same results should be obtained. However, interpretivists say that complete objectivity is not possible, because researchers are people and are bound to be personally involved in their research. For example, their values and interests may affect what they choose to study and how they interpret findings. This means that objectivity cannot be essential.

Commentary and task

This is an evaluation question. It requires at least two arguments for the view in the question, at least two arguments against the view in the question and a conclusion. The answer so far gives only one argument on each side. Complete the answer by adding another argument for and another argument against, and a conclusion.

PRACTICE QUESTIONS

Research methods, identity and inequality

1 Read **Source A** and then answer the questions that follow.

Source A

A team of researchers led by Sarah Cant investigated the views of sociology teachers in schools in England on the teaching of sociology. Their methods were a survey and group interviews.

To obtain their sample, the researchers first contacted all schools in England to ask whether they taught sociology; then they asked for the email addresses of sociology teachers. Not all schools replied and some schools had policies that meant they could not share the email addresses of their staff.

The survey questionnaire was sent to 963 schools that had been identified as teaching sociology. Automatic entry in a prize draw was offered as an incentive to complete the questionnaire. A reminder was sent to those who did not reply. In total, 212 respondents returned the completed questionnaire.

The main finding was that although sociology is a popular choice for learners, sociology teachers feel their subject is seen as having lower status than some other subjects and that they do not get enough support as a result.

(Savage, M. and Chatterjee, A. 2020)

a	i	From **Source A**, identify **two** methods used in this research.	[2]
	ii	Using information in **Source A**, explain **two** ways in which the researchers tried to ensure there was a good response rate.	[4]
	iii	Using information in **Source A**, explain **three** reasons why the responses may not be representative of all sociology teachers in England.	[6]
b		Identify **two** practical issues affecting sociological research.	[2]
c		Explain **one** strength and **one** limitation of covert observation.	[4]
d		Evaluate the view that objectivity is essential in sociological research.	

Your answer should include:

- at least **two** arguments for and **two** arguments against the approach

- a conclusion. [10]

e Explain the research methods and evidence that you would choose to investigate how schools use online learning. Give reasons for your choices.

Your answer should include:

- **two** primary methods with relevant sampling

- **one** source of secondary evidence. [12]

SELF-EVALUATION CHECKLIST

After studying this unit, complete this table:

You should be able to:	Needs more work	Almost there	Ready to move on
1.1 How do sociologists approach the study of society?			
Understand the positivist approach			
Understand the interpretivist approach			
Understand approaches that combine different research methods and evidence			
Analyse and evaluate research choices			
1.2 What types of data and evidence do sociologists use?			
Evaluate the strengths and limitations of primary and secondary sources of data			
Evaluate the strengths and limitations of qualitative and quantitative data			
Evaluate the strengths and limitations of secondary data			
Analyse, interpret and evaluate data from qualitative and quantitative sources			
1.3 How do sociologists investigate society?			
Explain the stages in research design			
Explain different sampling frames and sampling techniques, including their strengths and limitations			
Evaluate the strengths and limitations of quantitative and qualitative primary research methods (surveys and questionnaires, interviews, observations)			
Explain different types of question			
Discuss the theoretical and practical issues affecting research			
Discuss the ethical issues affecting research			

> **Unit 2**

Identity: self and society

LEARNING INTENTIONS

In this unit you will learn how to:

- Understand the key terms culture, norms, values, roles, beliefs and identity; appreciate that these are social constructions and understand how they influence human behaviour

- Describe and account for diversity and variations in human behaviour and culture, including the relativity of culture

- Explain the different agencies of socialisation and their impact on individuals, including the consequences of inadequate socialisation

- Assess the different views in the nature/nurture debate

- Understand the terms 'conformity' and 'non-conformity' and how agencies of social control work

- Recognise examples of rewards and sanctions applied in different societies and organisations

- Explain the nature of sub-cultures and how they impact on consensus and conflict

CONTINUED

- Assess the role of age, gender, ethnic group and class as influences on social identity

- Explain the ways in which childhood is socially constructed

- Assess the view that globalisation is creating a global culture.

Introduction

This unit considers the relationship between the individual and society, what constitutes our identity and how identity and behaviour are shaped by social processes. You will consider ideas about how individuals are socialised into their culture and how they may be socially controlled. This unit will introduce three main sociological perspectives on these processes, which have differing views on whether social control, for example, is a good or a bad thing.

What makes us human? For sociologists, what makes us distinctively human is our relationships with other people, how we live in groups and societies, and how we reflect and act upon our lives. This unit explores the relationships between individuals and societies, and how much our identities are shaped by the social influences and people around us.

Figure 2.1: The family is usually the main agent of socialisation during childhood.

2.1 How do we learn our identity?

Society as a product of social construction

This section examines the **social constructions** of culture, norms, values, customs and roles. It also investigates how they are created by, and then influence, human behaviour.

There is no single definition of the term **culture** but it is used in two main ways. In everyday speech, it usually refers to things such as art, music and literature – sometimes called 'high culture'. It can also refer to things such as the media, fashion and advertising – sometimes called 'popular culture'. In this unit, we will use the term 'culture' in a broader way, to mean a society's whole way of life. Every aspect of human life is influenced by culture in this sense, because we constantly refer – whether consciously or unconsciously – to our society or social group for guidelines about how to think and behave. Culture includes:

- what you eat and drink, with whom and when

- how you dress and the care you take over your appearance

- the language, spoken and unspoken, that you use to communicate with others

- the way you spend your leisure time

- the kind of home and family you live within

KEY TERMS

social construction: the idea that social situations and events are made by societies; they do not exist in nature as independent things

culture: the way of life of a society

- the kinds of work that people do
- religious and spiritual beliefs and practices
- festivals and celebrations.

All societies have ideas about the right and wrong ways of doing these things.

Society and culture are very closely related and the terms are sometimes used interchangeably. However, they are different – although they cannot exist without each other. Society is made up of institutions, both formal ones (such as the legal and educational systems) and informal ones (such as families). Culture is about how these institutions work; how they set norms and expectations about the roles people should play.

Society and the institutions within it are made up of individual people, and every individual within a society has their own sense of identity. Identity refers to our sense of who we are, how we see ourselves and the ways in which we think we are similar to and different from other people. An important part of this relates to how other people see us and judge us. In other words, our sense of self or identity is heavily influenced by others. Other people may give us feedback about ourselves and our behaviour, but even without feedback, we can put ourselves in the position of others and imagine how they would see us.

Elements of culture: norms and values

Two important elements of any human culture are **norms** and **values**.

- **Norms.** Norms are the kinds of behaviour that a society expects of its members in particular situations. There is a wide range of norms; some are more widely observed than others, and some carry more of a sense of what is right or wrong. For example, there are different norms about how to greet someone you are meeting for the first time. In some societies, the norm is to shake hands but in others, it is to bow. People visiting a place with a different culture need to be aware of the norms so they do not cause offence. Norms that are widely accepted and continue over time are sometimes called **customs**. In addition, some norms are given extra importance by being used as the basis for rules, regulations and **laws**. Norms are usually enforced by informal means. Laws are usually enforced by formal means.

- **Values.** Values are standards of what is considered good and right. They act as guides for what people should think and believe, and how they should act. Many people claim to have their own values but these values will be shared with other people.

Both values and norms provide guidelines for how people should behave. Values relate to ideas which we see as important, and they might relate to things such as personal space, respect and privacy. Norms are expected ways of behaving which are based on these values. Knowledge of key values allows us to work out what the norms will be, even in a new situation. For example, norms based on the value of personal space might include how far away you stand when talking to someone and where you sit, for example, on a bus or in a train.

Values and norms vary across society. This shows that they are socially constructed. They are not part of a universal culture and people are not born knowing them. They have to be learnt and passed on to the next generation. Think again about the example of the value of personal space. In some societies, people stand closer to each other when talking than in other societies. There are also societies where it is normal to sit next to a stranger on a bus, even if there are empty seats available, whereas in other societies, this would be seen as strange behaviour. These are norms based on values about personal space.

One distinctive value in some modern industrial societies is the desirability of being wealthy and owning material goods.

KEY TERMS

norms: the behaviour that societies expect of their members in particular situations

values: standards shared by members of a culture and used to judge whether behaviour is right or wrong

customs: norms in a particular society that are widely accepted and continue over time

laws: rules, usually formalised by government, that are used to order the way in which a society behaves

Someone who is able to buy an expensive car, live in a large house and travel widely for pleasure is usually seen as successful and has a high status. Indigenous Americans (people living in America before Europeans arrived) also placed a high value on possessions but this was not for personal enjoyment. At festivals known as potlatch celebrations, wealthy Indigenous Americans gave away lavish gifts to their guests. In return, the gift giver received the approval of the recipients and was looked up to and highly respected. Possessions were considered to have little value other than to be given away; by which the owner could acquire status and respect. An individual in a modern industrial society who gave away most of their possessions in this way would be considered eccentric or even insane. This shows how values can vary enormously between cultures.

KEY TERM

status: a position that someone has in a society; status can be ascribed (fixed by others) or achieved

---

Figure 2.2: Shopping for material goods.

Norms and values also change over time in a society. In his book *The Civilising Process*, Norbert Elias described how in Europe during the Middle Ages, there were fewer limits on individual behaviour than there are today. The state was weak and unable to control individual behaviour to any great extent, so people with power could more easily use violence and force to get their own way. As the state grew in power, however, this led to a 'civilising process'. During the Middle Ages, for example, it was common for strangers to share a bed in an inn, for people to eat with their fingers from common bowls and for people to go to the toilet in public. By around 500 years ago, books on etiquette were advising the nobility that burping, breaking wind, spitting and picking your nose in public were rude acts, signifying bad manners. By the 19th century, such behaviour was unacceptable in all but the lowest classes and children were taught these norms.

In modern societies, there are more norms that cover more areas of life. Elias also suggests that it has become the norm to control emotion. People still have violent and intense emotions but, in most societies and situations, they do not show them in public.

Because norms and values are different in different societies around the world and also vary depending on the period of history, we can say that they are socially constructed and relative. Norms and values are made by societies, not by individuals, and they are not natural in the way that, for example, scratching an itch is natural.

People in a society share values and norms so, most of the time, social life is orderly and predictable. We know what other people are likely to do and how they will respond to what we do. Not everyone shares all the values or conforms to all the norms but societies have ways of expressing disapproval of those who break the norms. Societies also have ways of encouraging, or forcing, people to conform.

Other aspects of culture which relate to norms and values include symbols and language. A symbol is something that carries a particular meaning, that is recognised by people who share the same culture. For example, a cross worn on a chain is a symbol of Christian religious beliefs, and a shirt with a particular colour and badge may show that the person wearing it supports a particular football team. Countries have national symbols, such as flags. The understanding of such symbols and their meaning is part of a culture's norms and values.

Language can be seen as a system of symbols, in which sounds and words carry meaning. Language allows people to communicate with one another and there are norms surrounding the use of language – for example, not swearing or using rude words in a formal situation.

Status and role

Most norms are associated with status, which is the position a person has in a society. For example, you have the status of a sociology student. Your teacher's status is that of a teacher. But you both have other statuses as well. For example, in your family, your status is son or daughter, brother or sister. Being a teenager gives you a lower status than your parents and other adults but this will change when you become accepted as an adult. In many societies, especially in the past, most statuses were ascribed. That means that they were decided at birth and individuals could not choose or decide their status for themselves. This still applies today, with statuses based on gender, age and ethnicity, for example. In modern societies, however, some important statuses are now achieved. Individuals can make decisions or take actions – for example, relating to the work they do – that lead to a particular status.

With each status comes a set of norms, called a role. The role of a student includes norms such as attending classes, asking questions and learning. Students are expected to sit at a desk and listen to what the teacher says. Having a role is like having a part in a play, but you have some choice over how you act that role. For example, you may be a good student or a lazy one.

KEY TERMS

gender: the roles and expectations associated with being male or female

age: a form of stratification based on how old people are; age is often looked at in stages rather than specific numbers – childhood, youth, adulthood and old age. There are particular roles and expectations associated with each age

ethnicity: the state of belonging to a particular group with a shared culture, including language, beliefs, history and traditions

role: the patterns of behaviour expected of someone because of their status in society

How these concepts influence individual behaviour and social identity

Social identities are how we perceive ourselves and how we are perceived by others. Everyone has different statuses and roles and most people have multiple roles. Roles are based on our relationships with others. For example, one of the authors of this book is a husband, a father, a lecturer and an author. He is also a customer for the businesses he uses and a patient to his doctor. Each of these roles is part of

his identity, although some roles are more important than others in particular social circumstances, and the relative importance of each role will vary depending on the situation. People experience role conflict when the norms attached to two or more different roles are incompatible with each other. For example, a parent may experience conflict between their work role (the need to be at the office, working hard) and their role as a mother or father (the need to nurture their children).

TIP

Remember that roles and identities are not fixed. They continually change as a person grows from a child to an adult, changes careers, has a family, etc.

Stereotypes

Within cultures, individuals learn the norms, values and statuses of different people, as well as their associated roles. This creates stereotypes – oversimplified sets of ideas about a particular type of person or social group. The media often use these one-sided, exaggerated images because they are widely understood and a convenient way of conveying ideas. Stereotypes are usually misleading but often contain some truth; they can be positive as well as negative. Media portrayals of particular groups often rely on stereotypes. For example, in the UK media, young people are often portrayed as disrespectful and reckless.

Such stereotypes are repeated so often that they seem to be accurate; as a result, they are often believed, especially by people who have no personal experience with which to challenge the stereotype. For example, someone who has no recent experience of being around young people is more likely to believe that they are all disrespectful and reckless. In contrast, a teacher who works with young people is more likely to reject the stereotype, since they will have personal experience of the differences between individuals and may know many respectful young people.

KEY TERMS

social identity: an individual's perception of themselves, based partly on ideas about how others see them

stereotype: an oversimplified set of ideas about a particular type of person or social group

The social construction of our identity

Our social identity, or image of ourselves, is therefore formed through interaction with others. Identifying ourselves as male or female is our gender identity. We also develop identities in particular groups and situations, such as in our family, at work, at school. We see ourselves as having certain characteristics, such as being a good friend or being a tough boss. Identities connect individuals to society in the sense that, through our identity, we can see ourselves in the context of our culture. This allows us to link our inner selves (who we think we really are) with the roles we occupy.

We can choose how to respond to the identities we see ourselves as having. For example, a person with a disability may see their disability as an important aspect of their identity because they are often treated differently from others. They can choose how they engage with this, for example by passively accepting inferior treatment or by rejecting the label and fighting back to emphasise their abilities. The sociologist Stuart Hall argued that in the 21st century, people are often more uncertain about their identities than they might have been in the past. For example, ethnic identities are no longer as clear as they once were; more people have mixed backgrounds and are familiar with different cultures. Many people also have more roles than they would have in the past and there may be more uncertainty about what these roles involve. Having more roles can be both positive and negative – it gives us more choices but can also make us feel confused or overwhelmed.

ACTIVITY: RESEARCH 2.1

1   Interview several older people (for example, members of your family or neighbours) and ask them how your society's culture has changed during their lifetimes. Before you start, look again at the section on interviews in Research methods in Unit 1 and decide how to conduct the interviews and what kinds of questions you will ask.

2   From what your respondents say, try to identify changes in values and norms.

REFLECTION

Consider the changes in values and norms you identified in your research. Were you aware of these changes in your society's culture before the interviews?

If you were, how? If you were not, why not?

What other topics in sociology could older people be a useful source of information about?

The nature–nurture debate

The **nature–nurture** debate is about the extent to which our personality, attitudes and behaviour are determined by our genes (our nature) or by our social environment (nurture). This is a long-running debate with arguments on both sides. Recent research suggests that there is a complex relationship between nature and nurture; in other words, both sides are partly right. Sociologists tend to concentrate on nurture, since they are interested in the impact of society and culture – rather than biology – on individuals.

The two extreme positions in the nature–nurture debate are called determinism. Biological determinists argue that nature is the most important influence on our behaviour. Social determinists argue that society is the most important influence. On the nature side of the debate, sociobiologists argue that all social behaviour is directed by natural instincts or biological drives. We have known for many years that aspects of our appearance – such as eye colour and hair colour – are determined

KEY TERMS

nature: (in the nature–nurture debate) the influence of biological factors on human behaviour

nurture: (in the nature–nurture debate) the influence of society and culture on human behaviour

by the genes found in our cells; they are inherited. The nature theory argues that traits and behaviour such as intelligence, personality and aggressiveness may also be inherited.

On the nurture side of the debate, sociologists argue that, while we may inherit tendencies, they do not determine how we behave. Through socialisation, people who are genetically very similar may become very different people. As conscious human beings, we are able to make decisions about how we behave and about the sort of person we are. For example, biological determinists would see aggression as an inherited trait. Social determinists, on the other hand, would look at the ways individuals are socialised to express aggression in their culture; for instance, in many cultures, it is more acceptable for men to show aggression than women.

One extreme example often used to support the nurture side of the debate is that of **feral children**. These are children who have had little or no human contact in early childhood. Sometimes they have been completely neglected; in other instances, they have spent more time among animals than people. When such children are found and studied, they often find it difficult to learn 'human' behaviours and adapt to their new surroundings. For example, they struggle to learn language and to interact with other children or adults. The study of feral children shows that much human behaviour is learnt from others, rather than being instinctive or natural.

ACTIVITY: RESEARCH 2.2

Use the internet to research the topic of feral children. Write a short summary of your findings. For each case you find, decide to what extent you trust the information.

The relativity of culture

Human cultures are very **diverse**. What is considered normal in one culture may be seen as strange, deviant or offensive in another. This shows the **relativity of culture**: all cultural norms and values are relative (they vary in relation to one another), not fixed.

Some areas of cultural relativity include:

- language
- norms of dress and appearance
- food and drink

- traditions, such as rituals and festivals
- ideas about morality.

Here are some cultural variations relating to food:

- Cultures have different ideas about what people should and should not eat, such as insects and certain animals. For example, horse meat is eaten in many countries in Europe but not (usually) in the UK.

- The main global religions have some followers who keep to dietary rules. For example, Muslims do not eat pork or drink alcohol. Jains believe in the sanctity of all life and so do not eat meat, poultry, fish or eggs; some even avoid eating root vegetables, as the whole plant is killed when the root is dug up.

- Meat and fish are usually cooked before eating but there are exceptions. For instance, raw fish is eaten in Japan and Rastafarians only eat lightly cooked food.

- There are cultural variations relating to mealtimes and who should eat with whom; for example, men and women eat separately in some cultures.

- Some cultures tend to avoid eating with their hands and instead use cutlery such as knives, forks and spoons. Others use chopsticks or eat with their hands.

In recent decades, knowledge about other cultures has spread rapidly, through travel and migration and through electronic mass communication. We are now more aware that we live in a diverse multicultural world, and many people are able to access and appreciate aspects of other cultures, such as their food, music and clothing. This has been called the 'global village', as we have all become closer. For example, people from all around the world are aware of and able to watch mega-events, such as the Olympic Games in Tokyo in 2021.

KEY TERMS

feral children: 'wild' children who have not been socialised

diverse: varied; cultural diversity refers to the wide differences between human cultures

relativity of culture: the idea that all cultures vary and change; culture is not fixed, but relative to time and place

CASE STUDY 2.1

The Amish

Figure 2.3: The Amish.

The Amish are groups of traditional Christians who live mainly in the USA and Canada. They have a distinctive way of life based on their religious beliefs and practices. The Amish reject many aspects of modern life, including most – but not all – modern technology, and largely keep themselves apart from mainstream society. They dress very plainly and the men wear wide-brimmed hats. The Amish place a high value on humility, calmness, rural living, simplicity and hard manual labour. They avoid using electricity, telephones and cars (they prefer horse-drawn carriages) and they refuse to perform military service. They have religious objections to commercial insurance and to social security, although they pay sales and property taxes.

If members of the community do not follow these rules, they may be **ostracised** (rejected socially) or excommunicated (permanently excluded from the community). These are forms of **social control**. In some Amish communities, teenagers are allowed a period called *rumspringa* (running around), when they can behave in ways that would result in ostracism for an adult.

TASK

1. In what ways is the Amish way of life different from that of most Americans today?

2. How might *rumspringa* be functional for the Amish way of life?

3. Do you know of any other groups who reject 'modern' ideas?

Figure 2.4: The Olympic Games in Tokyo in 2021.

There are now very few groups of people with **lifestyles** that are relatively isolated from other cultures.

The main flow of culture has been from Europe and the USA to the rest of the world: elements of European or American influence can be seen in all cultures. Some people fear that this may lead to cultural uniformity, where all cultures around the world are similar (for example, speaking the same language and eating the same kinds of foods).

KEY TERMS

ostracise: exclude someone from a community or group

social control: ways in which members of society are made to conform to norms and values

lifestyle: the typical way of life of an individual, group or culture

Some people are concerned that **globalisation** is reducing cultural diversity and may be leading to the development of a single human culture based on Western values. This view is considered in the discussion of globalisation in section 2.3.

Socialisation, norms and values

Socialisation is the process by which the norms and values of a culture are passed on by **agencies of socialisation**, which include the family, the peer group, education, media, religion and the workplace.

Socialisation happens throughout life. However, the most important period is **primary socialisation**, which takes place mainly within the family, from birth to infancy. This is when children learn the basics of interacting with other people. For example, they learn how to smile and how other people will react to this. Human beings are born helpless and have to become aware of themselves, learning to live in the culture they have been born into. This makes it possible for societies to survive over time. In early childhood, we learn the norms and values of the culture we live in – for example, how to eat and ideas of good and bad behaviour.

The main agencies of **secondary socialisation** are education, religion, workplaces, the media and **peer groups**. Each time a person faces a new situation –

such as starting school, starting a new job or getting married – they have to learn new roles and accompanying norms; these are learnt through secondary socialisation. In some situations, people need to change their behaviour a lot. For example, if a person joins the armed forces, emigrates to another country or is sent to prison, they will have to learn a completely new set of norms and values to fit into their new environment. In these situations, resocialisation takes place.

Socialisation is not a simple process of absorbing ideas and messages. We are actively involved in our own socialisation, thinking about how the messages apply to us, how others see us and how we can or should amend our behaviour. We can reject some messages and choose which norms and values to follow if there are conflicting messages from different agencies of socialisation. For example, a child's peer group may encourage them to follow different norms and values to those of their school or family.

Key agencies of socialisation

Figure 2.5: A family.

The family

The family is usually the main agent of socialisation during childhood. There are many types of family, so children can have very different experiences. Many children spend most of their early years in a family of mother, father and siblings. Others are brought up by only one parent, grandparents and step or adoptive parents.

KEY TERMS

globalisation: the complex process by which different cultures around the world are increasingly aware of, interact with and influence each other

socialisation: the process of learning the norms and values of a culture

agencies of socialisation: the groups and institutions which carry out the process of socialisation

primary socialisation: the process by which infants and young children absorb the basic norms and values of their culture. This is the first and most important stage of socialisation, which usually takes place in the family during early childhood

secondary socialisation: later socialisation, when people learn more specific norms for particular statuses and roles

peer group: people of the same status (for example, people the same age)

The **social class** and ethnicity of the family are also important. Children internalise the language and behaviour of their parents and others in the family, so they become part of who they are. The family may continue to act as an agent of socialisation in adulthood.

Many sociologists see the family as the most important agent of socialisation. Some sociologists argue that children who are not brought up in a stable family with two parents will suffer from inadequate socialisation, which may have negative consequences for them and for society as a whole (such as criminal behaviour and mental health problems).

Education

The education system of schools and colleges is another important agent of socialisation. Children learn the formal curriculum but they also learn about the organisation of the classroom and the school and the behaviour expected of them. This is the **hidden curriculum** described in section 2.1. In modern industrial societies, many children now attend pre-school institutions, where they begin to learn these things. In traditional societies, children may be educated by adult members of the family and community.

For many children, education is the first formal institution they come into contact with, and the norms and values it teaches are usually more consistent than those learnt in the family. Most children spend at least ten of their most important, formative years in education of some kind, and what they learn there will have a big impact on the path they take in their adult life. For this reason, many sociologists see education as the most important agent of socialisation: what is learnt through the hidden curriculum is important in shaping adult behaviour, including values such as respect for authority and acceptance of a hierarchy.

Peer groups

Peer groups are made up of people of the same age and status. They may include friends but not all peers will be friends, or even people you know personally. Peer groups are seen as having the most impact on children because, during their time in education, children tend to mix almost exclusively with people of a similar age. The desire to fit in and belong is particularly strong for children and teenagers, so the peer group is often a very effective agent of socialisation, working alongside the school to shape young people's norms and values. Peer groups may also apply **peer pressure**, encouraging people to act in ways that are approved of by their friends.

Figure 2.6: A child experiencing peer pressure.

Media

The media is now an important part of socialisation throughout life. In traditional societies, the equivalent of the media is the oral storytelling tradition, in which many stories have messages that children learn from. Today, the media includes 'traditional' media forms such as television, radio and newspapers, but also digital and **social media**, which can be accessed online and arguably have an enormous influence on people's lives.

KEY TERMS

social class: a shared economic and social status; for example, working class, middle class or upper class

hidden curriculum: what learners learn in school, apart from the content of lessons, such as the importance of following rules and the consequences of not doing so

peer pressure: the influence of a group of people of the same age and status, to force or persuade its members to conform

social media: internet-based applications for sharing content and communicating online, such as Instagram and Weibo

---

The media provides most of our ideas and information about other parts of the world, and about what is important in our own culture.

As mentioned previously, the media often portrays social groups in stereotypical ways; as a result, this form of socialisation can be very effective but also quite divisive.

STRETCH AND CHALLENGE

In what ways could you argue that the media is now more important than ever before as an agent of socialisation?

Religion

Religious organisations, such as mosques and churches, are often important agencies of socialisation. Many children learn moral values by attending places of worship with their parents and other believers, or from hearing and reading holy books and teachings. Some religious organisations have a formal process of becoming a member and, once an individual becomes a member, the organisation's rules and guidance may strongly influence them. For individuals who are part of a religious community or have a strong belief, religion can be a very effective form of socialisation, since the values promoted come from a higher authority and are therefore unlikely to be challenged or questioned.

However, in some countries – particularly those in Europe – religion is losing its significance. This decline in the importance of religion is some societies is called secularisation. As societies become more secular and less religious, the effectiveness of religion as an agent of socialisation is declining. However, it remains very strong in some communities and in large parts of the world.

Workplace

When a person starts a new job, they learn the expectations of their role and modify their behaviour based on what their employer wants and expects them to do. They may go on training courses and learn how to get on with fellow workers. There is pressure on workers to conform to the norms of their workplace, to gain acceptance and approval from their employer and peer workers, and perhaps to keep their job or be promoted. Most adults spend the majority of their time at work, so the workplace can be an effective agent of socialisation. Every workplace has its own 'canteen culture'. This term relates to people (maybe mixing in the workplace canteen) influencing each other and developing their own set of norms and values in relation to their workplace.

MAKING CONNECTIONS

Do any of the agencies of socialisation described so far overlap? Which ones?

Processes used by agencies of socialisation

From a very early age, children try to conform to social expectations. They learn from parents and others, often through imitation: young children see someone doing something and copy it. They are more likely to imitate behaviour that is positively sanctioned (rewarded in some way). When parents or others apply **sanctions** to behaviour, this is called reinforcement.

Another process which has been identified in the family is **canalisation**. This is a way in which children learn their **gender roles** through socialisation, when parents channel their children towards certain activities and hobbies based on gender expectations. For example, girls may be taken to dancing lessons while boys are pushed more towards sport.

Role modelling

Older children and adults may act as **role models**: people that someone looks up to and tries to imitate. For example, a child may see their mother being polite or kind and copy them, because they have learnt that this is

KEY TERMS

sanctions: ways of rewarding or punishing acceptable or unacceptable behaviour; usually used in the sense of punishment (negative sanctions)

canalisation: channelling children towards activities that are considered appropriate for them (for example, because of their gender)

gender roles: the roles and expectations associated with being male or female

role modelling: when someone acts as an example, so their behaviour is copied by others

role models: people someone looks up to and tries to be like

good behaviour. Role models can also be people the child sees or learns about through the media, such as sports players, celebrities and influencers.

Hidden curriculum

At school, children do not only learn the formal curriculum of subjects such as science and mathematics. They also learn a hidden curriculum, relating to the organisation of the school and classroom and the things that are taught alongside formal lessons such as respect, conformity and punctuality. Children absorb a range of norms and values from the hidden curriculum, such as their status in relation to adults, and the importance of consideration for others.

Figure 2.7: A school.

Media representations

Today, the media is increasingly important because people spend more time using it; this is especially true with the rise of digital and social media. There are many films and television programmes aimed at children, and young people spend more and more time interacting via digital and social media. For a long time, sociologists have tried to find out whether the socialisation of children by the media might have negative effects. For example, children might watch violent content and copy it, thinking such behaviour is acceptable. In fact, research suggests that children can be thoughtful and discriminating viewers who do not passively accept media messages. Instead, they try to make sense of them, often with help from their family and peers.

The importance of the media continues throughout life. For example, news coverage of crimes and court cases reminds people of the limits of acceptable behaviour and the consequences of breaking the law.

Advertising socialises people into being consumers; they are encouraged to want things, even when they cannot afford them or do not need them. Various forms of media present stereotypical representations of groups of people, including women, young people and immigrants; if an audience does not have access to alternative information, they might accept these portrayals as accurate.

Peer pressure

Peer groups are very important in the socialisation of children and young people; they can also influence adults, since most people want to be accepted by their peers. Peer groups have a particularly strong influence on teenagers, who may behave in ways that help them fit in with friends, sometimes in opposition to the ways expected by parents and school. There are two main types of peer pressure:

- Active peer pressure is when a group of peers encourage or even demand certain behaviour from others to be accepted into their group, or to prevent harsh treatment. This can be seen as a form of bullying.

- In other circumstances, an individual may choose to change their behaviour to confirm and fit in, because they want to be accepted by a particular peer group. This is a form of **social conformity**.

> ### KEY TERM
>
> **social conformity:** acting in accordance with norms and social expectations in order to fit in with others

Peer pressure is now commonly seen on social media platforms. Many people – both young and old – are anxious about the numbers of 'likes' or 'shares' their posts receive, while negative comments are often used to negatively sanction behaviour or opinions expressed online.

Religious teachings

Attending a religious institution or being exposed to religious teachings can be an important part of socialisation. Many people hold strong religious beliefs, so religious teachings will have a strong influence on them. The world's major religions all give instruction or advice on how to behave; for example, the Ten Commandments in Christianity and the Five Pillars of Islam.

Workplace training

Workplaces often make new workers take training courses, and further courses may be needed for promotion or more pay. Workplace training can help workers adapt to the expectations and requirements of a job, both in terms of the work itself and to fit in with other workers.

The debate between sociological perspectives and their theories on socialisation

Sociologists have different views on the nature of society and social life. These are referred to as perspectives and relate to underlying ideas about **conflict** and **consensus**. Different sociological theories – functionalism, Marxism and feminism – use their different perspectives to explain things which happen in society. This section will introduce these three sociological theories, then consider their differing views on socialisation.

KEY TERMS

conflict: disagreement; this term is used to describe a perspective on society which assumes there are basic disagreements between social groups (for example, based on social class or gender differences)

consensus: agreement; this term is used to describe a perspective on society which assumes that people generally share values

Consensus and conflict

Different sociological perspectives emphasise social consensus and social conflict to differing extents.

There is social consensus (agreement) when people generally share values and there are no major disagreements between the main groups.

This is only possible if all the groups in a society have similar levels of wealth, status and power or if it is widely accepted that it is right for each group to have the current level of wealth, status and power. A society built on consensus will be stable and harmonious. The shared values may be based on a religion or belief system, or perhaps on political ideas; there are likely to be shared practices and rituals that bring everyone together and give them a sense of belonging so they identify strongly with their society and its values.

Social conflict occurs when there are major disagreements about important issues such as wealth, status and power. In a society based on conflict, there will be significant and important differences between groups and there will be no overall set of shared values held by all groups. A society based on conflict may be unstable, though the groups with power may find ways to ensure that other groups do not recognise the differences in values and interests and instead accept their situation.

Some perspectives in sociology do not focus on consensus or conflict. Instead, they take a more micro (small-scale) approach to understanding society, sometimes known as interpretivist approaches. For example, interactionism is an interpretivist approach and one of its main ideas is labelling theory (covered in Unit 5). Because interpretivists are more interested in individuals and small-scale social interactions than in the overall nature of a society, the debates about conflict and consensus are seen as irrelevant. However, interpretivists are sometimes criticised for not taking into account the wider issues such as power, which may influence the situations they study.

ACTIVITY: DISCUSSION 2.1

In a small group with other learners, discuss this question:

Is your society today based more on consensus or on conflict?

REFLECTION

Were you able to reach a consensus within your group? What kinds of evidence did you consider to reach any decision you made? Do you think that comparing your society with other societies would make a difference to your answer?

Functionalism

Functionalism is the main sociological theory based on a consensus perspective. Functionalists emphasise functions and ask, 'What function does this aspect of society perform, that keeps this society stable and allows it to continue?' They might say, for example:

- The function of schools is to give young people the skills they need for work, which helps the economy of a society.

- The function of families is to socialise children into the norms and values of the society, so the next generation will have these values.

- The function of prisons is to (temporarily) remove from society people who do not follow the laws and who therefore upset the smooth running of society.

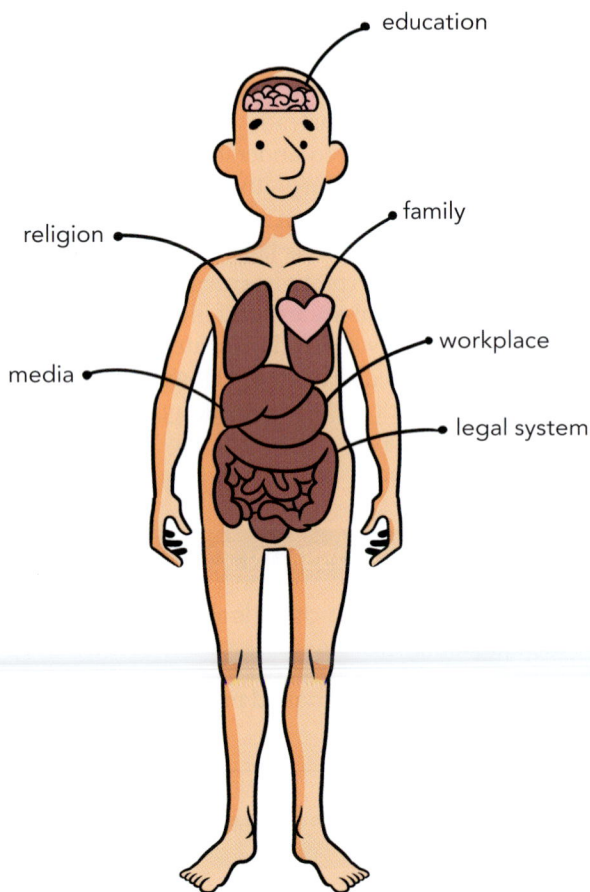

Figure 2.8: The functionalist idea is that if all the systems (organs) in society are functioning in harmony, it will remain healthy.

Functionalists see human society as being like the human body. This is called the organic or biological analogy because it compares society to a living organism. The different parts of the human body – the brain, heart, liver, skin and so on – all have jobs to do to keep you healthy. In the same way, each part of society is seen as having functions that help the society as a whole to be healthy and survive.

If something goes wrong in one part of your body, it may affect other parts. It can also be a warning sign that you need to change something. So, in a human society, an increase in crime might become a problem that needs to be addressed, perhaps by schools more effectively teaching children to obey the law.

Functionalism was the most important theory in sociology for many years, especially in the early and mid-20th century. Most sociologists thought societies worked in this way. The main sociologist associated with this theory is the American Talcott Parsons (1902–1979).

Inadequate socialisation

Functionalists see socialisation as essential; the example of feral children shows what can happen if children are not socialised into human society. Most functionalists see the family as the most important agent of socialisation, since it teaches the basic norms and values of society to children and helps them to become fully functioning members of society. Feral children have clearly had **inadequate socialisation**, but functionalists would also be concerned about families that do not teach their children the correct norms and values. For example, some functionalists worry that children who grow up in one-parent families may not have proper role models; or that families that do not promote the importance of education or following the rules may be inadequately socialising their children for their future lives. This could have a negative impact on society in terms of poor performance in school or high crime rates, for example.

KEY TERM

inadequate socialisation: socialisation that does not fully instil the shared norms and values of a society; individuals who are inadequately socialised are more likely to become deviant

---

Social cohesion and value consensus

According to functionalists, socialisation ensures that almost everyone in a society shares the same norms and values. This creates a feeling of belonging (social cohesion) because there is widespread agreement on values (value consensus). It makes it possible for people to predict how others will behave. This is true even in new situations, where you may not know all the norms that apply: you will be able to work out some of the most important ones by knowing the underlying values. For functionalists, social cohesion is very important because it ensures that all individuals accept society's rules and also, when necessary, accepts things which do not feel functional (such as failure at school or at work, or price rises). The sense that 'we are all in it together' and that everything works for the good of society is very important in ensuring that society survives.

Marxism

The theory of Marxism argues that modern industrial capitalist societies are based on a conflict between different social classes. The economic system of capitalism promotes private ownership of property and wealth, encouraging the accumulation of profit. Marxists refer to two main classes in capitalist societies:

- The bourgeoisie are the owners of wealth and property, sometimes referred to as the ruling class. They have power and wealth and they exploit and oppress the proletariat.
- The proletariat (the working class) are 'wage slaves'. This means they must work to survive, but they are never paid the full value of their work – this is taken by the ruling class as profits.

KEY TERMS

social cohesion: the sense of belonging and amount of connectedness between groups in society

value consensus: widespread agreement on values

Marxism: a theoretical perspective that sees conflict between classes as the most important feature of society

bourgeoisie: in the theory of Marxism, the bourgeoisie are the owners of wealth and property, sometimes referred to as the ruling class

proletariat: in the theory of Marxism, the proletariat are working-class people who must work to survive

---

Where functionalists look at how the parts of society keep society stable and harmonious, Marxists look at how these parts of society allow the bourgeoisie to keep their wealth and power. Marxists say, for example:

- Schools ensure that working-class children fail and that they think this is their own fault, so they then accept a low position in society.
- The media distracts people's attention from what is really going on, directing their interest to celebrities, sport and trivial issues.

Therefore, Marxists agree with functionalists that parts of society have functions, but they disagree completely about who benefits from these functions.

Marxism is much more than a sociological theory. It is also important in politics, history and economics. Marxism inspired the political movements of socialism and communism, which involve attempts to create new societies based on equality rather than class divisions. Marxists are in favour of radical social changes that would end exploitation and make everyone equal. Critics of Marxism argue that this is probably impossible and that many attempts to create equal societies have led to even greater oppression.

Marxism is named after Karl Marx (1818–1883). However, Marxist ideas have developed considerably since his time, as later Marxists have tried to adapt his ideas to explain societies today and the issues they face. Modern Marxist writers are often called neo-Marxists.

Socialisation into capitalist ideology

Like functionalists, Marxists believe that socialisation has a function. However, they see that function as being in the interests of the bourgeoisie only, based on capitalist norms and values ('capitalist ideology'). The Marxist approach focuses on how people are controlled through socialisation; this is explored further in section 2.2.

Reproduction of social class

According to Marxism, socialisation functions to enable the survival of capitalist society. It does this by ensuring that capitalist norms and values are passed from one generation to the next. Again, this is similar to functionalist ideas but sees the process as functional for only one class (the bourgeoisie), rather than for the whole society.

The reproduction of social class applies to both the main classes. The children of the working class are socialised to accept that society is unequal but that this is fair, because those at the top of society deserve their position. They are taught to accept that their low position is their own fault and not to question it. The children of the bourgeoisie are socialised to believe that they are superior to the working class and deserve their higher position. For example, they may go to schools which are only for children from their social class background; here, they may be taught that they will be leaders and should behave accordingly, expecting obedience from those with a lower social status.

Feminism

Feminism is another sociological theory that emphasises conflict. Like Marxists, feminists see a fundamental division between two groups in society; for feminists, this division is between the two sexes, rather than two classes. Feminists argue that men control society and have wealth and power in relationships, families, the world of work, education, and so on. A society which is controlled by men in the interests of men is called a **patriarchy**. Feminist sociologists conduct research on gender differences; for example, they are interested in why, although girls in some countries tend to do better in school than boys, men still end up in higher-paid jobs.

Like Marxism, feminism is much more than a sociological theory; it is a broad social and political movement with a long history. Feminists have campaigned for equality between men and women for many years. They have made progress in many societies but argue that there is not yet full equality. Feminism has sometimes been seen as 'anti-men'. However, many feminists argue that equality will bring benefits for everyone and many men today identify as feminists, supporting the goal of gender equality. Feminism covers such a wide range of ideas that there are several strands within feminism. They include:

- liberal feminists, who believe that major advances have been made and that equality can be reached through further changes such as new laws

- radical feminists, who believe that despite these advances, societies remain fundamentally patriarchal and men still have power

- Marxist (or socialist) feminists, who bring together the insights of both Marxism and feminism, focusing on how class and gender work together to produce fundamental divisions in society.

MAKING CONNECTIONS

You have now been introduced to the three key sociological theories of functionalism, Marxism and feminism. Can you predict what they will say about the following topics? Create a table like this one to record your ideas.

	Family	Education	Crime and deviance
Functionalism			
Marxism			
Feminism			

Gender role socialisation into masculinity/femininity

Feminists argue that socialisation helps to maintain the differences in power and status between men and women. From an early age, children are socialised into their gender roles, which are based on expectations of **masculinity** and **femininity**.

KEY TERMS

feminism: a political movement and sociological perspective advocating equality between the sexes

patriarchy: a society or organisation (including the family) in which men are dominant and women are subordinate; the dominance of men over women and children in society

masculinity: the attitudes and behaviour associated with being a man in a particular culture

femininity: the attitudes and behaviour associated with being a woman in a particular culture

The feminist sociologist Ann Oakley argued that children learn the social expectations that go with their gender roles (that is, the behaviour expected of their gender) in four main ways:

- **Manipulation.** Parents encourage and praise some activities and discourage others. For example, a boy may be praised for taking part in a hazardous physical activity while a girl might be discouraged from even trying.

- **Canalisation.** Parents channel their children towards activities they consider appropriate. Boys may be encouraged to play football, and girls to take up ballet dancing. Girls may be encouraged to take greater care over their appearance than boys.

Figure 2.9: Girls may be encouraged into certain activities, such as ballet.

- **Verbal appellations.** These are the ways in which parents address their children. For example, the word 'naughty' may be used more often with boys than with girls; 'pretty' may be used for a girl and 'handsome' for a boy.

- **Different activities.** Boys and girls will be encouraged to take part in different activities; for example, girls help their mother with cooking while boys help their fathers with do-it-yourself tasks around the home.

THINK LIKE A SOCIOLOGIST

Think about the ways in which parents socialise their children into gender roles. How can this affect the choices those children make as adults?

Since the 1970s, when Oakley developed these ideas, there have been significant changes in the way children are brought up. Some parents, especially in Western countries now try to avoid gender stereotypes. However, this can be very difficult because other agencies of socialisation may give conflicting messages. For example:

- **Media.** The media often convey stereotypical ideas about gender, although this is beginning to change.

Feminists argue that media gender stereotyping reinforces gender roles in society, by focusing on male actions and achievement and on female appearance

- **Peer groups.** Feminists point out that boys or girls who deviate from gender expectations – for example, boys who cry or girls who fight – are often sanctioned by their peers.

- **Education.** Schools often treat boys and girls differently. Some subjects are studied by one gender more than the other; for example, when learners have a choice of subjects, sociology is chosen by girls more than boys. Boys are often encouraged more to consider maths- and science-based subjects. Teachers may also treat boys and girls differently and the leadership roles in many schools are dominated by men, despite more class teachers being women.

- **Religion.** Some religions have teachings that require or recommend different behaviour from males and females. For example, in Islam, females are expected to dress in particular ways.

Feminists are interested in all the different ways that we are socialised into gender roles, and the implications of this for continuing inequalities in society. They suggest that until gender role socialisation changes, society will remain unequal, serving the interests of men.

CHECK YOUR UNDERSTANDING 2.1

1 For each of the following, write the definition and give three examples:

  a norms

  b values

  c roles.

2 In a group of three, take it in turns to explain the three sociological theories – functionalism, Marxism and feminism – and what they say about socialisation. Can you all remember the main ideas of each theory? Give each other feedback.

3 Create a table with two columns: one for nature and one for nurture. In each column, explain the view and write down evidence which supports it.

KEY POINTS

- Society is a product of social constructions.
- Each society has a culture, which includes:
  - norms
  - values
  - customs
  - roles
  - statuses
  - stereotypes.
- All of these influence individual behaviour and social identity.
- There is a debate about whether nature or nurture has more influence on our behaviour.
- Culture is relative. This means that cultures vary between times and places and are not fixed or universal.
- Socialisation is essential for the transmission of norms and values.
- The key agencies of socialisation are:
  - the family
  - education
  - peer groups
  - media
  - religion
  - workplaces.
- These agencies use processes such as:
  - canalisation
  - the hidden curriculum
  - media representations
  - peer pressure
  - religious teachings
  - role modelling
  - workplace training.
- There is a debate between different sociological perspectives and theories regarding socialisation:
  - Functionalist ideas include inadequate socialisation and social cohesion/value consensus.
  - Marxist ideas include socialisation into capitalist ideology and the reproduction of social class.
  - Feminist ideas include gender role socialisation into masculinity/femininity.

2.2. How does society control us?

Social control

Most people conform to most norms most of the time. They conform because, through socialisation, they have internalised the norms and values of their culture. There is a value consensus; most people in a society agree on shared values and on the norms related to those values. Even criminals often disapprove of the actions of other criminals; this suggests that the criminals share part of the overall value system, even though they break its rules. However, societies need ways of ensuring social conformity. There are two types of social control: formal and informal.

Differences between formal and informal types of social control

Informal social control is exercised by individuals and groups who do not have any official power to do this. For example, if you disapprove of something a friend has done, you might give them a disapproving look, make a negative comment, or refuse to speak to them until they apologise. These are forms of informal social control. Informal social control can seem minor but it is often very effective.

KEY TERM

informal social control: ways of controlling behaviour imposed by people without a formal role to do this (such as peers)

One common form of informal social control in peer groups of young people is ostracism or social rejection: an individual is excluded from the group and made aware that they are not welcome.

The agencies of informal social control are the same as the agencies of socialisation: family, peer groups, education, media, religion and workplace. These agencies informally control our behaviour in different ways, for example through peer pressure or the hidden curriculum.

Formal social control is imposed by an institution or person who has authority in that situation, such as a police officer or judge. Agencies of formal social control include the police and the criminal justice system. They can impose a wide range of formal sanctions, such as fines and imprisonment.

Figure 2.10: Formal social control being applied by the police.

Some agencies have both formal and informal roles in terms of social control. For example, in education there will be informal social control via the hidden curriculum. However, schools also have an official role and exert formal social control; for example, they might exclude a learner for serious misbehaviour. Similarly, informal control may occur in the workplace via canteen culture, but an employer can also exercise formal social control, using the company's disciplinary procedure to officially warn an employee who behaves unprofessionally.

KEY TERM

formal social control: social control imposed by people or organisations who have the authority to implement rules or laws

Positive and negative sanctions

There are two main ways of achieving social control. Positive sanctions reward behaviour that is approved of.

- Informal positive sanctions include praise from parents, a smile from a friend, and or a social media 'like'.

- Formal positive sanctions include a medal or award, a work promotion or good exam grade.

Figure 2.11: The formal positive sanction of a study award.

Negative sanctions are punishments for behaviour that is seen as wrong.

- Informal negative sanctions include a frown or an angry look, a parent sending a child to their room and a child being ostracised by their peers.

- Formal negative sanctions include being arrested by the police, punishments given by a court (such as a prison sentence or a fine) and a work dismissal.

Effectiveness of these processes in producing social conformity

The methods used by the agencies of formal and informal social control are considered in the following section. All these methods have advantages and disadvantages, and there are disagreements about their effectiveness.

MAKING CONNECTIONS

How does social control link to socialisation (covered in section 2.1)?

The debate between consensus and conflict views of social control

Consensus views: functionalism

Some sociologists believe that social control is most effective when it persuades people to conform by convincing them that this is the right thing to do. If persuasion does not work, there is the threat of sanctions. Consensus views, such as functionalism, believe that this kind of informal social control is positive and essential to the continued stability of the society. Functionalists such as Emile Durkheim believe societies need a set of shared values to hold them together and to prevent anomie. Anomie is the chaos that occurs when individuals cannot regulate their behaviour because there are no norms to guide them; this leads to the breakdown of bonds between individuals and of the society as a whole. Durkheim argued that societies need a collective conscience that is shared by all (or nearly all) members.

Conflict views: Marxism and feminism

Marxism takes a conflict perspective on society and sees social control as a way for the ruling class to maintain their power over the working class. The Marxist Louis Althusser argued that capitalist societies have two types of institution that apply social control: the ideological state apparatus (similar to informal agencies of social control) and the repressive state apparatus (formal agencies of social control).

Althusser referred to schools, the media and religion as the ideological state apparatus – institutions that make people believe it is right to conform. However, he believed that the norms and values promoted by these institutions suit the ruling class and help to keep them in power.

For example, working-class people might be 'taught' that people who are born into a high status deserve that status and should be respected and obeyed. This is a form of indoctrination, by which the working class are conditioned to accept beliefs that act against their own interests.

If the ideological state apparatus fails to make the working class conform, then the repressive state apparatus – the police, the criminal justice system and the armed forces – will be used instead. For example, if there is a protest demanding change, those in power might first try to convince the protestors that they are wrong to protest, via media coverage. If this does not work, the police or armed forces may be sent in to break up the protest, perhaps using force.

Feminism, another conflict perspective, focuses on the ways in which women are socially controlled by men in patriarchal societies. Feminists believe that many family expectations reinforce the role of women as housewives and mothers, controlling women's choices. In the education system, the subjects girls are encouraged to study and the careers they are encouraged to pursue are ways of socially controlling the position of women in a patriarchal society, to the benefit of men. This social control makes it difficult for women to achieve independence and equality.

ACTIVITY: WRITTEN 2.1

List the main points about consensus and conflict views of social control. Identify the main similarities and differences between the two sets of views. Then write an essay with the title, 'Compare and contrast different views of social control'. Include six paragraphs:

1 A short introduction saying what the essay will be about

2 Consensus views

3 Conflict views

4 Similarities

5 Differences

6 A conclusion that briefly sums up what you have written.

REFLECTION

If you had been given this essay title with no suggested structure or content, how would you have approached it?

Did you find it helpful to list the main points, similarities and differences? If so, why?

Write some tips for writing good essays, based on your work in this task.

The effectiveness of agencies of formal social control

> **THINK LIKE A SOCIOLOGIST**
>
> In what ways are people discouraged from committing crime in your society? How do formal and informal agencies of control help to discourage crime?

The main agencies of formal social control include the government, the police, the courts, the penal system (including prisons) and the armed forces. These agencies usually work together. For example, the police arrest a suspect who is suspected of breaking a law passed by the government. The suspect is put on trial in a court and, if convicted, enters the penal system, perhaps being sent to prison.

The existence of these agencies is a form of social control, acting as a deterrent: people are aware that their actions will have consequences. Their effectiveness varies according to conditions in different countries. However, because they have legal authority, they can be seen as an immediately effective way of controlling individual behaviour.

Some sociologists argue that it is more effective to control people's behaviour by consent, using the informal agencies of social control. They feel that the formal agencies of social control should only be used as a last resort. Many people break the law and may reoffend even after being punished; this suggests that the formal agencies are not fully effective in controlling the behaviour of a minority of people in most societies. It is also very costly – both financially and socially – to use formal sanctions such as imprisonment.

Methods of control used by formal agencies in achieving social conformity

Law making

Laws are rules made by an organisation that has authority, usually the government. The purpose of laws is to control what people can do, usually so they do not harm other people or their interests. Laws vary between countries and so do the ways of enforcing them. In some countries, laws based on religious teachings become the basis of the law for the whole society. For example, Sharia law (based on Islamic religious principles) is the basis for the legal system in Iran and Saudi Arabia.

When there is a change in society, governments can respond by making new laws or by repealing (abolishing) old ones. For example, the rapid growth of the internet has led governments to introduce new laws about online activities.

Coercion

Coercion is when someone is compelled to do something they do not want to do, often through threats or by force. Coercion can happen between people; for example, a bully might demand money from others and make threats. Coercion in this sense usually involves acting against laws or rules. However, formal agencies of social control are often allowed to use coercion to some extent. For example, the police may put handcuffs on someone and lock them in a cell against their will, or they might use a weapon such as a Taser against a suspect. The armed forces have a range of equipment they can use to coerce people; for example, they might use tear gas and water cannons against protesters.

> **KEY TERM**
>
> **coercion:** the use or threat of force or violence

Surveillance, including digital surveillance

Surveillance is not new – people have always watched what others are doing. But in the late 20th century, developments in information and communication technology led to increased and more formal surveillance. In many countries, especially in cities, an individual is filmed by surveillance cameras many times a day. All aspects of everyday life – shopping, driving, going to school, using a phone or the internet, or just walking – are now monitored or recorded. This has changed how agencies of social control work. The police can respond quickly to crimes when a building or other location is being monitored. They can also use technology to identify suspects and track their movements. **Digital surveillance** also operates online. Internet use and the websites an individual visits can be tracked and monitored – often by advertisers. In some countries, digital surveillance is carried out by government agencies who monitor any online activity that could threaten the government or break the law.

> KEY TERM
>
> **digital surveillance:** the use of digital technology to observe and control behaviour

Figure 2.12: A CCTV surveillance camera.

Arrest

Arresting someone involves apprehending and detaining them on suspicion of committing an offence. In most countries, only the police can arrest someone and they must have valid reasons for suspecting the person. There are also rules about how long a person can be detained before they are charged and their case is considered by a court.

Sentencing, including imprisonment

The sentences a court can impose vary depending on the country, and on other factors such as the severity of the crime committed and the offender's previous record. Sentences range from a discharge (where the offender is free to go) for the most minor offences, to imprisonment for serious offences. In some countries, capital punishment – the death penalty – is still used for the most serious crimes.

> ### ACTIVITY: DISCUSSION 2.2
>
> Is there too much surveillance? Some sociologists say we now live in a 'surveillance society'.
>
> 1   In a small group, discuss how much surveillance there is, considering both online and offline surveillance. Collate your ideas and make a list.
>
> 2   Now discuss how you feel about this level of surveillance. Do you feel you should have more privacy? Or is surveillance a good thing (for example, helping to prevent crime)? Make sure everyone contributes to the discussion.
>
> 3   Finally, as a group, design a large poster about surveillance and what you think about it.

The effectiveness of agencies of informal social control

Agencies of socialisation are also agencies of informal social control. They pass on norms and values but they are also able to make people conform. The main agencies of informal social control are the family, education, peer groups, the media, religion and the workplace.

Informal control can be seen as more effective than formal social control since it avoids any official confrontation or conflict. If individuals choose to conform due to informal sanctions, they are less likely to break the law or become a threat to society. As a result, things will run more smoothly.

In the previous section on socialisation, we have seen how these agencies can influence, and so control, behaviour. For example:

*   In families, parents or guardians use positive and negative sanctions, such as giving treats for good behaviour or telling children off if they misbehave. Canalisation is also a form of informal control in relation to gender role socialisation.

*   In education, the hidden curriculum is a key form of informal social control. Other influences include informal rewards and punishments (such as a gold star or being sent out of the classroom) and peer pressure exerted by peer groups.

All of these agencies are effective in shaping an individual's behaviour, encouraging them to repeat or avoid certain things in the future based on the sanctions received and ensuring they learn the behaviour expected in any situation.

> **TIP**
>
> Some agents of social control use both formal and informal methods to control deviance. For example, schools have formal punishments such as detentions, but also control behaviour in more informal ways (for example, a disapproving look or a warning from a teacher).

Methods of control used by informal agencies in achieving social conformity

This section describes some key methods used by informal agencies of social control.

Ostracism

Ostracism was a common form of social control in societies in the past. When a member of a community does something that is seen as unacceptable, the community does not involve agencies of formal social control. Instead, they reject and isolate the offender. For example, they might not speak to the offender or allow them to buy what they need to survive. This form of punishment aims more to stabilise the community that has been upset by the offence, than to punish the offender.

Ostracism was more common in the past, when formal agencies of social control were less common and, for example, there was no equivalent of prison. However, it does happen today – for example, a group of school friends might exclude and reject one member of the group.

Parental rewards

Within the family, parents can punish their children or give them rewards such as treats and special privileges. Rewards also include words of praise, which encourage good behaviour and can be more effective than punishing bad behaviour.

Social media 'likes'

'Likes' on social media are a new type of informal social control. They are important for businesses and brands, but also for people. People enjoy getting 'likes' and this can be very important for self-esteem, especially for teenagers. 'Likes' can be a sign of popularity, which makes people feel good about themselves; as a result, many people modify what they say and how they behave to get more 'likes'. Those who get few 'likes' may feel rejected – a new form of ostracism.

Figure 2.13: Social media 'likes' are a type of informal social control.

Religious rewards/sanctions

For people with religious beliefs, the idea of being punished by a god after death can act as a form of social control. For example, many Christians believe that living a good life (which usually involves following laws) will lead to them going to heaven when they die; in contrast, those who behave badly will go to hell and be punished for eternity. These beliefs can strongly influence behaviour. They can even be stronger than the fear of being caught and punished by the criminal justice system: if there is a god that can see what you do all the time – and may even know what you are thinking – there is no possibility of 'getting away with' a crime.

School punishments

Most schools display their rules on noticeboards and have policies relating to rewards and negative sanctions. In modern industrial societies, rewards are often emphasised more than negative sanctions, because schools have found it is more effective to reinforce positive behaviour than to punish negative behaviour. Informal rewards include verbal praise, positive comments on written work, positive letters to parents, merit badges, stickers or positive points. More formal rewards include certificates of achievement and success in exams.

Informal negative sanctions include looks of disapproval or verbal comments by teachers, negative comments on written work, making learners sit or work alone, sending them out of the classroom or keeping them in at break. More formal punishments include official detentions after school, contacting parents to report misbehaviour, confiscating property (such as mobile phones) or even excluding a child from school for a fixed time or permanently in the case of repeated or very serious misbehaviour. In the past, and in some countries today, corporal punishment may be used. This is physical punishment, such as being caned by a teacher.

Figure 2.14: Disapproving verbal comments by a teacher.

ACTIVITY: RESEARCH 2.5

What forms of social control do teachers use?

1   Ask one of your teachers if they are willing to be interviewed by you. Using the advice and ideas in the section on interviews in Unit 1, write some questions to ask the teacher about how they get learners to follow the rules. Ask them which ways they think work best and why. Make notes on what they say.

2   Compare your findings with those of other learners who interviewed different teachers.

REFLECTION

Do you feel you were able to build up a good relationship with the teacher so they opened up to you and gave honest, valid answers to the questions you asked? What factors may have prevented the teacher being fully open with you in their answers?

Dismissal from a job

Like schools, workplaces have rules, for example about starting and finishing times and about what to wear. The ultimate negative sanction is being dismissed ('fired'). There are laws to prevent workers being fired unfairly; there may be a disciplinary hearing before a dismissal, allowing the worker to present their point of view. If the worker belongs to a trade union, the union can offer support in this process.

Other negative sanctions include the loss of pay, having to face a disciplinary hearing, being closely monitored at work, being demoted to a lower position and being given less pleasant work. Rewards in the workplace include promotion to a better job, a pay increase, performance-related pay, bonus payments, commissions or being given shares in the company.

Resistance to social control through protest groups and sub-cultures

Sub-cultures are groups of people whose norms and values deviate in some ways from those of the rest of that society. People belonging to sub-cultures may display different value systems, non-conformist behaviour and different styles of dress and appearance. The members of a deviant sub-culture reject or rebel against cultural

KEY TERM

sub-culture: a group of people within a larger culture which has its own distinctive norms and values

aspects of the society in which they live. They do not conform to many of the norms and values of the society as a whole. They do, however, conform to the norms and values of their own specific sub-culture. Sub-cultures are often associated with teenagers – referred to as youth sub-cultures – who may form these sub-cultures as a way of expressing their individuality and identity as they move from being children to becoming adults. Sub-cultures often use informal social control to regulate the behaviour of members, for example by ostracising them until they conform.

The existence of sub-cultures suggests that not everyone in a society holds the same values and norms in all circumstances. However, there will be dominant norms and values to which members of sub-cultures still conform. For example, members of a youth sub-culture might rebel against norms relating to fashion or hairstyles, but still speak the same language and follow the main value system of a country.

Protest groups

A protest group can be seen as a type of sub-culture, consisting of a group of people who want to bring about a change in society. In many countries, there are protest groups campaigning for change on a wide range of issues, such as:

- voting rights
- poverty
- human and civil rights
- environmental issues, such as the climate emergency and the loss of biodiversity
- animal rights
- wars and the arms trade
- policing.

Some protest groups organise transnationally, when issues are not confined to one country. For example, the School Strike for Climate – associated with the Swedish environmental activist Greta Thunberg – has involved students in about 150 countries protesting for action to prevent climate change. This protest movement brings together thousands of people who have their age and their fears about climate change in common. Another recent example is the Black Lives Matter movement, which originated in the USA but then spread globally, leading to protests and demonstrations in many countries, particularly in 2021.

Figure 2.15: A Black Lives Matter protest.

Youth sub-cultures

Adolescence is a difficult period for many young people, who need to develop a sense of autonomy and independence from their parents. From a functionalist point of view, sub-cultures offer an outlet for people – especially teenagers – to express their emotions and frustrations. In this respect, youth sub-cultures are functional both for individuals and for society as a whole. Strong peer groups of young people may have norms and values that are different to some extent from those of the rest of society. Young people can experiment with their identities and styles, and even participate in reckless behaviour, without any serious consequences before they settle down to have families of their own.

The term youth sub-culture is mainly associated with groups of young people who adopt a style and culture that is partly at odds with the main culture of a society. Some visible youth sub-cultures are:

- gyaru
- mods
- hippies
- punks
- goths.

All these youth sub-cultures attracted considerable media attention.

KEY TERMS

youth sub-culture: a sub-culture of adolescents or young adults who are usually distinguishable by their style, dress and/or musical preferences

protest group: a group of people who protest in order to bring about a change in society

They were often identified as threats by the main culture, because their values and behaviour were seen as deviant.

Figure 2.16: Clothing, music, appearance and speech can act as symbols of sub-cultures.

Joining a youth sub-culture can be functional for young people whose route to success seems to be blocked – for example, if they have not done well at school or cannot find a job. The sub-culture gives them a group in which they can win status and respect, providing an alternative opportunity structure. The members of the sub-culture may start by having the same values as everyone else but develop their own values and norms because they cannot achieve their goals by socially acceptable means. Most people belong to youth sub-cultures for a limited period only. They leave as a result of employment, marriage and adult responsibilities and readopt mainstream norms and values.

Neo-Marxists who studied some of the youth sub-cultures from the 1960s and 1970s felt that they were ways for working-class youths to resist the social control of society based on their social class position. For example, in the 1960s, working-class youths had few opportunities to progress in education. They may have become mods, who dressed in designer suits as a way of showing that they were just as good as their middle-class peers. This neo-Marxist approach is different from the functionalist one because it is not concerned with the transition from childhood to adulthood generally. Instead, it is focused on young people's place in the economic system and class structure. Neo-Marxists therefore see youth sub-cultures as revealing the deep conflicts within society.

Although youth sub-cultures attract a lot of media and sociological attention, it is important to remember that most young people never belong to any of these sub-cultures. Some writers have suggested that youth sub-cultures are now little more than fashion,

created by the mass media and marketing. As a result, the sub-cultures' values have little depth; they are more style than substance. They may have begun as real rebellions – as suggested by Marxists – but, over time, they are incorporated into the system. For example, early punks rejected fashion by making their own clothing from ripped old clothes, safety pins and even bin liners. Before long, however, mass-manufactured punk clothing could be bought in fashion shops.

The highly visible sub-cultures identified in the UK in the 1960s and 70s were usually associated more with males than females. Sociologists tried to explain why girls did not seem to form sub-cultures as boys did. Some feminists suggested that it may have been because girls' behaviour was seen as less deviant or threatening and so got less media attention, or because the male sociologists studying these sub-cultures did not see the girls' sub-cultures as relevant or interesting. Parents also tended to keep greater control over girls than boys. Angela McRobbie suggested that there were female sub-cultures but that girls got together in their homes, not on the streets, and so were less visible. She called this a bedroom sub-culture. Youth sub-cultures today are much more mixed in relation to gender, possibly because girls now have greater freedom and because of changing gender roles in society.

STRETCH AND CHALLENGE

How relevant do you think the idea of youth sub-cultures is in your society today? If they exist, are they just fashions, with very little connection to people's values? Refer to examples from your society to support your points.

Online sub-cultures

The internet and social media platforms such as YouTube and Instagram have made it much easier for geographically distant people to share their enthusiasms, via online communities, forums and chat rooms. As a result, **online sub-cultures** have grown stronger, allowing

KEY TERM

online sub-cultures: groups of people who connect with each other online, through social media or other websites. They share distinct norms and values, often related to a particular interest or issue

people to connect with others from around the world who share their interests or values. This has led to the development of transnational communities. For example, people who play a particular online game, or follow a particular band or influencer, share an interest that may be strong enough to be described as a sub-culture. There is also an overlap between online sub-cultures and protest groups, with the growth of clicktivism (online activism). This is sometimes based on the use of hashtags to spread information about a particular issue or a planned protest. This can explain how protest movements such as #BlackLivesMatter spread so quickly around the world.

CASE STUDY 2.2

K-Pop – an online youth sub-culture

K-pop is the term used to describe Korean popular music, which has had a huge global impact over the last few years, helped by digital platforms such as YouTube. The K-pop group BTS have enjoyed worldwide success, with over 18 million followers on Twitter.

Figure 2.17: K-pop band BTS.

The fans of K-pop ('K-poppers') can be seen as an online youth sub-culture, with many different websites connecting fans from all over the world. Like the youth sub-cultures of the 20th century, K-poppers adopt certain fashions and hairstyles and share certain attitudes and interests.

One significant feature of the K-pop fan sub-culture is its diversity: it includes people from different countries, languages and cultures, and is very inclusive and socially aware. The initial love of the music can lead fans from around the world to increase their awareness of many issues affecting young people today.

The bands themselves are often also engaged with global issues. For example, BTS have spoken at the United Nations General Assembly on more than one occasion about young people and their need to have a voice. This sub-culture challenges common views about young people being disengaged from social issues. It also challenges the view sometimes presented in sociology that visible youth sub-cultures are a thing of the past. They may look different today but many young people are still engaged and passionate when it comes to expressing their identities and joining with others to share a love of music.

TASK

In what ways are K-poppers similar to and different from the youth sub-cultures of the past, such as skinheads or punks?

Religious sub-cultures

Many religious beliefs and practices fit into the dominant culture. Some, however, can be seen as sub-cultures – for example, some sects place strong demands on members and require them to conform to different norms and values. An example of a religious group with distinctive values is the Amish (see Case study 2.1). Membership of a **religious sub-culture** may influence behaviour, dress, diet and other norms and values.

KEY TERM

religious sub-culture: a sub-culture based on religious faith and practices which are distinct from those of the wider culture

CHECK YOUR UNDERSTANDING 2.2

1   Make cards. Write the name of an agent of social control on one side of each card; include both formal and informal agents. Put these cards face down in a pile. In a small group, take turns to pick up the top card and say what methods of control that agent uses. The rest of the group can give marks for accuracy and examples.

2   Write definitions for each of the following terms:

   a   ostracism

   b   coercion

   c   protest group.

KEY POINTS

- Social control can be formal or informal and can involve positive and negative sanctions.

- There is a debate between consensus (such as functionalist) and conflict (such as Marxist and feminist) views of social control.

- Formal agencies of social control are:

  - government

  - police

  - courts

  - penal system

  - armed forces.

- Formal agencies of social control use methods such as:

  - law making

  - coercion

  - digital surveillance

  - arrest

  - sentencing

  - imprisonment.

- Informal agencies of social control are:

  - family

  - education

  - peer groups

  - media

  - religion

  - workplace.

- Informal agencies of social control use positive and negative sanctions, such as:

  - ostracism

  - parental rewards

  - social media 'likes'

  - religious rewards/sanctions

  - school punishments

  - dismissal from a job.

- Social control can be resisted by:

  - protest groups

  - youth sub-cultures

  - online sub-cultures

  - religious sub-cultures.

2.3 What influences our social identity?

Key aspects of social identity

Sociologists are particularly interested in certain aspects of identity that we all have. This section considers the relationships between identities and age, gender, ethnicity and social class.

Age and identity

Different societies divide their members into age groups in different ways; the roles assigned to these age groups vary and are not always directly linked to biological abilities. In modern Western societies, children spend a relatively long period (compared with other societies) becoming socialised before they enter the adult world. Older people enter a phase of retirement at a legally specified age. In some other societies, children start working alongside adults at a much earlier age and there is no formal retirement age; people work for as long as they are physically able.

It is thought that, in the past, many people did not know exactly how old they were; birth dates were not always remembered or records of births kept. As a result, the age group to which a person belonged was more important – for example, childhood, adulthood or old age.

In some African societies in the past, and still today in some more traditional tribal communities, there were three main stages in men's lives – children, warriors and elders. Boys of roughly the same age and maturity were initiated into adulthood, often in group ceremonies. During this initiation, they might have learnt about the traditions of the group and the expectations and responsibilities of an adult. There might also have been a challenge or ritual to perform; for example, killing an animal in a hunt or running across the backs of cattle. In some societies, there were equivalent ceremonies for girls. Older people were seen as a source of knowledge and experience. Because they had lived through many changes, they were able to give advice in situations that younger people had no experience of, such as what to eat if a crop failed. Older people were therefore valued members of the community, integrated into extended families and looked after by them. The oldest members of a community or tribe – the elders – were often leaders, respected for their wisdom.

Industrial societies place more emphasis on age in terms of years, rather than maturity. Children become adults at a specific age, usually 18. At other ages, different rights and responsibilities are acquired. Table 2.1 shows the ages at which certain rights are acquired in the UK.

Age	Right or responsibility
10 (12 in Scotland)	Age of criminal responsibility (can stand trial and be convicted of a criminal offence)
13	Can work for limited hours that do not interfere with education
16	Can join the army (with parental consent)
17	Can drive a car
18	Can vote in elections
21	Can drive a bus, lorry or train

Table 2.1: Ages at which rights are acquired in the UK.

Members of the same age group are called a generation. The difference between generations is usually thought to be about 25 years. In modern industrial societies, there can be significant differences in experiences and attitudes between generations and this can lead to conflict. This kind of difference is called a 'generation gap'. For example:

- Teenagers may think that older people are out of touch with modern society and culture, while older people may see teenagers as rebellious and disrespectful.

- Today, different generations have very different experiences of smartphones and other new technologies. Children and teenagers have grown up with these technologies and find them easy to use, while older people may struggle to understand them. The young are digital natives; older people are digital immigrants, who often find the culture of today's digital society confusing.

Members of an age group who share a common experience of growing up at the same point in history are an age cohort. Belonging to a particular cohort can have important consequences, because each cohort experiences different events and social changes. For example, people born in the 'baby boom' in Europe and North America after the Second World War experienced dramatic social changes in the 1960s.

These included: increasing wealth and standards of living in these countries; the Cold War and its end; more effective birth control; the arrival of computers and other new technologies; and growing concern about the environment. As a result of the high number of people in this age cohort, companies made many products aimed specifically at this generation. For example, there were new kinds of popular music such as rock and soul, with more artists and more records released. An ageing population and increasing costs in health care and social services are occurring as this cohort grows older.

> **TIP**
>
> The terms 'generation' and 'age cohort' are often used as if they mean the same thing. It is useful, though, to make the distinction: the word 'generation' draws attention to the common features of, say, being a teenager, while the term 'cohort' draws attention to the particular experiences that come from being born at a particular time. So while there is always a young generation, there is only one age cohort born in the 2010s.

ACTIVITY: DATA INTERPRETATION 2.1

	USA	UK	Japan	China	Mauritius
Driving a car	Varies between states; the lowest is 14 years 3 months in South Dakota	17	18	18	18
Drinking alcohol	21	18	20	18	18
Leaving school (ending compulsory secondary education)	16	18	15	15	16
Marriage	Usually 18 but varies between states	18 (16 with parental consent)	20 (18 for boys and 16 for girls with parental consent)	22 for men, 20 for women	18, sometimes younger with parental consent
Voting	18	18	20	18	18

Table 2.2: Comparison of legal ages for activities in different countries.

1   Look at the information in Table 2.2. In which of these countries is:

    a   the voting age the highest?

    b   the minimum age for driving the lowest?

ACTIVITY: WRITTEN 2.2

'Who is considered an adult is different in different countries.' Use the information in Table 2.2 to explain this statement. Write about 250 words and try to refer to each country at least once.

Cohorts since the 'baby boom' have been given letters to identify them. In Europe and North America, various attributes are said to apply to cohorts but in reality there are no real boundaries between cohorts. Recent cohorts are shown in Table 2.3.

Cohort	Approximate birth years
Generation X, children of baby boomers	1965–1980
Generation Y, also called Millennials	1981–1996
Generation Z	1997–2010
Generation Alpha	2011 onwards

Table 2.3: Recent cohort names and birth years.

ACTIVITY: DISCUSSION 2.3

Add a third column to Table 2.3, headed 'Childhood experiences'. In a small group, discuss what you know about what life was like when the people in each cohort were children. For example, you could discuss these questions:

a   What important events took place, in your country and globally?

b   What entertainment and media were available for children?

c   What were people in your country, or globally, concerned or worried about?

You can ask people from these generations what they remember of their childhood, or use the internet for research.

REFLECTION

What sources of information did you use? Why did you choose them? How trustworthy do you think they are? How did your group decide what to put in the table? Did you leave anything out, and if so, why?

In past societies, the transition from childhood to adulthood might have been a single event such as an initiation ceremony. In societies today, however, it takes a period of years for children to become adults. Adolescence (the period between being a child and an adult, usually when people are teenagers) is seen as a difficult time because it involves status anxiety. Modern industrial societies emphasise achieved statuses over ascribed statuses. Young people feel pressure to achieve status and to establish who they are as individuals. One response is to rely on your peer group, who are going through the same problems and anxieties as you. As a result, young people tend to share norms and values and this can lead them to form youth sub-cultures (see section 2.2).

Gender and identity

In many societies in the past, and in some today, gender roles were fixed and there was little scope for individuals to negotiate them. There were set norms and expectations for both males and females, who were expected to follow them. This influenced the ways in which people saw themselves – their gender identity – and acted as a strong form of social control.

Biology is the starting point of the functionalist Talcott Parsons's analysis of gender roles and gender identity. He argues that because mothers give birth to and nurse children, they have a closer and stronger relationship with them. In a modern industrial society, this is reinforced by the absence of the father, who goes to work. Parsons describes the woman's role as expressive: she provides emotional warmth and security. These expressive qualities are also shown in her relationship with her husband – the second function of the wife and mother is to provide love and understanding to the husband, whose role at work is instrumental. This functionalist view of gender suggests that gender identities – our sense of ourselves as male or female – are based on biology and are universal.

However, these ideas of a fixed and universal gender identity have been challenged. Sociologist Ann Oakley uses the example of the people of the island of Alor in Indonesia. In this culture, women are not tied to their offspring and this separation has no harmful effects. Oakley accuses Parsons of basing his analysis on the beliefs and values of his own culture (that of the USA in the 20th century). She argues that the expressive role taken by women is not necessary for the functioning of the family but exists for the convenience of men.

The anthropologist Margaret Mead also found surprising variations in gender roles and identities in traditional societies in New Guinea:

- Among the Arapesh people, both men and women were peaceful and neither men nor women made war.

- Among the Mundugamor people, both men and women were warlike; the opposite of the Arapesh.

- Among the Tchambuli people (now known as the Chambri), the women left the villages to work while the men stayed at home and spent time on their appearance.

In contrast to these examples, we could look at Western or American society at the time of Mead's research. Here, the gender roles of the Chambri are reversed, with men working and women being more concerned with appearance. Mead's findings have been taken as proof of the importance of nurture rather than nature (see section 2.1). It seems that men and women can have different temperaments and different roles depending on the culture in which they are brought up.

STRETCH AND CHALLENGE

How useful do you think cross-cultural research like that carried out by Ann Oakley and Margaret Mead is? Can you think of any problems with research like this?

In modern industrial societies, gender is still an essential aspect of identity. It is helpful to distinguish sex from gender, although they are closely interconnected. Sex relates to the body and biological characteristics; in particular, male and female humans have different chromosomes. Gender is about how these biological differences affect our social lives.

Until recently, it was commonly thought that there were two sexes – male and female – which align with two genders, man and woman. Babies were assigned to one category or the other at birth, based on physical features. However, gender and sex do not coincide for everyone; some people identify with a different sex to the one they were assigned at birth.

There have always been people who do not easily fit into the binary (two-part) categories of male and female based on sex; for example, transgender, gender non-conforming and nonbinary people. Awareness of these variations has increased in recent years and more people choose a different gender identity based on their understanding of their gender and how they want others to see them. Some argue that it is more useful to think of gender as a spectrum, rather than an 'either/or'. Many people see themselves as being at one or other end of the spectrum – identifying themselves as male or female – but there are many possibilities between these ends.

Many non-Western cultures have a long history of accepting people who do not identify as one sex or gender or the other. Examples include:

- the Hijra in South Asia, officially recognised as a third gender

- the Two Spirit people in American indigenous communities, who are biologically male but take on female gender identities and roles.

Western cultures have been less accepting, with people who do not conform to binary sex and gender identities often being ostracised and discriminated against. Recently, there has been some progress towards equal rights in some countries. For example, in the UK, transgender people can change their passports and other official documents to show their preferred gender; however, this is still a binary choice between male and female.

Until recently, gender roles and identities in modern industrial societies were quite strict. Men took what functionalists call the instrumental role, looking after the practical and economic needs of the family, such as food, shelter and money. Women took the expressive, domestic role, looking after the home and the emotional needs of the family.

Men who conform to the expected gender role of their society are seen as masculine, while women who conform to the expected gender role are seen as feminine. In modern industrial societies, masculinity and femininity are often thought of as opposites (as in 'the opposite sex').

These stereotypical ideas can be seen in some of the words commonly used to describe the two sexes:

- masculinity: strong, competitive, aggressive, unemotional, active, confident, hard

- femininity: weak, emotional, passive, quiet, dependent, soft.

These are stereotypical ideas, although in many parts of the world and at times in history, people would have wanted to live up to these stereotypes. Today, such ideas may seem unrealistic, particularly in North American and European societies. There have been huge changes in gender in the last 50 years or so, and sociologists now talk about *masculinities* and *femininities* to show that there are different ways of being masculine or feminine.

In business, politics and culture, more women now reach senior positions and are important decision-makers. Young women increasingly expect to work and have financial independence; they do not see their futures only in terms of becoming a wife and mother. However, the situation is still far from equal and patriarchal culture is deeply embedded. Women who work in previously male-dominated areas may be thought of as unfeminine.

For men in modern industrial societies, the traditional and expected role was to be strong – both physically and emotionally – in order to support the family. This has been referred to as **hegemonic** masculinity – an idea about what a 'real man' should be like. For example, boys were expected to be able to fight, to be interested in competitive sports such as football and to think of themselves as better than females. Men were also expected to have the role of breadwinner – to support their family by earning a good income from their job. Males who could not live up to these expectations could be seen as failing to achieve masculinity, or not being 'real men'.

Figure 2.18: A senior businesswoman.

Among many groups, these ideas have changed over time. It has become much more acceptable for males to behave in ways that might once have been seen as feminine, such as:

- showing emotion publicly, such as crying

- taking care over their appearance

- talking about their relationships and emotions

- fathers having a close emotional bond with their babies or infants.

Figure 2.19: A father showing a close bond with his child.

More men are 'stay at home' dads, and those who work full-time spend more time with their children and help more with housework. These changes are seen as a good thing in many ways, freeing men from a restrictive role and allowing individuals to negotiate the form of masculinity that is right for them. They might also lead to a reduction in domestic violence by men against women and children and to greater willingness to talk and negotiate, rather than fight.

There has, however, been a negative side to these changes and there are now new pressures on men. For example, the old hegemonic male took little care over his appearance but today, value is placed on looking good. The cosmetics industry for men has grown and advertising pushes males to care more about their appearance.

This can lead to feelings of inadequacy shown, for example, by the rise in eating disorders among boys. There can also be greater role conflict, as men try to combine success at work with being a good husband and father.

Ethnic group and identity

Throughout history, when one group has encountered another, they have responded by making a distinction between themselves and the other group. The Romans saw everyone who lived outside the Empire as 'barbarian', in contrast to supposedly civilised Roman citizens.

> **TIP**
>
> Remember that everyone has an ethnicity. Those who belong to a majority ethnic group have an ethnic identity, just as much as those who belong to a minority. Ethnicity refers to a person's cultural background, which can include their norms, values, language, traditions, religion and shared cultural history.

Ethnicity is a social construct; this means that ethnic groups exist only because people identify themselves and others as members of groups. In most modern industrial societies today, there is much greater ethnic diversity than in the past because of migration. For example:

- the UK has significant African-Caribbean and Asian ethnic minorities, indigenous English, Welsh, Scottish and Irish ethnic groups, and people with origins in many other countries

- in Mauritius, Indo-Mauritians (of Indian/ Pakistani descent) make up about two-thirds of the population. Other ethnic groups include Mauritian Creoles (of mixed descent), Franco-Mauritians (of French descent) and Sino-Mauritians (of Chinese descent)

- in Kenya, the largest ethnic group (the Kikuyu) make up less than 20% of the population. Other ethnic groups (often referred to in Kenya as tribes) include Luhya, Luo, Kalenjin, Kamba and Meru peoples, and there are also European, Arab and Asian minorities.

In some countries, there is a majority ethnic group. Smaller groups are referred to as minority ethnic groups. Often, members of a majority group occupy most of the leading positions in politics, business and society;

there may be discrimination and prejudice against members of minority groups. This has been the case in the UK and USA, for example, where the white majorities (themselves made up of different ethnicities) have had a dominant position over minorities. In countries such as Kenya, with a number of groups of similar size, power is often more evenly distributed. Sometimes there are formal arrangements to ensure that a group does not feel disadvantaged. Occasionally a minority group has all the power. This was the case in South Africa under the apartheid system, which ended in the early 1990s. The white minority held all positions of power and treated the black majority (made up of several ethnic groups) as second class.

In the past (during the period of slavery and afterwards), racism was based on physical differences such as skin colour. More recently, cultural variation has become a greater source of difference. This is why, in sociology, we now usually talk about ethnicity rather than race.

Common differences between ethnic groups include:

- language or dialect

- customs and traditions

- religion and mythology

- ancestry and history

- food

- costume.

Over time, as people from different ethnic groups live alongside each other and perhaps marry, they tend to adopt some of the features of other groups. This can create hybrid cultures – cultures formed by a mixing or blending of different ethnic traditions. A good example in the UK is British Bangladeshis. They are descendants of people who migrated from Bangladesh to the UK, who are now both British by citizenship and Bangladeshi by part of their culture. Having grown up in the UK, they are British; at the same time, they may also follow Bangladeshi culture. Today, there are increasing numbers of people from mixed backgrounds (with parents from different ethnic groups), who live in both cultures. These individuals have some choice in creating new identities for themselves.

For many people, a shared ethnic identity is important and a source of pride. However, minority ethnic groups may experience discrimination and inequality compared to the majority group. The reactions of others may damage the pride they feel in their ethnic identity. This is a common experience for recently arrived migrants, who are often treated with suspicion and may even be seen as a threat to the way of life of the majority. This can be counterbalanced by the effects of globalisation, which has made it possible for people around the world to stay in contact with family and ethnic group members elsewhere. For example, someone who migrates to work in another country can, through social media, still be a part of the life of the family they are away from. They will continue to speak their language and follow their celebrations.

National identity is closely related to ethnic identity. Some people expected globalisation to lead to the end of the nation-state and to national identities. In fact, in recent years, nationality has become a more central part of many people's identities. For example, nationalism has been a factor in both world wars, in anti-colonial struggles, in the fall of communism in Eastern Europe and in debates over the future of Europe.

Figure 2.20: Indian flag and passport.

Nationalism developed in modern times as a way of uniting the diverse peoples of nation-states. For example, the UK needed to unite the people of England, Scotland, Wales and Northern Ireland, who had different religions, languages and cultures. Benedict Anderson argues that nations and nationalism are socially constructed; he calls them 'imagined communities'. In real communities, people know each other or interact regularly but nations are too big for this to happen. Creating a sense of national identity is particularly important where:

- there are several sub-cultures or ethnic groups within the nation. In these situations, the sense of national identity needs to be stronger than loyalty to the sub-culture. Some civil wars start when a group rejects the national identity and tries to break away

- the national boundaries are artificial (they do not correspond to natural dividing features such as

rivers and mountains, or to areas where people actually live). In Africa, the borders drawn by European states during the colonial period have led to problems, because the boundaries on maps divided people of the same group from each other.

States persuade people to accept a national identity, using means such as:

- national symbols such as flags, emblems, money and postage stamps

- a head of state such as a king or queen or a president, who acts as the national figurehead

- national anthems

- national rituals such as parades, festivals and holidays, either regularly or for special occasions

- national sports teams; for example, the nationality of the competitors is always emphasised in the Olympic Games

- broadcasting and mass media; these often involve a national broadcaster, such as Doordarshan television in India.

Social class and identity

Social class can be less immediately obvious from an individual's appearance than their age group, ethnic group and gender. Sociologists have different ways of deciding which social class people belong to. Neither sociologists nor the people concerned always agree about how the distinctions should be made. This is partly because there are no clear boundaries between classes. However, our social class decides many of our life chances – the opportunities we have to improve our lives – and this is widely recognised.

Sociologists usually refer to three broad classes: upper, middle and working class. These groups can be subdivided. For example, the middle class can be divided into those in professional careers (such as doctors and lawyers) and people who own or manage businesses. Within the working class, there are people working in offices and people in factories or doing outdoor work, such as building.

Members of the upper class are likely to think of themselves as belonging to a sort of exclusive club, based on their ability to spend considerable amounts of money. Conspicuous consumption – spending money on luxury items and making sure other people know you are doing this – can be a way of signalling wealth to everyone else;

for example, by owning luxurious houses, expensive cars and jewellery, or travelling around the world.

In most countries, the middle class has grown considerably in the last hundred years or so. Rising living standards have allowed this expanded class to show its new status in many ways. Members of the middle classes often try to show their class status through conspicuous consumption (in the same way as the upper class do). For example, they might show their class through their house or car, the type of holiday they go on and the types of shops they visit. People who have experienced upward social mobility – moved into a higher social class position from the one they grew up in – may be most keen to prove their new status.

During the 20th century, being working class was a powerful source of identity for many people. In the UK, there were strong working-class communities based on industries such as coal, steel, car-making and ship-building. Boys often followed their fathers to work in the local industry and many marriages were made within the community. Membership of trade unions and shared working and living conditions created a strong sense of collective identity – stronger than in other classes. The working class were aware of their lower living standards but, by asserting their values, they placed a strong positive value on their way of life. These collective identities have been weakened by the loss of jobs in these industries and by the fragmentation of the communities that were based on them. In the UK, media reporting of the working class has become very negative, stereotypically portraying them as lazy and relying on welfare payments rather than earning their own income. It has become harder to claim being working class as a positive identity. In a society that claims to be meritocratic – based on merit and equal opportunities – it can be seen as a sign of failure to remain in the same social class as your parents.

The digital self and online identities

A significant recent change in society is the development of digital technologies, such as the internet and smartphones. These have become part of everyday life for many people, affecting cultures and identities. Many people now create a **digital self** and one or more **online identities** in addition to their offline identity. However, people have choices about how they use digital technologies – or even whether they use them at all.

Digital technologies have affected daily life in many ways. For example:

1 Everyday life is faster. Many people carry a smartphone at all times. They can access information and contact people quickly at any time.

2 People can contact other people all over the world. For example, family members who live in different parts of the world can easily keep in daily contact. This includes speaking to relatives, seeing them (via a phone or webcam) and even taking part remotely in the events of day-to-day life or special occasions, such as birthday parties.

3 Increased contact with people all over the world makes it easier to find new friends, new communities and new interests. One example of this is online dating – choosing possible new romantic partners online. Communities that only exist online are called **virtual communities**.

4 New ways of communicating online are developing all the time, and many people have a presence on several social media platforms such as Facebook, WhatsApp, Instagram and Twitter.

5 Digital technologies have their own status systems. A person's digital status may relate to the digital technology they own (for example, the latest model of smartphone is a status symbol) and to their behaviour online (for example, how many 'likes' they get or how many followers they have).

It is possible for people to display different aspects of their identity online. They can even create new identities and have multiple online identities.

Positive impacts include:

- People can choose new identities and display them online. For example, a person can identify their gender or ethnicity, give their age or occupation, state whether they are in a relationship and so

> **KEY TERMS**

digital self and online identity: the way that someone presents themselves online, and the personae they adopt in online communities, such as forums and social media

virtual community: an online group of individuals who share interests, personal opinions or backgrounds

on – but they do not *have* to give out any of this information, or be honest. People can choose who they want to be and what they want to make public, and differences in gender, ethnicity and age are often less important.

- Being physically present is no longer as important. For example, a sociologist working in Mauritius can take part remotely in a conference in the USA. They can feel part of, and be accepted by, a global community of sociologists in a way that would not have been possible before. Another example is that a person with a physical disability may be able to participate fully and equally in an online community, without the barriers that might prevent them from doing this in face-to-face situations.

- People can find new interests and new communities to join, which may be significant enough to become a part of their identity. There are huge numbers of online communities, covering every possible aspect of human interests. This makes it possible to feel a shared identity with people around the world whom you may never meet. These online communities can be very positive; for example, people with a rare disease can share ideas and information about sources of support, treatments and medical developments related to their condition.

- Digital communication can help families stay in contact, despite being far away. A migrant worker can keep in contact with family in their home country or elsewhere. This will allow them to maintain the identity based on their family role.

- Digital communication can maintain identities based on ethnicity around the world. Migrants find it easier to stay in contact with their home culture; for example, Chinese people around the world can access Chinese media, including social media, and feel part of a global Chinese diaspora community.

- Digital communities can help people who face prejudice and discrimination: they can join together with others in the same position and support each other. Digital communities can also enable protest, with people coming together online to campaign for change.

Some negative aspects include:

- There are digital divides. Many people do not have access to new and social media and so miss out on the opportunities they can provide.

These divides take many forms; they might relate to what people can afford, to their gender, age or other aspects, or to geographical limitations (for example, areas where there is no internet or phone connection).

- There is a lot of disinformation. People may click on links that take them to areas of the internet – including online communities – that spread dangerous and misleading information. For example, there were many online conspiracy theories about COVID-19 vaccinations. It can then be difficult to break free of this. The internet relies on algorithms, which track people's online activity and direct them to sites that are similar to ones they have previously visited. As a result, they might not come into contact with alternative views. Instead, the internet can be like an echo chamber – the same ideas are bounced back to each user, like an echo.

- Online communication can bring people into contact with ideas that influence them negatively. For example, ideas about what bodies should look like can lead to 'body shaming', where people are made to feel ashamed of how they look. Online bullying, like offline bullying, can be very damaging to an individual's identity.

Figure 2.21: Online hate

- As people spend more of their time online, they have less time for the 'real' world. As a result, identities based on neighbourhoods where people live may become less important.

- Some people feel the term 'digital communities' is misleading, because they are not real communities. Real communities – such as a village or an urban neighbourhood – have a range of people of different ages and characteristics who have to get on together. There may be conflicts but there will also be negotiations and solutions.

CASE STUDY 2.3

Figure 2.22: A Filipina nurse.

Filipina migrant workers in the UK

Madianou and Miller carried out research with Filipina women who were in the UK as care workers and nurses. The women had families in the Philippines. Digital technologies allowed them to be heavily involved in their families' lives, in a way that was not possible for earlier migrants.

For example, Greta had three children at home. She called them on Skype, first thing in the morning and then as she was going to bed so she could wake them up for school in the Philippines. She also helped them with homework, knew what they were having to eat and advised their grandmother (who looked after them) on caring for them. Digital technologies allowed these women to maintain their identity as mothers and family members in quite an intensive way, despite the geographical distance and time differences.

Task

1 How would earlier generations of migrant mothers have kept in contact with their families? How might this have affected their identities?

2 'Digital technologies make it difficult for migrant women to be free of responsibility for families back home.' Do you agree with this view? Why or why not?

In contrast, online communities can have only one type of person. As a result, opinions become entrenched and alternative views are unwelcome; if there is any conflict, people just leave the group. Digital communities can also be very large and individuals may not be committed to the group.

- There is a lot of concern about children and others who are vulnerable. When children have smartphones, or any internet access, it can be difficult for parents and teachers to monitor their use. Children may be less able than adults to put what they see into perspective, or to realise when their responses are being manipulated. This is why some social media platforms, such as Facebook, have age restrictions.

- Although people are not always aware of it, their online activities are monitored – sometimes officially by a government, but also by the platform owner (such as Telegram). These organisations collect data about users. This is digital surveillance and it can happen even when users have encrypted their data. This type of surveillance can be used to prevent

crime and offensive behaviour but it can also be used, for example, to track political dissidents.

Globalisation

The influence of globalisation on individual and social/cultural identities

Globalisation is a concept used by sociologists to describe the process by which the world is becoming increasingly interconnected. It involves the feeling that the world seems to be getting smaller, because people and cultures around the world have more contact with each other and are more aware of each other. Globalisation is often described as involving changes in politics, economics and culture. In practice, it is very difficult to separate these changes because the globalisation of culture is made possible by economic and political changes. Examples of cultural globalisation include:

- world information systems, such as satellite communications, the internet, telecommunications and email

Figure 2.23: A globalised, interconnected world.

- global mass media such as news, films, television programmes and recorded music being available around the world

- global patterns of consumption and consumerism, where people have cosmopolitan lifestyles and feel at home in different cultures

- global sport, such as the Olympic Games and the football World Cup

- world tourism, where people now travel long distances for tourism

- clothing and appearance; for example, people all around the world wear T-shirts, jeans and baseball caps

- food; the types of food and styles of cooking from different places are available everywhere

- some brand names associated with cultural goods are global, such as McDonalds, Coca Cola and Walt Disney.

Many people now see the world as one place – a global village sharing one **global culture**. This perception is encouraged by the media (for example, we can now see news from around the world as it is happening) and by people's personal experiences. This change in thinking can be seen even in popular media; for example, science fiction films often show all humans united against an enemy, such as alien invaders or an asteroid heading for the planet.

However, if there is a global culture, many people are still excluded from all or some of it. Much of the writing about globalisation is by people in the developed world where, for example, a much greater range of food is available and fruit and vegetables that are out of season are flown around the world to meet demand. The global travel industry has created opportunities for exotic holidays, and global influences on the creative arts – such as the music industry – have enriched people's choices and experiences. However, the experience of globalisation in developing countries is more economic than cultural – working hard for little reward to supply the rich world.

Some sociologists view cultural globalisation as the spread of Western, or specifically American, culture; they see the flow of culture as one-way. This can lead to the view that globalisation is being *done by* some countries and *done to* other countries: Western culture is imposed on the rest of the world. This can either be seen as good, because it spreads values about human rights, freedom and gender equality, or as bad, because it leads to exploitation and the end of local cultures. When it is seen as a bad thing, it is often referred to as cultural imperialism. This implies that, rather than ruling the rest of the world directly (as they did in the age of colonialism), the rich countries now dominate the world through their cultural influence.

There are similar debates about **cultural appropriation** as a consequence of globalisation. For example, there is some debate about whether white, Western people should wear their hair in dreadlocks for fashion reasons, when dreadlocks have a cultural significance in parts of the Caribbean. Some people see this as disrespectful and even ignorant; it has also been related to previous times of Empire and colonialism when natural resources from the Americas, Asia and Africa were collected and taken back to European countries.

KEY TERMS

global culture: the idea that, as a result of globalisation, there is or will be a single culture shared by people all around the world

cultural appropriation: where culturally significant practices and artefacts from one part of the world are adopted by people in another part of the world, in a way that uses them as a fashion statement and strips them of their meaning

New media and technology may have gone global but they are not used in the same way in all cultures. Each culture makes different use of what is available. For example, mobile phones are used in different ways in parts of Africa and in Europe. In Africa, phones are often shared and they are used, for example, by farmers to find out prices at markets and to spread news about the dates of weddings and other festivities. In European countries, in contrast, phones are mostly used to access the internet and especially social media.

Cultural defence

Some countries and peoples have reacted vigorously to defend their culture against globalisation and to reject outside influences and ideas. Here are some examples:

- The small Himalayan kingdom of Bhutan has tried to minimise some modern influences; for example, it did not allow televisions until 1999.

- Religious fundamentalists such as the Taliban in Afghanistan and Boko Haram (which means 'Western education is sinful') in Nigeria violently reject Western culture.

- Some countries try to block access to the internet and censor media (such as magazines) from other countries, to prevent their people being 'corrupted'. For example, China's Great Firewall blocks access to selected foreign websites.

- France limits the amount of English language television that can be broadcast and English language music that can be played on the radio (to protect the French language).

Hybrid identities

Globalisation sometimes seems to weaken local cultures by bringing in American influences. However, the flow of culture is not always one way. Europe and North America are influenced by other cultures, in music, food, fashion and much more. Philosophical and religious traditions and practices from Asia, such as meditation and yoga, have become popular. Some sociologists describe what is happening as the creation of hybrid cultures; new cultures that have features of two or more others. People can also combine aspects of different cultures, developing **hybrid identities**. This can be seen as positive and even exciting. We cannot expect traditional cultures to remain the same (it is unlikely that they ever have) but elements of them will survive and enrich new, emerging cultures. For example, aspects of traditional cultures can acquire a new value when they are used

for tourism. An African dance that celebrated a harvest or coming of age ceremony may not be used for those purposes anymore; instead, it may be performed for tourists, creating an income for the dancers.

Homogenisation of identities

One view is that globalisation will lead to cultures and identities being the same all around the world. For example, in the future, people everywhere may speak the same language, dress in the same kinds of clothes and eat the same foods – there will be a single global culture. When culture and identities are the same everywhere, they are homogenised. This is the opposite of cultural diversity, where a range of different cultures co-exist.

In theory, a homogenised global culture could be a mixture of all the cultures of the world. In reality, if a **homogeneous** global culture is spreading around the world, it is based on American culture. This spread of American culture is sometimes called Americanisation. Those who are against it argue that it involves a destructive way of life; for example, Americanisation encourages people to want a consumer-driven lifestyle and aspire to possess goods they do not need. People who have always drunk water may come to think that fizzy drinks are better, because they are associated with the desired American lifestyle. This may have long-term health consequences and may be something they cannot afford. The globalisation of American culture can seem like a vigorous attempt by powerful transnational corporations to persuade the rest of the world that it needs and wants to adopt American consumerism and materialism. The spread of the American lifestyle is also bad for the environment, as it depends on the heavy use of energy that reduces natural resources and contributes to climate change. Finally, Americanisation may lead to the loss of many valuable things, such as the rich diversity of languages and traditions in other cultures.

KEY TERMS

hybrid identities: when people combine and mix aspects of different cultures to create new identities

homogenisation of identities: when the differences between identities of people around the world disappear, so they become similar

---

Table 2.4 summarises some of the key evidence for and against a homogenised culture and identities.

Evidence for	Evidence against
Hollywood films are seen all over the world and they tend to glorify an American way of life and American values. They are also accompanied by merchandising, such as toys, which may particularly influence children.	Other countries have film industries, for example, India has Bollywood and Nigeria has Nollywood. Bollywood films are watched globally but mainly by audiences of Indian origin.
Most of the world's most successful music performers are American or European.	Bob Marley, from Jamaica, was the first superstar from a developing country. The Korean group BTS are among the world's biggest music stars.
An American style of dress, with T-shirts, jeans and trainers, has become almost a young people's uniform around the world.	Many people still value traditional styles of dress, such as the sari, *salwar kameez* and *dhoti* in India, Pakistan and Bangladesh, or kimonos in Japan. Some fashion and jewellery from non-Western cultures have become popular in Western cultures, such as the use of henna as body art. This shows that global influences are not just moving in one direction.
English has become a global language. Most websites are in English.	There are still thousands of languages, although some of them are dying. In terms of numbers of internet users, Mandarin is close behind English.
Some American foods have become popular globally, led by brands such as McDonalds and KFC.	Many foods from other parts of the world are everywhere; most countries now have many restaurants that offer Chinese, Indian, Thai, Japanese and other food, and the ingredients of food from different cultures are on sale in shops.
Football originated in Europe and has become the world's most popular team sport. European teams often win the World Cup.	Brazil has won the football World Cup the most times. American sports such as basketball and baseball have not become globally popular.
World news is supplied mainly by a small number of American companies and press agencies, and tends to reflect American interests.	News organisations from non-Western countries, such as al-Jazeera, based in Qatar, are increasingly important.
Most global tourism is by American and European tourists to destinations designed to cater for them.	There are increasing numbers of tourists from non-Western countries visiting many other parts of the world. For example, tourism from China and Japan has increased over the last few decades.

Table 2.4: Key evidence for and against a homogenised culture and identities

Positive and negative impacts on identity of global culture, cultural diversity and multiculturalism

As we have seen, global culture and cultural diversity can have both positive and negative influences on identity. A global culture could lead to the homogenisation of identities or it could create diverse and hybrid identities. Cultural diversity, with a variety of cultures co-existing, can give individuals a lot of freedom and choice, and create more tolerance of a range of identities.

In modern society, there is increased movement of groups of people between regions and countries. As a result, different cultures now exist in many countries. For example, in the UK there are at least four cultures based on national identities (English, Scottish, Welsh and Northern Irish) and there are also cultures of immigrant groups, such as African-Caribbean, Asian and Eastern European. In some countries, this has happened to a much lesser extent; for example, Japan has relatively few immigrants.

People and societies can adapt to the co-existence of cultures in different ways.

Assimilation and integration take place when immigrant cultures (or other cultures) gradually lose their separate identity and become part of the dominant culture. This has happened with some groups that immigrated to the USA: the USA in the 18th and 19th centuries was described as a 'melting pot'. This means that immigrants from all over Europe, and elsewhere, gradually became more American than German or Russian or whatever their national origin. They were assimilated into being American, which involved conforming to American norms and values. Some aspects of their culture blended with American culture, so the original American culture was also changed by absorbing these new influences.

Many people felt that important aspects of the original cultures were lost in this process. A response to such concerns has been the promotion of multiculturalism. A **multicultural society** is a society made up of many different cultures that exist alongside each other without losing their distinctive features. Each group keeps its own language and cultural practices, and people do not have to abandon their heritage to be accepted. In the USA, some immigrant groups have held onto the culture of their country of origin; if they feel their culture is under threat, they may even assert it more strongly than they would have done if they had stayed in their country of origin.

KEY TERM

multicultural society: a society in which many different cultures or sub-cultures exist alongside each other

Two multicultural countries are India and Mauritius. In India, an astonishing variety of cultures and sub-cultures exist alongside each other. Some aspects of this diversity are:

- religions: while most Indian people are Hindus, there are followers of many other faiths, including Islam, Christianity, Buddhism, Sikhism and Jainism

- regions: because of India's great size, there are significant differences in culture between states and regions

- languages: Hindi is the official language and English is a subsidiary official language, but more than 30 native languages are spoken by more than a million Indians. Hundreds of other languages are also used and there are several different writing systems based on different languages.

The population of Mauritius is very ethnically diverse. Most Mauritians are of Indian, African, Chinese or European descent. Mauritian Creole is the most widely used language but many people are multilingual, speaking French, English or Asian languages.

In some modern industrial societies, there has been a movement away from multiculturalism in recent years. This is connected to concerns about immigration. Some politicians and others have argued that it is not desirable to have distinct ethnic cultures in a nation-state. This is something that functionalists would agree with, because they suggest society needs a value consensus to run smoothly. Some of the criticisms of multiculturalism include:

- It gives too many rights to minority communities; for example, it would be expensive to provide opportunities for all children to be educated in the language of their country of origin.

- Minority communities may choose to remain separate from the host community; this leads to insufficient integration.

- It is too idealistic. It is unlikely that very different cultures can exist alongside each other in peace, harmony and equality.

- The host culture becomes just one of many cultures, when it should provide the value system that holds the society together.

- It may lead to conflict between groups.

As a result, some countries have moved towards assimilation – where immigrant groups adopt the host culture – rather than multiculturalism. They might do this in the following ways:

- Citizenship tests. Many countries require immigrants to pass a test before they are given the right to remain in the country. These tests often ask potential citizens about the history and culture of the country they wish to live in, as well as assessing their language skills. Such tests can be controversial, because all cultures are diverse. As a result, there are disagreements about which aspects of a culture are the most important for immigrants to learn.

- Acting against the expression of some aspects of minority cultures. For example, in 2010 France banned the wearing in public of anything that covered the face. The effect of this was to prevent the wearing of the *niqab*. Thus, an aspect of Muslim culture was banned.

- Increasing nationalism. In some countries, nationalism has been based on asserting a single culture. This happens when a region wants to break away from a country and the people from that region are ethnically, linguistically or religiously distinct from the national culture. Examples include the province of Quebec in Canada, Catalonia in Spain and Scotland in the United Kingdom, which all have nationalist movements that wish to gain independence. It can also take the form of opposing immigration and wanting to expel minorities.

Postmodernist views of identity as chosen rather than given

The 20th century was the modern period. People looked back at earlier periods of history as pre-modern. Now, society and life have changed. Some sociologists say that we have moved into a new and different period of history, a new type of society. They are called **postmodernists** and they call the period we now live in postmodernity. Different postmodernists emphasise different things that have changed, but they all agree that mass communication and digital technologies are transforming our lives.

Postmodernists believe that people now have much greater choice over their identities. In the past, identities were given or ascribed, based on statuses such as gender, age and ethnicity, or life events such as being married or a parent. There were some limited choices, such as when people took on a new occupation. In general, however, individuals had little freedom in terms of how they performed the roles associated with their identities.

Today people have wider choices. They might not choose some of the traditional aspects of identity – for example, more people choose not to marry or have children, or opt out of traditional gender roles. In addition, there are now more identities that are considered important. For example, being a vegan or vegetarian has become an important identity for some.

Digital identities and identities linked to consumption patterns and lifestyle in a pick-and-mix society

Postmodernists think that these changes to identities are linked to **consumption**. They say that the modern world was based on production (making things) but the postmodern world is a consumer society, based on what

people buy and use. As a result, the work someone does may be a less important aspect of their identity than how they spend the money they earn from work. Someone who might once have said they were an office worker or a salesperson may now think of themselves more as the owner of a particular type of car, or the wearer of a particular fashion brand. Thus, through consumption individuals are constructing their own unique identities and **lifestyles**. Studying **consumption patterns** can inform us about the ways in which cultures and identities are evolving, according to postmodernists.

Postmodernists also describe society today as a **'pick-and-mix' society**. Society is like a big supermarket, where each customer can choose what they want.

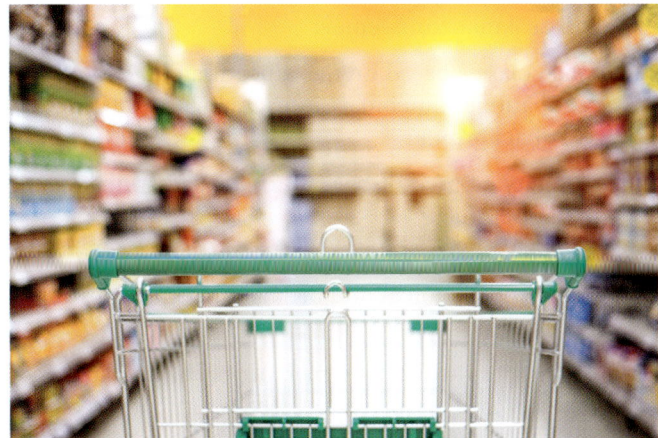

Figure 2.24: A 'pick-and-mix' society.

KEY TERMS

postmodernism: the view that we now live in a new type of society, different from the modern society that came before

consumption: the buying and use of goods and resources

consumption lifestyle: a lifestyle based on what people buy and consume (rather than, for example, the work they do)

consumption patterns: variations in consumption depending on time, place and group

pick-and-mix society: in a postmodern society, people can choose from a range of options and select what suits them best

From the shelves, they might choose a football team to support, a car to drive, a type of diet, a favourite influencer, a set of religious beliefs and so on. Every one of these choices can be an aspect of identity in a pick-and-mix society, but the shopper decides whether to choose them and how important they are to their overall identity. It has also become much easier to change identities. To extend the analogy, a shopper can go back to the supermarket at any time, give back anything they do not want any more and choose new items instead.

Through their choices, individuals in a postmodern society can create and shape their lifestyles, deciding who they want to be and how they want to live. In modern societies, lifestyles were very much linked to:

- gender – based on the choices and opportunities you had as a male or a female
- social class – based on the educational and occupational outcomes associated with your social class background
- ethnicity – based on the cultural expectations related to your ethnicity
- age – based on the expectations surrounding appropriate choices and behaviour related to your age group.

In a postmodern world, however, people have many more choices and opportunities. Teenagers can become millionaire entrepreneurs and influencers, women can head up global companies, and people can now choose to change career, work from home or relocate to another country at any point in their lives.

The problem with this postmodern view of consumer society is that many people do not have access to these options, either in the real world or online. Some people have far more choice than others. This is often because of wealth and income – and, therefore, social class. Many people cannot afford digital technologies or many consumer goods. Other sociologists say that postmodernists do not acknowledge the continued differences in social class, gender, ethnicity and age, which still decide important parts of our lives (as you will see when you study other topics).

CHECK YOUR UNDERSTANDING 2.3

1 Work with a partner and make sure you can both explain the following terms:
   a globalisation
   b the homogenisation of identities
   c hybrid identities
   d multiculturalism

2 Write down three ways in which each of these aspects of identity has changed in the last 50 years:
   a social class
   b age
   c gender
   d ethnicity

KEY POINTS

- Key aspects of social identity are:
  - age
  - gender
  - ethnicity
  - social class.
- These aspects impact on individuals and social groups in different societies.
- People today can create a digital self and have online identities.
- Social networks, social media and virtual communities have positive and negative impacts on identity.
- Cultural diversity, multiculturalism and global culture have positive and negative impacts on individual and social/cultural identities.
- Postmodernists view identity as chosen rather than given.
- In postmodern societies, people can have digital identities linked to consumption patterns and lifestyle in a pick-and-mix society.

SUMMARY

- Individuals learn their identity through primary and secondary socialisation.

- There is a debate between sociological perspectives about socialisation.

- People are controlled by formal and informal agencies of social control, which use a variety of methods.

- Some people join groups to resist and protest against social control.

- There is a range of influences on social identity.

- These influences are increasingly online.

KEY SKILLS EXERCISES

1 Knowledge and understanding

Without using this book or your notes, see if you can list the **four** key aspects of social identity. Check your answer. Now, for each aspect, give **three** examples of how it might affect people.

2 Interpretation and application

How much are digital technologies used today? Design a social survey asking about the digital devices people own or use, and what they use them for. Ask a range of people in your school or college (teachers, other staff, your peers, younger learners) to take your survey. Present your data in a chart or table.

What have you learnt about how much the people in your sample use digital technologies?

3 Analysis and evaluation

Write up to 500 words to answer the question: 'To what extent has social media changed the way people construct their identities?' In your essay, try to use these terms (and any others you think are relevant): digital self, virtual communities, globalisation, social networks, postmodernism, pick-and-mix society.

IMPROVE THIS ANSWER

Research methods, identity and inequality

Evaluate the view that age is the main influence on identity. Your answer should include:

- at least three arguments for and three arguments against the view

- a conclusion.

The importance of peer groups is one example of how age is a strong influence on identity. These groups of friends are often based on age, and shape the way we see ourselves (in relation to the group). This is especially important for young people; the peer group provides an identity (based on age). Another example is the fact that age is seen as important by society. There are different social expectations for different age groups; for example, there are restrictions on what young people can do. In most countries, young people cannot work, get married or vote until they reach an age at which they get the same rights as adults. This means that age is bound to be an important part of a young person's identity. A third example is that there is now a greater generation gap than in the past, so the experiences of different age groups are very different, and it is more likely people will identify with a particular age group. Social and technological changes such as the internet and social media mean that different age groups have different experiences, which influence their identities.

Commentary and task

This is an evaluation question, so it requires several arguments for the view in the question, several arguments against the view in the question and a conclusion. The answer so far gives several arguments in favour of the view that age is the main influence on identity. Improve this answer by adding a new paragraph with at least three arguments against the view. Try to include some sociological concepts and refer to sociological theories such as Marxism and feminism. Finally, add an evaluative conclusion.

PRACTICE QUESTIONS

Research methods, identity and inequality

a Define the terms:

    i   stereotype   [2]

    ii   peer pressure   [2]

b Give **two** examples of types of sub-culture.   [2]

c Explain **three** ways in which formal agencies of social control achieve social conformity.   [6]

d Explain **three** aspects of the feminist view of socialisation.   [6]

e Discuss the view that identity is now chosen rather than given.

   Your answer should include:

- at least **three** developed points with evidence.   [8]

f Evaluate the view that age is the main influence on identity.

   Your answer should include:

- at least **three** arguments for and **three** arguments against the view

- a conclusion.   [14]

SELF-EVALUATION CHECKLIST

After studying this unit, copy and complete this table.

You should be able to:	Needs more work	Almost there	Ready to move on
1.1 How do we learn our identity?			
Understand how society is a product of social construction			
Understand the social construction of identity			
Understand primary and secondary socialisation and the processes used by the key agencies involved			
Evaluate the effectiveness of each agency in the socialisation process			
Understand the debate between sociological perspectives and theories on socialisation			
2.2 How does society control us?			
Understand types of social control			
Understand the debate between consensus and conflict views of social control			
Understand the methods used by the formal and informal agencies of social control			
Evaluate the effectiveness of agencies of formal social control			
Evaluate the effectiveness of agencies of informal social control			
Understand the reasons for and forms of resistance to social control			
2.3 What influences our social identity?			
Explain the key aspects of social identity: age, gender, ethnicity and social class			
Explain the digital self and online identities			
Understand globalisation and its influence on individual and social/cultural identities			
Evaluate the positive and negative impacts on identity of cultural diversity, multiculturalism and global culture			
Explain postmodernist views of identity			

> ## Unit 3
Social stratification and inequality

LEARNING INTENTIONS

In this unit you will learn how to:

- Understand social stratification in open and closed societies

- Explain differences in life chances in education, employment, health, housing and life expectancy as affected by age, gender, ethnicity and social class

- Understand the intersectionality of age, ethnicity, gender and social class in understanding the impact of inequality on individuals

- Understand different sociological theories of social inequality

- Explain the use of legislation within societies to reduce inequality

- Explain the development and impact of welfare states on life chances

- Explain the work of non-governmental organisations (NGOs)

- Understand sociological views of the success of attempts to reduce social inequalities

- Explain the impact of migration on societies

- Explain the impact of global ecological issues on societies

- Evaluate sociological explanations for global inequalities.

Introduction

Living together as members of a society brings many benefits to individuals. People can achieve more together than they can alone. Our media and culture tend to imply that great achievements in society are the work of individuals – scientists, inventors, discoverers, writers, artists and composers. In reality, the accomplishments of such people are made possible by their social background and by building on the earlier work of others.

Not everyone has an equal chance to achieve. Most societies are organised so they are unequal. They have systems of stratification by which individuals and groups are ranked or graded in a hierarchy that gives some an advantage over others. This unit explores the nature of **social stratification** and **social inequality**, focusing on inequalities both within societies (between men and women, between social classes and between age and ethnic groups) and between societies.

KEY TERMS

social stratification: a hierarchy in which groups have different statuses and different levels of privilege

social inequality: the differences between groups in a stratification system; for example, in income or wealth

3.1 What is social stratification?

Social stratification in open and closed societies

Human beings living in groups have always divided functions and labour for greater efficiency. In hunter-gatherer groups, long before recorded history, different individuals performed the tasks needed by the whole group, such as gathering food, preparing food, constructing shelters and watching for danger. In all societies, women bear the children. Beyond this, however, **statuses** and roles are socially constructed: groups and societies make decisions about who does what. This is called **social differentiation**. Societies become more differentiated as they develop, because there are more tasks to be done and therefore more statuses and roles.

Social differentiation refers only to differences in role and status. It does not mean that some individuals are considered superior to others. Social differentiation does, however, lay the foundations for a hierarchical system in which people are ranked; some are seen as superior, or they have greater **power** or more possessions than others. At this point, differentiation becomes stratification. (The word stratification is borrowed from geology, where strata are the different layers of rocks, laid on top of each other. Sociologists use the word to describe how social groups are like layers in society, with some higher than others.)

Social stratification is found in all societies. It is based on rules, norms and values that can be enforced by sanctions. Societies may be described as open or closed.

- In **open societies**, individuals can change their roles and status, perhaps through education or hard work. Modern industrial societies tend to be open. As a result, stratification is dynamic rather than static. There are constant changes as groups try to improve their status and power relative to others.

KEY TERMS

status: a position that someone has in society; status can be ascribed (fixed by others) or achieved

social differentiation: the assignment of different roles and statuses to groups and individuals within a society

power: the ability to influence people's behaviour

open society: a society in which individuals can move between social roles and change statuses

- In **closed societies**, an individual's role and status are fixed, usually by being born into a particular social group. Some traditional societies are closed, at least in some aspects of stratification, such as gender or social class. For example, in some societies, women are prevented from attending school or becoming financially independent.

The main forms of stratification are by **social class**, **age**, **ethnicity** and gender. In practice, many individuals are stratified in several different ways. For example, a young, working-class female from a minority ethnic group may lack power and status in society, but it will be difficult to identify which characteristic has the most impact on her status.

Achieved and ascribed status

Ascribed statuses are given to people by their group or society, and individuals usually have little control over them. Age, sex, ethnic group, religion and social class are ascribed to people at birth, although some can be changed later; for example, it is possible to change religion. Ascribed statuses are common in traditional closed societies, where people's life chances are largely determined at birth.

Age differs from other ascribed statuses in that it changes over time. Adults have a higher status than children and, in many societies, there are rites of passage (ceremonies or rituals) to mark the transition to adulthood. In traditional societies, age often brings greater status: the younger members of a group look after the elders, value their experience and treat them with great respect. In modern industrial societies, in contrast, old age often brings a loss of status. Statuses that are attached to work are lost when someone retires, and older people are often victims of **ageism**. (Strictly speaking, the term 'ageism' refers to **discrimination** against any group based on their age. However, it is usually used to refer to discrimination against older people.)

Achieved statuses are those that people gain through choice and competition. They are commonly the main form of status in open societies. Some statuses that are ascribed at birth – such as social class and religion – can be changed in open societies; for example, a person may convert to a different religion. Other achieved statuses include occupational status, such as a teacher or an engineer.

Poverty

It is very difficult to define poverty. Living standards are higher in modern industrial countries than in developing countries, but there are poor people in both types of society. One way of defining poverty is to talk about absolute and relative poverty. People living in absolute poverty do not have some of the basic necessities of life such as:

- food
- safe drinking water
- sanitation (toilets near the home)
- shelter (somewhere to live)
- health (access to treatment for serious illnesses and in pregnancy)

KEY TERMS

closed society: a society in which individuals' social roles and statuses are fixed

social class: a shared economic and social status; for example, working class, middle class or upper class

age: a form of stratification based on how old people are

ethnicity: the state of belonging to a particular group with a shared culture, including language, beliefs, history and traditions

ascribed status: a position in society that is given to an individual by their society or group; people usually have little or no control over ascribed statuses

---

KEY TERMS

ageism: prejudice and discrimination against people based on how old they are

discrimination: treating a person or group of people differently to other people, often based on prejudice

achieved status: a position in society that an individual acquires through their own effort

- education

- information (access to the media).

Absolute poverty is a standard that can be applied in all times and places. The global measure of absolute or extreme poverty used by the World Bank is living on less than $1.90 a day. This figure is adjusted when it is applied globally, to account for the different prices of essentials in different countries. By this measure, in 2017, about 700 million people around the world were living in extreme poverty. In 1990, this figure was well over a billion, so extreme poverty on a global scale has gradually reduced. However, the COVID-19 pandemic is thought to have increased the number of people living in extreme poverty by around 100 million and climate change is also pushing more people into poverty. In the last quarter of 2022, the World Bank updated the global measure of poverty (called the Global poverty line) to $2.15 per day, to reflect the increase in prices in low-income countries since 2017.

Relative poverty is a way of measuring poverty that takes social context into account. A person living in relative poverty can be considered poor in comparison to others in the same society. In a modern industrial society, people can be considered poor if they do not meet the basic standard of living of that society – even though, in a different society, they might not be considered poor. People living in relative poverty may have the basic necessities of life, such as food, shelter, water and sanitation. However, they do not have the material goods which others in their society would see as necessities. In modern industrial societies, the groups most likely to live in relative poverty include:

- lone parents and their children

- unemployed people, especially the long-term unemployed

- workers who are low paid

- chronically ill or disabled people

- people who are dependent on welfare **benefits**

- refugees, asylum seekers and recently arrived immigrants.

In addition, women, children, older people and members of ethnic minority groups have a high risk of living in relative poverty.

Many people who live in absolute or extreme poverty as measured by the World Bank live in South Asia and Sub-Saharan Africa. In countries in South Asia, economic growth is lifting many people out of poverty. However, in many African countries, economic growth is often slower and starts from a lower base.

KEY TERM

benefits: money paid by governments to people who are ill, unemployed or poor

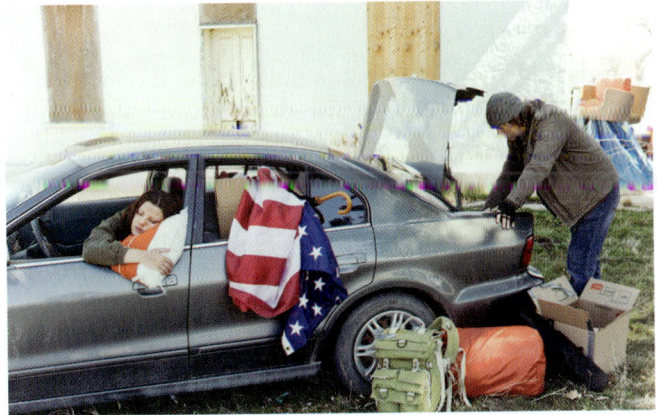

Figure 3.1: Experiences of poverty vary between societies.

This means that many people there will continue to live in poverty. The world's poorest people face many risks, including the following.

- People living in city slums often have temporary homes with few services and facilities and no security. At any moment, city authorities may decide to destroy their home and reclaim the land.

- People living in rural areas often have limited access to health, education and other services.

- Political instability and civil wars often affect poorer people the most. Wealthier people can afford to escape dangerous situations.

- Climate change is affecting poor people first and worst. The areas where poorer people live are often at risk of flooding, landslips and pollution and affected by rising sea levels. Poorer people cannot afford to move away from these risks.

Poverty is a complex phenomenon that does not have a single cause. Some of the main reasons for people being in poverty are:

- being born into a family living in poverty

- not having opportunities to gain qualifications or employment to improve their situation

- not having paid work or a source of income

- being in low-paid work

- welfare benefits are not sufficient to help people move out of poverty.

An adult is more likely to live in poverty if they were born into poverty.

The **cycle of poverty** refers to families that have been in poverty for at least three generations, because the factors causing their poverty do not change and instead keep them in poverty. For example, a child born into poverty is unlikely to do well at school. As a result, they will not gain the skills and qualifications they need to move up the social class ladder.

Many poor people do not have the resources to get out of poverty and they suffer disadvantages that keep them in poverty. They tend to lack social and cultural capital (see Unit 5), as well as money. A similar phenomenon occurs at the other end of the scale: the children of wealthy parents are likely to become wealthy adults.

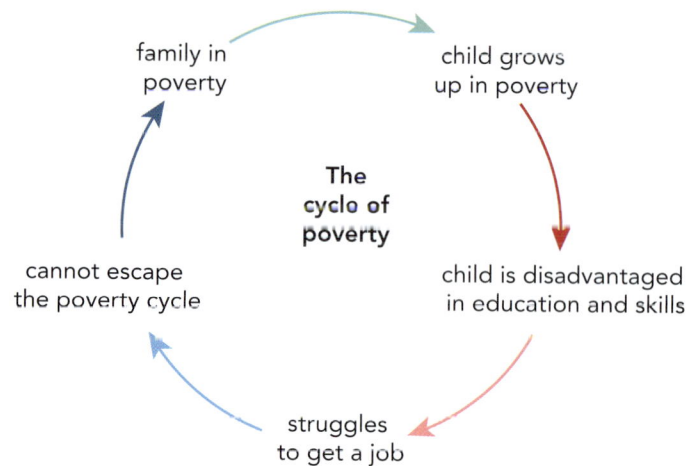

Figure 3.2: The cycle of poverty.

It is very difficult – or even impossible – for poor people to change their situation, because they do not have the opportunities and resources necessary to escape from poverty. This is known as the **poverty trap**. One reason for this is that it is expensive to be poor. People have to spend a high proportion of their income just to maintain a basic standard of living. For example:

- Poor people cannot afford to travel to cheap supermarkets, so they have to use more expensive local shops.

- They cannot afford to buy products in bulk (buying large quantities of a product at one time), which would be cheaper in the long term.

- They cannot afford to insulate their homes, so they pay a lot for fuel.

- They buy old or second-hand goods that are likely to break down and need to be replaced.

KEY TERMS

cycle of poverty: when poor families become trapped in poverty for at least three generations because they have no access to the resources or qualifications to lift themselves out of it

poverty trap: when poor people are unable to escape from being poor

- They cannot afford facilities that would enable them to take up opportunities; for example, to pay a childminder so they can work longer hours.

- They may be unable to borrow from a bank due to their low or unstable income. As a result, to pay their bills, they may have to borrow from someone who will charge high rates of interest.

One explanation for the cycle of poverty is that there is a **culture of poverty**; that poor people have a set of values that tend to keep them in poverty. Characteristics that have been said to be part of the culture of poverty include:

- having low levels of literacy and education

- being unable to plan for the future

- wanting immediate gratification (wanting rewards instantly; in contrast, deferred gratification involves investing time in something – such as working hard at school and going on to higher education – in the hope of greater rewards later). This is sometimes linked to working-class children underachieving in education (see Unit 5)

- **fatalism** (not believing they can change their lives for the better)

- feeling they do not really belong in society.

The idea of a culture of poverty is controversial. Some research has shown that poor people have the same values as the rest of society and the suggestion that they have different values could be seen as a form of victim blaming – implying that it is their own fault they are poor. In addition, some characteristics – such as poor education – are not the fault of the poor person. The idea of a culture of poverty has been used by some politicians as a reason for not attempting to tackle poverty; such politicians argue that spending money helping poor people will make no difference if the culture does not change.

KEY TERMS

culture of poverty: when poor people have a different set of values to the majority, which keeps them poor

fatalism: an individual's belief that they cannot control what happens to them

ACTIVITY: DISCUSSION 3.1

In a small group, discuss the following questions:

1   What could be done to prevent the cycle of poverty? Should governments do more to help families get out of poverty?

2   Do you think there is a culture of poverty in your society? Do poor people have values which make it more likely that they will stay poor?

3   Does the existence of poverty in a society affect everyone? In what ways?

Wealth

Wealth refers to the ownership of financial savings and of things that can be bought and sold to generate income. There are many different forms of wealth other than money. Some of the most important forms of wealth are:

- stocks and shares in companies

- land

- houses and other buildings

- works of art, jewellery and other valuable items.

Having these forms of wealth is an important indicator of social class. Some forms of wealth also create more wealth. For example, shares produce dividends and works of art often grow in value. The very wealthy do not need to work because their wealth creates more wealth. Wealth is often inherited (passed down to individuals from their parents or other relatives), not earned.

It is difficult to be sure how wealthy people are because wealthy people tend to be secretive about their wealth. They might also employ tax advisers to help them appear less well off, so they pay less tax.

KEY TERM

wealth: money, savings and property that can be bought and sold to generate income

In some developing countries, there is a very wide gap between the rich and poor. This can lead to striking contrasts when rich and poor people live close to each other. For example, India's richest man, Mukesh Ambani, is one of the wealthiest people in the world, with a fortune of $103 billion. He owns a 27-storey house in Mumbai, a city where millions of people live in slums.

Figure 3.3: Mukash Ambani's house in Mumbai.

The world's wealthiest and most powerful people can move easily from one country or continent to another. Increasingly, they share cosmopolitan lifestyles based on the consumption of luxury goods and services. They are likely to use private transport, live in gated communities and go to exclusive clubs, restaurants and resorts. The sociologist Leslie Sklair conducted interviews with some of these people. He identified a fairly new transnational capitalist class that consists of the following main groups:

- owners and controllers of transnational corporations

- politicians and bureaucrats, such as those working for the United Nations and other global organisations

- professionals

- consumerist elites (such as those in the media).

This class is a sort of global bourgeoisie, in Marxist terms.

More broadly, most inhabitants of the more developed countries have a significantly higher standard of living than the majority of the world's population. Their lifestyle is based on consumerism and they consume a high proportion of the world's energy and other resources. Inhabitants of the more developed countries are the one billion or so most privileged people in the world. Large numbers of people in modern industrial societies would not consider themselves wealthy, but they have a lot more money and assets than most people in developing countries. Many people have bank or building society savings accounts; smaller numbers have other personal investments. Most households also own consumer goods such as televisions, computers and cars that are a form of wealth. The following are common forms of wealth:

- Housing: Many people own their own houses; this is often their main form of wealth. However, it is difficult to turn this into useful money if it is your only house and you need to live there.

- Pensions: Many people now have pensions to provide an income when they retire. The money saved is a form of wealth, but it is kept in pension funds and cannot be used before retirement.

- Shares: Today, more people own shares in businesses than in the past. However, the largest numbers of shares are usually held by a small number of very wealthy investors.

Power

Discussions about inequality tend to focus on wealth and poverty: how much, or how little, money and resources people have. But inequality is also about power. People who have power can achieve what they want even if others are opposed to them, whereas powerless people cannot.

Power comes from different sources. An individual may have power due to their occupation. For example, the police and judges have power through their jobs and a manager has power over more junior workers. Those in government have power to change laws and make policies which directly affect people's lives. Power may also come from other forms of status, such as a person's gender, age, social class or ethnicity. It can be argued that men have power over women; adults have power over children, youths and the elderly; the middle class have power over the working class; and people from the dominant ethnic group in a society have power over those from other ethnic groups.

Power can be used in different ways. It might allow an individual to use force or threaten legal consequences if others do not do what is expected. This may include the threat of losing a job, imprisonment or even violence.

Power can also be used in less obvious ways. Those with power can manipulate situations or withhold information to ensure people do what they want – without having to use the threat of direct consequences.

People without power may experience **social exclusion**: this means they are systematically excluded from rights, opportunities and resources that are available to others. Social exclusion refers to a wider set of disadvantages than material poverty and these disadvantages prevent people from fully participating in the life of their society. Socially excluded groups do not have people to support them. For example, politicians are not interested in them, either because they do not vote or because they are considered unimportant.

Individuals who have little or no power may still try to challenge those who do. They will find it easier to resist if they do so with others, since a larger group will have more power. For example:

- Groups of workers can form trade unions to try to improve their pay and conditions, or they can go on strike. They have more power to challenge their employer collectively than as individuals.

- People can form protest groups, working together to try to force those with power to act differently. For example, after the killing of George Floyd by a police officer in Minnesota, USA in 2020, the Black Lives Matter movement protested against racism and for reform of the police. The numbers involved in these protests ensured that governments could not ignore their grievances.

- **Non-governmental organisations (NGOs)** (see section 3.2) often act in the interests of powerless groups.

Social mobility

Social mobility is movement between classes. Types of social mobility include:

- upward social mobility, which involves moving up the social class hierarchy; for example, from the working class to the middle class

- downward mobility, which involves moving down the social class hierarchy; for example, from the middle class to the working class

- intergenerational mobility, which involves children moving to a different social class from their parents; for example, a child of working-class parents who is successful in education might enter a middle-class profession

- intragenerational mobility, which involves an individual changing social classes within their lifetime; for example, someone may start their working life in a working-class job, but moves up to become a manager.

Social mobility happens in open societies, but is not possible in closed societies. In a **meritocracy**, where people achieve the social position they deserve through talent and effort, we expect to find a lot of social mobility – both upward and downward.

Factors that lead to social mobility include:

- getting education and qualifications to improve your chances of being upwardly mobile

- getting promotion and career advancement

- marrying someone of a different class

- changes in wealth; for example, becoming wealthy through inheritance or winning a lottery.

Upward mobility is more common than downward mobility. This is because of changes in the numbers and proportions of different kinds of jobs. In many countries today, there are fewer unskilled manual jobs and more middle-class jobs. This change, as well as greater educational opportunities, has allowed people to move up the social hierarchy. Most mobility is short range; for example, an individual is unlikely to move from the very bottom of the hierarchy to the upper class or the other way around, but they might move from the top of the working class to the bottom of the middle class.

KEY TERMS

social exclusion: when society does not provide a group with the rights and benefits available to others in the same society

non-governmental organisations (NGOs): non-government, non-profit making bodies that address social and political issues

social mobility: the movement of individuals or groups up or down the social hierarchy

---

KEY TERM

meritocracy: a system in which individuals reach the social positions they deserve, based on their educational achievement, talent and skills

---

It could be argued that this is not really mobility at all, since it involves little change in lifestyle, life chances or class identity.

Marxists see social mobility as a sort of safety valve. If people could not move between classes, there would be more anger and increased chances of class conflict. However, the fact that there is some mobility allows people to believe (mistakenly) that the system is open and fair.

From a functionalist perspective, it is natural for most middle-class positions to be taken by people from middle-class origins, because they tend to be more talented, as their parents and grandparents were. This talent allowed their parents and grandparents to move up the social ladder before them. The functionalist perspective thus assumes that intelligence is largely inherited. This is a controversial idea, challenged by many other sociologists. Those who believe that ability and intelligence are spread equally throughout the classes argue that the present system prevents a lot of talent from being realised, leading to a waste of human resources.

Meritocracy

The idea of a meritocracy is that each individual reaches the level they deserve, based on their talent, ability and effort. Many modern, open societies claim to be or want to be meritocracies. In a meritocracy, there are equal opportunities in the education system and the employment market: people with talent who work hard can achieve, whatever their background.

Meritocracies are not equal societies – they do have inequalities in terms of outcomes. However, opportunities should be equal. Supporters of meritocracy say that inequalities in terms of outcomes are justified because everyone can compete equally for the rewards offered by society – such as wealth and jobs – and so people get what they deserve.

There are two problems with the idea of meritocracy:

1   Meritocracies are unfair. They reward people who already have more than others (such as talent and ability). An alternative would be to reward those who cannot achieve success because, by chance, they were born without the natural talents required. Meritocracies seem to reward those who already have and punish those who do not.

2   Societies that claim to be meritocracies are not. People who already have wealth and privilege find ways of passing these advantages to their children. For example, societies that claim to be meritocracies say their education systems provide **equal opportunities**. In reality, however, wealthier parents can send their children to private fee-paying schools rather than state-funded schools. This means that those with more money can buy advantages for their children.

Social class is important in modern industrial societies. However, social stratification in closed societies can take other forms, such as **slavery** and **caste** systems.

Modern slavery

Many early, closed societies were stratified into citizens and slaves, where citizens had rights that slaves did not (including the right to own slaves). Slaves were treated as property; they were forced to work and had no freedom. Most countries abolished slavery in the form of legal ownership of people in the 19th century. However, slavery still exists today, in less obvious forms. Slavery today is referred to as **modern slavery**. It includes:

*   Debt bondage. This is when someone in poverty has to borrow money. To pay back the debt, they have to work for the person or organisation they borrowed from. Because the pay is low and interest is charged on the debt, it can be almost impossible to pay off the debt.

KEY TERMS

equal opportunities: when everyone has the same chance of succeeding

slavery: a stratification system in which one group or individual is treated as the legal property of another group or individual

caste: a closed stratification system in which a group's status is fixed at birth and cannot be changed

modern slavery: the severe exploitation of vulnerable people for personal or commercial gain

- Human trafficking. This is when people are forced into work they do not want to do. People may be kept almost as prisoners and cannot escape their situation.

- Forced marriage. The victim has no choice but to marry and is usually made to carry out demanding domestic tasks for the family they have married into. They are treated more like a servant than a family member.

Modern slavery only comes to light when a serious incident occurs, such as slaves dying because of unsafe working conditions.

Many victims of modern slavery are children. This is because children's relative lack of power is often combined with other disadvantages – such as belonging to a minority group which experiences prejudice and discrimination. For the same reasons, females are more likely than males to be in slavery. In 2022, the NGO Anti-Slavery International estimated that there were 40 million people in slavery worldwide. Of these people, 25 per cent were children and 71 per cent were female.

The caste system

This was the stratification system in India and in some other places for many centuries. In the caste system, people inherit their status at birth and cannot change it. This form of stratification is found in closed societies.

Caste affected what jobs people could do and who they could marry; they had to marry within their caste. India's caste system was officially abolished in 1950 but the social hierarchy associated with caste still exists in many aspects of life there. There were thousands of castes (mostly based on particular occupations) but five broad categories – shown in Figure 3.4. Members of lower castes were considered inferior by the higher castes and there were strict rules about ritual, purity and contact between different castes. Having contact with someone from a lower caste was thought to pollute a higher caste member.

Slavery and caste are to a large extent closed systems, in which it is very difficult for people to change their status. Social class – which has largely replaced these systems in modern industrial societies – is more open, because it allows some mobility between classes. No systems are completely open or closed. In most modern industrial societies, competition for statuses is limited to some degree by gender, ethnicity and social class. This is considered later in this unit. Although there is some movement of individuals and even groups in open systems, the system itself remains stratified.

In all societies, gender adds another dimension to social stratification. There are inequalities between men and women in every society. In many societies today, there are also ethnic and racial divisions, as well as inequalities between age groups.

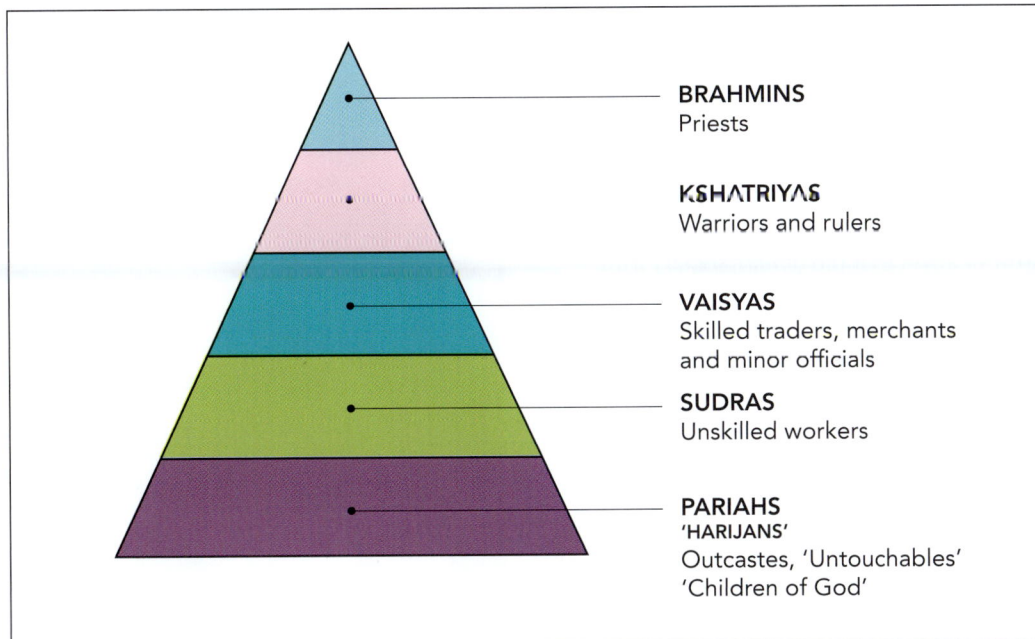

Figure 3.4: The Indian caste system.

- BRAHMINS
  Priests
- KSHATRIYAS
  Warriors and rulers
- VAISYAS
  Skilled traders, merchants and minor officials
- SUDRAS
  Unskilled workers
- PARIAHS
  'HARIJANS'
  Outcastes, 'Untouchables'
  'Children of God'

Social class, gender, age and ethnicity work together to produce patterns of inequality. The combination of stratification and inequality is known as **intersectionality**.

> **KEY TERM**
>
> **intersectionality:** ways in which different forms of stratification and inequality interact with each other

> **TIP**
>
> Be careful when thinking about and using the term 'traditional societies'. In this book, we often distinguish between traditional societies and modern industrial societies. However, all societies change constantly; what appears to be a long-held tradition may in fact be fairly recent. Modern industrial societies also keep some traditions from their past.

Differences in life chances affected by age, gender, ethnicity and social class

This section explains what **life chances** are and discusses how and why they differ between and within stratified groups.

Life chances are the opportunities people have to improve their lives. They depend on aspects of stratification such as social class, age, gender and ethnicity. People who share these aspects are likely to have similar life chances. Life chances are affected by the nature of stratification in a particular society and by norms, values and laws.

Life chances include opportunities for:

- education
- employment
- health

> **KEY TERM**
>
> **life chances:** the opportunities people have to improve their lives

- housing
- life expectancy.

Taken together, these factors indicate an individual's quality of life.

Age

Age and education

Because school is for children and young people, gender, ethnicity and social class are more relevant than age when considering life chances in education. However, many older people in developing countries did not go to school; they are more likely to be illiterate and unable to do basic maths. This is because universal and free education is relatively recent in some societies. Within societies, and even within families, there may be older people who did not go to school, while young adults and children did or do go. The life chances of those who missed out on school will be negatively affected by this.

In parts of Africa, Asia and elsewhere, there are projects to improve adult literacy – classes for adults who missed out on school or left education early. Such projects are often run by NGOs and based in local schools. These classes give adults a chance to gain skills and knowledge they missed out on.

During 2020 and 2021, the COVID-19 pandemic disrupted the education of many children and young people around the world. Many schools were closed, often for weeks or months. Different countries have tried to help the children affected catch up in various ways.

Figure 3.5: An adult literacy class in India.

Online lessons were run by individual schools and teachers but, in many countries, resources were also made available nationally. For example, in Mauritius, online lessons were provided for older learners and, at primary level, educational programmes were broadcast on television for children and their parents to access. Nonetheless, this disruption may have negatively affected the life chances of many children and young people across the world.

Age and employment

Education is seen as the most important thing for children. Although children around the world do work, many countries limit the amount of paid work children can do, because education is seen as more important. For example, children aged 14 and over in the UK can do some kinds of part-time work, as long as they still go to school and their education does not suffer.

In poorer countries, children often need to contribute to their family's income by working, for example by helping on the family farm or selling produce at a market. Many children also do work at home, such as looking after younger siblings. The International Labour Office (ILO) calls these children 'working children'.

The ILO makes a distinction between working children and child labourers. Child labour refers to children working long hours for low pay, and usually not going to school at all. This is seen as an abuse of children's rights that deprives them of their childhood and holds up their development. Most countries have laws against child labour. These laws are difficult to enforce, partly because the work is often hidden from public view but also because it is difficult to decide whether a particular case is child labour; it will depend on the child, the type and hours of work and on local and cultural factors. The ILO estimates that in 2020 about 160 million children were in child labour (about one in ten of all children worldwide). The great majority were in developing countries and far more boys than girls were involved in child labour.

The worst cases of child labour are forms of modern slavery. Campaigners against child labour face a dilemma, because if a child is not allowed to work, their family may lose an important source of income and fall further into poverty. Laws may be passed to ban child labour, with the expectation that these children will then be able to go to school. However, if families need the income made by their children, they will allow them to keep working illegally.

Older people sometimes face ageism at work. For example, they may not be considered for promotion, or they might find it difficult to change jobs because they are seen as less adaptable, energetic, dynamic or willing to learn new skills. Their accumulated skills and experience may not be valued if younger workers are thought to be more productive. In countries with **welfare states**, people who reach a certain age (usually between 60 and 70) are able to stop working and receive a pension to replace some of the income they lose (see section 3.2).

> **KEY TERM**
>
> **welfare state:** a system in which the government of a country provides services (such as free education and healthcare) and gives financial support to those who need it (such as the unemployed and the long-term sick), paid for by taxes

Age and health

Life chances of children globally have been increased by improvements in hygiene, sanitation and nutrition, as well as by vaccination programmes. The risk of transmissible diseases (such as polio, cholera, hepatitis and typhoid) and airborne diseases (such as tuberculosis, pneumonia, meningitis, whooping cough, diphtheria and influenza) has been reduced. Most children are now protected by vaccination against some of the diseases which killed many children in the past. However, malaria is still a major problem in some parts of the world, especially Africa. The World Health Organization (WHO) estimates that there were 241 million cases of malaria worldwide in 2020, and 627,000 deaths. Of these deaths, 96 per cent were in Africa and 80 per cent were children under five.

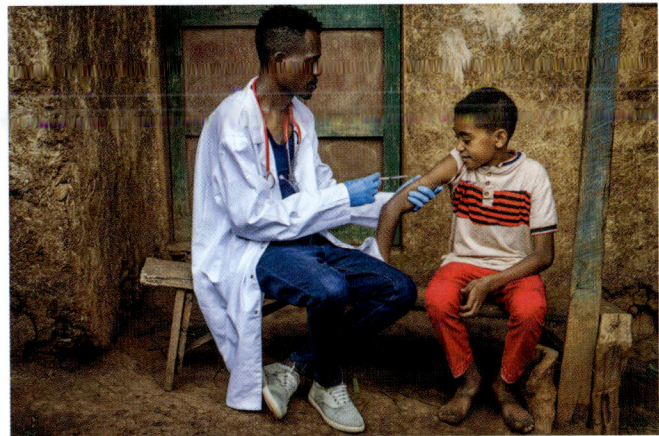

Figure 3.6: A child receiving a vaccination in an East African village.

Malaria and other diseases keep children away from school and so reduce their chances of success in education. Children from poorer backgrounds may also do less well at school because of poor nutrition, which leads to lack of energy and inability to concentrate.

Like children, older people are vulnerable to many diseases. This was shown in the COVID-19 pandemic, in which many of those who died were older people. Some health problems in older people come from physical changes; for example, it takes longer for broken bones to heal. There are also conditions which tend to specifically affect people as they age, including dementia. Many countries now have specialised health services for both children and older people. There are debates about how health resources should be allocated in some countries, especially those with ageing populations. With a limited amount of funding, some argue that resources should be focused on younger people who experience health problems rather than older people who have already lived a long life. However, this is controversial: others argue that every individual deserves access to treatments if they are available.

Age and housing

Children usually live with their families, so housing is affected more by factors such as ethnicity and social class (which children share with their families) than by age. This also applies to older people who live with their families. However, many older people do live alone, following the death of their husband, wife or partner. Today, many countries are unsure how to provide social care for older people who need help with day-to-day living but who are not actually ill. Some older people, especially in developed countries, live in accommodation designed for older people, with health and other services that may be needed close by. For older people who need more support, specialised care, provided in care homes, can improve life chances.

Age and life expectancy

Life expectancy is the average number of years a person can expect to live. In 1800, the average life expectancy globally was about 30; today, it is 72. Average life expectancy was lower in the past because many infants and children died, often of infectious diseases. This brought down the average age significantly. The number of babies who die per 100,000 live births is called the infant mortality rate. This has declined sharply over the last two centuries, although it remains higher in developing countries. In the past, children who survived into adulthood were likely to live into their 40s or 50s.

The global infant mortality rate has been greatly reduced by:

- vaccinations against diseases
- improvements in nutrition, hygiene and living standards
- developments in antenatal and postnatal care (care before and after birth), including information about diet and health for expectant mothers and scans and tests for genetic conditions. All of these factors can lead to better health outcomes for babies and children.

The decrease in the infant mortality rate has increased average life expectancy. It has also contributed to families having fewer children, since they are all likely to survive. The life chances of children with fewer siblings are likely to be better, since they may grow up with more resources than children from very large families.

Life expectancy also affects older people. People used to retire from work with, at best, a few years of life ahead of them. However, it is now common for people in developed countries to live for several decades after retirement, reaching their 80s or 90s, and to be healthy and active for most of that time. The number of people who live to be 100 years old has also increased dramatically: the United Nations estimates that there are now more than half a million centenarians worldwide, nearly four times as many as in 2000. All this means that the life expectancy of children and young people today is much higher than in the past.

Gender

Gender is perhaps our most basic ascribed status. It has huge implications for the rest of our lives. All societies are, to some extent, **patriarchal**; that is, men have a higher status than women and some degree of power over women.

Gender and education

In the past, almost all school education was for boys. Families wanted their boys educated to improve their prospects, whereas girls were usually expected to become

> **KEY TERM**
>
> **patriarchy:** a term used by feminists to describe societies and organisations (including the family) in which men are dominant and women are subordinate

wives and mothers, with domestic responsibilities. The assumption was that women would be supported by their husbands, so they did not need to be educated.

In many developing countries, girls are still less likely than boys to go to school and to complete their education. This limits their life chances because they do not gain qualifications; for example, two-thirds of people who cannot read or write are female. This situation is changing; for example, the UN identified universal primary education as one of its Millennium Development Goals. According to UNICEF, two-thirds of countries now have equality in the numbers of boys and girls in schools. However, in Chad, only 74 girls go to primary school for every 100 boys; in Pakistan, it is 84 girls for every 100 boys. In Afghanistan, the Taliban – who returned to power in 2021 – continues to disapprove of education for girls.

In countries where there is equality in school admissions, girls do at least as well as boys – and often better. More girls are also continuing their education to university level, improving their chances of a professional career. The reasons for these developments are explored in section 5.3.

Gender and employment

Women have always worked but their main traditional role was to be responsible for the home and family; in contrast, men worked to meet their family's economic needs. Women who did work were often paid low wages for jobs which were not highly valued (sometimes because they were seen as women's work), such as cleaning and caring for children or older people. Today, women play a greater part in the workforce and their roles have changed as a result. The traditional female gender role of housewife and mother has not disappeared, but it is now more likely to be combined with paid work. Men often take on a greater share of housework and childcare to accommodate women's greater role in the workforce.

However, women still face discrimination in employment. They are more likely than men to work part-time. Part-time work often attracts lower pay, is less secure and is less likely to include benefits such as sick pay or a private pension. Women are also more likely than men to spend time away from work when children are born and while the children are young; this can affect their opportunities for promotion. Many women experience role conflict between the demands of their family and the demands of work.

Paid employment affects women's life chances in the following ways:

- Women earn less than men and are less likely to be financially independent.

- Women are more vulnerable to poverty. Many more women than men earn such low wages that they are in or close to poverty. This is particularly true of women who are the only wage-earner in their households.

- Women's careers are often interrupted by pregnancy, childbirth and family responsibilities.

There are two main types of segregation in workforces.

- **Horizontal segregation** describes how men and women tend to have different types of occupation and work in different employment sectors. For example, secretarial, nursing and primary school teaching jobs are mostly held by women. Other roles traditionally associated with women include preparing food, cleaning and shop work. These employment sectors tend to have a fairly low status and include many low paid jobs. Men, on the other hand, are more likely to work in employment sectors such as IT, finance and law, which tend to attract higher status and higher pay.

- **Vertical segregation** means that, even when they work in the same occupations or workplaces as men, women tend to be concentrated in the lower levels of the hierarchy. In schools, for example, many teachers are women but most head teachers and senior managers are men.

Taken together, these factors lead to a **gendered division of labour**.

KEY TERMS

horizontal segregation: differences in the number of people from different groups (such as the sexes) in different employment sectors

vertical segregation: differences in the number of people from different groups (such as the sexes) occupying different levels within an employment hierarchy

gendered division of labour: the way in which societies expect women to be responsible for some tasks (such as cleaning and preparing food) and men for others

Towards the end of the 20th century, the numbers of working women grew significantly in most modern industrial countries. Some of the reasons for this are as follows:

- More women wanted to work. They wanted to break away from the restrictions of traditional gender roles and gain some independence through employment.

- There were changes in the socialisation of girls. More girls saw their future in terms of work as well as, or instead of, being a housewife and mother.

- Changes in the economy meant that skills and jobs traditionally associated with women became more numerous and more valued.

- Equality legislation, such as laws preventing sex discrimination, led to changes.

- Increased availability of birth control, especially the contraceptive pill, gave women more control over when and if they had children. This meant women could more easily fit children around a career.

- There were changing attitudes in workplaces, as employers began to value their female staff more.

- There were more female role models in occupations for girls and young women to aspire to.

Despite these advances, there are still many areas of work where women are unable to reach the very highest level, regardless of their qualifications and achievements. This has been called the 'glass ceiling': it is as if there is an invisible barrier preventing their advancement. Some aspects of the glass ceiling are as follows:

- Women who apply for promotion are not seen as serious candidates.

- Women have not held the highest positions before, so employers see appointing a woman as a risk.

- The appointments are made by existing managers, who may have sexist attitudes.

- The small group of men at the top of a company or organisation may not want to work with someone they see as different to them.

- Men may believe that, because of family responsibilities, a woman will not be able to commit fully to the job. For example, they may not be able to work at certain times (such as the weekend) because they want to spend time with their children.

Gender and health

Men's and women's health needs and problems can be different. Men and women often have similar health problems but the rates can vary by gender. For example, Alzheimer's disease and other forms of dementia are more common among females.

Pregnancy and childbirth present serious risks to health where medical facilities are inadequate. These risks are increased when girls marry at a very young age. Many women do not have access to the medical care they need in pregnancy and childbirth – either because there are no suitable facilities nearby or because they cannot afford them. UNICEF estimates that, in 2015, there were 303,000 deaths of women worldwide due to complications in pregnancy and childbirth. The risks are higher for women who have low levels of education or live in poverty. They are also high for girls aged 15 to 19, for whom conditions related to pregnancy and childbirth are the main cause of death.

Another threat to women's health comes from domestic violence and abuse within the home. Men can also be victims of domestic violence and abuse, but this is less common. There are dangerous practices, such as female genital mutilation, which endanger the health of women and girls. Domestic violence and abuse are considered in section 4.2.

Men's work outside the home can expose them to more health risks than women. Many occupations have hazards, such as using dangerous equipment or materials, or the risk of a road accident. There can also be longer term risks to health; for example, miners breathe in dust that damages the lungs.

STRETCH AND CHALLENGE

Some researchers have identified differences in the ways that men and women think about and talk about their health. What differences might there be and what impact might they have on health outcomes for men and women?

Gender and housing

As with children, men and women usually live in families. Housing is more affected by factors such as ethnicity and social class (which both men and women usually share with their families) than by gender.

Gender and life expectancy

Women live longer – on average about five years longer than men in most societies. Possible reasons for this are:

- Men are more likely to be in high-risk situations, so they have a higher risk of accidental death, including car accidents.

- Men in many societies consume more alcohol, tobacco and other drugs than women. This means they are more likely to suffer from serious disease.

- Men's work exposes them to risks, such as accidents in mining and factory work.

- There are biological reasons for differences in life expectancy between men and women.

ACTIVITY: RESEARCH 3.1

Interview an older female member of your family or someone you know. Ask how life chances, especially with regards to family and work, have changed for women in her lifetime. This will be an unstructured interview – look back to Unit 1 to remind yourself about these.

REFLECTION

Did you find out anything you did not know? Did you ask the right questions to find out what you wanted to know? What could you have done better?

Ethnicity

The life chances of minority ethnic groups are affected by racism and racial prejudice. Racial prejudice refers to beliefs that another racial group is inferior in some way.

KEY TERMS

racism: prejudice or discrimination against an individual or group because of their perceived ethnicity or race

prejudice: an unfair and unreasonable opinion or feeling, especially about a particular group of people, that is formed without knowledge and often based on stereotypes

Racial discrimination is when someone is disadvantaged because of their perceived ethnic or racial group. Someone who is prejudiced may be in a position to discriminate against people, for example, by not giving them a job or a promotion. Racism is a more general term used to refer to both beliefs and behaviour. **Institutional racism** refers to racism that is built into the way that an organisation or system works, so discrimination is not merely the result of an individual's prejudice or discriminatory actions. For example, police forces can be institutionally racist. This would be demonstrated by **police targeting** of minority ethnic groups. Institutional racism in the police is discussed in detail in section 6.2, and institutional racism in education is discussed in section 5.3. **Cultural racism** refers to prejudice and discrimination based on perceived cultural differences between people of different ethnicities. This is common in many societies today. Instead of suggesting that a particular racial group is *biologically* superior or inferior, cultural racism implies that a particular culture and its associated language, beliefs and lifestyle are superior or inferior. For example, the belief that immigrants should adopt the culture of their host country, abandoning their original culture, is a form of cultural racism.

Minority ethnic groups tend to be low down the socioeconomic scale, so they are affected by the same factors that influence social class and life chances.

Minority ethnic groups may face discrimination in terms of education, employment, health, housing and life expectancy. There are laws against racial discrimination in all three areas but in practice, it can be very difficult to prove that discrimination has occurred.

KEY TERMS

institutional racism: when the functioning of an institution or organisation involves systems and expectations that lead to discrimination against an ethnic group

police targeting: when the police focus on a particular group of people, believing that they are more likely to be involved in criminal behaviour than others

cultural racism: racism based on differences between ways of life, such as religion and customs, rather than supposed biological differences

Ethnicity and education

In education, teachers are likely to be from the majority group and they might stereotype minority ethnic learners as lazy or deviant. These learners might then internalise those views, so they are less likely to succeed in education. The school may also have an ethnocentric curriculum based on the history and culture of the majority group. Together, these factors disadvantage children from some minority ethnic groups, limiting their ability to improve their life chances through qualifications. These ideas are explored more fully, with examples, in section 5.3.

Ethnicity and employment

People from minority ethnic groups are often in low-paid, low-skilled and temporary work. When applying for jobs, they may face discrimination. For example, they might not be selected for an interview if their name suggests they are from a minority; or they might not be offered the job after an interview, even if they are the best candidate. When they are in employment, they may be given fewer opportunities to take training courses and they might not be promoted. Many of the disadvantages experienced by women in employment, including vertical segregation and the glass ceiling, also apply to minority ethnic groups.

Ethnicity and health

Minority ethnic groups can face inequalities in health. These overlap with social class factors, such as poor housing and high levels of poverty – but the health problems faced by minority ethnic groups are often greater than those for the majority ethnic group in the same class. This may be due to the following factors:

- Some health conditions are more common in people of certain ethnicities. For example, Britain's African Caribbean population has much higher rates of sickle cell anaemia (an inherited blood disorder) than the average for the population. This can be a problem if health service staff know little about the condition and do not treat it appropriately.

- There may be health differences arising from lifestyle, such as higher rates of cigarette smoking, or a diet high in fats, which may lead to obesity and heart disease.

- There may be reluctance to seek medical help from outside the minority community, or a tendency to reject help.

- Racism and discrimination lead to unhealthy and stressful daily lives, with a higher rate of health problems, including mental health problems.

Ethnicity and housing

When local government has houses available for rent, members of minority ethnic groups may find that they are not offered these houses. In areas of privately owned housing, members of minority ethnic groups may be made to feel unwelcome. This can lead to informal segregation, as different ethnic groups choose to live in different areas. This has occurred in some parts of the USA, where some areas have an overwhelmingly white population and others have a primarily black population. Los Angeles is an example of an American city with informal ethnic segregation, where neighbourhoods often have a large majority from one ethnic group.

Because of racism and discrimination in employment, members of minority ethnic groups are more likely to be in low-paid, unstable and temporary work. This makes it more difficult for them to get adequate housing. Minority ethnic groups are usually more likely than the majority to be in housing:

- which is poor quality

- from which they can be evicted

- with more people sharing the house ('overcrowding').

Immigration has led to people from other parts of the world forming communities in particular areas of many larger cities in developed countries. Many cities have a Chinatown, ThaiTown or Little Tokyo, for example. New immigrants settle where there are people they know, who can offer help with jobs and housing. A community develops, with shops and services provided by and for the ethnic group.

Ethnicity and life expectancy

There are differences in life expectancy between ethnic groups. These are linked to the health inequalities described already. One of the disadvantages faced by members of minority ethnic groups is a lower average life expectancy.

Social class

Social class is more difficult to define and measure than other dimensions of stratification. It is possible for individuals to define themselves as being in one social class, when a sociologist might decide they belong to another.

CASE STUDY 3.1

A European ethnic minority: the Roma

Figure 3.7: Romani people celebrating International Romani Day in Berlin, Germany.

There are around 8 million Romani or 'Roma' people in Europe. All across Europe, Romani people face prejudice and discrimination.

They are usually among the most disadvantaged groups in terms of health, education, housing and employment. They also have high rates of imprisonment. They used to have a nomadic lifestyle, moving from place to place, but many now stay in one place. Romani people are often victims of racial violence by neo-Nazis.

Find out more by visiting the website of the European Roma Rights Centre (ERRC). The ERRC is an NGO which takes up court cases on behalf of the Romani people, carries out research and campaigns for change.

TASK

1   The Romani might have high rates of imprisonment because they commit more crimes. What other reasons could there be?

2   Romani children do not usually do well at school. How might a sociologist explain this?

For Marxists, there are only two main classes: the bourgeoisie (the ruling class) and the proletariat (the workers). In most countries today, however, the broad categories of working class, middle class and sometimes upper class are used. There is no agreement on the best way to measure which class someone belongs to. Most sociologists operationalise (see section 1.3) the idea of social class by identifying indicators for each class, for example:

* wealth
* income
* housing (number of houses, size and location)
* occupation
* level of education and qualifications
* status
* lifestyle – some research has even used the type of car people drive or their choice of shops to buy their goods.

Occupation is the most common indicator, used by many governments to group their populations into social classes.

Social class and education

In many countries, people from different social classes go to different schools or types of school. This is partly because of area: a school in a middle-class area will have mainly middle-class students, for example. In most countries, state schools educate the majority of children but there are also often private schools for which parents pay fees. These school are able to charge fees because they claim to offer a higher quality of education. Because they charge fees, most students are from well-off families. Private schools allow middle-class parents to increase the life chances of their children, so they are less likely to be downwardly mobile. Different types of school are discussed in section 5.3.

Even within state schools, working-class children do less well on average than those from higher class backgrounds. There are various reasons for this, discussed in more detail in section 5.3.

Social class and employment

Sociologists most often use a person's occupation to identify their social class. This is because occupation is closely linked with income, status and living standards.

Occupations can be ranked in a hierarchy, with the highest-paid and most rewarding occupations at the top, and others below. Occupations are often classified as either non-manual or manual. Non-manual jobs involve mental rather than physical work. This includes 'the professions', a term used to refer to occupations associated with a higher level of education, status and pay (such as medicine and law) as well as lower status, office-based occupations. These are sometimes called white-collar occupations, referring to a white shirt collar; they are seen as middle class. Manual jobs are sometimes called blue-collar jobs, referring to blue overalls. They involve some physical effort. Examples include mechanics, miners, builders and other tradespeople. They are seen as working class. These two broad groups can be further divided according to the level of skill involved and the qualifications or training required.

The upper class are at the top of the social class hierarchy. These people are very wealthy and may not have to work. They often have very cosmopolitan lifestyles; they travel widely and may live (or have homes in) several countries. The upper class includes these groups:

- the landowning aristocracy – people with inherited wealth and titles, including, in countries that have them, royal families.

- the new rich or super-rich – people who have very high earnings based on their own achievements. This group can be seen as a new and growing part of the upper class. The super-rich may include people from the world of sport, media and entertainment, such as film stars, popstars and elite sportspeople. This category also includes successful entrepreneurs who have founded and run international businesses, for example, Bill Gates (Microsoft), Jeff Bezos (Amazon), Mark Zuckerberg (Facebook/Meta) and Elon Musk (Tesla). People who have reached the very top of their professions as politicians, judges, lawyers and company directors, etc. will also be part of this group due to their money, status and power. This group is distinct from the aristocracy because their wealth and status are achieved rather than inherited (although some of the super-rich will have come from privileged backgrounds).

The term middle class covers people in a very wide range of occupations, from office clerks or secretaries to lawyers or architects. There are three broad groups within the middle class:

- owners of small businesses, such as shops and workshops, landlords and small farmers

- professionals and managers – the upper middle class. Their high income and status are associated with the education and training they have received. This group grew in the 20th century, especially in the public sector and welfare state, with professionals working in schools, hospitals, social services and national and local government.

- the lower middle class, working in a very wide range of jobs, including routine office jobs and jobs in the retail sector.

The working class is also a diverse group. It is usually divided into three categories:

- skilled – those in manual work who are highly trained and qualified, for example electricians or plumbers

- semi-skilled – those who required some training, such as those working in the building trade or in factories

- unskilled – those who require minimal training, including cleaners and those doing physical labour in various types of industry.

Differences between the classes in employment affect life chances in several ways:

- Middle-class occupations are usually safer and take place in clean and hygienic workplaces, such as offices. Work in factories and mines, for example, can be more hazardous with risks to health.

- Middle-class occupations have better pay, enabling people to afford a better standard of living and to save money, for example, for retirement.

- Middle-class occupations have more opportunities for promotion.

- Middle-class occupations usually have better conditions and benefits, such as paid holidays and paid leave for ill health. Working-class occupations often lack these benefits.

Social class and health

There are significant inequalities in health between social classes. There are social, economic and environmental reasons for this. Health inequalities are the result of differences in living conditions (such as quality of housing), income and employment. Working-class people are more likely to experience a wide range of health conditions, from risk of still and premature births to types of cancer.

People from working-class backgrounds may be unable to afford a healthy diet. They might also live in poor housing in an unhealthy environment and work in jobs that are stressful or dangerous. The stress of living in poor conditions can lead to behaviour that further damages health, such as smoking and not exercising. All of these factors lead to poor health.

The areas where working-class people live have fewer health services. Working-class people are less likely to be near a health centre, doctor or hospital. They are also less able to pay for medicines and treatment in countries where these are not free.

Social class and housing

Middle-class people usually live in better-quality housing, which is less likely to be cold, unventilated, damp or overcrowded. The housing is also likely to be in an area with less pollution, better air quality and less crime.

Figure 3.8: High-rise flats are a common type of housing in working-class areas in some industrialised countries.

Social class and life expectancy

Working-class people have a lower life expectancy than middle-class people in the same society. For example, in the UK in 2017, life expectancy for males who lived in the most deprived areas was 74 years, compared with 83.1 years for those who lived in the least deprived areas. For females, the equivalent figures were 78.9 years in the most deprived areas and 86.1 years in least deprived areas. There are several possible reasons for this:

- Working-class occupations are more dangerous, so there are work-related risks.

- Working-class people may live in unhealthy environments, such as near sources of pollution or in damp, cold houses.

- Working-class people may be unable to afford good health care.

- Working-class people may lead less healthy lifestyles, for example in terms of diet and exercise.

> **TIP**
>
> A lot of the ideas in this topic link to other topics you will study, including Family, Education, and Crime, deviance and social control. Make sure you think about sociology as a whole and be confident using ideas and examples from other topics in your answers, if they seem relevant.

The intersectionality of age, ethnicity, gender and social class in understanding the impact of inequality on individuals

Age, ethnicity, gender and social class cannot easily be separated as factors that lead to inequality. Every individual has an age and a gender and belongs to a social class and an ethnic group, so there are many possible combinations. For many sociologists, social class is the most important of the four factors; however, its impact on any individual depends on the other factors as well. For example, working-class people are at a disadvantage to middle-class people in terms of the life chances considered in the previous section, but a working-class person from the majority (or privileged) ethnic group in a society may experience advantages due to their ethnicity, despite the disadvantages caused by their social class. If they are also male, their advantages will be increased further. The way in which the different characteristics – age, gender, ethnicity and social class – can combine to affect individuals is called intersectionality.

> ### THINK LIKE A SOCIOLOGIST
>
> How does the intersectionality of your age, gender, ethnicity and social class affect you and your life chances in your society? How will your employment prospects be affected by these characteristics?

Different sociological theories of social inequality

Labelling theory (part of interactionism)

Labelling theory is a set of ideas put forward by interactionism. It is a micro approach to sociology, which relates to small-scale social interaction. Unlike the other theories, interactionism does not look at the bigger picture of societies or the whole world in terms of inequalities related to age, ethnicity, gender or social class. However, it does help us to understand how inequalities can start and be reproduced in micro situations. Labelling theory uses the following key terms:

- **Stereotypes.** These are representations of groups in popular culture, or views held by individuals, that assume all members of a group have the same characteristics. Negative **stereotyping** can lead to discrimination and prejudice against some groups.

- **Master status**. When a person is labelled, that label may become the main way that others think about them. It might also be internalised by the labelled person, who starts to think of themselves in this way. This idea helps to explain why some people find it difficult to resist a label, or to change their behaviour.

- **Self-fulfilling prophecy.** People who have been labelled may begin to act in certain ways, making the expectations of the label come true. Labels can be difficult to resist.

The interactionist Howard Becker, who developed labelling theory, argued that people from powerless groups (such as those from the working class, women, minority ethnic groups and some age groups) would be disadvantaged because people with power might label them based on stereotypes and treat them differently. Labelling theory has particularly been applied to educational achievement and crime. It is explored further in Units 5 and 6.

> ### MAKING CONNECTIONS
>
> In what ways can labelling theory help to explain inequalities in terms of education and crime? Who has the power to label? Which groups might they label, and which labels might they apply? What effect might this have?

Marxism

Marxism sees inequality and extremes of poverty and wealth as inevitable consequences of **capitalism**: 'the rich get richer and the poor get poorer'. Marxists focus on inequalities of social class. Other aspects of inequality are seen as part of social class inequality; for example, a minority ethnic group are disadvantaged because they

> ### KEY TERMS
>
> **labelling:** defining a person or group in a particular way
>
> **stereotyping:** applying and acting upon an oversimplified set of ideas about a particular type of person or social group
>
> **master status:** when a label becomes the single most important thing about a person in the eyes of others, and is then internalised by the labelled person
>
> **self-fulfilling prophecy:** when people are aware of certain expectations and so they act in ways that make those expectations come true
>
> **Marxism:** a theoretical perspective that sees conflict between classes as the most important feature of society
>
> **capitalism:** the economic system of most countries today; based on private ownership of the means of production

are part of the working class. Capitalists (the bourgeoisie or ruling class) will always try to pay their workers as little as possible to increase their profits. They will also try to bring in automation and keep wages low to save costs. As a result, the wages of the working class fall and some become unemployed. Marxists use the following key terms:

- **Exploitation of the proletariat.** The nature of capitalism is that the bourgeoisie exploits the proletariat. They do this by paying workers less than the full value of the work they do. The bourgeoisie make a profit by owning what Marxists call the means of production – factories, land, mines, etc. Workers have to work to support themselves and their families, so they have to accept what the bourgeoisie will pay.

- **Ideological control.** Capitalism is clearly an unfair system. There are far more workers than capitalists, so why do the workers accept this situation most of the time? The Marxist answer is that the workers' thoughts and beliefs are manipulated. The capitalists use propaganda through the ideological state apparatus (see section 2.2), so the workers believe that the system is fair – that the capitalists deserve their wealth and power and that nothing can be done to change the situation anyway.

- **Poverty trap.** This idea was explained in the section on poverty and wealth. Marxists use it to explain how a part of the working class is always kept in poverty. Capitalists use their power to make it difficult to escape from poverty. The working class then work hard, for low pay, to try to avoid the poverty they see around them.

- **Reserve army of labour.** Capitalists can keep wages low, to maximise profits, by having unemployed workers ready to take the jobs of others. Workers who cause trouble for the capitalists – for example, by forming trade unions and demanding better pay and conditions – can be replaced by others who will work for lower wages. The unemployed, often low-skilled, working-class people are a **reserve army of labour**. These people can also be used if there is an economic boom and more workers are needed; they will be made unemployed again when they are

no longer needed. Other groups have also been used as a reserve army of labour to meet the needs of employers and the economy. For example, during the Second World War, many women were brought into factories to replace the male workers who had gone to fight. When the men returned, these women were often sacked and had to go back to being housewives. Older and younger people at the end and beginning of their working lives may also be used as a reserve army of labour, as may new immigrant workers.

These ideas can be applied globally, as well as to individual societies. For example, when rising wages in Europe and North America began to affect profits, capitalists moved their factories to countries where wages were lower. Less developed countries provided a reserve army of labour willing to do work that was previously done in the developed countries, for less pay.

Feminism

Feminists draw attention to the inequalities women face compared with men. For example, more women than men live in poverty. This is partly caused by the poverty of lone mothers, but it is also because women are paid less on average than men, and because women have more limited employment opportunities. Feminists use the following key terms:

- **Division of labour.** Gender inequalities start in the home, where there was traditionally a division of labour. Females were responsible for the home and for looking after children and older people, while males were responsible for meeting the economic needs of the family by providing money, food and

> ### KEY TERM
>
> **reserve army of labour:** people who are employed when an economy is booming or when they are needed, but who find themselves out of work when they are not required

Figure 3.9: Many women have to combine housework and childcare with their career.

other essentials through paid work. This division of labour restricted women's opportunities to work outside the home, and to be financially independent.

- **Dual burden.** This refers to people who have to work to earn money to support themselves and their family, while at the same time being responsible for all or most of the domestic work in the family home. Women have usually had this **dual burden** and this limits their opportunities. The sociologist Arlie Hochschild called this the 'second shift' in her book of the same name. Those who have the dual burden effectively have two jobs: they work a shift outside home in an office or factory, then come home to work a second shift cooking, cleaning and caring for others. In a married couple, the man often expects to relax after work while the woman has to perform the second shift. Feminists point out that the second shift is essential for the family and society but women do not get paid for it and it may not even be noticed. The dual burden can lead to stress and long-term effects on health.

- **Triple shift**. This is a development of the dual burden, used to highlight a further aspect of women's lives. As well as paid and domestic work, women are expected to take on responsibility for the emotional well-being of the family. This involves caring for children and for the male partner.

- **Horizontal and vertical segregation.** As explained previously, work is segregated in two ways. Men and women tend to be in different types of work (horizontal segregation) and, within the same work organisation, men tend to be at a higher level in the hierarchy (vertical segregation).

Functionalism

Functionalists see inequality as a positive thing that is functional for the whole society.

To make the best use of the people's natural qualities and abilities, society has to reward some people more than others. The existence of poverty means that unpleasant or poorly paid jobs will be done, because poor people have no choice but to take them. Poverty reminds the rest of society of the importance of values such as hard work, honesty and a stable family life, and warns them of the consequences of straying from these values. It also increases social solidarity among people who are not poor, showing that they are different from those who deserve charity or blame. Functionalists use the following key terms:

- **Social mobility.** Movement between social classes is an important part of the functionalist view of society. The education system 'sorts out' who is right for different kinds of work. People can be upwardly mobile, usually through success in education.

- **Meritocracy.** Success in achieving upward social mobility is part of a meritocratic system. Those with talent and ability who work hard will be able to move up.

- **Legislative change.** If the system is not working as it should, it might become dysfunctional. Functionalists would expect society to adjust by bringing in new laws to ensure equal opportunities and meritocracy.

ACTIVITY: WRITTEN 3.1

Compare and contrast the four theoretical approaches to inequality. Which has the strongest explanation of inequalities today? Write a 300-word answer giving reasons for your choice.

CHECK YOUR UNDERSTANDING 3.1

1   Make a set of cards with one of the key terms listed below written on one side of each card. Put them face down in a pile. In a small group, take turns to draw the top card and say which of the sociological theories (interactionism/labelling theory, Marxism, feminism and functionalism) would be most likely to use this term. The rest of the group can give marks for accuracy and examples.

CONTINUED

Key terms to use: capitalism; culture of poverty; dual burden; equal opportunities; fatalism; gendered division of labour; horizontal segregation; labelling; master status; meritocracy; patriarchy; police targeting; poverty trap; power; reserve army of labour; social exclusion; social mobility; stereotyping; triple shift; vertical segregation

2   As quickly as you can, write down:

a   three types of life chances

b   three ways women are disadvantaged at work

c   three reasons why minority ethnic groups have health disadvantages compared to the majority

d   three reasons why life expectancy has gone up in the past 200 years.

CONTINUED

- The intersectionality of age, gender, ethnicity and social class help us to understand the impact of inequality on individuals.

- There is a debate on social inequality between these sociological theories:

  - labelling theory (interactionism)

  - Marxism

  - feminism

  - functionalism.

3.2 What attempts have been made to reduce social inequalities?

The use of legislation within societies to reduce inequality

Different countries have different levels of inequality. In many modern industrial societies, including the UK, there was a trend during the 20th century towards a reduction in inequality; that is, the **distribution of wealth** and income became more equal. This was helped by the expansion of the welfare state in these countries, and by governments that were committed to making society more equal. This trend was reversed towards the end of the century and inequality widened in most countries. Those at the lower end of society continued to be better off, because of economic growth, but those at the top pulled further ahead.

KEY POINTS

- Open and closed societies are stratified in various ways, linked to:

  - achieved and ascribed status

  - poverty and wealth

  - power

  - social mobility

  - meritocracy

  - modern slavery

  - the caste system.

- Life chances include:

  - education
  - housing
  - employment
  - life expectancy.
  - health

- Life chances are affected by:

  - age
  - ethnicity
  - gender
  - social class.

KEY TERM

distribution of wealth: the way in which the wealth and income of a society are divided among its population

Japan, Norway, Sweden and Finland are some of the more equal modern industrial societies.

In these countries, the richest 20 per cent of the population are about four times richer than the poorest 20 per cent. In Singapore, the richest 20 per cent are about 10 times richer than the poorest 20 per cent, and in the USA they are more than eight times richer.

The effects of inequality on societies have been studied by Wilkinson and Pickett in *The Spirit Level* (2010). They argue that many aspects of society are decided not by how wealthy a country is, but by how equal or unequal it is. Societies in which there is a considerable gap between rich and poor people score poorly on a range of measures, such as:

- physical and mental health and obesity

- educational performance

- levels of violence and other crime, and the number of people imprisoned

- lack of opportunities for social mobility.

These negative consequences also apply to those at the higher end, so greater equality benefits everyone in a society.

Governments do not see inequality as a problem in itself. In modern industrial societies, which see themselves as meritocracies, it is widely accepted that people should be rewarded according to their talent and effort. However, it is also widely accepted that inequalities should not be extreme; governments are seen as having a duty to ensure that the living standards of the poorest are not too low. Governments have used legislation to achieve this in different ways, including those described in the following section.

Progressive taxation

Progressive taxation means that people who are wealthy or have a high income pay a higher rate of tax on some of their earnings than those who have lower incomes. For example, the rate of income might be 20 per cent for earnings up to a certain amount, and 30 per cent for income above that level. Often, people on low incomes pay no tax at all.

> ### KEY TERM
>
> **progressive taxation:** when those who earn more pay a higher rate of tax on some of their earnings than those who earn less

However, not all taxes are progressive. For example, in many countries there are taxes on goods which are sold in shops, and on petrol. These taxes are the same for everybody, which means that poorer people pay proportionally more of their income on those taxes than wealthier people. Also, wealthier people are often able to find ways of paying less tax. Those with multiple sources of income, such as income from stocks and shares or property, often pay an accountant to help them avoid paying tax on some of this income, perhaps by registering it in another country. People whose income is directly taxed – that is, most normal working people – are not able to do this.

Redistribution of wealth though benefits

Most of a government's income comes from taxes, and this income is spent on the needs of all government departments. This includes funding the welfare state. Through progressive taxation, the government can **redistribute wealth**, providing welfare benefits and subsidised housing to those who need them. People who receive welfare benefits are usually from these groups:

- the unemployed

- people with long-term illness or disability, especially if this prevents them from working

- those whose income is below a set level

- those who cannot work because they are a lone parent or a carer.

Redistribution of wealth can ensure that people in these groups do not fall into extreme poverty.

> ### STRETCH AND CHALLENGE
>
> To what extent can progressive taxation and the redistribution of wealth be seen as fair?

Minimum wage

A minimum wage means that employers are not allowed to pay their workers less than a certain amount per hour.

> ### KEY TERM
>
> **redistribution of wealth:** the transfer of some of the income and wealth from richer individuals to those who are poorer, through systems such as taxation and welfare payments

A minimum wage should mean no one is paid so little that they cannot support themselves. The cost of living changes all the time, so governments update the minimum wage to make sure it is still at the right level. Supporters of a minimum wage say that it prevents poverty and reduces inequality. Opponents say it increases unemployment, because companies would employ more workers if they could pay them less.

Most developed countries have a minimum wage. However, to maximise their profits, some companies try to avoid paying the minimum wage to their workers. Companies may do this by classifying their workers as independent contractors, rather than employees. These workers are not employed by a company but sell their services to it. Companies pay for a specific task, rather than per hour, so the workers are often paid at a lower rate than the hourly minimum wage for the work they do. Also, the company does not have to give these workers the benefits that employees are usually entitled to, such as a guaranteed number of hours of work, paid holidays and paid leave for ill health.

Equal opportunities laws

Equal opportunities legislation tries to prevent discrimination against disadvantaged groups and ensure that everyone has the same opportunities. Without laws like this, there could be discrimination based on sex and gender, age, disability, race and ethnicity, religion and other characteristics. Equal opportunities laws vary between countries and have been passed at different times. Examples include:

- In Mauritius, the Equal Opportunities Act was passed in 2008. This prohibits discrimination in employment on the basis of a person's status, including their age, ethnic origin, race, sex and sexual orientation.

- In the UK, the Equal Pay Act 1970 was passed to ensure equal pay for equal work by men and women. Several other laws have been passed over the decades to address discrimination in terms or race, sex and disability. The Equality Act 2010 replaced previous anti-discrimination laws relating to sex, race, religion, age, sexual orientation and disability with a single Act, making the law easier to understand and increasing protection in some situations.

- Many other countries now have Equal Employment Opportunities (EEO) principles embedded in their laws or constitutions, including the USA, Nigeria and Pakistan.

Equal opportunities laws apply particularly to employment. They mean that every individual should be treated in the same way in terms of:

- applying for and being selected for jobs

- being trained and having opportunities for promotion

- day-to-day treatment within the workplace by employers and colleagues

- termination of employment; all processes regarding the ending of an employment contract or dismissal from a job should be fair and equal.

Equal opportunities laws give rights to workers. At the same time, they give employers responsibilities to treat everyone equally. Employers need to implement policies and practices to ensure fair treatment. However, it is important to note that equal opportunities laws are not always followed and are often difficult to enforce.

THINK LIKE A SOCIOLOGIST

How will your own employment prospects be affected by equal opportunities laws? Are these laws enforceable?

Other government measures

Governments can take a range of measures to reduce social inequalities. They can subsidise goods or services, or provide them free of charge, for poorer members of society or for everyone. In some countries, the price of basic foods is set by law, for example the price of bread in Egypt and Mauritius. This ensures that everyone can afford to buy food. It also prevents companies from making very high profits, for example, by raising prices during Ramadan. Another example is that, in the UK, people who receive a state pension can travel on buses for free during the day, and get financial help towards fuel bills in winter so they can keep warm. Children from poorer families are also given free meals at school.

Some other government measures are considered in the following section on welfare states.

The development and impact of welfare states on life chances

Modern states are all welfare states to some extent. This means that they take some responsibility for the security and well-being of their citizens. Most working people pay taxes on their earnings and this money funds the welfare state, helping those in need. While most welfare is provided by the government, voluntary organisations such as NGOs, charities, religious organisations and informal social groups often provide a large amount of financial and social support for vulnerable people.

Welfare states were introduced and continue today for:

- **Moral reasons.** It is seen as wrong to let some people live in poor conditions and on low incomes while others prosper. All the major world religions see charity as a virtue.

- **Political reasons.** Welfare is seen as necessary to prevent people uniting in anger against an unjust system that creates inequalities and injustices. Governments and political parties can also win support and votes by giving benefits to particular groups. Functionalists see welfare as essential to maintaining a society's value system and preventing it from becoming dysfunctional.

The strongest welfare states are probably those of the Scandinavian countries – Sweden, Norway, Denmark, Iceland and Finland. There are differences between these countries but they all provide significant benefits to those in need. These benefits are paid for by taxing the wealthy and high-income earners more than in other countries; as a result, Scandinavian countries have relatively low levels of inequality. In these countries, and elsewhere in Europe, welfare states have often been expanded by social democratic parties, who see welfare as a way of reducing class conflict and achieving redistribution of wealth. In contrast, the USA's approach, based on its value system of individualism, encourages people to look after themselves with the support of their family and religion. It provides only basic welfare – a safety net for the people most in need – rather than trying to reduce inequalities.

The welfare state in the UK started just before the First World War with the introduction of old age pensions and national insurance. Workers, employers and governments all paid into a fund that could support the sick and unemployed. The welfare state was greatly extended by the Labour government after the Second World War, with the introduction of free universal secondary education, a free National Health Service, extended benefits and pensions, and better and affordable housing. While some benefits were means tested (given only to those who met certain financial criteria), many were universal, meaning that everyone was entitled to them.

The high levels of welfare established in the UK in the mid-20th century were difficult to maintain, as costs went up and the economic situation declined. Right-wing politicians and writers argued that the welfare state was too expensive and encouraged a **dependency culture**, making it easy for people to become dependent on benefit payments, rather than encouraging them to support themselves. After the global financial crisis of 2008, the UK government cut many benefits, restricting them to those who met strict criteria. They also privatised some parts of the welfare state so the government was not directly responsible for them. More benefits are now means tested. For example, there are controversial new tests to determine whether people with disabilities should work to support themselves or receive support. These changes moved the UK closer to the type of welfare state in the USA, rather than those in Scandinavia.

The COVID-19 pandemic was very expensive for all governments; at the same time, they received less money from taxes because many workplaces closed down for long periods of time. Countries with strong welfare states, including free health services, were able to help their citizens most. But government resources were stretched and the situation was made worse by the effects of the Russian invasion of Ukraine in 2022. Russia is a major exporter of oil, food and other commodities, and the sanctions which many countries imposed on Russia led to shortages, driving up prices across the world. In such times of financial crisis, governments must choose between cutting spending – including welfare – and raising taxes, which is unpopular with voters.

> ### KEY TERM
>
> **dependency culture:** a set of values leading people to lose the desire or ability to look after themselves, so they become dependent, for example, on welfare benefits

The following aspects of the welfare state can affect life chances:

Free and universal education

In most countries, governments now provide basic education for all children. Before this, many children did not go to school at all, or only went for a few years. Schools are usually free, although there may be school fees and other costs, such as for uniforms, that some parents cannot afford. Universal primary education is offered by all countries but poorer countries do not have the resources to offer universal secondary education as well. As a result, it is not unusual for children in poor countries to leave education after primary school. The NGO The Borgen Project estimates that, across Africa, only about 28 per cent of children will go to secondary school.

Free **universal education** improves life chances in many ways, by giving children opportunities to:

- acquire skills, qualifications and experience that will help them in later life

- improve employment prospects

- develop literacy skills, which help people to be aware of their rights and reduce the risk that they will be taken advantage of

- better understand health and nutrition, so they are more able to look after themselves and their families. Children who go to school, but whose parents did not, will educate their parents, for example about hygiene and diet. If they have their own children, they will be better prepared to be good parents themselves.

Free universal primary education has only recently become normal for all countries. This is a result of concerted efforts by many countries to achieve universal primary education as one of the Millennium Development Goals (a set of goals agreed by all countries at the United Nations). These efforts involved NGOs as well as governments.

Because these changes are quite recent, many developing countries still have large numbers of adults who did not go to school. Many of these adults cannot read and write and this has limited their life chances. Countries with very low rates of adult literacy include Chad (22 per cent) and Somalia (5 per cent).

Often, schooling is prevented by wars or other disruptions. The COVID-19 pandemic led to the closure of many schools around the world during 2020 and 2021; this disrupted the education of many children. We will not know for some time how much this has affected their life chances.

KEY TERM

universal education: schooling provided for all children, regardless of their background

MAKING CONNECTIONS

How might the existence of a welfare state in a country affect the global differences in educational achievement discussed in section 5.3?

Unemployment benefits

Many countries have policies to help people who are unemployed. Being unemployed means being available for work but unable to find a suitable job. Sometimes, people find new work quickly and need little or no help. Governments are more concerned about long-term unemployment.

Unemployment benefits are payments made to people while they are unemployed. As a condition of receiving these benefits, people usually have to register as unemployed, look for work and take any suitable work available. If they fail to do any of these things, they might lose their benefits. Unemployment benefits are usually low and may be difficult to live on; this is to discourage people from deliberately avoiding work. Unemployment benefits can, however, help people to survive during a difficult period. In most countries, the taxes paid by people in work are used to fund unemployment benefits.

Pensions

Pensions are payments to older people who meet the retirement age set by a government. Before pensions were introduced, and in countries without a pension system, older people had to carry on working or rely on their family to support them.

Part of the taxes paid by working people is used to contribute to pensions. In some countries, a separate form of tax is taken directly from people's earnings to cover social security, including state pensions, sick pay and other benefits. In the UK, this tax is known as National Insurance. France and Germany have much higher rates of tax for their social security systems than the UK's National Insurance tax; it can be argued that their pensions and welfare systems are better funded as a result. State pensions are meant to protect people from poverty so, as with unemployment benefits, the amount paid is not high. Many people, especially in developed countries, will have a private pension as well. This means that they and their employers pay into their personal private pension fund while they are working, so they have more income when they retire.

When state pensions were first introduced, life expectancy was low and governments did not expect many people to live long enough to receive their pension. Now life expectancy has increased, so more people receive a pension and for longer. This is more expensive for governments. Some countries have increased the retirement age and encouraged people to work for longer, to reduce the cost for the government.

Without pensions, older people as a group were at risk of poverty. Pensions reduce this risk and therefore improve life chances. However, some older people are still at risk, including older people who need expensive care and those who have no private pension or other savings to add to their state pension. Women who did not work, or only worked for short periods because of domestic responsibilities, made few tax contributions when they were of working age. As a result, they may only be entitled to a small pension.

Low-cost housing

Some governments have tried to improve the life chances of disadvantaged people by providing better housing at an affordable cost. For example, in the UK and other countries after the Second World War, there were extensive house building schemes. Local councils built and owned housing, which they provided at a low cost to people who would otherwise struggle to buy a house or pay rent.

Free healthcare

People who do not have much money may not be able to pay to see a doctor or have hospital treatment. Medical treatments are often expensive and even middle-class people might be unable to afford a serious operation. To improve life chances for everyone, some governments provide free healthcare as part of the welfare state. This is funded by taxes and ensures that everyone can access the health services they need without having to worry about the cost. An example of this approach is the UK's National Health Service (NHS).

Countries vary in how much free healthcare they provide. Some only provide basic or emergency care, and even this may not be free; people are encouraged to take out private insurance to cover the cost if expensive treatment is needed. For example, the USA and China do not provide universal free healthcare. Instead, they have systems of health insurance – which the poorest people may not be able to afford. Even in countries with free provision, there are usually private health services available for those who can afford to pay. These provide better and faster treatment.

Universal basic income

This is a new idea which is an alternative to welfare payments. It has so far been tried in only a few countries, on a small scale. **Universal basic income** (UBI) is when the government pays everyone a set amount of money, usually each month. This means that everyone has a 'safety net' so no one will be poor. Those who want to can work to add more to their income, but they do not have to.

Supporters of UBI say it ensures no one lives in poverty. It also prevents the benefit trap, in which some people cannot take a low-paid job because they would lose some or all of their benefits and end up worse off as a result. Clearly, a lot of money needs to be paid out. However, the large government departments that manage benefits are also expensive and this money will be saved. UBI would also reduce the costs associated with poverty – including additional healthcare costs and extra costs relating to crime and policing in poor areas. As a result, money would actually be saved in the long-term.

Opponents of UBI say it might encourage people not to work. They feel it is better to use the welfare benefits system to help get people into work. Trials in Finland, Kenya and Wales will show how it works in practice.

KEY TERM

universal basic income: when the government pays everyone a fixed amount of money as a regular income.

ACTIVITY: RESEARCH 3.2

1 Use the internet or other sources of information to find out about the main forms of welfare provided by the government in your country. These may include education and healthcare. Design a poster to show your findings.

2 If you were in charge, and money was available, what changes would you make?

The global work of non-governmental organisations (NGOs)

There is a very wide range of non-governmental organisations (NGOs). They are not part of the government and they are not businesses that exist to make a profit. They are voluntary organisations of people who want to help others. There are many NGOs that work within one country, but others are global. Well-known examples of global NGOs are Oxfam, Christian Aid, Save The Children and Médecins Sans Frontières (Doctors Without Borders).

NGOs provide aid in the form of money, resources and expertise. The amount of aid they provide is small compared to governments, but they are seen as important. Governments often distribute their aid through NGOs, though NGOs also raise a lot of money themselves, through fundraising appeals. Many NGOs use a lot of their resources to help people after disasters, such as war, flooding or earthquakes. They also work for longer-term development in the following ways.

Reducing poverty

NGOs carry out a wide range of activities to reduce poverty. Most try to help people to help themselves, providing opportunities for people to move themselves out of poverty. For example, they might give money to a farmer for seeds or new livestock. The aim is that the farmer will then be able to support their family and will not need further aid. This avoids creating a dependency culture.

Providing medical assistance

Health services are often limited in poorer countries: there are few health centres and doctors, so many people are not near them. NGOs work to improve health services, by training health workers and providing equipment and medicines. Volunteer doctors and other medical staff may also be sent to support local health services.

Promoting business

One way of helping people to support themselves is to ensure they have a way of making money. Where jobs are few and poorly paid, NGOs can help people out of poverty by providing what they need to establish a small business, such as selling food at a market. Often a small investment, such as a refrigerator to keep food fresh, can make a big difference. NGOs can provide a loan, with low or no interest, to help someone make their business more likely to succeed. Recently, some NGOs have created websites that allow people in developed countries to loan money directly to people in developing countries who are trying to start small businesses.

CASE STUDY 3.2

A health NGO: Médecins sans Frontières (Doctors without Borders)

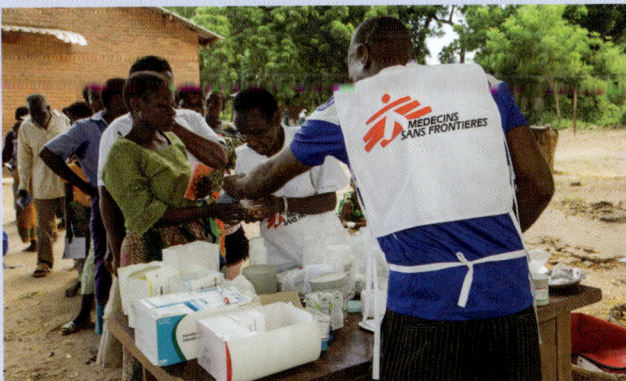

Figure 3.10: People waiting to see doctors from Médecins sans Frontières in Madagascar.

Médecins sans Frontières (MSF) is a health NGO which began in France. It specialises in working in war zones, and in areas where there are endemic diseases such as tuberculosis, HIV and AIDS. It provides medical assistance, especially in crisis situations and where existing health services are insufficient. It works in 88 countries and has tens of thousands of employees, mainly local doctors, nurses and other medical professionals. Other doctors and professionals work as volunteers, for example to train local people. As well as medical treatment, MSF helps to provide access to clean water and shelter.

CONTINUED

TASK

Read more at the MSF website. Then answer these questions:

1 MSF likes to hire most of its staff locally. Why do you think this is?

2 Why would a health NGO think it was important to provide clean water and shelter?

Improving education

NGOs work to improve education in many ways. They can provide money, equipment and buildings for schools. Education is often seen as a priority for NGOs because it can transform people's life chances and affect society more widely.

Sociological views of the success of attempts to reduce social inequalities

New Right criticisms of the welfare state/underclass

Welfare states have been strongly criticised by conservative and right-wing politicians and writers. The sociologists associated with this view are called the New Right. They argue that:

- welfare encourages a dependency culture in which people feel they do not need to look after themselves; they expect to be looked after

- welfare payments have become too generous, for example discouraging unemployed people from looking for jobs

- the welfare system has become expensive because it now provides for more people; it should support only those who are most in need

- welfare produces an **underclass**, whose values are based on reliance on welfare

KEY TERM

underclass: a group below the working class that is effectively cut off from the rest of society

- the system is open to abuse, with some people fraudulently claiming benefits to which they are not entitled; this is really an argument for reform and clamping down on fraud, rather than against the welfare state in general

- the state has become a 'nanny state'; it interferes too much and does more than the state should do.

Right-wing thinkers such as the New Right identify an underclass – a marginalised group at the bottom of society, who cannot be seen as part of the working class because most of them do not work. These sociologists argue that people in the underclass have different values to the rest of society. The term is relatively new but the idea is not: in the 19th century, Karl Marx said that there were other groups besides the working class at the lower end of society. These included older workers who had lost their jobs, farm workers trying to move into industrial work, people in casual and irregular employment, people who could not work (such as the disabled) and also what he called the lumpenproletariat – criminals, prostitutes and vagrants.

The underclass is seen to be clearly separate from the working class, characterised by:

- multiple deprivations, such as low income, unemployment, poor housing and poor education

- social exclusion – they do not have the normal means of voicing grievances; they are less likely to vote and less aware of their rights than the working class

- a culture of fatalism and despair – they feel alienated and are suspicious of the police and authority in general

- dependency on the welfare state.

The American Charles Murray, from a New Right perspective, defines the underclass by their behaviour. For Murray, the signs of an emerging underclass are:

- increasing reliance on welfare benefits

- increase in illegitimacy (births to unmarried mothers)

- rising crime rates, increasing anti-social behaviour and increasing use of illegal drugs

- a growth in those unwilling to take jobs (related, he says, to the availability of state benefits).

This kind of definition seems to blame members of the underclass for the position they are in. It also blames governments for providing benefits that encourage people to be irresponsible.

The term underclass has also been used by left-wing thinkers, who see the underclass as victims of their circumstances. However, these writers have mostly stopped using the term, because it has become linked to the New Right view and is now seen as a negative label. Marxists prefer not to use the term underclass at all. They say that the underclass is just the part of the working class which has suffered most during an economic downturn, and been pushed out of work. Many people argue that governments should be doing more, through the redistribution of wealth, to help those who are in poverty and socially excluded to rejoin society and improve their life chances.

ACTIVITY: DISCUSSION 3.2

Is 'underclass' a useful term? Is there an underclass in your society? How can you be sure? Discuss these questions in a small group.

The culture of poverty and the dependency culture

Debates about the underclass and the welfare state are linked with concerns about the culture of poverty and the dependency culture. As we have seen in section 3.1, some people argue that a culture of poverty can develop among the poor: they develop particular values to cope with their poverty – such as focusing on the present rather than planning for the future – and these values can contribute to keeping them in poverty.

New Right thinkers argue that the welfare state encourages this culture, because the poor are able to live week by week on their benefit payments so they are not encouraged to work, plan or save. This can combine with a dependency culture in which people lose any sense of responsibility for their own lives.

The New Right argue that working for a living gives people a sense of pride and self-worth, whereas the welfare state creates dependency and laziness. They see the welfare state as actively discouraging people in poverty, or the underclass, from helping themselves.

Marxist criticisms of the welfare state

There are also Marxist and left-wing criticisms of welfare. For Marxists, welfare softens the harshest effects of the capitalist economic system and so reduces demands for radical change. It gives the impression that the system is less unjust than it really is. Welfare can be seen as a form of bribery, making radical change less likely. From this point of view, it would be better if there were no welfare; this would make the unjust nature of the system clear to everyone, and make a revolutionary change more likely. However, many left-wing writers support the welfare state. They argue that a complete overthrow of capitalism (as favoured by Marxists) is unlikely. Therefore, the welfare state is the best way of making society more equal, redistributing wealth and helping those at the bottom of society to improve their lives.

Criticisms of NGOs

Aid provided by NGOs can seem to be a good thing. However, as with welfare states, there are several problems associated with this type of aid.

- Aid prevents people in poorer countries supporting themselves. It can be seen as teaching people to depend on handouts, taking away their initiative and their ability to help themselves. It encourages people – and perhaps countries – to be lazy and inefficient.

- The aid that is provided is sometimes inappropriate and does not help. NGO staff from developed countries may not understand the culture of the country in which they are working. They may set up projects that are intended to help but do not work.

- Some NGOs have been involved in scandals, such as their staff abusing or taking advantage of local people. NGO workers from developed countries are much better off than people from the countries they work in, and this can cause resentment.

- Marxists argue that all aid is a way for the developed world to control and exploit the developing world. It keeps things the way they are: developing countries rely on charity to run what should be basic services, such as health and education.

- Feminists say that NGOs sometimes forget to consider how an aid project will affect gender relations within a community. For example, loans to women to help them set up a small business may not be approved of by their husbands, because this alters the relationship between them.

Feminist criticisms of equality legislation

Feminists campaigned for laws that would bring about gender equality, for example:

- equal pay for equal work – women should be paid the same as men for the same work

- ending gender discrimination – making it illegal for women to be discriminated against at work because of their sex, for example when applying for promotion or due to pregnancy

- enabling women to work in the same jobs as men, such as the armed forces.

Soon after such laws were passed in most developed countries, it became clear that they had not solved all the problems. Feminists argue that more still needs to be done to bring about full equality, because women are still treated unequally in some ways. For example:

- women's pay is still significantly less than men's, on average

- women have not been able to gain equal access to areas of work dominated by men

- some aspects of the new laws are difficult to enforce and easily avoided by employers; for example, an employer who rejects a woman for a job because of her sex can easily say she was unsuitable for other reasons

- it can be time-consuming and expensive for a woman to use the law and take her employer to court if she believes she has been discriminated against; as a result, women may simply find a new job instead

- laws do not do enough to help women who are pregnant or have young children. The laws focus on employment but, to tackle inequality, they must consider women's lives as a whole.

CONTINUED

- These have an impact on people's life chances.

- Non-governmental organisations (NGOs) work globally to help reduce social inequalities, aiming to:

  - reduce poverty

  - provide medical assistance

  - promote business

  - improve education.

- There are debates between sociological perspectives about the success of attempts to reduce social inequalities. These include:

  - New Right criticisms of the welfare state, claiming that it creates an underclass, a culture of poverty and a dependency culture

  - Marxist criticisms of the welfare state

  - criticisms of the aid work done by NGOs

  - feminist criticisms of equality legislation.

3.3 How has globalisation affected inequalities between societies?

The impact of migration on societies

Immigration/emigration

Migrants are people who move from one country to another. People who move for a short time only, such as for a holiday, and intend to return home afterwards, are not usually thought of as migrants.

Emigration is when people leave their original country and settle somewhere else. **Immigration** means arriving and settling in a new country. All migrants are, at the same time, both emigrants from one country and immigrants to another.

People also move within countries, for example from the countryside to a city. These people are sometimes described as 'internal migrants'. Internal migration is easier than international **migration** because it does not involve crossing an international border. Most of this section is about international migrants.

Human migration has always happened. Early in the history of our species, long before records were kept, groups of people moved out of Africa, where humans originated, and spread around the world.

For several centuries before the Second World War (1939–1945), the main pattern of migration was from Europe to other parts of the world. People from Europe settled in North and South America, Australia, New Zealand and parts of Africa and Asia. This was mainly as part of **colonialism**. In some places, most of the indigenous people were killed, either by violence or by diseases brought by Europeans. There was also significant forced migration of people from Africa as slaves.

Since the Second World War, more migration has been from the former colonies to Europe and to North America. This is because of persecution and poverty in the former colonies, and the higher standards of living in more developed countries. Countries to which migrants are attracted have immigration policies, which define the kinds of people they will accept. These policies favour people from some countries over others. For example, it has become very difficult for people from African countries to migrate to Europe.

KEY TERMS

emigration: moving away from your home country and settling in a new country

immigration: arriving and settling in a new country

(international) migration: moving from one country to another, to live

colonialism: the policy or practice in which one country controls another country, exploiting it and occupying it with settlers

As a result, many people try to migrate by unofficial routes, often putting themselves in danger. People from developed countries migrate too, but by official routes. They will find it easier to obtain visas to travel wherever they want to.

The most common migrants are unmarried male adults. It is easier for single males to travel; there are often more restrictions, and greater risks, for women. Many men are the first person in their family to migrate. If they are successful in finding work and housing, they will bring family members to join them. In some countries, such as the Philippines, it is common for a married woman with children to emigrate alone; she will send money home to support her family, where the children are often looked after by grandparents. Migrants often migrate to an area in another country where people from their home country are already settled, so they can get support and advice from this community when they arrive.

Figure 3.11: Immigrants arriving in the UK from Jamaica, a former colony, on the HMT *Empire Windrush* in 1948.

There are four main types of migrant today.

Economic migrants

These are people who migrate to gain a higher standard of living. Many countries have agreements with other countries about whether their citizens can travel, live and work there. Often, countries require migrants to have a visa (permission to enter and work). It can be time-consuming and expensive to apply for and gain a visa. Visa applications are closely scrutinised and often rejected. Visas are usually given by embassies that, in effect, act as border controllers.

Highly skilled migrants

Most developed countries want to attract workers with skills needed for their economies. They try to attract workers who have particular skills, such as health professionals, engineers and computer programmers. They attract them by offering incentives such as being able to bring family with them or to apply for citizenship.

Refugees and asylum seekers

Refugees are people who leave their homes because of wars, disasters and persecution to seek refuge somewhere else. Many refugees move within their own countries, to a safer area where they may have friends or relatives. Many international refugees go to a neighbouring country, where the culture may be similar and from where it may be easy to return home. Others travel much longer distances.

The term 'refugee' is often used to describe anyone in this type of situation. However, there is also a legal status of refugee. This is when someone who has applied for asylum – an asylum seeker – has their claim accepted. The United Nations works with national governments to find ways to help refugees.

Students

Universities in developed countries accept many students from other countries. For example, many young people from China study in the UK. The universities benefit from this, as they are able to charge high fees. Students are treated differently from other types of migrant because the university is to some extent responsible for them. Students are temporary migrants: they are expected to return to their country of origin at the end of their studies. Some gain qualifications which may allow them to stay on as highly skilled workers. In this way, temporary migration can become permanent migration for highly skilled work. One outcome of this is that some countries lose some of their most talented people, who move abroad to study and then remain there permanently.

Push and pull factors

Some migration has always been forced while some has always been a choice. People thinking of migrating today may consider a range of factors. **Push factors** are reasons for leaving a country, **pull factors** are reasons for moving to another country. Some common push factors are:

- **Poverty.** For many people living in poverty, moving away offers a chance of a better life.

- **Lack of opportunity.** Some countries have few opportunities for education or employment, so people cannot have a good standard of living for themselves or their families.

- **Famine and environmental problems.** As the effects of climate change grow, more people will be forced to move because it will no longer be possible for them to make a living or survive where they are.

- **Violence and persecution.** Some people migrate to escape conflicts, or because they are being persecuted for their ethnicity, sexuality, religion, political views or other factors.

Pull factors include:

- **Better education.** Many people believe that education is the key to future success. The opportunity to get a better level of education, for themselves or their children, can be a strong pull factor.

- **Employment.** Many migrants move to take up work opportunities that do not exist in their own country, or which will be paid more highly. Even if they do not have skills or qualifications, migrants may find work with better pay and conditions in their new country.

- **Living standards.** Even for people on low wages or in unskilled work, the country of arrival may offer higher standards of living, for example in housing and healthcare.

- **Western consumer culture.** Many people in less developed countries aspire to the lifestyle and the consumer goods of wealthier countries, because they have been socialised to see them as desirable.

KEY TERMS

push factors: reasons for leaving a country

pull factors: reasons attracting people to a new country

- **Hope of better treatment.** Many migrants believe – sometimes incorrectly – that they will be treated with respect and will be able to fit in and adapt to their new situation. For example, being able to speak English or French may encourage people to think they will be able to integrate.

These push and pull factors are important but many sociologists think that people's decisions about migration are more complicated. Because of globalisation, many people have networks of family and friends that spread across several countries. Each person's network is different but they all offer opportunities. People may hear stories of life in other countries, often from people who have migrated there, and make decisions based on these and other factors.

ACTIVITY: DISCUSSION 3.3

1 Which are more important – push factors or pull factors? Or does the idea of networks explain migration better? In a small group, discuss these questions and agree on one position.

2 Now create and practise a brief role play in which one member of your group plays someone from your area who is thinking of emigrating from your country. The other members of your group should play this person's friends, giving advice about why they should go, based on different push and pull factors. Perform the scene for other members of the class.

REFLECTION

Did you feel comfortable taking part in the role-play activity? Did it help you to understand the influence and importance of different push and pull factors on someone's decision to migrate?

Increasing cultural diversity

As a result of international migration, some countries have become increasingly diverse, both ethnically and culturally. Countries in Western Europe and North America, in particular, now have more groups of people of different ethnic backgrounds living alongside each other; these societies have become multicultural. Often, migrant groups gradually blend with the culture of the country they have moved to: they keep their own culture to some extent, but also adopt aspects of the host culture. The children or grandchildren of migrants often have hybrid identities, which combine both cultures. An example in the United Kingdom is British Bangladeshi people – the children or grandchildren of people who migrated from Bangladesh to the United Kingdom. They are British by birth and citizenship and have adopted many aspects of UK culture, but they also retain some Bangladeshi culture, such as language and religion, and may have strong family ties to Bangladesh.

MAKING CONNECTIONS

Multiculturalism is discussed in section 2.3. Revisit this section and the countries discussed. Consider your own country and whether it is multicultural.

Economic consequences

Economic consequences for countries from which people emigrate

One of the main patterns of migration is from poorer countries to wealthier ones. This is because migrants see opportunities for education, employment and a better life. Many emigrants are young, healthy people. Their departure changes the population of their home country, leaving fewer young adults and a higher proportion of older people. This can be seen within countries as well, where internal migration leads to an older population in rural areas and more young people in cities.

International migration can leave countries short of workers, particularly when the people who emigrate are highly skilled workers. This has been called a 'brain drain'. For example, a country might train people as doctors, only for those people to emigrate to a country that can offer higher pay and better living standards. The decision to emigrate may be the right one for the individual, but their country of origin loses valuable assets.

Emigrants often send money they have earned back to their families in their country of origin. Amounts of money sent in this way are called remittances. Remittances have become important to the economies of many countries. They bring in foreign currencies – dollars, euros and pounds – and put money into the local economy.

Economic consequences for countries to which people immigrate

Developed countries often need more workers for some sectors of the economy.

They have ageing populations and fewer young people of working age to work and pay taxes.

Some of the work may be highly skilled, attracting qualified professionals. Other work is temporary and low paid, such as picking fruit at harvest time, and may not appeal to local people. Migrants are often prepared to work for low wages, because the pay is still better than in their country of origin or because it is a way of settling in before finding better work. The means that the presence of migrant workers can keep wages low for other workers. This is unpopular with trade unions, who fight for improvements in workers' pay and conditions but see these being taken away because of migrant workers.

Most analyses show that migrants contribute to the economy of the country they move to. However, mass migration can cause problems – at least initially – by leading to strain on local resources such as housing, schools and healthcare. This may cause resentment from the local population.

Negative perceptions of migrants

Immigrants are seen in different ways but perceptions can be negative. For example, people emigrating to Europe from Africa and parts of Asia, and people migrating to North America from Central and South America have sometimes been met with suspicion, resentment and hostility by people in the host countries. Negative stereotypes of immigrants are spread via media representations and in the speeches and actions of politicians. For example, former president Donald Trump of the US wanted to build a wall all along the US border with Mexico to prevent anyone crossing from Mexico into the US.

The varying responses to migrants are complex. On an individual level, and when a migrant's story is known, people in host countries can be very welcoming. However, on a more abstract level, many people are concerned about the idea of mass migration into their country or local area, and the impact this might have on their lives. Some migrants are welcomed based on where they have come from and why; this was the response of many people in European countries to refugees from Ukraine during the Russian invasion in 2022. However, immigrants have a different culture which is often seen as a threat by local people. For example, some people object to immigrants speaking a different language or having a different religion. These defensive reactions are more likely when large numbers of migrants arrive in a short period.

Politicians may be against immigration because they believe this stance will win them votes. Governments try to control immigration, allowing in migrants with the skills they want or need, and keeping others out. They try to keep out immigrants they see as 'illegal' – people travelling without required official documents, such as a visa. Many migrants from Africa try to enter Europe, for its opportunities and higher standard of living. Some are escaping from wars, others from poverty and the effects of climate change. They travel long distances, often across desert and sea. They usually have to pay large sums of money to human smugglers who promise to help them get into Europe. Those who do manage to enter have very few rights; they may be detained in conditions similar to prison, then sent back to their country of origin.

Impact of global ecological issues on societies

Globalisation leads to ecological issues that affect inequalities between societies. As the climate crisis grows and human activities continue to damage the environment, the effects are felt most by poorer people and poorer countries. This section explores some of the connections between ecological issues and inequalities within and between societies.

The influence of transnational corporations

Transnational corporations (TNCs) are businesses which operate around the world. They employ people, source materials and sell goods and services in different countries. Globalisation has led to there being more and larger TNCs. Many are extremely wealthy, and as powerful as nation-states. Some are well-known global brands, such as CocaCola, Nestlé, Shell and Toyota. Others are less well-known because they do not sell directly to consumers; these include, for example, the mining corporation Glencore and the shipping company Maersk.

TNCs are part of the global capitalist system. Their purpose is to make as much profit as possible without breaking the law. Many now have policies about protecting the environment, because they know they might lose customers if they are seen not to care about environmental issues. However, their actions still cause environmental problems, which then affect inequalities.

Developing countries try to attract TNCs to invest in them – for example, by setting up factories – because this will bring money into the economy, create jobs and help economic growth. To attract TNCs, however, they have to offer ways by which TNCs can make higher profits. These ways can include, for example, removing controls on pollution and construction. The low pay and poor conditions for workers in developing countries may also be attractive to TNCs, helping them to minimise their costs. This reinforces and increases the inequalities between developed and developing countries.

The actions of TNCs can damage the environment in the following key ways.

- **Farming.** TNCs use the best agricultural land for cash crop production. Cash crops are produced to sell on the global market for profit, often to developed countries, rather than to feed people in the country itself. They include cocoa, coffee and tea. This pushes small farmers onto marginal, less fertile land. TNCs may also use pesticides and other chemicals that pollute the ground.

- **Plastics.** Some TNCs manufacture plastics, while others use large amounts of plastic in packaging and for goods they make. The production of plastics depletes natural resources. Pollution from plastics is now affecting life in seas and rivers. It also affects the livelihoods of people who rely on fishing.

Figure 3.12: Plastic waste washed up on a beach.

- **Fossil fuels.** The continued use of oil, coal and gas by TNCs in their production of products such as cars and airplanes is contributing to global warming.

- **Oil.** Spills and leaks pollute air, land and water.

- **Mining.** Mining often leads to chemical pollution, acid in water, soil erosion and exposure to hazardous materials.

- **Deforestation.** Logging for timber and land clearance for construction reduces forests. This affects wildlife and contributes to climate change.

- **Fishing.** Large-scale fishing by TNC-owned factory ships is reducing the diversity of ocean life. It also leaves few fish to be caught by people who have traditionally fished from small boats. This contributed to the problem of piracy off the coast of Somalia: Somali fishermen could no longer make a living because so many fish had been taken by factory ships, so they began holding ships to ransom instead.

- **Consumer lifestyle.** TNCs seek profits by persuading people to continually buy new products, and to get rid of items that can still be used. This 'throwaway' culture puts more pressure on the world's resources and increases the number of products which go to landfill sites, causing more environmental damage.

- **Waste.** When the goods made by TNCs are no longer useful, they are often exported as waste to developing countries. For example, many old computers and other digital devices are sent to Agbogbloshie in Ghana. Here, some materials are extracted and recycled. However, toxic chemicals are released at the same time; these damage the health of the people taking the devices apart and pollute the ground and water.

Some TNCs are adapting their practices. The way they operated for many years was not sustainable in terms of resources used or environmental impacts such as pollution, and this is now being recognised. However, there has already been a lot of damage to the environment and the effects of this will continue for many years.

Climate change

Climate change as a result of human actions is now accepted as a threat. Global warming (attributed mainly to carbon emissions from factories, power plants, cars, airplanes, etc.) is affecting the climate in different parts of the world in unpredictable ways, with effects on societies. These effects include:

- **Changing rainfall patterns.** Farmers rely on predictable weather; for example, in West Africa, the arrival of rain is essential for growing crops.

The start of the rainy season has become less predictable, so farmers are unsure when to plant crops.

- **Desertification (the growth of deserts).** This occurs as climate change and soil erosion make it more difficult for vegetation to grow.

- **Loss of biodiversity.** Species become extinct or at risk of extinction due to changes in their ecosystems.

- **Weather events.** Chanes in global climate lead to more violent and less predictable storms and other weather events.

- **Natural disasters.** Many people live in areas at risk of mudslides, flooding or wildfires, all of which occur more often with global warming. The people most at risk are often the poorest and most disadvantaged, for example those living in shanty towns where homes are built from whatever is available.

- **Rising sea levels.** Some small island states in the Pacific and Indian Oceans, such as the Maldives, Kiribati and Tuvalu, are very low-lying. As polar ice melts and sea levels rise, these lands will be submerged. Some large cities are also at risk, including Kolkata and Mumbai in India, Dhaka in Bangladesh and Bangkok in Thailand.

Pollution

Pollution occurs through the actions of TNCs, governments and consumers. By the second half of the 20th century, it was recognised that pollution is a serious threat to health: it can reduce people's quality of life and how long they live. Its effects are experienced most by people who cannot afford to move to a less polluted environment. Pollution can take many different forms. Some are very long-lasting, such as plastic in oceans. With other forms of pollution, such as an oil spill, the pollutant is gradually dispersed; however, land may be unusable for years afterwards.

Pollution can be thought of as affecting three aspects of the environment, though these are all connected:

- **Land pollution.** Pollution in the ground affects plant life, crops and livestock who eat vegetation. Waste from the developed world often ends up in poorer countries; some is recycled but it also brings pollution and health problems.

- **Air pollution.** Sources of air pollution include emissions from factories and exhaust fumes from motor vehicles. Some cities, such as Delhi in India, have very high levels of air pollution;

this affects the health of people living there, causing breathing difficulties and blocking out sunlight. Small particles in polluted air can affect the lungs and cause many diseases. The World Health Organization estimates that 4.2 million people died prematurely in 2016 because of air pollution.

- **Water pollution.** Wells, lakes, rivers and oceans can be polluted by, for example, oil, chemical waste and plastics. In some places, people have to drink or use polluted water because they have no other source.

Most countries have some laws to prevent pollution, but these are difficult to enforce (see section 6.1 on corporate and green crime). Developing countries give priority to economic growth and industrialisation, which cause further environmental degradation. China, for example, has large reserves of coal which it is using to meet its citizens' energy needs, even though this causes pollution and contributes to global warming. More sustainable practices are being introduced and many countries are moving towards renewable forms of energy, such as solar and wind power. However, a lot of environmental damage has already been done and it will be a long time before existing pollution, such as plastic in the seas, can be eliminated.

Figure 3.13: Air pollution from a petrochemical plant.

Urbanisation

Urbanisation refers to the process by which the proportion of a country's population living in cities increases. A city is usually defined as having over 100,000 inhabitants. Urbanisation is happening most quickly in less developed countries, especially those in Africa.

City populations grow partly because people move in from rural areas, due to the same push and pull factors as for international migration. They also grow because they have lots of young people who are likely to have children.

Cities in developing countries often pull in all kinds of resources from the countryside, because they are centres for exports, jobs, education, etc. Cities extract food, water and other resources from large areas around them. They have large 'ecological footprints'. This means that the growth of cities changes the environment and has big effects on how people live.

Some people see cities as 'magnets' which are dynamic centres of innovation and growth. However, they can also be seen as 'drains', soaking up and wasting a country's natural and human resources.

In urban areas in developing countries, poor people usually have no access to regular housing. Instead, they build their own. These areas are known by different names in different countries, for example shanty towns, barrios, favelas, bidonvilles and bustees. They are often on illegally occupied land, so people do not have a right to live there and can be moved out. Governments often see shanty towns as a problem and want to hide them from tourists. For the people who live there, shanty towns provide cheap accommodation and access to work. New migrants to the city will often settle there, creating communities which connect people and provide support.

In spite of these advantages, shanty towns have many problems. In less developed countries, the living conditions of the poor in cities are often worse than those of the poor in rural areas. Such conditions in cities include:

- overcrowding, with many people sharing a small space

- contaminated water. In cities in poorer countries, piped water that is clean and treated is usually provided for a minority, in wealthier areas. The poor buy their water, which is often of poor quality, or use water from sources that are likely to be contaminated and may be a risk to health

- lack of decent sanitation; sewerage systems are rarely provided for the residents of shanty towns

- threat of floods or landslides, because poor people often live on unstable land

- indoor pollution from cooking and heating, made worse by inadequate ventilation.

Together, these conditions mean there are high risks of infectious diseases spreading, and of other risks such as fire.

CASE STUDY 3.3

An African shanty town: Kibera, Kenya

Figure 3.14: Kibera, Kenya.

Kibera is a huge shanty town in Nairobi, the capital city of Kenya. About a million people live there, in a small area, and it is one of the biggest shanty towns in the world. The government owns the land and the people have no right to live there. Most live in shacks with mud brick walls and corrugated iron roofs. Until recently there was no water, but there are now two pipes. There are a few toilets that are holes in the ground. There are no government clinics or hospitals. Only 20 per cent of Kibera has electricity. Many young people are unemployed and bored, so cheap illegal alcohol is a common problem. A railway runs through Kibera; children play on the tracks and people sleep next to them. Although living conditions are poor, Kibera has some of the things you would expect in a town – a railway station, several schools, youth organisations and a football team. The government has plans to improve Kibera and rehouse people.

Task

1   What are some of the health risks in a shanty town like Kibera?

2   Some people living in Kibera might not want to be rehoused. Why might this be?

ACTIVITY: WRITTEN 3.3

Write 300 words to summarise the advantages and disadvantages of living in shanty towns.

Sociological explanations for global inequalities

As you can see, globalisation has affected inequalities between societies in many ways. In this section, we will consider some sociological explanations for this.

Marxist views of capitalist exploitation

The Marxist view is that inequalities between richer and poorer countries are caused by the capitalist economic system. Capitalism creates inequalities between social classes, both within countries and on a global scale. The inequalities between the developed world and poorer countries are a global version of the division between the ruling class and the working class.

Inequalities are created by exploitation. Developed countries use their greater wealth and power to take advantage of poorer countries. This process began in the past, with colonialism (see next section), and continues today with trade and capitalism.

A closely related view, often put forward by neo-Marxists (newer Marxists who have updated Marx's ideas), is known as dependency theory. This view argues that capitalism has created a chain of dependency. This is like a food chain, in which large animals eat smaller animals who, in turn, eat insects and plants. In the chain of dependency, wealthier countries exploit countries who are just below them and they, in turn, exploit countries just beneath them. This pattern continues down to the poorest countries.

Colonialism

Early traders and explorers from Europe began to have more contact with people around the world about 500 years ago. For example, European explorers crossed the Atlantic Ocean to the Americas in the 15th and 16th centuries. The trade was on very unequal terms, with the European countries benefitting much more.

Part of the trade was in people, with slaves taken from Africa to work in the Americas.

The Europeans established trading posts which, over time, became fortified and permanent settlements. The trading posts were often used as bases from which much larger areas were controlled. Contact with European settlers was disastrous for the original inhabitants, who were often wiped out by violence and by diseases brought by Europeans, to which they had no immunity. For example, the civilisations of the Inca in Peru and the Aztecs in Mexico were eradicated by European colonists.

European powers then began to compete for control of large areas. Eventually they took political control, brutally crushing any resistance. Large parts of the world became colonies of European countries such as Britain, France, Spain, Belgium, Germany and the Netherlands. Often these countries ruled over populations much bigger than their own. The colonists imposed borders between countries which did not relate to the natural borders between different peoples. Old civilisations were destroyed and cultures wiped out. Industries were also destroyed; for example, Britain destroyed India's cotton industry so that it could not compete with its own. The people of the colonies had very few rights and were often treated very badly. At its greatest extent, the British Empire was the largest ever, containing about 450 million people (20 per cent of the world's population at the time) and covering about a quarter of the world's land.

The European countries used their colonies to provide resources and cash crops (see the section on TNCs). People were not allowed to grow crops for themselves; instead, they were made to grow crops which they had to sell and export to the colonial power. In this way, people were forced to become workers in a capitalist economy, earning money and paying taxes.

By the mid-20th century, the European colonial powers had been weakened by the two world wars and countries began to see their colonies as a burden. The colonies gradually became independent, although they often had to fight wars to achieve this. The colonial period ended but the newly independent countries were left in a disadvantaged position:

- They remained economically dependent on the ex-colonial power (for example, having to sell cash crops to it).

- They struggled for stability and growth because they had no tradition of self-rule or democracy. Their people had been prevented from having an education, so they did not have the skills to run the government and economy.

- They inherited colonial borders which did not reflect traditional ethnic groupings and settlements. This made it difficult for many countries to develop a sense of national unity. In some former colonies, these ethnic divisions caused further upheaval and unrest, even civil war. In some cases, new countries emerged; for example, Pakistan and Bangladesh were formerly part of the British-ruled India under colonialism.

- The culture of the colonial power had deeply influenced society. For example, English is still used as the language of government and education in Britain's ex-colonies in Africa, such as Sierra Leone and the Gambia.

The remnants of the colonial system still create disadvantages for the former colonies. This is often referred to as neo-colonialism.

ACTIVITY: RESEARCH 3.3

Work by yourself to answer the following questions:

a   Was your country a colony in the past? If so, research how this has affected your country today – for example, in terms of language, religion and governance.

b   If your country was not a former colony, was it a colonial power? If so, research which countries it colonised and how it may have benefitted from this.

c   If your country was neither a colony nor a coloniser, choose a country which was and research it more fully.

REFLECTION

How did it make you feel when you found out more about the impact of colonialism on your country or another which you researched? Were you previously aware of this history and how it may still affect countries today?

Feminist ideas of patriarchy

One of the most striking aspects of global inequality is the difference between the life chances of males and females. Most feminists accept some of the points in the Marxist and colonialist explanations, but they argue that gender should be considered too. As well as capitalism, the patriarchy leads to women being disadvantaged in many areas of life. The United Nations, NGOs and global social movements now take gender issues very seriously. However, by the measures used by global social movements, women are still a long way from equality with men. For example, there has been slow progress towards gender equality in work, which often gives women financial independence. Similarly, although more girls now go to school worldwide, there is still a gender gap in access to education in some countries.

The following questions can be used to judge progress towards equality:

- Can women decide whether and whom to marry, and can they end a marriage?

- Do women have freedom of movement?

- Do girls and women have access to education on the same terms as boys and men?

- How much power do women have within families and households?

- Are women able to decide whether and when to have children?

Feminists argue that the global spread of capitalism requires the exploitation of women. They draw attention to newer forms of exploitation – for example, it is mainly young women who are employed in sweatshop factories in South East Asia and elsewhere to make cheap clothing for the developed world. TNCs pay little and treat female workers poorly, partly on the (false) grounds that the work is unskilled. This work can sometimes help young women to achieve financial independence; often, however, the money goes straight to a man, either the female's father or her husband. The boss at work is usually a man and training and job security are rarely provided. This means the limited progress towards financial independence is partly blocked by the patriarchal nature of society.

CHECK YOUR UNDERSTANDING 3.3

1   What are the four main types of migrant today? For each one, write a sentence or two explaining why they decide to migrate.

2   In a small group, share ideas about images and text to include in a wall display on the theme: 'Global ecological issues and inequalities'. Design and produce your display, dividing the tasks fairly. Ask other learners to look at and comment on your display.

KEY POINTS

- Immigration and emigration, caused by push and pull factors, affect societies through:

  - increasing cultural diversity

  - economic consequences

  - negative perceptions of migrants.

- Global ecological issues have an impact on societies. These issues include:

  - the influence of transnational corporations

  - climate change

  - pollution

  - urbanisation.

- Sociological explanations of global inequalities include:

  - Marxist views of capitalist exploitation

  - dependency/underdevelopment theory

  - colonialism

  - feminist ideas of patriarchy.

SUMMARY

- Social stratification involves differences in life chances affected by age, gender, ethnicity, social class and the intersectionality of these factors.

- Attempts have been made to reduce social inequalities through legislation, welfare states and NGOs.

- Globalisation has affected inequalities between societies through migration and global ecological issues.

KEY SKILLS EXERCISES

1 Knowledge and understanding

Write a paragraph explaining what is meant by differences in life chances. Include some examples of how life chances may vary based on age, social class, ethnicity and gender.

2 Interpretation and application

Interpret the examples below from at least one of the following sociological perspectives: interactionism, Marxism, feminism, functionalism

- A woman is not considered for promotion because her employer assumes she will not want to work longer hours due to her children.

- A teacher assumes that a boy from a minority ethnic background is likely to behave badly and do less well in his lessons.

- Children from a privileged family follow their parents into well-paid careers in law and medicine.

3 Analysis and evaluation

Identify two criticisms of each of the following:

- the New Right view on the welfare state/underclass

- the aid work of NGOs

- the functionalist view on social inequality and meritocracy

- the Marxist view on global inequalities and capitalist exploitation.

IMPROVE THIS ANSWER

Research methods, identity and inequality

Evaluate functionalist views of social inequality. Your answer should include:

- at least three arguments for and three arguments against the views

- a conclusion.

Functionalists argue that social inequality is functional for the whole society. It is the result of rewarding some people more than others based on their contribution to society. This encourages people to conform to social norms and values in order to, for example, get well paid employment, which helps the economy. The way that society does this is through meritocracy, that is, the education system filters and sorts people according to their ability and how hard they work, and rewards those who are successful with higher status. This makes inequality functional for these people and for society.

On the other hand, Marxists argue that inequality is wrong and that we should have an equal society. They point out that meritocracy is a myth; there is very little upward social mobility and few

CONTINUED

opportunities to move up based on merit. Those born into wealthy, privileged families tend to stay there. Inequality may be functional for the bourgeoisie, because it allows them to keep their wealth and power, but not for the working class. Feminists also object to the functionalist view, saying that functionalists ignore the importance of gender. There are inequalities between males and females in patriarchal societies. For example, women cannot reach the highest levels in employment because of the glass ceiling — an invisible barrier based on male prejudice and discrimination.

Commentary and task

This is an evaluation question, so it requires several arguments for the view in the question, several arguments against the view in the question and a conclusion. The answer so far gives two arguments in favour of the view in the question and two against. Improve this answer by adding one more argument in favour and one more argument against. Try to include some sociological concepts and refer to sociological perspectives. Finally, add an evaluative conclusion.

PRACTICE QUESTIONS

Research methods, identity and inequality

a   Define the terms:

    i   social mobility [2]

    ii   distribution of wealth. [2]

b   Give **two** key terms used in labelling theory [2]

c   Explain **three** ways non-governmental organisations have tried to reduce social inequalities. [6]

d   Explain **three** features of colonialism as a sociological explanation for global inequalities. [6]

e   Discuss how global ecological issues may have an impact on societies.

    Your answer should include at least **three** developed points with evidence. [8]

f   Evaluate functionalist views of social inequality. Your answer should include:

    • at least **three** arguments for and **three** arguments against the views

    • a conclusion. [14]

SELF-EVALUATION CHECKLIST

After studying this unit, complete this table:

You should be able to:	Needs more work	Almost there	Ready to move on
3.1 What is social stratification?			
Understand social stratification in open and closed societies			
Explain differences in life chances in education, employment, health, housing and life expectancy as affected by age, gender, ethnicity and social class			
Explain the intersectionality of age, ethnicity, gender and social class in understanding the impact of inequality on individuals			
Understand different sociological theories of social inequality			
3.2 What attempts have been made to reduce social inequalities?			
Describe the use of legislation within societies to reduce inequality			
Describe the development and impact of welfare states on life chances			
Explain the global work of non-governmental organisations (NGOs)			
Understand sociological views of the success of attempts to reduce social inequalities			
3.3 How has globalisation affected inequalities between societies?			
Explain the impact of migration on societies			
Explain the impact of global ecological issues on societies			
Understand sociological explanations for global inequalities			

> # Unit 4
Family

LEARNING INTENTIONS

In this unit, you will learn how to:

- Describe the different types of family

- Discuss the influence of culture, social class and ethnicity on family diversity

- Discuss views on family diversity, including the New Right and postmodernist views

- Describe the role and functions of the family from functionalist, Marxist and feminist perspectives and understand the 'loss of functions' debate

- Describe alternatives to the family

- Describe cross-cultural differences in marriage and alternatives to marriage

- Explain roles and relationships within families, how they have changed and how they vary

- Discuss negative aspects of family life

- Explain how industrialisation and urbanisation affect families

CONTINUED

- Outline demographic trends and how they affect families, including the consequences of an ageing population
- Explain changing patterns and trends in marriage, divorce and cohabitation.

Introduction

Sociology is about how people interact with others in social groups. These social groups come in many forms and sizes: nations, organisations of different kinds, communities, schools and so on. But perhaps the most important social group in our lives is our family. This unit explores the sociology of the family, looking at different kinds of family, family structures and patterns, and the changing roles and relationships in families.

Because people live in families, we might assume that we know a lot about them. But there are many types of family. Over a lifetime, each person will probably live in several different types of family, because the family is changed by births, marriages, deaths, divorces and separations, remarriages, adoptions and changes of residence. In many societies over the last 50 years or so, there has been an increase in the number and proportion of different types of family and a decline in nuclear families.

4.1 What are the different types of families?

Different family structures

There are two main types of family: the **nuclear family** and the **extended family**. This section discusses these two main types, as well as variations of them and other types of family. Different types of family include the reconstituted or step-family, the lone-parent family and the same-sex family. Not everyone lives in a family; for example, groups of friends may live together. We will look at alternatives to the family later in this section.

The nuclear family

A lot of sociological writing in the 20th century took it for granted that there was one main type of family: the nuclear family. The nuclear family is made up of an adult man and an adult woman, living together with dependent children. This was seen as the normal kind of family in the USA, the UK and industrial societies at the time. It was thought to be not only the most common kind of family, but also the best.

In 1949, the functionalist sociologist George Murdock argued that the nuclear family of a mother, father and dependent children was the basic family unit worldwide. He based this claim on research carried out around the world on many different cultures and societies. Types of family that seemed to be different, he argued, had a nuclear family at their heart. For example, family units of mother, father and children exist within extended families.

However, Murdock's ideas were challenged by many sociologists; they suggested that he misinterpreted and even ignored evidence that challenged his claim. Whether or not Murdock was right at the time, it is clear that since at least the 1970s, other types of family have become more noticeable and widespread.

Extended families

It is often thought that extended families were more common in the past and are now in decline because they are less suited to life in modern industrial societies. Extended families include more relatives than the nuclear family, usually living in the same household. A family with more than two generations, usually including grandparents, is a **vertically extended family**.

KEY TERMS

nuclear family: made up of an adult man and an adult woman who are married or in a relationship and living together with dependent children

extended family: a family with parent(s) and children living with or close to other relatives, such as grandparents or aunts and uncles

vertically extended family: a family with parents(s) and children living with relatives from one or more other generations (for example, grandparents)

A family with aunts, uncles and cousins (that is, people of the same generation as the parents and children) is a **horizontally extended family**. The term 'extended family' is usually used when all the relatives share a household – they live together under one roof. However, it can also be used to describe a nuclear family living close to relatives in the same street or area, with lots of contact and support between them. In modern industrial societies, with better communication and transport, relatives who live far apart are more able to stay in contact; when there is regular contact (for example, by social media) and mutual support between family members, they can be described as a **modified extended family**.

Many couples, especially in industrialised countries, now have fewer children – so children have fewer siblings, if any. As a result, the next generation has few, if any, aunts and uncles. Increased life expectancy can mean there are several generations in a family, but only a few people in each generation. This type of 'tall and thin' family is called a **beanpole family**. This could be seen as a type of vertically extended family with few people in each generation (though the term beanpole family does not imply that the generations live together).

Reconstituted family

If a person marries for a second time after **divorce** or the death of their first partner, a new family is formed. The new family is called a **reconstituted family** or

step-family. There are many versions of this type of family, for example: one or both partners may have been married before; one or both partners may have children; children from previous relationships may live with the new family or with their other parent. Remarriage creates new relationships, such as step-parents, step-children, step-siblings and step-grandparents. This situation is relatively new, so the norms and values are often unclear; for example, a step-parent may be unsure about the extent to which they should correct the bad behaviour of their partner's children. Equally, the children may be unsure what authority this new person in their lives should have.

Same-sex family

Same-sex families are formed when two adults of the same-sex – that is, two males or two females – raise their own or adopted children. In the past, families like this were often not accepted, but modern industrial societies increasingly give same-sex couples the same or similar rights and responsibilities as opposite-sex couples. These rights include property rights, parental rights and rights to welfare benefits. For instance, women who have left their husband to live with a female partner are finding it easier than in the past to gain custody of their children. This is because research in the UK and in the USA has found that children raised by gay parents are no more likely than others to grow up gay or to suffer bullying at school; this had been a concern. When deciding who should bring up a child, parents' sexual orientation is increasingly seen as less important than factors such as the strength of the parent–child bond. Research also suggests that children brought up in same-sex families are no different to children from opposite-sex families in their **gender roles**, identities and attitudes to life.

KEY TERMS

horizontally extended family: a family with parents(s) and children living with other relatives of the same generations, such as aunts, uncles and cousins

modified extended family: an extended family who have close ties but do not all live together

beanpole family: a vertically extended/multi-generational family with only one or two children in each generation; this creates a tall and thin family tree (rather than a 'bushy' one with lots of siblings, aunts, uncles and cousins)

divorce: the formal, legal ending of a marriage

reconstituted family: a new family created when someone remarries after divorce or the death of a partner

KEY TERMS

same-sex family: two adults of the same-sex – two males or two females – raising their own or adopted children

gender roles: the roles and expectations associated with being male or female

In some parts of the world, same-sex relationships are disapproved of and may even be against the law, making it difficult for same-sex-families to exist openly. However, there is a growing opinion in most parts of the world that a loving and stable environment – regardless of the gender of the parents – is the best environment in which to bring up children.

Figure 4.1: A family.

Lone-parent family

There have always been lone-parent families, also known as single-parent or one-parent families. In the past, lone-parent families were usually the result of the death of one of the parents, leaving the other parent to raise the children on their own. This situation was often temporary, until the surviving parent found a new partner and formed a reconstituted family. However, there has been an increase in the number of lone-parent families in modern industrial societies, especially since the mid-20th century. Some still result from death, but many now result from separation, divorce or choice.

KEY TERM

lone-parent/single-parent/one-parent family: one parent and their dependent children living together

Here are some reasons why there are more lone-parent families today than in the past:

- Divorce has become common and it can leave one parent looking after the children.

- Women have greater financial independence, due to increasing gender equality in most societies. They are more likely to have qualifications that allow them to work to support their family. If they cannot work or earn enough to support their family alone, they may be able to receive welfare benefits, so they do not need a man to bring in an income.

- Some women now choose to raise children on their own, without support from the father.

TIP

Be aware that people in different societies think about their families and kinship in different ways. In this book, the terms used are those from an Inuit system of kinship classification, which is used in Europe, North America and elsewhere. Although this system has become the most common, it is only one of six systems described by the anthropologist Lewis Henry Morgan. For example, in the kinship system of Hawaii (before explorers arrived), the brothers and sisters of your parents – your aunts and uncles under the Inuit system – were also called mother and father, so individuals had several mothers and fathers. The children of these other mothers and fathers were then sisters and brothers, rather than cousins. The Inuit system emphasises the nuclear family bond, rather than extended kinship ties.

Polygamous families

Some families have more than two people in a marriage, either a man married to two or more women or a woman married to two or more men. These families are discussed later in the section on types of marriage.

KEY TERM

marriage: the formal joining of a man and a woman in a relationship with rights and responsibilities; some countries now allow same-sex marriage (involving two men or two women)

Empty-nest families

In modern industrial societies, adult children usually leave the family home to live independently, eventually marrying and starting a new family. This leads to empty-nest families, with a parent or parents living at home after their adult children have moved out. As life expectancy has increased, parents often live for many years in this type of family. However, it is becoming more common for adult children to return to the family home, often for economic reasons; this means empty-nest families are only temporary for some people. Adult children returning to live with their parents are referred to as boomerang children, and this type of family is called a boomerang family.

Childless families

Childless families are couples who do not have children. In the past, when the primary role of an adult woman was to be a mother, women who did not have children were stigmatised or pitied. However, developments in modern medical technology mean that couples who might not have been able to have children in the past are now able to do so. As a result, childless families are often childless by choice. This can be for many reasons, including financial ones – people are aware of the high cost of having children in modern societies. A woman might decide not to have children so she can pursue her career. Many people are also less optimistic now about the world that children will live in; the future looks increasingly dangerous because of climate catastrophe. Because families choose not to have children, the term 'child-free' may be better than childless.

KEY TERMS

empty-nest family: parents living at home after their adult children have moved out

boomerang family: a family where an adult child has returned to the family home to live with their parent(s)

childless families: a couple who live together and have no children

---

The strengths and limitations of different types of family

The previous section has discussed some of the reasons for, and the strengths of, different types of family. The nuclear family is often seen as the most widespread and functional type. A nuclear family can be geographically mobile – small enough to move to where the work is – and provides stability and role models for the children. However, some sociologists – such as Ann Oakley – have criticised the nuclear family as being oppressive to women. The benefits of greater family diversity are considered in the next section.

Extended families have many benefits in terms of support, both for the couple in raising their children and in providing care for older generations. This could explain why modified extended families are becoming more common. As we will see in section 4.3, the role of grandparents in the family is increasingly important.

Although some sociologists criticise them, lone-parent families are increasingly common and often very successful in bringing up children. Many parents feel that they provide a better environment for a child than one in which two parents remain together but constantly argue or are not happy together. Reconstituted families often bring challenges – as two existing families learn to live together – but many are very successful. Children of divorced parents may spend their time between two reconstituted families, widening their support network in a positive way.

Despite these general points, however, every family is unique. It is impossible to generalise and claim that one type of family is better or worse than another type. Each individual family will have its own strengths and limitations.

ACTIVITY: DISCUSSION 4.1

1 In a small group, discuss the possible challenges for people living in:

   a   nuclear families

   b   extended families

   c   lone-parent families

   d   reconstituted families

   e   same-sex families.

2 Is one type of family 'better' or more desirable than other types?

Variations and diversity in the family

The changes in the number and types of different families, or **family diversity**, are related to culture, social class and ethnicity.

Cross-cultural

The sociologist Göran Therborn suggested that there are seven broad types of family system, shown in Table 4.1.

There is an assumption that Therborn's Christian-European family is spreading worldwide. However, although some aspects of this family type are becoming more common, other family types remain strong. There is no sign that there will soon be one globally dominant family type.

Name	Main characteristics
Christian-European	The least patriarchal and the most open to change. Based on monogamy. New couples form new households.
Islamic West/North African	Marriage and religion are deeply connected. Male superiority is shown in rules, e.g. about male guardianship. Women are seen as individuals with rights.
South Asian	Strong patriarchy and strong rules about who can marry whom, e.g. within castes in India.
Confucian East Asian	Strongly patriarchal, with an emphasis on sons' duties to fathers and to ancestors.
Sub-Saharan African	Polygamy is common. Fertility is highly valued, leading to high birth rates. Male power is a dominant theme, but women have some financial freedom.
South East Asian	Less strongly patriarchal than the other Asian types.
Creole	Arose from European invasion and oppression of African and indigenous American peoples. There are low rates of marriage, high rates of births outside marriage and female-centred families.

Table 4.1: Therborn's seven types of family system.

CASE STUDY 4.1

Families in Niger

Niger is a landlocked country in West Africa, with a history of colonisation and slavery.

It has a very high fertility rate of 7.2 births per woman. It also has the highest infant mortality rate in the world. Nearly half the population are under 15.

In rural areas, a typical household is a very large extended family whose livelihood is farming.

Figure 4.2: Women in Niger.

CONTINUED

A married father will be at the head of the household. His wives (up to four are allowed) live with him, as do his sons and their wives and children. Child marriage is common; marriage is legal at 15 but many people marry at a younger age. More than half of all girls are married and pregnant by the age of 16. Marriages are arranged and it is very unusual for anyone to marry someone their family disapproves of.

Task

1   Look at Table 4.1. Which of Therborn's family types do you think Niger has? Why?

2   Make a list of ways in which the family in your country is the same as or different from that in Niger.

Social class

In some countries, there is a link between family types and social class; that is, people in different social classes tend to live in different types of family. In the UK in the 20th century, the extended family was strongly associated with the working class. Areas with older industries such as coal, steel and shipbuilding had strong working-class communities in which it was normal for young men and women to marry and stay close to their parents, creating modified extended families. With secure jobs, there was no reason for them to move away. These industries declined in the late 20th century and factories, mines and docks closed or were automated. As men lost their jobs, people moved away in search of work and extended family ties were weakened. This pattern has also occurred in other countries where there is migration to cities for employment. Globally, families in poorer regions are more likely to be extended, relying on relatives to support one another; poorer families are also likely to have more children who can contribute to the family's income.

Ethnicity

In some societies, different ethnic groups are associated with particular types of family. There may be differences between ethnic groups in, for example:

- family size, where different ethnicities tend on average to have more or fewer children or more extended family members compared to others

- marriage, for example between ethnic groups where arranged marriages are common and those where participants have greater choice

- the division of labour between genders.

ACTIVITY: WRITTEN 4.1

Write a summary (around 200 words) explaining how family types may vary based on culture, social class and ethnicity. Use examples to support your answer.

Sociological perspectives on family diversity

The New Right view

The New Right view on family diversity developed in the late 20th century. It was a response to the increase in family diversity and the perceived decline of the nuclear family in North America and Europe; it was also prompted by the changing roles of men and women in families and the increase in lone-parent families. New Right ideas and policies have been put forward by journalists and politicians, but also by some sociologists such as Charles Murray.

New Right thinkers say that we need to return to the nuclear family because the new diverse types of family cannot carry out important functions. In particular, they argue that children need to be raised in nuclear families, with both a mother and a father. According to the New Right, the changes that have undermined the family's functions include:

- the growth of lone-parent families

- the easier availability of divorce in some countries

- **cohabitation** (because the couple are not married, cohabiting relationships are seen as unstable and unsuitable for bringing up children)

- the rise of feminism (seen by the New Right as making women unhappy with their roles in the family)

- women going out to work (seen as having negative effects on children).

The New Right believes these changes are related to or responsible for several social problems, such as children failing in school, rising rates of crime and delinquency, and a dependency culture in which people rely on welfare benefits and are not interested in working. The welfare state, together with these other changes, disturbs the 'natural' order of family life, interfering with relationships between men and women and the way that children are raised. This creates **dysfunctional families**. In particular, the New Right argues that boys brought up by a lone mother do not have a role model for how males should behave – working to support a partner and a family, whom they treat with respect and restraint. New Right politicians support cutting welfare benefits, encouraging women not to work and strengthening the nuclear family headed by a male breadwinner.

The New Right view has been strongly attacked by other sociologists, particularly those who take a feminist view, including Pamela Abbott, Claire Wallace and Melissa Tyler. They argue in favour of people's right to live however they wish – including living alone, in a same-sex couple, in a lone-parent family or with a female breadwinner supporting a househusband who cares for the children. Different kinds of family work for different people, and children can be brought up just as well by a lone parent as by two parents; this may even be better if the absent partner provided unreliable economic support, behaved violently or was an alcoholic. They argue that lone parents (in particular, lone mothers) usually struggle because of poverty and so they need *more* financial support, rather than reduction of any welfare benefits.

Postmodernist view

While the New Right see the growth of new family types as causing social problems, postmodernists see it much more positively. People are no longer held back by traditional values and practices. They can make decisions for themselves as individuals, rather than having their choices constrained by family, gender, social class or religion. This gives them a range of possibilities for how to live – whether in families or in alternatives to families – that have not been available to people before.

Other sociologists say that postmodernists exaggerate how much diversity there is now and how much choice people have. Many people live in communities and societies where they are still expected to follow conventional family patterns and roles, and those who do not may be ostracised or stigmatised. There are also many people who find the number of new options overwhelming and prefer to do what worked for their parents and grandparents.

MAKING CONNECTIONS

How does the postmodernist view on family diversity link with the postmodernist view on identities, seen in section 2.3?

The extent of family diversity and the dominance of the nuclear family

The views of the New Right and postmodernists assume that family diversity is far greater now than in the past. But how much diversity is there really? Diversity is greatest in Europe and North America. Even there, however, more traditional types of family are still common. In the UK in 2021, an opposite-sex married couple with dependent children was the second most common family type. The most common was an opposite-sex married couple with no children – which would include married couples who have not yet had children, and married couples whose children have left home.

KEY TERMS

cohabitation: when two people who are not married to each other live together in a sexual relationship

dysfunctional family: a family that fails to carry out the expected functions; for example, where children are neglected

So, even in countries where diversity has increased, most people spend a large part of their lives in nuclear families. This is also what many people in these countries think of when they imagine a family: a mother and father and their children.

> ### STRETCH AND CHALLENGE
>
> How far is it true to say that most people still see the nuclear family as the ideal type?

Alternatives to the family

This section describes alternatives to the family, including other types of household. Not everyone lives in a family. Some people live alone or with friends who are not their family. Sociologists are interested in the different living arrangements people have. When a family lives together, there is a family household. But there are other types of household and ways of living that are, in some ways, strikingly different from families.

Single-person households

In many societies, there are growing numbers of **single-** or **one-person households**. For example, in Germany more than 40% of households are one person; in the Swedish city of Stockholm, it is over 60%. This has been a trend since the mid-20th century. It is not an even pattern around the world, however; in countries such as Pakistan and Myanmar, there are very few single-person households.

Four main types of people live alone:

- Older people, who are widowed and whose children have moved away. About half of people living alone are older people.

- Young adults who have moved out of their parents' home but are not yet married or living with a partner.

- People who choose to live alone. These are often women who have chosen to focus on a career rather than a relationship. Some may be men or women who have never found another person they want to live with.

> ### KEY TERM
>
> **single-person/one-person household:** when only one person lives in a residence

- People who are separated and divorced. This group is mainly made up of men: the woman often stays in the family home with the children, becoming a lone-parent family, while the man moves out. There are also smaller numbers of women who move out and live on their own, while the father stays with the children.

In Europe and North America, the number of single-person households has increased as a result of greater opportunities for women, the decline in the pressure to marry and the increased number of divorces.

Shared households

Some people share a household with people they are not related to. By sharing, we usually mean they use a common entrance to the property and share the use of some rooms, such as the living room, kitchen or bathroom. This could include groups of students sharing a house at university, and groups of young professionals sharing a house to save money early in their careers.

Friends as family

Figure 4.3: Friends as family.

For some people, a friendship group functions in the same way as a family, providing love and support. This idea of **friends as family** may be important for

> ### KEY TERM
>
> **friends as family:** when friendships between people who are not related to each other form a support network similar to a more traditional family

people who live far away from their relatives, who do not have any close family or who do not have any contact with their family for some reason. Some sociologists argue that, because family life is more uncertain than it used to be, people may rely more on their friends than on their family. For example:

- Friends have become very important for young people who are establishing their independence from their parents.

- Friends may play a greater part in emotional, practical and social support.

- Friendships with other unattached people become important for divorced and separated people.

Young people in particular tend to rely on friends from their own age group. Groups of young people sharing a house have become more common. Shared households often exist for economic reasons; buying or renting a house with a group of friends may be the only way people can afford to live somewhere. But the change also reflects the importance of friends in young people's lives. Friendships are different from family ties in several ways. Family relationships are sometimes very unequal, while friendships are often based strongly on equality and usually involve people of similar age. However, the family is still important in many ways, with commitments which rarely apply to friends, for example care of older people and the inheritance of property.

Variations in types of marriage

Arranged marriage

In some cultures, parents or other family members decide who their children will marry or provide them with a choice by arranging introductions to potential partners. The bride and groom have usually agreed that their parents will do this, often with the help of a matchmaker. **Arranged marriages** were once the norm in many countries, and still are in countries such as Pakistan and Egypt. Because they are based on negotiations between families, they often involve the traditional practices of dowry (money paid or property given by the bride's family to the groom or his family) and bride price (payment by the groom or his family to the bride's family). Supporters of arranged marriages today point out that **love marriages** are based on feelings which can decrease over time; arranged marriages, in which the partners do not have expectations based on being in love, are more likely to last.

Love marriage

Arranged marriages have been common throughout history, but love marriages were unusual until fairly recently. Love marriages are decided by the couple, with or without the consent of their families. Today, the term is rarely used in Europe, North America and South America – where it is assumed that all marriages are love marriages. Where arranged marriages are still the norm, as in India, Pakistan, Sri Lanka and Nepal, the term is still used.

> **TIP**
>
> Laws about same-sex partnerships and marriages have recently changed in some countries and there will have been further changes by the time you read this book. As with all information in textbooks, it is worth making sure the facts you use in your answers are up to date.

Same-sex marriage

Same-sex families, where both parents are either male or female, are becoming more common and more acceptable in many countries. At the time of writing (in 2022), 31 countries allowed same-sex couples to marry. Most of these countries are in North America, South America and Europe, but same-sex marriage is also recognised in Australia, New Zealand, Taiwan and South Africa. In other countries that do not recognise such relationships, same-sex couples may cohabit but do not have the same legal rights. There are also countries which allow **civil partnerships**, in which a couple has a legally recognised relationship with many or all of the same legal rights as marriage.

> **KEY TERMS**
>
> **arranged marriage:** a marriage in which the partners are chosen by older family members, rather than people choosing their own marriage partner
>
> **love marriage:** a marriage where the couple decide to get married, with or without the consent of their families
>
> **civil partnership:** a relationship between two people, often of the same sex, that has been formally registered, giving them the same or similar legal rights to married couples

These were mainly introduced before the legalisation of same-sex marriage, to provide legal rights for same-sex couples. However, in some countries, including the UK, opposite-sex couples can now also form civil partnerships.

Empty-shell marriage

An **empty-shell marriage** exists when a married couple continue to live together – and may appear to the outside world to be a 'normal' married couple – but they no longer have an intimate relationship or affectionate feelings towards each other. The couple may remain together, rather than separate or divorce, for financial reasons; they may be unable to afford to live apart. Other couples stay together because they have dependent children and they do not want to disrupt their lives.

Monogamy

Monogamy is the practice of marrying one person at a time. In many countries, it is the only legal type of marriage. If either person tries to marry again without their first marriage coming to an end – through death or divorce – they are committing a criminal offence and the second 'marriage' would not be legally recognised.

Serial monogamy

In the UK and other modern industrial societies, the **divorce rate** increased during the 20th century. As a result, **serial monogamy** has become more common. This is when a person has several marriage partners over their lifetime, but only one at a time. Today, many people are married more than once in their lives because they remarry after the death of a partner or after divorce.

Polygamy

Polygamy is a marriage that involves at least three people. It can take two forms: polygyny is when a man has more than one wife, and polyandry is when a woman has more than one husband. These arrangements can be a rational adaptation to unusual circumstances, for example if there is an imbalance between the numbers of men and women. After a war has reduced the numbers of men of fighting and marrying age, a group can grow more rapidly if the surviving men are allowed to marry and have children by several women.

Examples of polyandry are rare and usually involve a woman marrying two or more brothers. This is known as fraternal polyandry. It has been practised in Tibet, where it helped to prevent the division of scarce farming land into areas too small to support a family: instead, the land

was shared between brothers and their children by the same wife.

Polygyny is far more widespread. It is allowed by law in most of Africa and the Middle East, and in parts of southern Asia. Islam allows a man to have up to four wives. However, even in these countries, most marriages are monogamous, because it is expensive for a man to support several wives and their children.

Jacob Zuma, the President of South Africa from 2009 to 2018, is one of the world's best-known polygamists. In April 2012, he married for the sixth time; at the time, he had three other wives, with one having died and another divorced. Polygamy is allowed in South Africa by the Customary Marriages Act.

Figure 4.4: Jacob Zuma and three of his wives.

KEY TERMS

empty-shell marriage: when a married couple continue to live together, but without love or affection

monogamy: being married to one person at a time

divorce rate: the number of divorces in a year per 1000 people in a population

serial monogamy: when someone has more than one marriage partner during their life, but only one at a time

polygamy: being married to more than one person at the same time; for example, a man with several wives or a woman with several husbands

TIP

Monogamy, and related terms such as polygamy, have in the past always referred to marriage. Today, however, they are often applied more generally to long-term relationships. For example, people may describe their relationship as monogamous if they are having only one romantic relationship at the time. When answering questions in sociology, it is best to use monogamy and polygamy in relation to marriage only, to avoid any confusion.

Group marriages are a fourth possible structure for relationships between husband and wife (after monogamy, polygyny and polyandry). In a group marriage, there are two or more husbands and two or more wives. Although unusual, this may be a recognised form of marriage, and being unfaithful with someone outside the marriage would be treated in the same way as infidelity in another form of marriage.

CHECK YOUR UNDERSTANDING 4.1

1   Write a paragraph explaining the differences between the following types of extended family:

- vertically extended family

- horizontally extended family

- modified extended family.

2   Working with a partner, take it in turns to explain the following types of family and marriage:

- beanpole family
- empty-nest family

- same-sex family
- reconstituted family

- dual worker family
- empty-shell marriage

- symmetrical family
- monogamy

- polygamy.

KEY POINTS

- Different types of family include:

  - nuclear

  - extended

  - reconstituted

  - same-sex

  - lone parent

  - polygamous

  - empty nest

  - childless.

- There are strengths and limitations to different types of family.

- There are variations and diversity in the family, depending on culture, social class and ethnicity.

- There are different sociological views on family diversity:

  - New Right view

  - postmodernist view.

- The extent of family diversity and the dominance of the nuclear family is debated by sociologists.

- Alternatives to the family include:

  - single-person households

  - shared households

  - friends as family.

- Variations in types of marriage include:

  - arranged

  - love

  - same-sex

  - empty shell

  - monogamy

  - serial monogamy

  - polygamy.

4.2 What is the role of the family for the individual and society?

> ## MAKING CONNECTIONS
>
> 1 What can you remember about the following three theories in sociology?
>
>   - functionalism
>   - Marxism
>   - feminism.
>
> 2 How is each of these theories likely to view the family, its roles and functions?

Functionalist views on the role of the family

How the family benefits its members and society: its functions

Functionalists argue that certain essential tasks or functions must be performed for society to work. They argue that the family is the foundation of every society because it carries out several vital functions. Most functionalists agree on the following **family functions**:

- **Reproduction.** Societies must produce new generations of children to survive, and marriage and the family are closely associated with having children. Reproduction within a stable family setting is encouraged.

- **Socialisation.** Children need to learn the norms and values of their society, and this happens through **primary socialisation** in their families. Families transmit the culture of the society to the next generation; they are the vital link between individuals and the wider society.

- **Social control.** This is closely related to socialisation and refers to the ways in which children's behaviour is controlled, so they conform to norms. For example, they may be punished for being 'naughty'

or rewarded for behaviour their parents define as 'good'.

- **Roles for family members.** Different family members have different roles – a father or mother, a husband or wife, a son or daughter, etc. Functionalists argue that the gender roles in nuclear families suit the nature of males and females. The natural role of the man is instrumental (the 'breadwinner') and the natural role of the woman is expressive. Because this division of labour is seen as natural by functionalists, carrying out these gender roles is functional both for society and for individuals.

- **Care of children and of older people and sick people.** Children need to be fed, clothed, sheltered and nurtured, intellectually and emotionally. In the family, people are given responsibility to ensure this happens, with older and younger members looking after each other in different ways at different times.

- **Status.** Families provide status for children, by involving them in a web of interpersonal and group relationships.

- **Regulation of sexual behaviour.** All societies seem to set rules about what kind of sexual behaviour is accepted, with whom and in what circumstances. Although sex outside marriage is tolerated in Western Europe and in parts of the USA, most societies insist that children are born to people in a socially approved sexual relationship.

Notice that some of these functions are for individuals and some are for society as a whole. Other functions are for both; for example, primary socialisation helps individuals to fit in and avoid conflict with others, but it also helps a society to survive by passing on its norms and values to a new generation. The roles of men and women in families help them to lead fulfilling lives, but also help to keep society stable. The family acts as a bridge between individuals and the wider society.

> ## KEY TERMS
>
> **family functions:** the functions of the family; the roles it plays and for whom, according to functionalist theory
>
> **primary socialisation:** the process by which infants and young children absorb the basic norms and values of their culture (see Unit 2)

The loss of functions debate and how family functions have changed over time

By the 20th century, the nuclear family was the main type of family in societies in Europe and North America. These societies changed rapidly because of industrialisation and urbanisation. The extended families of pre-industrial society were ideally suited to the demands of family-based subsistence farming. As industrialisation spread, however, extended families were replaced by nuclear families that were better suited to the new ways of life. Nuclear families allowed people to move to jobs in the new and growing towns and cities.

At the same time, there was a big increase in the number and influence of some large organisations: more school and colleges, more hospitals and health services, expanded transport systems, etc. The state also began to provide more support for people in need; pensions and the welfare state began.

The functionalist sociologist Talcott Parsons suggested reasons why the nuclear family can be said to fit modern industrial societies so well. In the past, people had to rely on the family to meet many needs; for example, to care for them when they were sick or old, to lend or give them money when they had none, and to teach them the knowledge and skills they would need as an adult. A large family made it more likely that help would be available. Today, these functions have been taken over, to a large extent, by other institutions. Modern economies also need workers who are willing to move to where the jobs are, and nuclear families can move more easily than extended ones.

Functionalists expect families to change over time because, to be functional, they have to meet the needs

Figure 4.5: Talcott Parsons.

of societies. The extended family fulfilled important functions in the past, when state-run education and healthcare were less common and the extended family could meet these needs instead. Today, the nuclear family fulfils important functions in many societies. For example, as societies industrialised they needed greater movement of labour into growing towns and cities, and nuclear families were better able to meet this need. This functionalist view is that each society will have the type of family that best fits its needs.

Function	Traditional societies: Extended families	Modern industrial societies: Nuclear families
Care of very young children	Parents supported by extended family members	Parents supported by professionals, such as nurses and nursery teachers
Care of the elderly	Extended family	Pensions, residential care, health services and social services
Care of the sick	Extended family	Health services, doctors, nurses, hospitals
Help with work, e.g. on a farm at harvest time	Family and neighbours	No longer usually required
Education	Family, community	Schools and media
Financial support in times of crisis	Extended family	Welfare state, savings, borrowing from banks and other institutions

Table 4.2: Functions of the family.

The loss of functions debate considers the extent to which the family has lost some, or even all, of its functions in society today, as other institutions of society have taken over. The extent to which this actually happens varies between societies. Parsons argued that the family's functions had declined but it still had two basic functions that no other institution could perform:

- primary socialisation
- stabilisation of adult personalities – by this, he meant the way that the family provides a role and a sense of responsibility for adults.

Parsons argued that the nuclear family was still essential for society and for individuals because of the importance of these functions.

'Warm bath' theory

Figure 4.6: The warm bath theory.

One need that arose with industrialisation and urbanisation was for male workers to have a place where they could recover from the stresses and dangers of working in places like factories and mines.

The working day was long and difficult. In order to keep returning to work each day, to earn a wage to support their families, men needed to be able to rest, relax and be looked after. The family took on this new role: women became housewives who looked after the home and their husband, cooking food, washing clothes and providing emotional comfort. The way in which the family does this is sometimes called the 'warm bath' theory, because a warm bath can relax you, leaving you refreshed.

Importance of the nuclear family

Functionalists argue that the important functions identified by Parsons (primary socialisation of children and stabilisation of adult personalities) are performed best in the nuclear family. The nuclear family also meets the emotional and economic needs of all family members. In nuclear families, mothers take responsibility for the emotional and home-based needs, and fathers take responsibility for the economic and material well-being needs of the family. However, other sociologists argue that these functions and needs can be met by other types of family – and perhaps by arrangements that are not families at all. For example, in the past, primary socialisation was often the responsibility of extended families and communities; in modern industrial societies, in contrast, some socialisation and childcare functions are performed by schools and other institutions.

Another challenge to functionalism is that, although the family may fulfil wider functions, it is dysfunctional for some people. The anthropologist Edmund Leach suggested that the nuclear family in modern industrial societies was, in fact, dysfunctional. The image of a happily married couple with healthy children – which Leach called the 'cereal packet' image of the family – was found everywhere in advertising and the media; it set up an ideal that many families could not reach, leading to pressure and tension.

KEY TERMS

'warm bath' theory: the functionalist theory that the family can act like a 'warm bath' for its members, especially men; for example, by soothing away the pressures of their day at work and making them feel relaxed and happy

cereal packet family: the stereotypical nuclear family of mother, father and children with traditional gender roles often shown in advertisements

Other evidence that nuclear families can be dysfunctional for at least some members comes from the perspectives of Marxism and feminism.

Marxist views on the role of the family

How the family benefits capitalism

Marxists agree with functionalists that families carry out important functions for society. However, they disagree with functionalists on what these functions are. For Marxists, the family functions for the benefit of capitalist society: as an institution, the family contributes to the continuation of an economic system. Friedrich Engels lived at the same time as Marx and collaborated with him. He showed that the family could only be understood in terms of its role within the economic system of a society. Before capitalism and the idea of private ownership, families were much looser sets of relationships, with no monogamy. In capitalist societies, where private property is owned and passed on, it was important for a man to know who his children were, so they could inherit his wealth. This led to the development of monogamous families.

According to Marxists, the following family functions benefit capitalism:

- With the family, each generation is socialised into accepting capitalism and its values. For example, many working-class people believe that the system is fair and their failure to succeed is their own fault.

- The family brings up children to be the next generation of workers, producing profits for capitalists.

- Workers with families are less able to go on strike (withdraw their labour in protest against their employer), because then they would not be able to support their families.

- Men who are oppressed and alienated at work can compensate for this in the family, where they are in control. They take out their anger and frustration from work on their wives and children.

- The family is the main unit of consumption: families support the capitalist system by buying and consuming goods.

- Part of women's role is to look after sick and old people. The ruling class therefore avoids responsibility for health and social care.

Exploitation of family members

In a capitalist society, according to Marxists, the bourgeoisie or ruling class oppress the proletariat or working class (all those who have to work for a living). In other words, workers are exploited. The proletariat make things from which the bourgeoisie can make a profit. But the proletariat are only paid a fraction of the value of what they produce. The family plays a part in helping this unjust system survive. According to Marxists, workers may be powerless at work, constantly told what to do by their bosses, but at home they can be patriarchs, demanding service and obedience. This may prevent them from rebelling against their employers, since they maintain some form of power and control over their lives, within the family. A counterargument is that the family provides a safe haven from exploitation at work, where the man can relax and recover – the warm bath theory in functionalism.

Reproduction of class inequalities

One of the functions of the family is the reproduction of the labour force. By having children, families provide a new generation of workers to be exploited by the bourgeoisie. Moreover, the children of workers see their parents' situation – and that of other families around them – and learn that there is little they can do to change this. Boys may grow up accepting that they have to do similar work to their fathers. Girls may grow up accepting that their role is to be the housewife, looking after home and family, sometimes with limited resources. A few exceptionally able or lucky people may improve their situation. For most, however, their class position will remain the same and the capitalist system will maintain class inequalities.

The family as a unit of consumption

Before industrialisation and urbanisation, the family was a unit of production and this production was the family's source of livelihood.

For example, if a family had a farm, the father and older boy children would plant, manage and harvest crops, and look after large animals such as cows or pigs. The mother and older girls would look after smaller animals (such as hens), collect eggs, make clothes and foods (such as cheese and butter) and also cook, fetch water and look after the home. A lot of what they used and ate came from the farm. Anything extra was sold at market and the money used to buy items they could not supply for themselves. There was often a gendered division of labour but the family worked as a unit to support each other.

This changed with industrialisation and urbanisation, because men and boys increasingly did other types of work outside the home, for example in factories and mines. Many working-class women also went out to work, but usually in different kinds of work to the males in their family. Rather than growing or making the things they needed, families now earned a wage so they could buy these items. As standards of living gradually improved, families began to buy more things for their homes as they became available, such as electric goods, cars and furniture. Families changed from being units of production to units of consumption. The Marxist view of the family as a unit of consumption is that it deepens the exploitation of workers: they are pressured by advertising to buy more and more things that they do not need or really want, which makes profits for the bourgeoisie.

Figure 4.7: Family consumerism.

Family and ideological control

According to Marxists, the family today plays an important role in the legitimisation and continuation of capitalism through ideology – a dominant system of ideas. Through the family, children absorb the capitalist ideology that justifies the way things are, learning their place in the world. They also absorb messages about

accepting the hierarchy, and about how they should want to buy and own more things. Some families try to resist – for example, parents may not want to buy toys for their children that they know will soon be broken or ignored. But this resistance is likely to be outweighed by the transmission of capitalist ideas by the media, peers and other agencies of socialisation.

Feminist views on the role of the family

How the family benefits patriarchy

Feminists see the nuclear family as functional for a **patriarchal** society. Within the family, men have more powerful and privileged roles, so it is a patriarchal institution.

Feminists see the family as having several functions. Traditional gender roles make men the breadwinner and head of the household. Men benefit from the family because they have a wife who is expected to look after their needs: to cook, clean, support her husband emotionally and put her husband's interests before her own. Families socialise both boys and girls into gender roles. A son or male heir traditionally inherits the family's wealth, so wealth and power stay with males. According to feminists, patriarchy in the family is the basis of patriarchy in wider society. The overall function of the family is to maintain the patriarchy, so families are functional for men.

There are three main strands in feminist thinking: liberal, Marxist and radical (see section 2.1). Liberal feminists believe that equality can be achieved without fundamental changes to the nature of society. Progress can be made by, for example, persuading men to do more housework, bringing up children in non-sexist ways and encouraging women to have careers. To both Marxist and radical feminists, such changes are unlikely to achieve much, because society would still be patriarchal. For radical feminists, society needs to change completely. If the relationships between men and women are based on male superiority, then women need to stay out of such exploitative relationships and live separately from men. For them, the exploitation of women within families is part of a wider exploitative system.

The domestic division of labour

Many feminists are concerned with the way in which women are expected to take on all or most of the responsibility for looking after the home and family members. The way in which tasks are divided within the home (such as who does the cooking and cleaning) is called the **domestic division of labour**.

Feminists in the late 20th century wanted the domestic division of labour in families to change and become more equal. They saw this as an important step in moving towards **gender equality** in society as a whole. Research suggests there has been some progress towards more equal families, but this has been quite slow. Feminists argue that as long as society remains patriarchal, the domestic division of labour will be unequal. Some men will help their wives with housework and childcare, but the main responsibility will stay with the woman. This view is supported by research showing that even when men and women do paid work for the same number of hours, the woman still does considerably more housework. Changes in roles and responsibilities are explored further in section 4.3.

KEY TERMS

domestic division of labour: the way in which tasks in the home (such as cooking, cleaning, childcare and repairs) are divided between men and women

gender equality: where men and women are treated the same and have equal outcomes in all aspects of society

CASE STUDY 4.2

A Marxist feminist view of the nuclear family: *The Anti-Social Family* (1982) by Barrett and McIntosh

In this book, Barrett and McIntosh argue that the nuclear family is antisocial because it is so widely seen and considered (by functionalists, for example) to be the only good kind of family. The media promote the idea that we should all aim for a nuclear family, and that the alternatives do not work.

According to Barrett and McIntosh, however, the nuclear family does not work for many people.

Figure 4.8: Family arguments.

CONTINUED

Relationships in the nuclear family often fail because families are unequal and create stress. But people – especially women – are made to feel that they are to blame for these failed relationships. Women are even paid less than men because of the family. In the past, men argued for pay increases on the grounds that they had to support their families; today, women's paid work tends to be seen as an extra for her family and is therefore underpaid and undervalued.

Task

1 What do Barrett and McIntosh mean by describing nuclear families as antisocial?

2 What is it about Barrett and McIntosh's views that shows they have a Marxist feminist perspective?

Domestic violence and abuse

One of the main concerns of many feminists is violence and abuse within families. For a long time, **domestic violence** was rarely talked about or dealt with effectively by the authorities. There was a widespread belief that what happened in the family home was private – a matter for the family and not for the police or social workers. It was also sometimes believed that men had a right to use physical force against their wives if there was some justification. In the 1970s, two sociologists, Russell and Rebecca Dobash, researched domestic violence in Scotland. They showed that it was widespread and so could not be explained as just the behaviour of a few disturbed individuals. They found examples of women being pushed, slapped, beaten, raped and even killed by their husbands. These incidents often occurred when the man thought his authority was being challenged – for example, if his wife asked why he was home late. Feminists argue that within marriage, the man has power and authority and

this can make violence against wives seem acceptable. Although many men condemn violence against women, some feminists argue that all men benefit from it, because it reinforces the patriarchal nature of the family and of society.

In most cases of domestic violence, the offenders are men and the victims are usually women and sometimes children. However, men are sometimes the victims. It has been suggested that cases of domestic violence in which men are the victims are the least likely to be reported, because men see it as a sign of weakness or a failure of their masculinity, so they may not seek help.

Domestic violence is now recognised as a crime in almost all countries. It can be difficult for the police and courts to act, however, because a lot of domestic violence is not reported. This may be because the victims:

- feel that the police will be unable or unwilling to do anything
- fear that the violence will become worse if they tell someone about it
- are afraid of losing contact with their children
- believe the abuse is normal or that they deserve it
- believe that they will be able to change the abuser's behaviour
- believe that the abuser is still a good person
- still love the abuser.

KEY TERM

domestic violence: violence within the family, usually – but not always – by males against females; the term refers not only to physical violence but also to patterns of controlling behaviour that may include emotional manipulation

Most victims are assaulted many times before they report the violence. They may feel trapped because they do not have friends or family to discuss their problem with or they do not have the money or independence to be able to leave the relationship.

Children can also be the victims of violence and abuse within families. Not all children experience the family as a loving place of safety. For some, the family is dangerous and exploitative. In modern industrial societies, there are many reported cases of child abuse and neglect; much of this is caused by parents or step-parents, often (but not always) by males. Some of these cases have received a lot of news coverage, becoming national scandals. It is likely that, as with domestic abuse, the increase in cases of child abuse and neglect is largely a result of increased reporting: there are not actually more cases, but more cases are known about.

Child abuse is usually seen as having four possible forms:

- sexual abuse
- physical abuse
- emotional abuse
- neglect.

In addition, many children live in difficult and even dangerous situations, for example living with someone with mental problems or being a carer for an adult or for other children.

Joint and segregated conjugal roles

Feminists reject the functionalist view of gendered **family roles** as fair and natural (discussed earlier in this section). Roles in a marriage – **conjugal roles** – can be classified as either **segregated conjugal roles** or **joint conjugal roles**. Segregated or separated roles are associated with the traditional nuclear family, with clearly different roles for men and women. Joint or integrated conjugal roles mean that men and women share instrumental and expressive roles; their roles are not separate. Feminists argue that the segregated conjugal roles found in many nuclear families – and favoured by functionalists – benefit men and show that the family is patriarchal.

The following features of the female domestic role make it different from paid work:

- It is unpaid.
- There are no starting and finishing times.
- There are no benefits, such as a contract, holidays and pensions.
- It is not seen as 'real' work, so it has low status.
- It is solitary and gives little sense of achievement because there is always more to do.

Dual burden and triple shift

Although the domestic division of labour is still unequal, men and women in Europe and North America today are usually expected to do both paid and domestic work. For women, this can mean a **dual burden**; they do paid work but they do most of the domestic work as well. Duncombe and Marsden found in their research that women actually do a **triple shift**: alongside paid work and housework, they perform emotional work, supporting all other family members with their worries and concerns.

Power inequalities

Feminists are greatly concerned with inequalities of power within the family. In patriarchal families, males have – and exercise – power over women and children. The extreme outcome of this can be seen in cases of domestic violence and abuse. Even in families which are not physically abusive, women often put their husband's interests before their own. One reason for power inequalities, besides the patriarchal nature of families, is that women have less financial independence. Even a woman who works is likely to earn less than her husband and so may be financially reliant on him.

Decision-making

Power inequalities affect decision-making within families. Decisions are usually made by the man; even when there is discussion, decisions are likely to be based on his interests. For example, when a couple who both work have their first child, the woman is likely to take more parental leave. This may be because of views about the importance of the mother; it is also likely that the woman earns less than her partner, so it will damage the family less financially. Another example could be deciding to move home: a family is more likely to move for the man's career than the woman's.

Women do, of course, make some decisions, but these are often about the home or children – the woman's traditional areas of responsibility. In these areas, the man can concede control with no threat to his dominant position in the family.

Gendered socialisation

Feminists are concerned with the ways in which boys and girls are socialised into gender roles within families. This has been considered in section 2.1.

STRETCH AND CHALLENGE

How far do you agree with the feminist view that the family has a negative impact on women but benefits men? How would you argue against the points that feminists make?

Debates about whether the experience of family life is positive or negative for family members

The experiences of family members are viewed differently by the main sociological viewpoints. Table 4.3 summarises these differences.

View	Positive experience	Negative experience
Functionalist	men women children	
Marxist		men women children
Feminist	men	women children

Table 4.3: Experiences of different family members according to sociological viewpoints.

TIP

When explaining each of the sociological perspectives on the family, try to present the view positively, as if you really believe in what it says. Then evaluate it by considering its limitations.

ACTIVITY: DISCUSSION 4.2

In a group of three, take one theory each (functionalism, Marxism, feminism). Speak for one minute each, explaining your theory on the role of the family to the other two members of your group. Then discuss all three views together in your group:

a   Which one is the easiest to explain?

b   Which one is the most convincing?

Strengths and limitations of functionalist, Marxist and feminist views of the role of the family

Table 4.4 summarises the strengths and limitations of different views of the role of the family.

View	Strengths	Limitations
Functionalist	• Most people still live most of their lives in nuclear families, which supports the functionalist view that they are normal or natural. • Recognises that families are a positive experience for many people and for society.	• This is how middle-class white American men (like Parsons) experienced families. It is idealistic and does not recognise the darker side of family life, such as violence and abuse. • Does not recognise that non-nuclear families can be better, and just as effective in carrying out family functions. • Outdated and sexist: women may not want to be housewives and mothers, and men may want to play a bigger part in family life.
Marxist	• Shows how nuclear families are linked with and support the capitalist economy. • Explains the importance of families in capitalist society. • Explains the role of families in consumerism.	• Does not offer a practical alternative to how we should live – even non-capitalist societies have families. • Narrow view concentrating on work and the economy. • Does not acknowledge the importance of families to people at a personal level. • Tends to overlook the oppression of women.
Feminist	• Draws attention to neglected aspects of families – especially power inequalities, violence, abuse and domestic work. • Challenges the functionalist view of nuclear families as functional for everyone. • Values different kinds of families and relationships, without assuming one is better. • Sees the positive side of changes such as more divorce, more cohabitation, etc.	• Many women seem content with nuclear families; they do not find them oppressive and they find motherhood a positive experience. • Feminists tend to see all male–female relationships as involving the exploitation of women, but many relationships are based on love and respect.

Table 4.4: Strengths and limitations of different views.

KEY POINTS

- Functionalist views of the family focus on:
    - how the family benefits its members and society
    - the functions of the family
    - the loss of functions debate
    - how family functions have changed over time
    - the 'warm bath' theory
    - the importance of the nuclear family.
- Marxist views of the family focus on:
    - how the family benefits capitalism
    - the exploitation of family members
    - the reproduction of class inequalities
    - the family as a unit of consumption
    - family and ideological control.
- Feminist views of the family focus on:
    - how the family benefits patriarchy
    - the domestic division of labour
    - domestic violence and abuse
    - joint and segregated conjugal roles
    - the dual burden
    - the triple shift
    - power inequalities
    - decision-making
    - gendered socialisation.
- There are debates between these views about whether the experience of family life is positive or negative for family members.
- Each view has strengths and limitations.

4.3. How is family life changing?

Demographic factors and their effects on family life

The family is affected by **demographic trends** (changes in a population). In this section, we discuss family size, birth rates, life expectancy, the ageing population and having children in later life.

TIP

Remember that trends refer to changes over time, whereas patterns are differences within the data, for example between countries or age groups.

Family size and birth rates

Historians have argued that in the past, children were seen as an economic benefit to the family. There was only a short period when parents had to support children – usually up until the age of six or seven. After this age, children were expected to work and contribute to the family. Children would also look after their parents in sickness and old age. Therefore, families would benefit financially from having more children. This argument has also been applied to less developed countries today.

In modern industrial societies, the **birth rate** has fallen dramatically and mothers are having fewer children (a falling **fertility rate**). This means that family size has become smaller. There are several reasons for this:

KEY TERMS

demographic trends: changes in a population, such as the birth rate and death rate

birth rate: the number of live births per 1000 people in the population in one year

fertility rate: the number of live births per 1000 women of child-bearing age in the population in one year

- It is now very expensive to raise children, because they can no longer do paid work and instead depend on their parents over a long period of education. They have become an economic cost rather than a benefit.

- Fewer children die so parents can have fewer children and be fairly sure they will survive.

- It is no longer essential to have children to look after you when you are old: pensions and investments mean that older people can support themselves, and health and social services can provide care.

- Contraception is widely available, especially the contraceptive pill for women, which has allowed people to control the number of children they have. In Western Europe and parts of the USA, contraception is also more widely used because of **secularisation** and the decline of religious views against contraception.

- Having a smaller family makes it easier to move geographically, for example for a new job opportunity.

- Opportunities for women in paid work are restricted if they have many children.

Some married couples choose not to have children. They may adopt a lifestyle focused on success in their careers and shared leisure activities that leave little time for children. There may be less pressure than in the past from other family members to have children. Couples who both work and who do not have children are referred to as DINK families – 'double income, no kids'. They are often much better off financially than those who have children.

Life expectancy

As the birth rate has fallen, so has the **death rate**.

> **KEY TERM**
>
> **secularisation:** the process by which religion has become less important in the daily lives of many people in modern industrial societies

> **KEY TERM**
>
> **death rate:** the number of deaths per 1000 people in a population in one year; also called the mortality rate

---

CASE STUDY 4.3

DINKs in China

A survey in China's main cities in 2003 found a significant increase in DINK families, with an estimated 10,000 such families in Beijing alone. Only 37 per cent of families in Chinese cities are now nuclear families.

In the past in China, childbearing was a family's top priority. Today, however, it is regarded as a personal choice by many young couples. According to the Chinese news website People Daily, Zheng Jian, a 38-year-old businessman, and his wife Xiao Yan, a graphic designer, think their two-person family is one of the happiest in the world. They have been married for more than 10 years and have no children. 'We always have so many plans to do things together,' Zheng said. 'It seems like we are two kids who like playing together.' They insist: 'We are satisfied with our present lives, so why bother with children?'

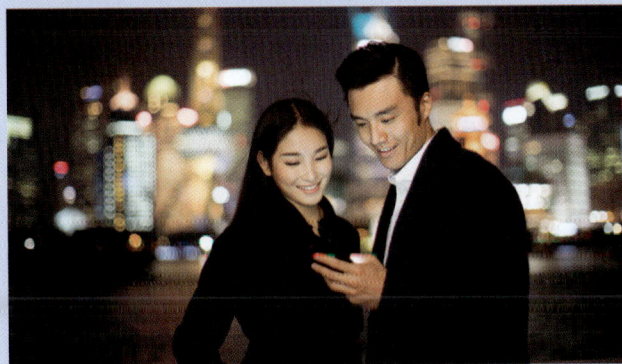

Figure 4.9: A young couple in China.

Task

1   What does the increase in DINK families suggest about traditional values in China?

2   What are some of the likely consequences if more couples decide not to have children?

Life expectancy all around the world has increased dramatically over the last two hundred years, despite wars, disasters and pandemics. In particular, the infant mortality rate (deaths of infants less than one year old) and the child mortality rate (deaths of children aged one to five) have fallen almost everywhere over the last century. The average life expectancy globally is now 73, with the lowest being the Central African Republic at 53 and the highest being Hong Kong at 85. There are many variations between countries; for example, life expectancy is 68 in Pakistan, 75 in Mauritius, 79 in the USA and 82 in the UK.

Some reasons for the fall in global death rates are:

- improved running water, sewage disposal and sanitation

- advances in preventing and treating diseases

- higher living standards, especially better diets

- fewer deaths related to work because of safer, healthier conditions

- better education and health care

- vaccination of children against diseases.

Developing countries tend to have higher death, birth and fertility rates than developed ones. These rates usually fall during industrialisation. The death rate falls first, so there is a growth in population, then the birth rate falls later. As we have seen, high birth rates are due to factors such as mothers' lack of education and access to contraception, as well as high infant and child mortality rates. Once the impact of these factors is reduced – for example, as more girls go to school and more people survive childhood – the birth rate falls.

Ageing population

In some countries, particularly in Europe and North America, the average age of the population is going up and older people make up a higher proportion of the population. This is known as an ageing population and occurs as life expectancy increases and fewer children are born.

Average ages vary significantly between countries. Most of Africa has low average ages, with high proportions of young people. In 2020, the average proportion of people over 65 in African countries was just 3.2 per cent; Mauritius has the highest proportion at 12.5 per cent, while Uganda has the lowest at 1.99 per cent. The UK, like many other modern industrial countries, has an ageing population. In 1901, under 5 per cent of the UK population were aged 65 and over.

By 2021, this was around 19 per cent. There has also been an increase in the numbers of very old people; for example, more people now live to be more than a hundred years old.

Old age is associated with retirement. In many countries, there is a legal age when people are expected to retire; they can then receive state benefits to help support them. Globally, retirement ages are increasing with life expectancy. Previously, many countries had lower retirement ages for women – and some still do – but these ages are more commonly becoming equal for men and women. The countries with the highest retirement ages include the Netherlands (68) and Greece, Italy and Norway (67).

Status depends to a considerable extent on occupation, so retirement brings a loss of status. This arguably affects men more than women because, for many women, status comes from their role as a mother, rather than from their occupation. However, occupation is becoming more important for many women as the main source of their identity and status.

Despite pensions, many older people rely on their children and, in particular, their daughters or daughters-in-law. In the past, one of the strongest reasons for having children was to ensure there was someone to care for you in old age; this remains important today. Many people – often those in the **pivot generation**, who have young children too – spend a lot of time and resources caring for ageing parents.

The consequences for families of an ageing population are likely to be:

- more older people living alone (single-person households) after the death of a partner

- a greater role for grandparents in supporting their children and grandchildren

- a greater burden for adult children looking after their ageing parents, perhaps even after they have reached retirement age themselves

- greater isolation and loneliness among older people

- a return in some families to the extended family, with three generations sharing the household.

KEY TERM

pivot/sandwich generation: middle-aged adults who care for their ageing parents, as well as for their children

Having children in later life

There is a trend for women to have their first child later in life. The UK Office for National Statistics found that there were twice as many pregnancies among the over 40s in 2018 than in the 1990s.

Having children late has some health risks for both the mother and the baby; however, these risks have been reduced by advances in medicine. New medical technologies also allow some women to have children at an age when this would not have been possible in the past.

A key reason for some women choosing to become mothers later is that they decide to pursue their education and a career before having children. This may also mean they are more financially secure. However, older parents may have less energy, and less support from their own parents, who will also be older.

The impact of industrialisation and urbanisation on family structures and roles

Functionalists argue that the modern nuclear family evolved from earlier types of family as society changed. An extended family suited the needs of pre-industrial societies, while the nuclear family is the most appropriate and beneficial form of family for modern industrial societies.

Urbanisation occurred at the same time as industrialisation, with large numbers of people moving to live in cities, which grew rapidly in size and number. For example, in the UK in 1800, 80% of the population lived in small villages, but by 1830, 50% of the population lived in towns. As farming became more difficult and manufacturing and trade became more important, people moved from villages to the new cities to earn a living. Urbanisation and industrialisation

KEY TERMS

urbanisation: the growth of cities; when a higher proportion of the population live in cities

industrialisation: the process in history in which societies changed from being mainly rural and based on agriculture to being urban and with more people working in industries

brought huge changes to the way people lived – including their family life. Families became smaller and more were nuclear.

These changes can be overstated. There were always some nuclear families in the past and, in the mid to late 20th century, sociologists Willmott and Young found that there were still strong extended families in working-class areas of London. Extended families lived close to each other – particularly mothers and their married daughters, who would live on the same street or very close by. This was possible because the men in these families worked in the same place, such as the docks.

However, when these old working-class areas were redeveloped, families moved out and the extended family bonds weakened. Women had less contact with their mothers because they lived further away. The nuclear family became the main form of family and the husband–wife bond became the main bond, replacing the mother–daughter one. Nuclear families had less interaction with neighbours, community and other relatives.

Explanations of changing patterns and trends in marriage, divorce and cohabitation

Marriage trends

Most people get married at some point in their lives. UN data shows that more than 90 per cent of people over 40 have been married.

Figure 4.10: A wedding in Mauritius.

Slightly more women than men are married, which reflects the pattern of women usually marrying men who are older than they are. This difference between the number of women and men who are married is seen more in younger age groups (for example, people in their 20s) and is much smaller for the over-40s.

Although most men and women eventually marry, the number of marriages has fallen in many countries in recent decades. For example, in the UK and Australia, the number of marriages has been falling for several decades. In the UK, the number of first marriages each year (between people getting married for the first time) fell by 50 per cent between 1970 and 2000. Over the two decades between 2000 and 2019, the marriage rate reduced by 23.7 per cent. In other countries – such as China, Russia and Bangladesh – marriages have become more common.

There are several key changes related to marriage. Compared with the period before 1975:

- more people now get married later in life. Between 1970 and 1999, the average age at first marriage worldwide was 24.3 for men and 21.1 for women; from 2000 to 2014, this had increased to 26.5 for men and 23.4 for women. These figures hide big differences between countries. In 2018, the average age of first marriage in Hungary was 34, whereas in Niger it was just 20.6.

- more people never marry at all

- more people divorce

- more people do not remarry after divorce or the death of their partner

- more couples live together without getting married (cohabiting). These partnerships are often long-term, and many cohabiting couples have children, but they do not appear in marriage statistics. Cohabitation is discussed later in this section.

A growing proportion of all marriages in modern industrial societies are now remarriages, in which one or both partners have already been married at least once. This has always happened to some extent, following the death of a partner, but today many people also remarry after divorce. Men are more likely to remarry than women. Remarriages create new reconstituted families with individuals gaining new relatives and new roles and relationships (see section 4.1).

Divorce trends

There has been a big increase in the divorce rate in many modern industrial countries. Large increases in divorce rates have occurred since laws changed, making divorce easier and more affordable. This suggests that many couples would have divorced previously if they had been allowed to.

Because divorce involves the legal ending of a marriage, the number of divorces can be recorded accurately. However, there are alternatives to divorce where the ending of a marriage is not officially recorded. This make it difficult to know the frequency of **marital breakdown**. Alternatives to divorce include:

- **Separation.** The partners stop living together. This often leads to divorce but it does not have to. Because separations are not recorded, it is difficult to know how many couples separate.

- **Desertion.** A type of separation in which one partner leaves the family. Again, there are no reliable figures for desertions.

- **Empty-shell marriage.** The couple continue to live together and appear to the outside world to be a married couple, but they no longer have an intimate relationship or affectionate feelings towards each other.

There are now more divorces globally than in the past. In 2020, the country with the highest divorce rate in the world was the Maldives, with a divorce rate of 5.52 per 1000 people. In the same year, Belgium had the highest divorce rate in Europe, at 3.7 per 1000 people, and the USA's divorce rate was 2.7 per 1000 people. Countries with the lowest divorce rates are mainly those where divorce is less acceptable, for religious or cultural reasons.

Islamic marriages can be ended by the man renouncing his wife. In European countries, however, it is usually women who decide to divorce their husbands, rather than the other way around. Women are also less likely to remarry after divorce than men.

Other features of divorce in Europe and North America today are:

- those who marry young are more likely to divorce

- middle-class people are less likely to divorce than working-class people (this is a reversal of the situation in the past, when only the well-off could afford divorce)

- those with strong religious beliefs are less likely to divorce; for example, Catholicism still forbids divorce, and a divorced person cannot remarry in a Catholic church.

It has been suggested that the following factors lead more people to divorce:

- Changes in laws have made divorce possible, or easier, in many countries.

- Changes in attitudes. The rise in divorce can be seen as part of a more general change in which individuals put themselves first and no longer feel obliged to do what was previously expected.

- The decline of religion (secularisation). The religious vows in marriage are no longer taken as seriously, at least by some, and more weddings are now civil ceremonies, not religious ones.

- Women have greater financial independence, so they no longer need to marry for economic support.

Women today do not have to accept the expressive role or the housework and chores that are part of the traditional role. They are also more likely to be able to support themselves after divorce.

- Because people live longer, they are married for longer and also for longer periods after their children have left home. Some couples divorce after many years of marriage because their dissatisfaction has grown over time, or because they want to embrace new opportunities.

- Extra-marital relationships are often a factor in divorce. It has become easier for people to meet potential partners because of internet dating apps and online messaging.

There are several broad explanations for changes in marriage, divorce and cohabitation over the past 50 years:

- **Legislation.** Laws have changed to allow easier divorce and, in some countries, to allow same-sex marriages.

- **Societal attitudes and values.** In many countries it has become more acceptable to cohabit, to divorce, to be unmarried or to be child-free.

- **Role of the internet.** Information on the internet has made people more aware of the choices available to them. The internet also provides new ways to meet potential partners.

- **Secularisation.** In many countries, religious beliefs now have less influence on people's behaviour.

- **Cultural expectations.** The pressure to conform, from family and community, is less strong in some countries. More people expect to be able to make their own choices about how they live.

- **Changes in the status and power of women.** Greater equality has allowed more women to make decisions such as prioritising their career over marriage, to initiating a divorce.

Alternatives to marriage

This section looks at four alternatives to marriage: cohabitation, singlehood, lone parents and civil partnerships.

Cohabitation

Cohabitation is when two people live together in a sexual relationship but are not married to each other. In many societies, there have always been relationships like this;

they were often accepted by the community as essentially the same as a marriage. Changing values in the last 50 years or so, especially in Europe and North America, have led to a wider acceptance of cohabitation and it is now considered normal.

According to Fulcher and Scott (1999), there are three different types of cohabitation:

- permanent or long-term relationships which only differ from marriage in that a formal ceremony has not taken place

- trial marriages, when a couple live together before marriage

- short-term relationships without commitment.

The first type – permanent or long-term relationships – is common in Scandinavian countries such as Sweden. This is probably because these countries have strong welfare states, so people are supported and looked after throughout their lives. Women are not dependent on the economic support of a male partner and so they do not feel the need for the formal contract of marriage.

The second type – trial marriages – seem particularly significant in the UK. More than half of all couples in the UK now cohabit before marriage. This suggests a change in marriage practice, rather than a rejection of marriage. Cohabiting couples are delaying marriage, not avoiding it. This is usually for economic reasons: more young people are now in higher education in their 20s and, as they are not earning an income, they are not financially independent enough for marriage (or unable to afford a wedding) until they are older.

The third type – short-term relationships without commitment – may become one of the other two types if the relationship proves to be more long-lasting. Many young couples choose to cohabit for financial reasons, because it seems wasteful to pay rent on two flats or houses when they spend most of their time together. Couples may also see cohabiting as a way of testing a relationship and seeing if they are compatible with their partner before making a longer-term commitment, such as marriage or having children. Some people cohabit with several different partners in succession before finding a relationship which is longer-lasting.

The increase in cohabitation helps to explain both the fall in marriage rates and the rising age of first marriage.

Singlehood

In section 4.1, you learnt about one-person households and the reasons for them. Some of these one-person households are people who have decided not to get married or cohabit; they have chosen singlehood. The greater independence of women has allowed more women to put their career before marriage and family. Women with a secure income may see marriage as a matter of choice, rather than an economic necessity. At the same time, it has become more socially acceptable for women not to marry or have children. Being single is not always a choice made in early adulthood 'for life'; some people never find someone they want to share their life with, or decide that they do not want to give up the independence which singlehood brings. Some single people live with friends or in shared households. Many people live alone after a divorce or separation. For those who do live on their own, social contact is important. The growth of the internet and social media have helped with this, particularly for people living outside cities.

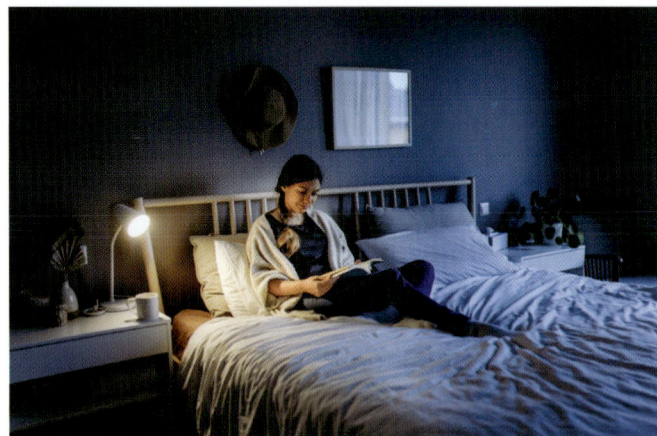

Figure 4.11: Singlehood.

Lone parents

There have always been some lone parents, usually after the death of the other parent. However, there are now two other factors that lead to lone parents:

1 **Divorce and separation.** Children may be better off with one parent than in a household where there are arguments and an unhappy atmosphere.

2 **Unmarried parents.** There are many lone parents who have never been married. For example, a woman may decide to raise children on her own. It is now easier for women to work to support themselves, and in countries with a welfare state, financial support is available (for example, for childcare costs).

In most countries, lone parents are now more socially acceptable and children of lone parents are less likely

Figure 4.12: A lone parent family.

to be stigmatised by their peers. This is partly because the reasons for lone parenthood (such as divorce) have become more socially acceptable, and partly because the numbers of lone parents have increased.

Many lone parents eventually marry or remarry and form two-parent families. Being a lone parent is, therefore, often a temporary stage in life.

Many children of lone-parent families have two living parents. The child may live with one of them but have regular contact with the other. Some spend half their time with one parent and half with the other. The amount of contact between children and parents they do not live with can vary, from every day to never. The amount of support, financial or otherwise, provided by an absent parent can also vary enormously. This makes it difficult to generalise about lone parent families.

As you saw in the discussion of the New Right in section 4.1, some people see lone parents as a social problem. They claim there is a link between children being raised by one parent and problems such as educational underachievement, involvement with petty crimes and unemployment later in life. But many children of lone parents experience no problems, while some children raised by two parents do experience them. An opposing view to the New Right suggests that the main factor is not the type of family, but poverty. Many social problems are associated with poverty and lone parents are more likely to be in poverty than two-parent families.

Civil partnerships

Same-sex families were explained in section 4.1. Currently, same-sex couples are allowed to legally marry in 31 countries, including Mexico, the UK, Denmark,

New Zealand and Taiwan. Other countries recognise a formal union of same-sex partners that is equivalent to marriage. These formal unions – called civil partnerships – give same-sex couples the same rights as heterosexual married couples, in terms of tax, pensions and inheritance. In other countries, there is no legal recognition of same-sex partnerships or relationships, and they may be socially disapproved of or even illegal.

In some countries, civil partnerships can also occur between opposite-sex couples, giving opposite-sex and same-sex couples the same options regarding their relationships. Opposite-sex civil partnerships have provided an alternative to marriage for couples who want to give their relationship a formal and legal status, but who may reject marriage due to its links with religion and traditional gender roles.

Changing family roles

This section examines the changes in family relationships, including conjugal roles and the changing roles of children and grandparents.

Changing conjugal roles

More diverse family types

Conjugal roles – the roles taken by the two partners, usually in a marriage – used to be fixed and individuals had little opportunity to move beyond them. However, the increasing diversity in families has allowed for changes in conjugal roles. For example, in same-sex families, it is not clear who should take which roles – or whether we can even identify roles in the traditional sense.

Segregated to joint conjugal roles

As discussed in section 4.2, functionalists believe it is best to have two clearly separate gender roles within the family: the expressive role for females and the instrumental role for males. Feminists have challenged this division of roles and suggest a move from segregated conjugal roles to joint conjugal roles, where men and women have more equal roles and share tasks.

A family in which the roles have become more equal in this way is called a **symmetrical family**.

KEY TERM

symmetrical family: a family in which the roles of the partners are equal

---

Many families today are **dual worker families**, in which both the man and the woman have paid work. In many families, men now do more of the traditional 'female' chores, such as cooking and cleaning. These men are sometimes referred to as 'new men'. A small number of families have a complete role reversal, where the woman goes out to work and the man is a 'househusband' who looks after the home.

KEY TERM

dual worker families: families in which both partners do paid work

The traditional female role in the family limits what women can achieve at work. Many women find that their responsibility for children constrains the amount of paid work they can do; for example, they may work part-time so they can collect their children from school. By taking time out of paid work to have children, women can also miss out on opportunities for training and promotion. This is why feminists are particularly concerned about conjugal roles and argue that they should be joint rather than segregated.

In the UK, the sociologists Willmott and Young found evidence of a new and more equal division of domestic labour based on joint rather than segregated conjugal roles. While there was still a clear division of labour by gender to some extent, both husband and wife were contributing equally to the family.

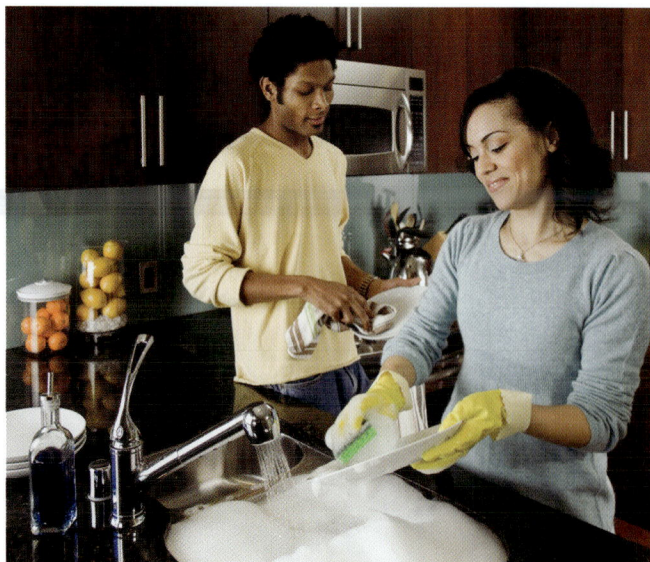

Figure 4.13: Joint conjugal roles.

TIP

Men have always done some household work, and tasks such as heavy gardening, house repairs and car maintenance are sometimes still seen as men's work today. These tasks are not generally classed as 'housework' (such as cleaning and cooking – historically seen as women's work) and they do not usually need to be carried out on a daily basis. Remember to consider the wide range of possible tasks when you talk about work in the home.

There are several possible reasons for the change towards more symmetrical families:

- Nuclear families became privatised, which means the couple organised their lives around the family home, rather than work and community. This was because homes had become more comfortable, with heating and with entertainment such as television. This encouraged a more equal partnership.

- The decline of the extended family meant there was less pressure from other family members to conform to their norms.

- Women have a higher status in society, so men are more likely to treat them as equals and women are more likely to insist that they do so.

- Women have greater independence as a result of paid work, which leads to more equality within the family (for example, joint decision-making). Women became more able to have paid work as the average number of children they had decreased.

- It has become easier for both men and women to choose their roles and to negotiate them with each other.

- Labour-saving devices in the home have reduced the time and effort involved in some housework, making the home a more attractive place to be.

THINK LIKE A SOCIOLOGIST

Do you think most families in your community are symmetrical? In which parts of the world do you think there may be more or fewer symmetrical families? Consider why this may be.

Other writers concerned with domestic labour have said that Willmott and Young are too optimistic about equal gender roles.

They point out that men tend to do tasks they have chosen, ones that are less dull and repetitive. For example, the man may prepare a special meal for guests, rather than taking on the day-to-day necessity of feeding children. Both men and women often overestimate the amount that men do around the home, and underestimate the amount that women do. Men's ideas of helping with children may involve the more pleasant and rewarding activities, such as playing or reading stories. Men still take most of the important decisions in the family, such as moving house or substantial spending.

Some household tasks are carried out by other family members, for example, children may be given specific jobs to do around the home. In some societies, it is common for families who can afford it to employ nannies or other staff to help with childcare and housework. The division of tasks by gender can be seen here, too; looking after children – for example, as a nanny or ayah – is seen as women's work, while a chauffeur to drive a car is likely to be a man.

Research on the domestic division of labour has several problems. Researchers have to decide what tasks should be covered and how they should be measured. It is also important who is asked about housework; a husband and wife may give completely different accounts of who usually does what. These problems mean that different research findings sometimes seem to contradict each other.

ACTIVITY: DISCUSSION 4.3

Working in a small group, make a list of household tasks traditionally done by women and girls, and those traditionally done by men and boys in your society. You can ask older family members or your teachers for help. Now discuss whether this situation is changing.

ACTIVITY: RESEARCH 4.2

Who is responsible for most of the domestic work in your family?

Draw up a list of tasks, including those that are needed only occasionally. Ask family members who carries out these tasks. Would you say your family has joint or segregated conjugal roles?

REFLECTION

Did you find it difficult to identify all the domestic tasks in your family? Were there more than you thought? Did it surprise you how much – or how little – some members of your family contribute compared to others?

The pivot/sandwich generation

Many middle-aged people have to look after the generation below them (their children) and the generation above them (their own parents). They are referred to as the sandwich generation or the pivot generation. Although this period of their lives is temporary, the demands on this generation's time and energy can be very intense. Today, more people have their first child at a later age. As a result, it has become more likely that their parents will need support before their children become adults. The responsibilities for caring for two generations often fall mainly on the woman, as they are part of the traditional expressive role of women.

Changing roles of children

To understand the roles of children today, we need to compare different societies, today and in the past. It is important to appreciate that the terms children and childhood have meant different things at different times.

What is meant by childhood?

Children are defined as people who have not reached the age of adulthood, which varies between societies. Children's lives are regulated by laws that organise them in particular ways; they are very different from adult lives. For example, in most countries, children must go to school and are not allowed to do paid work. Adult rights and responsibilities are gradually acquired throughout childhood but the ages at which rights and responsibilities are gained vary between societies.

Many traditional societies mark the change from childhood to adulthood with a ceremony, a rite of passage. Adolescent boys were removed from their family homes for a period, during which they underwent a series of rituals to initiate them into adult life. Before the ceremony, the individual is a child; after it, he is a man and a full adult member of the community, regardless of his age. For girls, the first menstruation is often taken as the sign of achieving womanhood. Among the Yanomami people of the Amazon rainforest, girls after their first menstruation are treated as adult women and will marry. In Shona society, in central southern Africa, women are traditionally not treated as adults until they have a child. If they die before they have a child, they are given the ceremony appropriate to the burial of a child.

Childhood has been very different in the past. According to the historian Philippe Ariès, in the Middle Ages in Europe, children worked alongside adults, dressed like adults, took part in the same games and festivals as adults, and were even punished for crimes in the same way as adults. Children were not seen as innocent or vulnerable and there were no attempts to protect them from the facts of death and sex. Many people did not know their exact age, so status did not depend on age. The small size of children was seen as making them suited for particular types of work, rather than making them fundamentally different from adults.

In modern industrial societies, children are subject to the authority of adults such as parents and teachers. They are expected to be respectful and obedient, accepting that adults have greater knowledge and that this will be used to help them. Children's time is closely controlled by their parents (for example, the time they spend on activities such as schoolwork, playing video games and times for bed and meals) and there are places where they can and cannot go. All this means there is a high degree of control over children, reinforcing the difference between childhood and adulthood. This difference is cultural, not natural. Much of this control is new, a response to the increased dangers to children perceived by parents and other adults. For example, in modern industrial societies, children today have less freedom to move around their home area in cities because of fears about traffic and danger from other adults. Whether the control is for the child's protection or not, it leads to a particular form of childhood, shaped by society.

On the other hand, new laws and regulations give some power to children, and children can find ways to win greater freedom. In many countries, corporal (physical) punishment is no longer allowed in schools and even physical reprimands by parents – such as 'smacking' – are unacceptable; they may be seen by the authorities as abuse. Most countries have signed the United Nations Convention on the Rights of the Child, which says that children have the right to be listened to, and to say what they think about decisions which affect them. Today, children usually have at least some say in decisions that affect them: for example, their views are taken into account in divorce cases, and many schools have pupil councils or representatives who act as the 'pupil voice'.

In some countries, however, children are still seen very differently to this. For example, they may be doing paid work from an early age rather than being in education. According to the UN in 2020, 72.1 million African children were involved in child labour; this has been increasing in sub-Saharan Africa.

Economic burden/cost

In the past, children were an economic benefit to the family – they worked as soon as they were able to, to bring extra income into the family. This is still the case in some African countries. However, in modern industrial societies, it costs a lot of money to raise children, for the following reasons:

- Children can no longer do paid work to add to the family's income.

- Childcare, preschool education and school education are expensive. In many countries, state schools are free but parents are expected to pay for uniforms, books and equipment.

- Parents are expected to provide higher standards; for example, in many countries children now expect to have a room of their own and new clothes (rather than items passed on from older siblings).

- Children want and put pressure on their parents to buy a range of consumer goods, such as toys and mobile phones.

- Children are dependent on their parents for longer. This may even extend into adulthood, in the case of boomerang children.

In modern industrial societies, children have become an economic burden. For some parents, how many children to have – or even whether to have children at all – has become an economic decision.

Child-centredness

Nowadays, childhood is seen as a period of innocence, when children should not have to work or experience other aspects of the adult world. New industries reinforce children's special status by producing specialised goods for them, such as clothes, toys and games, food, television programmes and television channels. Children put pressure on their parents and other adults to buy things for them, and many parents want to do this so their children do not miss out (for example, on having the same toys as their peers). In the past, children were producers; today, they have become important consumers in most societies. Modern industrial societies are **child-centred**: children have a central place in society and in the lives of many adults.

KEY TERM

child-centredness: when a child's needs and wishes are the most important considerations

Societies have become more child-centred because:

- families are smaller, so each child can have more attention

- children spend more time with their parents. This is partly because parents work fewer hours than they used to but also because many parents want their children at home, where they know they are safe

- standards of living have improved, so more money can be spent on children

- companies and advertising target children (and their parents) as consumers

- adults are put under pressure to be 'good' parents, devoting themselves to their children. There are, for example, many websites and books offering advice on parenting

- laws designed to protect children can force parents to look after their children more. Allowing children to explore their local area – as they might have done in the past – may be seen as neglect.

ACTIVITY: RESEARCH 4.3

Use the internet to research the average costs of raising a child in different parts of the world. Choose a country in Europe, a country in North America, a country in Asia and a country in Africa. Also include your own country if it is not in one of these categories. In what parts of the world is it most expensive to raise a child?

Boomerang children

Parent–child relationships continue after the child is 18 years old. Recently, it has become more common in Europe and North America for adult children to continue living with their parents. Some leave home – for example, to go to university – but then return, often because they cannot afford to live alone or to marry. They are sometimes described as boomerang children, and the family is known as a boomerang family. Families in this situation have a 'full nest' rather than an 'empty nest'. As a result, many parents today are financially responsible for their children for longer than in the past.

In Italy, well over half of 18- to 34-year-olds live with their parents. In other societies, this practice is disapproved of. In China, graduate children are expected to make a substantial contribution to their parents' living expenses; it is considered a disgrace if an adult is still being financed by their parents after their parents have retired.

STRETCH AND CHALLENGE

To what extent is the increase in boomerang families a positive thing for:

- the parents
- the adult children?

Changing roles of grandparents

Before the mid-20th century, few people lived long enough to become grandparents. Today, however, many more people live into old age and so most children know their grandparents. Many grandparents live long enough to see their grandchildren become adults and even to become great-grandparents.

There is a very wide variation in the ages at which people become grandparents, from late thirties to advanced old age. The role of the grandparent – especially the active, healthy grandparent – is new and important. All of the developments in families studied so far have affected the role of grandparents.

- Many grandparents have children who divorce, become lone parents or remarry.

- Divorce and separation also affect the relationship between children and their grandparents; for example, grandparents can 'lose' their grandchildren. Family feuds can also separate grandparents from their grandchildren.

- There are now many step-grandparents, resulting from the growth of reconstituted families.

- There are grandparents of children with lesbian and gay parents, of children who have been adopted or are in care, and of children who have been neglected and abused.

- Many children have grandparents from more than one ethnic group.

- Grandparents are themselves more likely to be divorced and remarried. They may start new families at an age when, in the past, they would have been considered too old to do so.

Figure 4.14: A child with their grandparent.

Childcare, economic support, wisdom and advice

Different generations within families support each other in many ways. Grandparents can support their children and grandchildren by:

- providing economic support – including giving and lending money

- providing practical support – for example, grandparents may look after their grandchildren while the children's parents work

- providing emotional and moral support – by listening, talking and giving advice; for example, many mothers rely on parenting advice from their own mother

- building a relationship with their grandchildren – many children have a strong bond with their grandparents, despite the age difference. Grandparents can listen and offer advice if children argue with their parents. They are often associated with treats as well; for example, grandparents may be more willing to give children unhealthy foods (such as sweets and ice creams), because they are not the primary caregivers.

Some forms of support are more likely to come from grandmothers than grandfathers. Far less is known about the role of grandfathers, because less research has been done. It is also likely that, in most societies, the mother's parents (maternal grandparents) play a bigger role than the father's parents (paternal grandparents).

MAKING CONNECTIONS

How might changes in the role and status of women in society link to the changing role of grandparents in the family?

Grandparents as dependents

Older generations do not always support younger generations. As grandparents age, they receive more help from their grown-up children (though they often continue to give support as well). Adult children may support their parents by providing:

- accommodation – grandparents may live with their children and grandchildren in a vertically extended family home

- personal care – helping with daily needs, such as eating and washing. Children, especially daughters, are a major support for their elderly parents. When the grandparents have mobility problems, or are forgetful, this can be an additional burden.

- economic support – grandparents with no income, or only a small pension, may need financial help.

ACTIVITY: WRITTEN 4.3

Write three paragraphs, one on each of the following changing family roles:

- conjugal roles (joint conjugal roles, segregated conjugal roles, symmetrical family, pivot generation)

- roles of children (child-centredness, boomerang children)

- roles of grandparents (ageing population, childcare, burden).

In each paragraph, make sure you include:

- the key terms given in brackets

- examples of the roles (including cultural differences)

- ways in which the roles have changed in recent years.

CHECK YOUR UNDERSTANDING 4.3

1   Write down three reasons for the decrease in the marriage rate.

2   Write down three reasons for the increase in the divorce rate.

3   Share your reasons with a partner and add to your lists.

KEY POINTS

- Demographic factors with effects on family life are:
  - family size
  - birth rates
  - life expectancy
  - ageing population
  - having children in later life.
- Industrialisation and urbanisation had an impact on families.
- Explanations of changing patterns and trends in marriage, divorce and cohabitation include:
  - legislation
  - societal attitudes and values
  - role of the internet
  - secularisation
  - cultural expectations
  - changes in the status and power of women.
- Alternatives to marriage are:
  - cohabitation
  - singlehood

  - lone parents
  - civil partnerships.
- Reasons why some people do not get married include:
  - changing norms
  - female empowerment.
- Changing family roles include:
  - conjugal roles
  - more diverse family types
  - changes from segregated to joint roles
  - the pivot/sandwich generation.
- Children:
  - as an economic burden
  - child-centeredness
  - boomerang children.
- Grandparents:
  - providing childcare
  - providing economic support
  - providing wisdom and advice
  - being dependent.

END OF UNIT SUMMARY

- There are many different kinds of family, as well as alternatives to the family.

- There are also different kinds of marriage.

- There are debates between functionalist, Marxist and feminist sociologists about the role of the family for the individual and society.

- Changes in family life include effects of demographic factors, alternatives to marriage and changes in the roles of husbands and wives, children and grandparents.

KEY SKILLS EXERCISES

1 Data interpretation and Knowledge and understanding

Statistical table

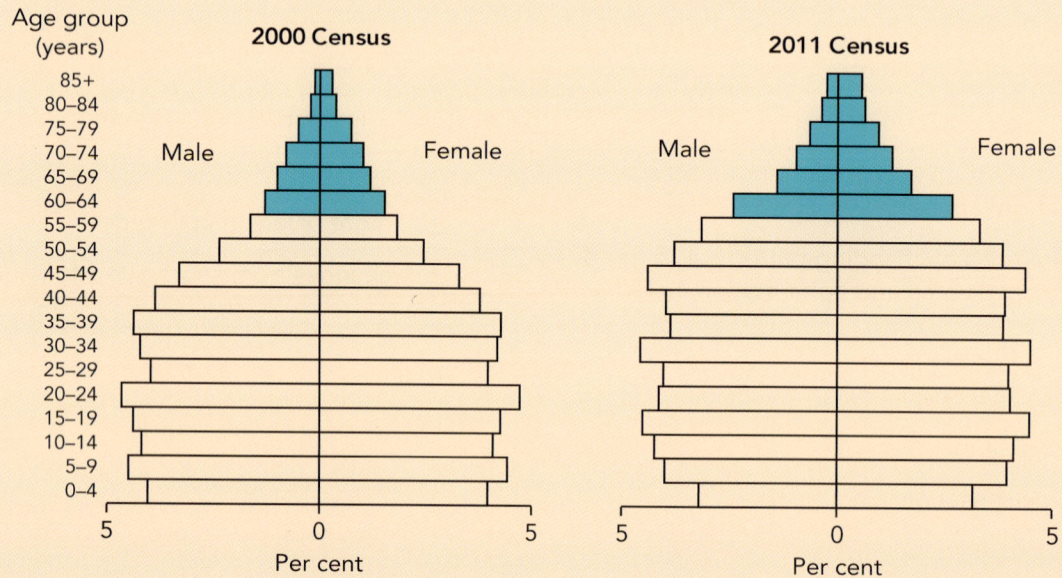

Figure 4.15: Population pyramids for Mauritius, 2000 and 2011. The darker areas show people over the age of 60.

Search for an animated version of this change on the population-pyramid.net website.

This animation goes up to the present day and also projects forward to 2099.

1. What do these population pyramids show about changes to the age distribution of the population of Mauritius?

2. What term is used to describe a population which is changing in this way, regarding its age distribution?

3. Give possible reasons for these changes.

2 Knowledge and understanding

Without using this book or your notes, see if you can list seven different types of family. For each one, write a definition. Check your answer.

3 Analysis and evaluation

Of the three main sociological perspectives – functionalist, Marxist and feminist – which do you think gives the most convincing account of the family today? Write a 250-word justification of your choice.

IMPROVE THIS ANSWER

Family, education and crime

Evaluate the view that marriage is still important today. Your answer should include:

- at least three arguments for and three arguments against the view

- a conclusion.

Supporting the view that marriage is still important today is that most people get married at some point during their lives. Despite the fact that, in some countries such as the UK, the number of marriages has fallen, it is still a popular choice, with many people deciding to get married, especially before having children. Marriage is seen as providing a stable home for bringing up children. This is a point made by functionalists. Also, even though many marriages end in divorce, people who are divorced often get married again, and sometimes more than once (this is called serial monogamy). Second and subsequent marriages are increasing in number, suggesting that marriage is still important. For people who do remarry, it is one

specific marriage that has failed, rather than the idea of marriage as a whole. The importance of marriage is also shown by campaigns by minorities for the right to marry. For example, when civil partnerships for same-sex couples were legalised in the UK, the campaign continued until, eventually, the Marriage (Same Sex Couples) Act of 2014 was passed, which allowed them to marry in the same way as heterosexual couples.

Commentary and task

This is an evaluation question, so it requires several arguments for the view in the question, several arguments against the view in the question and a conclusion. The answer so far gives several arguments in favour of the view that marriage is still important. Improve this answer by adding a new paragraph with at least three arguments against the view. Read the answer closely and you will see that it acknowledges how marriage has changed in ways that could make it seem less important; you may be able to expand these ideas into arguments. Finally, add an evaluative conclusion.

PRACTICE QUESTIONS

Family, education and crime

a   Define the terms:

  i   serial monogamy [2]

  ii   dual burden [2]

b   Give two examples of alternatives to the family [2]

c   Describe **three** ways the family can be patriarchal. [6]

d   Explain **three** criticisms of the functionalist view of the family. [6]

e   Discuss reasons why families have become smaller in size.

   Your answer should include at least **three** developed points with evidence. [8]

f   Evaluate the view that marriage is still important today.

   Your answer should include:

- at least **three** arguments for and **three** arguments against the view

- a conclusion. [14]

SELF-EVALUATION CHECKLIST

After studying this unit, complete this table:

You should be able to:	Needs more work	Almost there	Ready to move on
4.1 What are the different types of families?			
Identify and explain different types of families			
Explain the strengths and limitations of different types of families			
Explain variations and diversity in the family			
Understand the debates between sociological views on family diversity			
Identify and explain alternatives to the family			
Explain variations in types of marriage			
4.2 What is the role of the family for the individual and society?			
Explain functionalist views			
Explain Marxist views			
Explain feminist views			
Understand the debates about whether the experience of family life is positive or negative for family members			
Understand the strengths and limitations of functionalist, Marxist and feminist views of the role of the family			
4.3 How is family life changing?			
Explain the effects of demographic factors on family life			
Explain the impact of industrialisation and urbanisation on family structures and roles			
Explain changing patterns and trends in marriage, divorce and cohabitation			
Explain alternatives to marriage and reasons why some individuals do not get married			
Explain changing family roles – conjugal roles, children and grandparents			

Education

LEARNING INTENTIONS

In this unit, you will learn how to:

- Understand the difference between formal and informal education
- Describe the effectiveness of different types of schools
- Describe alternative approaches to education
- Assess functionalist, Marxist and feminist views of the role and functions of education
- Describe patterns in education achievement and experience according to social class, ethnicity, gender and global differences
- Assess explanations for differences in levels of educational achievement and experience, based on social class, ethnicity and gender
- Describe global differences in educational achievement.

Introduction

At home and in their families, through primary socialisation, children learn the skills, knowledge and values they need to live in their society. This continues throughout life via secondary socialisation (Unit 2); we are all learning every day. In modern societies, a lot of learning happens in schools and in other educational institutions such as colleges and universities. Around a century ago, few children globally went to school. Today, the majority of children do. The sociology of education is concerned mainly with schools. It considers questions such as: What is education for? What happens in schools? Why do some groups seem to do much better than others in the education system? In a world where education is seen as essential for a successful life, such questions have become very important.

> **KEY TERM**
>
> **socialisation:** the process of learning the norms and values of a culture

5.1 What is education and schooling?

Formal and informal education

For most of history, children learnt what they needed to know from their parents, families and communities, by watching, listening and being shown what to do. There were usually no schools so education was informal. Until relatively recently, this was still the case for people in poorer countries and communities.

Formal education takes place in schools and colleges, with professional teachers and agreed subject content. This has developed gradually, becoming more widespread over the past 150 years. In many societies, there has been resistance to the growth of formal education. For example, some political leaders felt

> **KEY TERM**
>
> **formal education:** education that takes place in classrooms, with professional teachers and set content to be taught and learnt

it would be dangerous to educate the poor, since it could give them ideas above their status in life. Some traditional communities also resisted pressure for their children to go to school, because they felt it would not teach them the skills they would need in the future, such as being able to work on the land and support their families. These views are still found in some parts of the world, especially in relation to the education of girls.

Although most children now go to school, **informal education** continues. Today, we use the term 'informal education' to refer to:

- education outside the classroom – for example, after-school activities
- things children learn at school that are not part of the formal content of lessons – for example, they might learn that they need to be on time or to follow instructions given by authority figures. This informal learning during lessons is called the hidden curriculum.

Official curriculum

The **official curriculum** consists of the subjects that are taught and their content. In most countries, the first years of primary education concentrate on reading, writing and mathematics, with an introduction to some other subjects. At secondary level, learners study a wider range of subjects, often taught by specialist teachers. After that, if they choose to continue in education, they study only a few subjects; many learners choose between arts and science subjects. At university level, it is normal to study only one subject, or possibly two.

Many countries have a national curriculum, in which the government outlines the subjects and content to be taught.

> **KEY TERMS**
>
> **informal education:** education that takes place outside the classroom or through daily interactions
>
> **official curriculum:** the subjects that are taught and the content to be covered

Figure 5.1: Children learning the official curriculum.

This means that all learners of a particular age or standard are taught the same things in every school. There may be national tests, taken by all learners to assess their progress. The results of these tests are used to measure the performance of different schools. In some countries, parents can also use this data when they are deciding which school to send their child to.

Having a national curriculum allows a government to decide what subjects and skills it wants for its future citizens. In most countries, language skills (such as reading and writing) and mathematics are considered to be the most important subjects. Once learners have basic skills in these subjects, they can study a range of other subjects. Some of the most common are:

- sciences (such as biology, chemistry and physics)
- literature
- religious knowledge
- history
- geography
- technology
- creative arts (such as art, music and drama)
- physical education/sports
- foreign languages.

At a more advanced level, even more subjects become available, such as sociology, economics and more languages. Sociologists would argue that everyone should know about their own society and others, so this should be taught to all learners from a young age. In some countries, such as Mauritius, all students learn about sociology as a core subject.

Within each subject, there is a range of content to be taught and learnt. Teachers have some freedom to decide what to teach and when, so they can consider the particular needs of their classes. However, in subjects which are assessed by public examinations, teachers must ensure they cover all of the content from the syllabus. For example, for Cambridge IGCSE™ and O Level, learners must be able to answer questions on all the topics from the syllabus.

Formal teaching in schools assumes that knowledge can be divided into labelled subjects – such as history, geography, science, etc. However, these divisions are social constructions: they are not natural but are the result of decisions made by people. This way of organising education may prevent learners from understanding the connections between different areas of knowledge. Interesting and important information can fall into the gaps between subjects, so it is neglected in schools.

Hidden curriculum

All learners know the official curriculum – the timetable of subjects and lessons they follow. But the *experience* of going to school is also a form of education, through which students learn **norms** and **values**, beliefs and attitudes. This is the hidden curriculum.

Part of the hidden curriculum is the structure and organisation of the school. Schools are places that are physically separate from the home. Classrooms are usually set out so with the teacher at the front and the learners seated, often in rows. All learners can see the teacher (but not all other learners) and the teacher can see all of them. This gives the message that the teacher is in control and the centre of attention. The ways in which teachers interact with learners, and the assumptions they make about them, are also part of the hidden curriculum.

Schools are hierarchies. Learners learn their place in the hierarchy and the norms that go with their role. Learners are at the bottom of the hierarchy, but older learners usually have higher status than younger ones;

KEY TERMS

norms: the behaviour that societies expect of their members in particular situations

values: standards shared by members of a culture and used to judge whether behaviour is right or wrong

Figure 5.2: The hidden curriculum includes learning about rules and conformity.

for example, they may have extra privileges. For adults within the school, the head teacher is at the top because they are responsible for the running of the school. Sometimes, the head teacher works with – or needs the approval of – a board of governors. Below the head teacher in the hierarchy are senior teachers (such as heads of department), junior teachers and other staff, such as office and maintenance workers.

Other features of the hidden curriculum include:

- competitive sports and testing of individuals. This gives the message that doing better than others is often more important than cooperating with them.

- the importance of punctuality and being on time for lessons. Schools follow a timetable and learners have to be in school – and in particular classrooms or other places – at set times, with little free time. This can be seen as preparation for the world of work because most jobs have set start and finish times.

- the importance of following school rules and expectations. Learners have to do what they are told by those in authority, even if they do not agree. They have to conform to rules about behaviour and expectations about school work and effort. This may be enforced by formal **social control** (for example, teachers may punish learners who do not follow rules) or informally (for example, the disapproval of others may encourage learners to conform).

- assemblies, which bring together large numbers of learners and staff. These gatherings reinforce the sense of the school as a community. They are often used to communicate shared values – for example, through stories and speeches.

- wall displays. These displays may reinforce hidden curriculum messages, by reminding learners how to act. They might also include flags or other symbols to show the importance of being part of a nation or community.

Figure 5.3: Children reciting the Pledge of Allegiance in a school in the US. This can reinforce a shared national identity, which is part of the hidden curriculum.

Functionalist, Marxist and feminist sociologists all engage with the idea of the hidden curriculum. However, they have different ideas about the main values and attitudes conveyed and how they should be interpreted.

TIP

The hidden curriculum is not necessarily a good thing or a bad thing; it is just the term used to refer to the learning done in school outside the official curriculum. You may need to evaluate the hidden curriculum and its function from different theoretical perspectives.

For functionalists, the hidden curriculum gives skills and attitudes that are essential, both for the smooth running of society and for the individual's future. It helps to fulfil the **functions of education**. Individual learners find out about their place in society, learn how to get on with others and what they should do as adults.

For Marxists, the hidden curriculum is about social control – the control of the working class by the ruling class through ideology. Through the hidden curriculum, working-class children learn not to have high expectations for work or of life. They learn to expect to be told what to do, to have their opinions ignored and to be bored a lot of the time. They become passive and conformist. Marxist sociologists are interested in how the ruling class maintains its power by persuading the working class to accept ideas and values that are against their interests. In particular, they focus on the different messages received by the different classes For example, working-class learners are likely to accept that they will do badly in school and that this is their own fault. In fact, the system has been designed to ensure that most of them fail. The way schools divide the curriculum into subjects makes it more difficult for learners to gain a full understanding, especially of the way capitalist societies work. This helps to maintain class privilege. The hidden curriculum for learners from upper-class backgrounds is very different. These children learn to expect to have a high-status occupation in which they will tell others what to do.

Feminists see the hidden curriculum as conveying messages about gender and **gender roles**. For example, boys and girls may have different uniforms, take different subjects and be treated differently by teachers. This encourages both boys and girls to conform to traditional gender stereotypes. Feminists argue that education can result in both boys and girls having stereotypical and mistaken views of what the two sexes are like and what they can achieve.

KEY TERMS

functions of education: the ways in which education contributes to society

gender roles: the roles and expectations associated with being male or female

---

ACTIVITY: RESEARCH 5.1

Interview an older member of your family about their education. Find out how schools and education have changed in your country. Ask about what subjects were taught, what lessons were like, what resources were used, how teachers interacted with learners and whether boys and girls were treated the same. Report back to your class, comparing your own experience with your family member's

---

The effectiveness of different types of schools

In modern societies, there are many different kinds of schools, and school systems vary between countries. This section discusses state, private, single-sex and faith schools, as well as selective education. However, types of schools may be known by different names. It is also possible that not all the types of school described here exist in your country.

One way of categorising schools is by the age of the learners. Children receive their first years of academic education in primary schools (called elementary schools in the USA and some other countries). In the UK, children usually start their primary education at the age of 5 and move on to another school at the age of 11. The starting age is higher in some countries; for example, it is 6 in China and Australia. Primary education usually involves an emphasis on reading, writing and mathematics, as well as an introduction to some other subjects. In a primary school, all subjects may be taught by one class teacher.

Many children have some education in a school-like setting before they start primary school. This pre-primary school-like setting is known as preschool. The aim of pre-primary education is to help very young children get used to learning in a school-like environment. It usually focuses on the children developing cognitive, physical, social and emotional skills. Preschools are often known as kindergartens or nursery schools.

Secondary school is the second period of education, usually for children aged 11 to 16, or older.

The term 'high school' is used in some countries; however, because education systems vary so much, 'high school' does not mean exactly the same thing as secondary school. At this stage, learners study a range of different subjects, with a different teacher for each subject. Secondary education often ends with examinations that determine whether the learner can move on to the next stage of education. In modern industrial countries, secondary education is compulsory. In some countries, learners who do not do well have to repeat a year. This can mean that there are learners of different ages in the same class.

Tertiary education, the third period of education, is not compulsory. It involves going to a university or college, and it is also referred to as post-compulsory education, further education or higher education. There may be some much older students, who are returning to education after some time working or having children; they are called mature students. Universities offer both undergraduate (or first) degrees and postgraduate (or higher) degrees, including doctorates. University staff members carry out research as well as teaching students. Different proportions of people in different countries study at this level. Almost all countries now have at least one university but there is a great variation in the number of subjects they offer. This means that some young people will have to go to another country to study their preferred subject. If a learner graduates at a university abroad, they may continue to live in that country; after several years studying in the country, it will have become a new home for them. As a result, the learner's country of origin will lose some of its brightest and best people – exactly the ones it needs to help its economy.

State/public and private schools

Schools can be categorised by who funds, runs and is responsible for them. The two main types are:

- **state schools** (called public schools in some countries), which are run and funded directly or indirectly by national or local government

- **private schools**, which are mainly funded by fees paid by the parents or guardians of the students who go

there. Because they are privately funded and run, private schools are free from restrictions placed on state schools; for example, they do not have to teach certain subjects or have qualified teachers.

In many countries, these two types of school exist alongside each other. In other countries, all education is state-funded; for example, Finland has no private schools.

Private schools are mainly for children whose parents can afford to pay for their children's education. However, there may be some scholarships or schemes that allow other children to attend without paying. Some private schools are run as businesses, which means the owners make a profit from running them. Others are charities whose main purpose is to provide an education – often to a particular group, such as members of a religion. Some of the top-rated private schools are also boarding schools, so the learners live there during term time.

In the UK, about 7 per cent of children go to fee-paying private schools. Two of the most famous private schools in the UK are Eton and Harrow. These two boarding schools have taught the children (usually boys) of the wealthiest families for several hundred years. Children educated at these schools have greater access to highly paid careers that attract power and status.

Figure 5.4: Students at a private school in the UK.

KEY TERMS

state schools: schools that are funded and run, directly or indirectly, by the government

private schools: schools that are funded by fees paid by the parents or guardians of learners; not run or controlled by the government

Limitations of private schools and strengths of state schools

- Few people can afford to send their children to private schools. Because of the strengths of private schools regarding class size, curriculum and facilities, children who attend private schools are likely to do better.

This gives them access to high-status universities and careers. This creates inequalities between children who attend state schools and those who can afford to go to private schools.

- It can be seen as wrong that the wealthy can buy a better education for their children.

- Private schools create a division between groups. Learners who go to private schools are likely to get top positions in society, while learners who go to state schools may have more limited opportunities.

- Governments control how much money is spent on state schools. The funds available to them are limited by what they can raise in taxes and how much they have to spend on other things (such as health services). Many middle- and upper-class parents spend large amounts of money on private school fees. This suggests that, if private schools did not exist, these parents could afford to pay more in taxes instead. This money could then be spent on improving education for *all* children through the state school system.

Strengths of private schools and limitations of state schools

- Classes in private schools tend to be smaller, so individual learners get more attention from the teacher.

- Private schools can choose what to teach, rather than following a national curriculum. This allows them to concentrate on teaching what learners and their parents want.

CASE STUDY 5.1

The American School of Dubai

More than 90 per cent of schools in Dubai are private schools. There is a large expat community – people who have moved from other parts of the world to live and work in Dubai and many of these people speak English. As a result, many of the private schools in Dubai follow either the US or the British curriculum.

One of the older private schools is the American School of Dubai, which has been established for over 50 years and has approximately 2000 students. The school is run as an independent not-for-profit community school, but the fees are high – around USD$26,000 per year for secondary school students. With this income, the school is able to provide impressive facilities, including two swimming pools, six tennis courts, two large playing fields, a theatre and two libraries. Class sizes are also small.

Around three-quarters of the students come from the United States and Canada, but 76 nationalities are represented in total.

The school has been criticised by school inspectors for its inconsistent delivery of the Arabic and Islamic Studies requirements from the Ministry of Education in Dubai. However, academic performance in the rest of the curriculum is very good.

Figure 5.5: An international school in Dubai.

Task

1   State-funded schools are available in Dubai. Why do you think so many parents are prepared to pay high fees for private education for their children?

2   What impact might the existence of schools like the American School of Dubai have on state-funded education in Dubai?

- Private schools vary widely, so parents can choose the school that best suits their children's needs.

- Because of their funding from fees, private schools usually have more money to develop good facilities, such as sports fields, swimming pools and ICT and science laboratories. They can also keep class sizes small, because they can afford to hire more teachers. In contrast, many governments have limited money to spend on state-funded schools, especially in developing countries. This has a negative effect on class sizes and the facilities they can offer.

ACTIVITY: WRITTEN 5.1

Write one paragraph arguing for and one paragraph arguing against the existence of private, fee-paying schools. Try to write as persuasively as you can, including examples to support your arguments.

REFLECTION

Read your paragraphs to another learner and listen as they read their paragraphs to you. Did you make similar arguments? Did they make any good points which you missed out? Which view did you find it easier to argue in favour of?

Selective and non-selective schools

In many countries, primary schools in a local area are able to accept most of the children who live there. At secondary level, the situation is more complicated. One of the main differences between types of secondary school is whether they select learners, or whether they accept all learners who wish to attend. In a **selective education** system, schools select their learners, usually based on academic ability. **Non-selective schools** accept all children; usually, the only requirement is that they live within a certain distance from the school – the

---

KEY TERMS

selective education: when schools choose their learners, usually based on their ability

non-selective schools: schools which accept all learners, regardless of ability

---

'catchment area'. Selective school learners will come from a wider area, so more of them will travel a long distance to school.

Selective schools use a variety of ways to choose which learners can attend. The most common way is to have an entrance examination. Learners who pass this examination are accepted into the school. Entrance examinations ensure that selective schools have the most able learners, who are most likely to do well in later examinations; the selective school will then claim the credit for their success. Learners who do not pass the entrance examination have to go to a non-selective school. These learners may feel that they have failed, or that they have let their families down. Entrance examinations often take place when learners are about 11 years old, and critics of selective schools say it is unfair for children to face such an important barrier at such a young age.

Strengths of non-selective schools and limitations of selective schools

- Non-selective schools allow equality of opportunity. All learners study the same subjects and have an equal chance of succeeding.

- Non-selective schools tend to have a strong community spirit, bringing together all the children in an area, regardless of class, ethnic group or ability.

- Many young people develop as learners after the age of 11, when entrance examinations usually take place. If a child fails an entrance examination, this can negatively affect their confidence. Without selective schools, this would not happen and learners would be able to develop at their own pace.

- Some parents can afford to hire private tutors to prepare their children for entrance exams. This gives those children an unfair advantage and may mean that selective schools admit more middle-class learners (whose parents can afford to pay for tuition). This can reinforce social class divisions in local communities.

Limitations of non-selective schools and strengths of selective schools

- Non-selective schools bring down standards, as learners who could progress more quickly have to work at the same speed as learners who need more support.

- Non-selective schools tend to be large and impersonal, and may have discipline problems. Selective schools may have a higher proportion of learners who are focused on studying and fewer who belong to anti-school sub-cultures.

- Selective schools ensure that learners with the most potential can achieve their best. This benefits the individual learners and society as a whole. These learners will be able to have jobs which are considered important for society.

- Some larger non-selective schools have a system of streaming or setting. These practices split learners into different groups for some or all of their subjects, based on ability; they are a form of selective education within one school. This can reduce the problem of everyone having to learn at the same speed. However, streaming and setting can also lead some learners to see themselves as failures (because, for example, they have been put in the bottom set). We will learn more about these systems in section 5.3.

THINK LIKE A SOCIOLOGIST

How does the existence of private schools and selective schools affect equality of opportunity globally? In what ways are employment opportunities affected by the type of school a child attends?

Single-sex and co-educational schools

Many early schools were single-sex schools. Boys and girls had very different futures ahead of them as adults, so it was assumed that different schools and different subjects were appropriate.

KEY TERMS

anti-school sub-culture: a group of learners whose norms and values reject those of the school

streaming: when children are taught all subjects in classes with other children of a similar ability

setting: when children are taught a particular subject with other children of a similar ability

single-sex schools: schools which only accept either male or female learners

There has been a lot of research into whether boys and girls do 'better' (this usually refers to exam results) in single sex or co-educational schools. There is some evidence to suggest that girls develop more confidence in single-sex schools, while boys behave better in co-educational schools. However, whether a learner goes to a single-sex or co-educational school does not seem to make a lot of difference in terms of educational achievement; it can be argued that factors such as the quality of teaching and the ethos of the school are more important.

Schools are not only about educational achievement. Discussions surrounding single-sex and co-educational schools should also consider social life and social skills. For example, does the type of school (single-sex or co-educational) affect whether boys or girls are more likely to grow up to have healthy relationships with people of both sexes? Or do boys at single-sex schools, who may have little contact with girls, develop stereotypical ideas? Again, there are strong opinions but the evidence is unclear.

Strengths of single-sex schools and limitations of co-educational schools

- Single-sex schools for girls may avoid some of the problems girls experience in co-educational schools – such as boys getting more attention from teachers, using science equipment more or dominating classroom discussions.

- Girls in single-sex schools may become more confident in subjects that are often seen as more for boys, such as mathematics and physics.

- Teenagers in single-sex schools are not distracted from their studies by the presence of the opposite sex.

Strengths of co-educational schools and limitations of single sex schools

- Bringing boys and girls together in one school is part of socialisation. It helps children to learn how to mix with others and how to behave with people of the other gender. For example, boys will gain experience of being around and talking to girls; as a result, they are more likely to treat girls and women with respect.

KEY TERM

co-educational schools: schools which accept both male and female learners

- It has been claimed that boys do better in co-educational schools because girls set them a good example by studying hard. It has also been suggested that boys want to do better than girls, so they push themselves more.

ACTIVITY: RESEARCH 5.2

If your school is co-educational, find out whether boys or girls get into trouble more. Are boys and girls punished for different things? Choose your own method for investigating this, using ideas from Unit 1. Write a brief report outlining your main findings, and your ideas about the reasons for your findings.

If your school is a single-sex one, try to obtain information about a school for the other sex to compare with your own.

REFLECTION

How did you plan this research and choose which research method to use? What difficulties did you experience when carrying out this research? If you had more time, how could you expand your research to explore the differences between boys' and girls' behaviour in more detail?

Faith schools

Some schools are run by, or have links with, religious organisations. In some countries, religious organisations – such as Christian churches – have always run many primary schools and some secondary schools as part of the state system. In primarily Christian societies, schools run by other religious groups and organisations are less likely to be state schools; for example, Muslim or Jewish schools are likely to be private.

Religious schools are referred to as **faith schools**. These schools are at least partly selective, because they choose children who are members of the school's faith.

KEY TERM

faith schools: schools which are linked to a particular religion or faith and promote that faith through their ethos and curriculum

Faith schools often have a distinctive ethos based on their faith. For example, the ethos of the Krishna Avanti School in London, UK, involves a lacto-vegetarian diet based on compassion for animals and an awareness of the ecological consequences of what we consume.

In Islamic countries, madrasas are faith schools. Part of the curriculum involves reciting the Quran, but madrasas teach many other subjects as well, such as the Arabic language, science and history. In some countries, madrasas are part of the state education system.

Figure 5.6: Boys studying at a faith school.

Strengths of faith schools

- Supporters of faith schools say that the children who attend them will acquire strong moral values, which will make them good members of society.

- Parents with strong religious beliefs can choose a school that shares their beliefs.

Limitations of faith schools

- Where there are several religious groups within a society, faith schools can segregate and divide children.

- It has been argued that faith schools promote the interests of their religion, rather than focusing on their learners' educational experience.

- Faith schools may teach that their religion is superior. This can create suspicion and mistrust of people from other religions.

- The values promoted by faith schools may clash with the values of the wider society. For example, a faith school may promote values that go against equality in some countries and cultures.

International schools

An international school delivers an alternative education to the local schools in a particular country. They are often attended by learners who are not citizens of the host country, but whose parents are working there, for example as part of the military, in an embassy or for a multinational company. International schools often follow a different curriculum to the local schools, offering qualifications such as the international baccalaureate or international GCSEs or A Level. They commonly deliver the curriculum bilingually, using the English language as well as the local language. There are also international schools that deliver their curriculum in French, German or Japanese, for example.

Strengths of international schools

- With increasing globalisation, more and more people work overseas, taking their children with them. International schools provide an education for these children which will be internationally recognised.

- International schools often achieve very good academic results – as good as, or better than, local schools.

- The diverse intake and curriculum of international schools allow learners to develop a global outlook, preparing them well for careers in the future.

- Local children may have the opportunity to study in international schools. This will allow them to gain internationally recognised qualifications, which may increase their future options.

Limitations of international schools

- They can be divisive. Learners who attend them may not integrate into local communities or adapt to local cultures.

- There is often a high turnover of learners as parents move on to different countries. This can affect children's learning and make it difficult for them to build lasting friendships.

- There is often a high turnover of teachers, who may choose to work in an international school for just one or two years before returning to their original country. This can affect learning and the relationships developed between teachers and learners.

- Most international schools charge fees, so most local families could not afford to send their children there. This can create a two-tier education system in countries with a large number of international schools.

ACTIVITY: RESEARCH 5.3

What types of school exist in your country? By using the internet and asking parents, teachers and others, find out the answers to these questions:

1   What is the most common type of school in your country? Why might this be?

2   What types of school are **not** found in your country? Why might this be?

3   Which type of school would you most like to go to? Why?

Alternative approaches to education

Online learning

Education and schools go together – but not as much as they used to. Increasingly, education happens online, rather than in physical classrooms. Some people have always educated themselves at home, by reading and research. But distance education – where a learners works in their own home, following a course designed by educationalists – is relatively new. One of the first examples was the UK's Open University (OU), which started 50 years ago. The OU sent books to adult students at home and also made special radio and television programmes for learners to listen to and watch. This idea has been widely copied since. There are now several groups of universities which offer free courses online; these are called MOOCs (massive open online courses) and they are far more interactive than the OU was when it started. In MOOCs, learners have opportunities to discuss and learn from people around the world, whom they will not physically meet.

Online learning was essential for many people during the COVID-19 pandemic, when schools and universities worldwide had to close. Many schools were able to adapt quickly, delivering lessons via the internet while learners at home joined on phones, tablets and laptops. Assignments were sent to teachers electronically, and they were marked and returned in the same way. The success of online learning means it will continue to grow. However, there is still the problem that many learners (and some schools) do not have the digital technology required for online learning, especially if several children in the same family need to access online lessons at the same time. During the COVID-19 pandemic, many learners also missed the social aspect of school – spending time with their peers; they felt that meeting online was not an adequate replacement.

Homeschooling

In **homeschooling**, children learn at home rather than at a school. Some homeschooled children are taught by one or both parents, while others have a tutor or tutors employed by their parents. In some countries – including Sweden, Germany and the Netherlands – homeschooling is illegal. In others, such as Canada and Denmark, it is regulated by the authorities and learners have to follow the official school curriculum. However, in many countries – including the UK, Australia and India – there is more freedom to follow the learners' interests. In the UK, children must have an education by law but this does not have to be at a school.

Homeschooling can be online. During the COVID-19 pandemic, the term homeschooling was used for parents who were at home (and often working from home) who took over the teacher role. These parents guided their children, who had attended school before the pandemic, helping them to complete work set by the school. In fact, this was more like distance education. Under the more traditional definition of homeschooling, parents and learners have more control over what is taught and when. Research suggests that some children have not returned to school since the COVID-19 pandemic because they prefer the homeschooling environment.

KEY TERMS

online learning: distance education delivered electronically, via the internet, using digital technology

homeschooling: education of school-aged children in the home, rather than at school

There are various reasons for homeschooling, for example:

- Parents believe that they can teach their children better than a school can.

- Parents are dissatisfied with schools; for example, they are concerned about their children being exposed to views they do not approve of.

- Parents want to protect their children from peer pressure or bullying at school.

- A child may have an illness or disability which makes it difficult for them to go to school.

- Children who live in remote areas or whose families travel constantly may find it difficult to settle in a school.

Homeschooled children have fewer opportunities to socialise with their peers. This can be seen as a good thing. Having people of the same age together in one place is a very artificial situation; it did not occur before schools and rarely happens during adulthood. At home, children will be with fewer people but they will interact more with adults, which may help them to become more confident. Homeschooled children are also protected from negative peer pressure and from being bullied.

However, these children also miss an experience that is a big part of most people's lives – and where many people make lifelong friends. Homeschooled children may also miss out on learning important social skills, including the ability to work with others and to cooperate with peers even when they do not have much in common with them. At school, children meet people from different backgrounds and with different upbringings and attitudes; this can help them to develop tolerance and flexibility, which will help them as adults. Homeschooled children do not have these experiences.

Unschooling

Unschooling is an alternative approach to education, based on allowing children to learn at their own pace and in their own time. Formal learning is kept to a minimum. Unschooling is usually a form of homeschooling, done

KEY TERM

unschooling: informal learning without lessons or a curriculum, in which the learner chooses what and how to learn at home with parents. Children are encouraged to learn how to learn, rather than learning subjects or particular knowledge.

Vocational learning

Vocational learning involves learning skills necessary for a particular area of work. Most schoolwork is academic, which means it does not have any immediate practical value. The idea of vocational learning is that not all learners are suited to academic work, so it is better for them to learn practical skills that will allow them to work in a skilled occupation later. For example, they might train to be an electrician or a hairdresser.

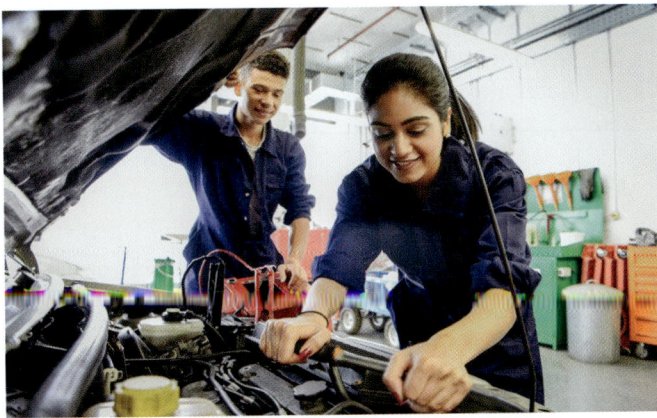

Figure 5.7: A teenage girl learning to be a car mechanic.

Progressive schooling

Progressive schooling describes a wide range of alternative types of school. They are progressive because they reject most of the assumptions that traditional schools are based on. For example, progressive schools emphasise:

- learning by doing things, rather than always from books
- thinking critically and solving problems, rather than memorising a lot of information
- group work and development of social skills; working and learning together
- taking decisions and being responsible
- helping others and the community.

A well-known type of progressive education is Montessori Education, based on the ideas of Maria Montessori. There are schools in many countries that follow these methods. In Montessori schools, learning is based on self-directed activities, creative approaches to learning and collaboration between children.

> **KEY TERM**
>
> **progressive schooling:** education which breaks away from traditional lessons and curriculum and focuses on experience

---

CASE STUDY 5.2

Summerhill School

This progressive school in the UK was started by A.S. Neill, who believed that normal schools failed to produce people who were free and happy. Neill wanted to create a school that was different and would produce more liberated individuals. Summerhill is run democratically: each member of staff and each learner has one vote in school meetings. Learners choose which lessons they go to – they can study any subject, at any level. It is a private, fee-paying boarding and day school, offering both primary and secondary education. Summerhill has been very controversial and in 2000, it had to go to court to fight criticisms made by inspectors.

Task

1   In what ways is Summerhill different from normal schools?

2   What are the advantages and disadvantages of Summerhill, for learners and for the wider society? You can do some research online to find out more about some of the criticisms and defences of Summerhill.

Strengths and limitations of alternative approaches to education

Strengths

- Alternative approaches offer choices to learners who find mainstream education difficult. They allow learners to find a style of learning that suits them.

- Alternative approaches make it possible for some learners to have an education who would not be able to do this in mainstream schools.

- Alternative approaches can give a second chance to learners who have rejected – or been rejected by – mainstream schools.

- Alternative approaches claim to make learners more rounded and capable individuals, with a wider range of skills than those who go to mainstream schools.

Limitations

- Alternative approaches may not give learners the chance to take examinations and earn qualifications; these are required for many careers.

- Alternative approaches usually require self-discipline from the learners; there is less control over what learners do and when. Some learners may not be able to cope with this. They might waste time or fail to learn.

ACTIVITY: DISCUSSION 5.1

Consider this statement: 'Students of different abilities and backgrounds should attend different types of schools, rather than all children going to the same type of school.' Do you agree?

First, on your own, think about this question and make some notes about your ideas. Then work in a group of three or four learners. Each of you has two minutes to share your views.

REFLECTION

When everyone has spoken, decide whether your opinion has changed. If so, why? If not, why not?

CHECK YOUR UNDERSTANDING 5.1

1 With a partner, take it in turns to explain the difference between:

   a formal and informal education

   b the official and the hidden curriculum

   c single-sex and co-educational schools

   d private and state schools

   e selective and non-selective schools

   f faith and non-faith schools.

2 Make a spider diagram to show the main features and any strengths and limitations of each alternative approach to education.

KEY POINTS

- Education can be formal and informal.

  - Formal education includes the official curriculum.

  - Informal education includes the hidden curriculum.

- Different types of schools include:

  - state/public and private

  - selective and non-selective

  - single-sex and co-educational

  - faith schools

  - international schools.

- These different types of school have strengths and limitations.

- Alternative approaches to education include:

  - online learning

  - homeschooling

  - unschooling

  - vocational learning

  - progressive schooling.

- There are strengths and limitations of alternative approaches to education.

5.2 What are the roles and functions of education?

The functionalist view: the positive roles and functions of education

Functionalist sociologists focus on the ways in which education contributes to the continued well-being of society. Functionalists believe that education has several roles and functions.

- **Socialisation.** Schools pass on the norms and values of a society from one generation to the next. They continue the process of socialisation that begins in the family. Education therefore acts as an agent of socialisation.

- **Social control.** In schools, children must follow rules; they learn to control their behaviour to avoid punishments.

- **Economic function.** The education system ensures that a society has enough people with training, qualifications, skills and abilities to maintain the economy. For example, the education systems ensures there are enough people to be doctors, lawyers and teachers.

- **Selective function.** By testing and grading learners and awarding qualifications, the education system ensures individuals can find work that is appropriate for them.

Meritocracy and social mobility

In most modern industrial societies, one of the main values that children learn – according to functionalists – is the importance of individual achievement. At home, each child has an ascribed status: their role is set, for example, by their gender or their place in the order of the children in the family. At school, however, they are judged mainly by what they achieve and this is measured by universal standards, such as exams. This makes achievement very important.

Functionalists say that modern societies are **meritocracies**, where each individual gets what they deserve based on their own talents and effort. In schools, this means that the best learners get the best grades, as long as they work hard. A meritocratic education system can create **social mobility** by giving learners the opportunity to study for the qualifications they will need for a well-paid career. This in turn may allow them to move up from one social class to another – referred to as upward social mobility.

Role allocation

One function of the education system is to produce people with the skills and abilities needed for the economy of that society. Meritocracy means that the best achieving learners should be able to enter their chosen career or area of work. For some jobs, learners will need to achieve particular qualifications or study particular subjects at school. For some careers (for example, in medicine, engineering or law), learners will need to continue their studies at university for several years after leaving school.

For a society, the education system prepares learners to fill the range of occupations needed and ensures that the learners' abilities match the requirements of these occupations. This is called sifting and sorting, or **role allocation**. By assessing children's abilities and how they do in tests and exams, the education system guides them to follow appropriate paths. A learner who passes exams with high grades may go on to study at university and then get a well-paid career as a result of their qualifications. Other learners with different abilities may train for more practical work. They may learn a trade, such as electrical work, or they might go into office work and administration. Learners who leave school with few, or no qualifications may have to accept low-paid jobs with little status – but this is functional too, because people are needed to fill these jobs.

KEY TERMS

meritocracy: a system in which individuals reach the social positions they deserve, based on their educational achievement, talent and skills

social mobility: the movement of individuals or groups up or down the social hierarchy

role allocation: sorting individuals into appropriate jobs and roles based on achievement in school

If the education system works well, it will produce the right numbers of people for the number of jobs available – a certain amount of doctors, engineers, teachers, craftspeople, manual workers, and so on.

Value consensus

The education system socialises children into a shared set of values. It can help them to feel that they belong to a particular society, and that they have shared interests with other members of that society. This creates a **value consensus**, where all or most people in a society share the same values. The shared values may be based on a religion but they do not have to be. It is particularly important to create a value consensus in societies that are ethnically diverse. There are many ways in which individuals can learn to adopt the value consensus of their society while at school. For example:

- being in the school with many other children, sharing the same experiences, learning together and uniting in assemblies

- singing the national anthem

- seeing the national flag or other national symbols (such as photos of the head of state) in classrooms and around the school

- learning patriotic slogans

- being taught about their society, its history and culture.

School acts as a bridge between the family and the wider society. According to functionalists, children spend their early years in their families, where they are valued as individuals and have an ascribed status. At school, they become just one person among many and they have to achieve a status. This is a step away from the family and towards the adult world of work.

Equal opportunities

As we have seen, functionalists argue that society in general, and the education system in particular, are meritocratic. A key feature of a meritocratic education system is that it provides **equal opportunities** for everyone.

If all children have the chance to go to school and they all study the same curriculum and take the same examinations, then according to functionalists, they have had equal opportunities to achieve. Any differences in their outcomes are based on their differing abilities or the amount of effort they made.

In a meritocracy based on equal opportunities, social background should be irrelevant. A child from a working-class background who has ability and works hard should be able to do as well as one from a privileged background. Most schools share and teach a value system which promotes the ideas of meritocracy and equal opportunities. As a result, most people accept the view that the education system is fair and that people who are successful deserve their success. Learners who are not successful blame themselves (for example, for not working hard enough), rather than the system.

Standardised testing

The functionalist view of meritocracy and role allocation relies on a **standardised testing** system in which all learners take the same tests. This is why examination boards, such as Cambridge Assessment, set exams which are taken by many learners, in many schools and countries. The marks and grades can be compared, so it is clear who has done well and who has not. Schools perform an important function in enabling learners to be judged by and to accept universal standards, which are essential for a modern industrial economy.

Figure 5.8: Children taking a standardised test.

KEY TERMS

value consensus: a widespread agreement on values

equal opportunities: when everyone has the same chance of succeeding

KEY TERM

standardised testing: when all learners take the same assessments, which are marked in the same way

Setting by ability

Among any group of children, there will be learners with different abilities. Despite the importance of equal opportunities, functionalists argue that it is unfair to delay learners who progress more quickly by slowing the pace of teaching for learners who need extra support. There is also the risk that a *slightly* slower pace will still not meet the needs of learners who find the work particularly challenging. One solution to this is 'setting' by ability: learners are put in different classes based on ability, studying at a different pace and sometimes studying different material.

Vocationalism

Vocationalism, or vocational education, is education that prepares a learner for a particular trade, craft or profession. Functionalists see this as an important part of education, because it supports role allocation. Most schooling is general academic schooling; many learners who succeed at school go on to higher education and obtain higher qualifications such as degrees before looking for work. Vocational education, on the other hand, gives people a different route into work. In secondary education and above, learners can take courses that lead directly to careers in, for example, car vehicle maintenance or health care. For functionalists, providing vocational education helps to ensure that there are trained people to carry out essential work roles.

The strengths and limitations of the functionalist view

Strengths

- The functionalist view explains how schools play a part in the continuation of societies, passing norms and values to the next generation.

- The functionalist view shows that education is an important agent of social control, teaching children to respect rules and those in authority. This is important for society.

KEY TERM

vocationalism: vocational education that prepares people for work or trains them for particular jobs or careers

- The functionalist view fits with the fact that, in most countries, access to education is free. This leads to equality of opportunity.

- The functionalist view fits with the practice of putting learners in sets based on ability, so that everyone can work at their own pace and not be held back by others.

- The functionalist view explains how occupational roles are taken by people with the necessary skills and abilities.

Limitations

Criticisms of the functionalist view come from different sources, including from Marxist and feminist perspectives. They include the following:

- Functionalists are wrong to say there is a shared set of values in education. Marxists say that the values passed on are those of the ruling class – the dominant ideology. Feminists say they are patriarchal values imposed by men.

- In reality, education is not a meritocracy. Many factors can affect a learner's grades, including the quality of the school, home background, gender, peers, social class and ethnicity.

- Functionalists are wrong to claim there is a strong connection between schools and work. As adults in work, many people use little of what they learnt in school. Some companies even complain that the literacy and numeracy skills of school leavers are not good enough: learners have been taught things they do not need, instead of things they do need.

- In some cases, people are selected for jobs based on factors such as their social class, ethnicity and gender, rather than their educational achievement. In these cases, it will not matter how well they did at school.

The functions of education: the Marxist view

Socialisation and social control as capitalist ideological control

Marxist sociologists see the functions of education in a very different light. They agree that the education system socialises people into a shared value system.

However, they see this as a capitalist value system based on the ideology of the ruling class – not as a set of values which reflects the interests of everyone in society (the functionalist view). The capitalist value system is based on the idea that people should accept their status and social position without challenging the existing hierarchy.

Marxists argue that socialisation into a capitalist value system through schooling works differently for the middle and upper classes. Working-class people are indoctrinated, not educated: they are taught a set of values that will make them 'good' workers for the capitalist system. To serve the ruling class, workers should be willing to come to work on time, work to the best of their ability, accept inadequate wages and not question orders from their superiors. According to the Marxist view, working-class people suffer from false consciousness. This means they are unaware of how they are being used and they do not realise that the shared values they learn are not in their interests.

In contrast, the children of the bourgeoisie often attend different types of schools, where they learn that they are superior to other classes and that they deserve privilege and respect. As described in section 5.1, wealthy children may go to fee-paying private schools. This makes it easier for them to access top universities and well-paid positions. In this way, according to Marxists, the ruling class ensures that its sons and daughters inherit its power and wealth, so the class system survives over time.

The hidden and official curriculum

According to Marxists, the capitalist value system is passed on through both the official curriculum and the hidden curriculum:

- The official curriculum does not teach children about the true nature of the society they live in, nor does it encourage them to think critically about it. Knowledge is divided into separate subjects, so it is difficult to put everything together and work out what is really going on. Sociology is one subject that does make people think critically about the nature of society and how people live – so Marxists would not be surprised that it is not taught to everyone in most countries.

- The hidden curriculum trains children to obey authority and accept hierarchies. In doing so, it prepares them for the world of work. Table 5.1 summarises the ways in which the experience of school is like the experience of work.

In all these ways, and others, Marxists argue that the children of the working class are trained to be reliable workers who do not complain.

STRETCH AND CHALLENGE

To what extent do you agree that the hidden curriculum is a way of controlling learners in school and preparing them for the world of work? Is this a good or a bad thing?

What is taught	Aspect of hidden curriculum
Conforming to rules and regulations at work	Schools have rules and punishments, such as detentions
Respect for authority, such as a manager at work	Learners have to show respect for teachers, e.g. they have to speak to teachers respectfully, ask for permission to leave the classroom and follow instructions
Acceptance of hierarchies	In schools, head teachers are at the top, and learners are at the bottom
Punctuality	Learners need to be on time for the start of school and lessons; there are punishments for being late
Lack of power at work	Learners have to do as they are told; they cannot choose what they learn or how
Differences in pay and status at work	Learners are graded by ability, being put in streams or sets; there may be rewards for academic achievement
Competition for jobs	Learners have to try to do better than others in study, sport, etc.
Accepting boring repetitive work	Learners have to do schoolwork, whether it is interesting or not

Table 5.1: Ways in which the experience of school is like the experience of work.

The middle-class culture in schools

Marxists see schools as middle class in almost every way, based on middle-class values. Teachers are middle class by definition, due to their occupation, so they praise and reward middle-class attitudes and behaviour. Marxists argue that this makes working-class children feel out of place. Their way of life and even the way they speak are not valued, and they may feel as though they have to be completely different at school and at home. It is not surprising then that some working-class children rebel by behaving disruptively, while others find it difficult to achieve academic success.

The sociologist Pierre Bourdieu used the term **cultural capital**. This refers to the amount of cultural knowledge people have, which may include taste, manners, an understanding of how to behave and how the middle-class education system works. Bourdieu argues that middle-class families have more cultural capital than working-class families. They pass this on to their children, allowing them to successfully navigate the middle-class culture of schools. Cultural capital is discussed in more detail in section 4.3.

The myth of meritocracy

Marxists challenge the ideas of meritocracy and social mobility. They argue that schools reproduce existing inequalities. In their view, success depends less on talent and effort and more on class background. Middle- and upper-class parents can provide advantages for their children, such as independent schooling, private tutors and access to books and other resources. If children are competing with each other to obtain prized occupations after school, those from working-class backgrounds start with a disadvantage. **Meritocracy is a myth**.

Figure 5.9: A child feeling unengaged at school.

Material factors, such as access to digital technology

According to Marxists, children from working-class families are disadvantaged in education by their lack of access to resources – referred to as material factors. This occurs both at home and in school. At home, children in poorer families are less likely to have access to digital devices or a high-speed internet connection. There may be fewer books in the home and poorer children are less likely to have their own room to do schoolwork in. Working-class children are also more likely to attend schools with few resources and equipment and may be unable to access additional learning (such as going on school trips) due to the cost involved.

Setting by ability

Marxists point to setting and streaming by ability as evidence that the school system has a social-class bias. According to Marxists, working-class learners are more likely to be put in lower sets and streams, which reduces their chances of educational achievement. This happens because of disadvantage from material and cultural factors – both in and outside school – and because of stereotyping by teachers. The potential ability of working-class learners is not recognised and assumptions are made about their attitude and potential, based on their social class background.

STRETCH AND CHALLENGE

How do you think Marxists would explain upward social mobility, where some children from working class backgrounds do achieve good qualifications and get middle-class jobs? Does this completely disprove the Marxist view?

KEY TERMS

cultural capital: the knowledge, taste and values associated with the higher classes

myth of meritocracy: the idea that equality of opportunity does not actually exist, so belief in meritocracy is false

Strengths and limitations of the Marxist view

Strengths

- The Marxist view explains why members of the working class accept a system that offers them few opportunities.

- The Marxist view explains how schools prepare working-class children for lower-paid and lower-skilled work.

- The Marxist view identifies many reasons why working-class children may be disadvantaged in the education system, showing that meritocracy is a myth.

- The Marxist view identifies how setting by ability can often disadvantage working-class children, who are negatively affected by material and cultural deprivation.

Limitations

- The Marxist view emphasises class inequality in education but does not pay enough attention to inequalities of ethnicity and gender.

- Some sociologists argue that the Marxist view exaggerates the extent to which schools produce a compliant workforce. At school, many learners rebel against the rules and authority.

- The Marxist view that the ruling class controls the education system can be challenged. Many schools are controlled locally, and teachers have some control over what they teach and how.

- It can be argued that the Marxist view is out of date, because factory workers are no longer needed as much. Many employers today want workers with a range of skills, such as those related to decision making and problem solving, and schools have responded by changing the way they teach.

The functions of education: the feminist view

Where Marxists see a division between social classes, feminists see a division between the two sexes. Education and schooling have always been affected by gender. In the past – and today in some countries – education is thought to be more important for boys than for girls. The content of education is also often different for boys and girls. Feminists argue that schools, like other secondary agencies of socialisation, send the message to both boys and girls that boys are superior. As a result, girls may learn to lower their expectations and accept traditional gender roles. This can happen for the following reasons:

- Girls are encouraged or even forced to take different subjects in school. Some subjects are seen as being more appropriate for the traditional female role, such as sewing and needlework, cookery and childcare. Girls may even be discouraged from taking 'harder' subjects, such as the sciences.

- Teachers have higher expectations of boys and encourage them to aim for a career, while assuming that the future for most girls is marriage and motherhood.

The feminist view of education is concerned mainly with achievement by gender in schools. This is discussed more in section 5.3. A brief explanation of the main themes is included here.

The patriarchal culture of education

The feminist view is that education is based on **patriarchy**. Assumptions about the roles of men and women are built into the education system. As a result, boys are seen as having priority over girls. Positions of authority in schools, from head teacher to head students, are often held by men or boys. Even boys' sport is given a higher priority than girls' sport.

Male power, gender hierarchy and role models

Feminists argue that education – including the curriculum, the organisation of schools and the teaching of lessons – reinforces male power. In many countries, although more teachers are women, more head teachers are men so men hold more positions of authority. This is referred to as a **gender hierarchy**

KEY TERMS

patriarchy: a term used by feminists to describe a society or organisation (including the family) in which men are dominant and women are subordinate

gender hierarchy: a system where one gender has a higher status than the other gender; in a patriarchal society, males benefit from the gender hierarchy and it is an example of male power, which sends an important message to the male and female learners in the school.

Role models, or the absence of them, can affect subject choices. For example, if most or all science teachers are male, girls may be less likely to choose science subjects. Role models in wider society also make a difference. For example, if a girl is considering a career in medicine, she may choose to become a nurse while a boy may choose to become a doctor. Both the girl and the boy may have been influenced by role models in school and in the wider society, in terms of which careers are appropriate for males and females.

Some feminist research suggests that, during lessons, boys are allowed to dominate the classroom space and take up more of the teacher's time and attention. This is another example of male power and gender hierarchy. Even a female head teacher could lead a school in which boys are prioritised over girls, because the underlying patriarchal nature of the school has not changed.

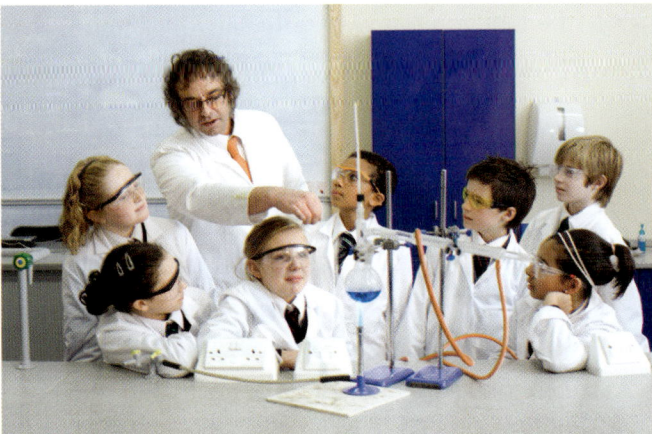

Figure 5.10: Science teachers are more likely to be male.

Access to education

Globally, girls are less likely to attend school than boys. This is explored in section 5.3, under the heading 'Global differences in educational achievement'.

> ### KEY TERM
>
> **role models:** people someone looks up to and tries to be like

Gendered curriculum and subject choices

Feminists argue that the official school curriculum is **gendered**: it involves a male-centered view of society. This is apparent in the following ways:

- Books studied in literature lessons are more likely to appeal to boys and to have male authors.

- Subjects such as history tend to focus on the achievements of men and on events seen from a male perspective.

- Images in textbooks show boys doing more interesting things than girls, or in a wider range of occupations.

- In the past, some subjects were only for girls (such as cooking or needlework) and others only for boys (such as woodwork or metalwork). In most countries, these barriers have now gone but boys and girls are still more likely to choose different subjects. These gendered choices can affect future career options. Subject choices are discussed further in section 5.3.

Teacher expectations

Teacher expectations vary by culture but, according to feminists, teachers are likely to have lower expectations of girls and are less likely to encourage girls to study hard. Some research in the UK has suggested that teachers also have different expectations for boys and girls in terms of behaviour. For example, girls may be punished for behaviour such as calling out in class or talking when they should be listening but boys are often allowed to behave in these ways without any sanctions. This may reflect wider expectations of the dominant or submissive roles of males and females in society.

Peer groups and social control

Girls' peer groups can influence their attitudes towards education. Studying at a higher level may involve moving away from home and community, so girls may discourage each other from doing this. They apply pressure to conform to the gender expectations of their society.

> ### KEY TERM
>
> **gendered curriculum:** when the content of the teaching has a bias towards one gender, usually boys

ACTIVITY: DISCUSSION 5.2

In mixed-gender groups of 4, discuss whether you agree with the following feminist statements:

a   Schools have a gender hierarchy, with most senior roles being held by men.

b   The curriculum is gendered, in favour of boys.

c   Teachers have higher academic expectations of boys but higher behaviour expectations of girls.

REFLECTION

If your group contained both male and female learners, was there a difference between the views of the males and the females?

Did all members of the group contribute equally to the discussion? If not, did male or female learners speak more?

Do you think your views on the issues discussed are influenced by your gender?

Strengths and limitations of the feminist view

Strengths

- The feminist view draws attention to the many ways in which girls are still disadvantaged at school, despite rising achievement.

- The feminist view shows how societies and education limit girls' and women's ambitions and achievements.

- The feminist view draws attention to the underlying sexism which can exist at every level of a school.

Limitations

- It can be argued that feminists exaggerate the extent to which schools and education are patriarchal. Many teachers, including head teachers, are women and provide role models. They work to ensure equal opportunities for girls.

- By concentrating on gender, some feminists may not pay enough attention to social class and to ethnicity.

- Some ideas are outdated. In many countries, teacher expectations of girls now outweigh their expectations of boys and girls achieve better grades in many subjects.

MAKING CONNECTIONS

What connections can you find between:

- the functionalist view of families and the functionalist view of education

- the Marxist view of families and the Marxist view of education

- the feminist view of families and the feminist view of education?

ACTIVITY: WRITTEN 5.2

Make a table comparing and contrasting the functionalist, Marxist and feminist views regarding the roles and functions of education.

CHECK YOUR UNDERSTANDING 5.2

1   Read the list of 20 terms and ideas below and identify which ones relate to functionalism, which to Marxism and which to feminism. (Note: Two terms are bold. These are referred to by more than one perspective.)

- meritocracy
- male power
- ideological control
- **setting by ability**
- vocationalism
- role models
- role allocation
- the myth of meritocracy
- **the hidden curriculum**
- social mobility
- gender hierarchy
- value consensus
- teacher expectations

- material factors
- gendered curriculum/subject choice
- equal opportunities
- the middle-class culture in schools
- the patriarchal culture of education
- standardised testing
- peer groups and social control

2   Make some cards, using three different colours of card or paper (one for each perspective). Write each term/idea on one side of a card; for example, if you choose pink for functionalism, write each functionalist term on a pink card. (If you only have card or paper of one colour, write in a different coloured pen for each perspective.)

3   On the back of each card, write a definition of the term/idea.

4   Work with a partner and use the cards to test each other on your knowledge and understanding of the three perspectives.

KEY POINTS

- There are functionalist, Marxist and feminist views on the role and functions of education.
- Functionalists see education as a meritocracy which has a key role in socialising children into the value consensus and allocating them to future roles.
- Marxists argue that meritocracy is a myth and that the education system reproduces class inequalities.
- Feminists think that the education system is patriarchal and reinforces gender inequalities.
- Each perspective has strengths and limitations.

5.3 What factors help to explain differences in educational achievement and experience?

Patterns in educational achievement and experience

This section discusses the patterns of educational achievement and experience in relation to social class, ethnicity, gender and **global differences in education**. These are patterns of **educational inequality**. Different groups may be treated differently in schools, educated in different ways, have different levels of **educational achievement** and generally experience education differently.

> ### TIP
>
> Sociologists deal with large groups of people – social classes, ethnic groups, gender groups and so on. There are always individuals who do not follow the broader patterns of these groups. For example, some people from disadvantaged backgrounds achieve very highly in education. Bear this in mind as you study this section.

> ### KEY TERMS
>
> **global differences in education:** differences in educational provision, outcomes and experience in different countries and regions of the world
>
> **educational inequality:** when different groups (based on class, gender and ethnicity) are treated or educated differently or have different levels of educational achievement
>
> **educational achievement:** how well individuals do in the school system, usually measured by exam results

Patterns and explanations for differences in educational achievement and experience based on social class

Social class is a major influence on educational achievement. In the past, schools were largely for children from the most privileged families. Until the 20th century, even in modern industrial societies, only a minority of lower-class children received an education and what they did receive was short and basic. There was essentially a two-tier system with no schooling or very basic schooling for most children and a privileged education for the few.

Early schools in countries like the UK were very much based on social class. There were basic primary schools for working-class children, often run by churches or charities, and private boarding schools for children from the upper class. In the 20th century, this system changed and now most children go to the same types of school. However, the continued existence of fee-paying schools for those who can afford them means that this does not always happen.

Children's social class is not usually recorded in the way that gender and ethnicity are. Statistics have to be treated with caution, because sociologists and statisticians have to operationalise social class; they have to decide how to measure who is in which social class. In the UK, one indicator used to measure social class in schools is learners' eligibility for free school meals. The welfare state provides free school meals for children from low-income families. Therefore, sociologists assume that children who receive these free school meals – whose families have a lower income – are from a lower-class background. Researchers have used this measure to see if there is a link between social class and educational achievement in the UK. For example, it has been found that 36 per cent of children who were eligible for free school meals achieved grade 4 or higher in Maths and English GCSEs, while 66 per cent of non-disadvantaged children did so. These figures suggest that social class is a bigger factor than gender or ethnicity in influencing educational achievement.

Material factors

One reason that working-class children underachieve is **material deprivation**. This refers to factors in the standard of living of children, especially those from working-class backgrounds, that may lead to them underachieving in school. Children living in (or close to) poverty are likely to be educationally disadvantaged in several ways, even when education is free. These disadvantages include:

- not having a quiet place to study because the home is small or crowded

- having an inadequate diet, so they have problems with concentration and tiredness

- being unable to afford extras – even when education is free, parents are often expected to provide school uniforms, sports kit, writing and other equipment and to contribute to the cost of trips

- not having had preschool education, because the family did not have the money to pay for this – they may then start primary school behind other children

- not having access to digital technology. Having a tablet or laptop has become increasingly important for success in education but many children do not have access to these items and may not have internet access at home. This became very important during the COVID-19 pandemic, when schools in many countries closed. Some children were able to study at home using the internet, following lessons set by their teachers and even participating remotely in lessons. Those without internet access found it difficult or impossible to study

- having few resources at home, such as educational books or materials

- having part-time jobs when they are old enough, to help with family income. This means they have less time and energy to study.

Cultural and social factors

Social factors including the cultural background of working-class learners may help to explain their underachievement in school. This is described as cultural, rather than material, deprivation. Cultural deprivation comes from values and attitudes, not from a lack of money and resources. Some sociologists have claimed that the following cultural aspects of the working class may cause disadvantage in educational achievement:

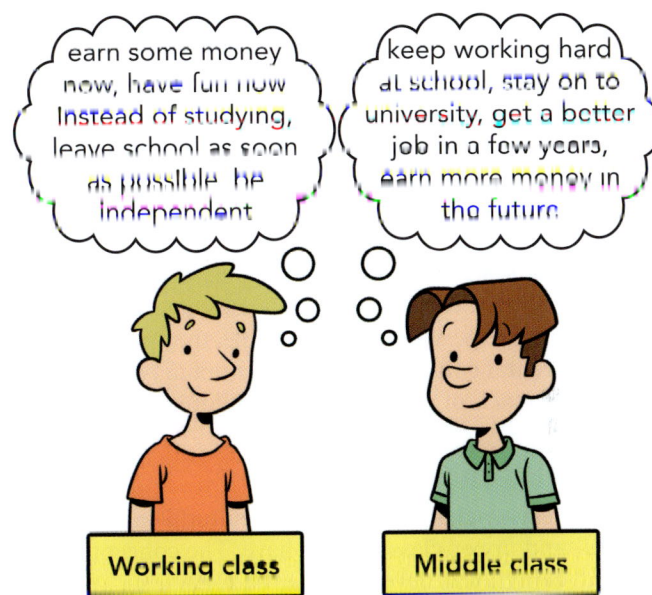

Figure 5.11: Immediate and deferred gratification.

- a fatalistic attitude. Working-class children may feel that they are not in control of their own destiny and cannot change their prospects. This might lead them to think there is no point studying at school.

- the need for immediate, rather than deferred, gratification. This means being unable to see the benefits of long-term rewards. For example, it is claimed that working-class children are more likely to want to start earning money as soon as they can (immediate gratification), rather than studying long-term, which will bring the reward of higher pay and a higher status career in the future (deferred gratification).

- a search for thrills and excitement. Working-class children may not be able to do expensive hobbies or go on holiday. As a result, boys in particular may turn to deviant or even criminal activities as a source of excitement in an otherwise boring life. This could be related to a culture of masculinity, which values excitement and rule breaking (see Unit 6). This may get them into trouble or lead to a negative label that affects their educational achievement.

KEY TERMS

material deprivation: being unable to afford material goods which most people in a given society would see as necessities

social factors: things that affect lifestyle and life chances, such as wealth, religion and occupation

---

- parents may not value education, perhaps because they had negative experiences at school themselves. Their children may learn this attitude from them.

However, many people have questioned the evidence that there is a different working-class culture. The term 'cultural deprivation' involves an assumption that working-class culture is inferior. Even if it is described accurately, this culture may be the best or only way of coping with disadvantages when people have very little control over their lives. Most working-class parents do see the benefits of education and are ambitious for their children to succeed. However, they may lack the knowledge and confidence that middle-class parents have; for example, to demand extra support for their child from the school. Some working-class parents are reluctant to have contact with schools because of their own negative experiences. For example, they may not attend parental consultations. The school may wrongly see this as a lack of interest in their children's education.

Cultural capital

Working-class parents may lack the cultural capital that middle- and upper-class parents have. The concept of cultural capital was developed by the French sociologist Pierre Bourdieu. In his theory, the advantages of middle-class and upper-class learners come from two sources:

- economic capital: they are better off financially, so their parents can spend more on a good education

- cultural capital, which includes such things as tastes, values and behaviour.

The advantages parents can give to their children in terms of cultural capital include:

- familiarity with books and reading

- visits to museums, concerts and art galleries

- a sense of the importance of education.

Middle- and upper-class parents also know how the education system works and how to use it to help their children. Working-class children have less cultural capital and teachers might see them less favourably as a result.

Home and community factors

Home factors and community factors tend to reinforce each other, making problems worse. For many working-class children, their home and local area may be barriers to their success in education. Related factors include:

- attending a disadvantaged school in a poor area. Such schools cannot offer as good an education as those in more prosperous areas, where parents

> **KEY TERM**
>
> **home factors:** factors in a child's home background that affect how they do in school

might raise extra money for the school and where fewer of the learners have additional social or behavioural needs.

- coming from a family that is not financially able to support a son or daughter through university or other higher education. If children are aware of this from an early age, they are likely to limit their ambitions accordingly.

- loyalty to the community or social class. It may be seen as wrong to want to move away from your origins by moving up the class ladder.

- an absence of successful role models in the family and community. If a child does not know anyone who benefited from doing well at school, they are likely to see education as unimportant, irrelevant or simply not for 'people like us'.

- problems with crime, drugs and gangs in some areas and communities. These interfere with the education of children from these areas, whether or not they become directly involved.

The children of middle-class parents are less likely to suffer from these problems. Middle-class parents are more likely to be able and willing to afford extras to help their children do well, such as buying books or even arranging a tutor for lessons outside school.

Linguistic factors

Another aspect of culture that can affect educational achievement is the type of language children speak. In 1971, Basil Bernstein argued in *Class, Codes and Control* that languages had two codes:

- The restricted code is used for informal everyday spoken communication with family and friends. Its vocabulary is limited and meanings are not always explicit, because the two parties share knowledge and assumptions.

- The elaborated code is used for formal occasions in schools, by teachers and in textbooks; learners get marks for using this in written work. It makes meanings explicit and can be used to express complex and abstract ideas.

Bernstein suggested that, because of their different exposure to types of language, middle-class children were more likely to be confident using the elaborated code than working-class children. This gave their teachers the impression that they were more able and allowed them to do better in school. It is important to note that the restricted code has its own strengths and uses and everybody uses it (including middle-class people): it is not simply working-class speech. The advantage middle class children have is being able to switch between the two codes easily.

Compensatory education

The relative lack of achievement by working-class learners is usually seen as a problem by governments; they want a well-educated workforce that will attract companies to invest. There have been many different attempts to raise the educational achievements of working-class learners. These attempts are known as **compensatory education** (compensating for perceived problems in the child's background). They include:

- extra support given to learners from disadvantaged backgrounds. For example, some governments give extra funding to schools in disadvantaged areas, or offer incentives such as higher pay to attract good teachers to work in these schools.

- schemes which offer free pre-school places and support to children from disadvantaged families, so these children do not start primary school without basic literacy and social skills.

In-school factors

Many explanations for working-class underachievement focus on the material and cultural factors outside school that affect children, before and during schooling. However, many sociologists argue that **in-school factors** are also important.

> ### KEY TERMS
>
> **compensatory education:** educational policies including financial aid, additional classes and tutoring which aim to support children from disadvantaged backgrounds and close the achievement gap between working-class and middle-class learners
>
> **in-school factors:** factors at school that affect children's educational achievement

Michael Rutter and his colleagues, in *Fifteen Thousand Hours: Secondary Schools and their Effects on Children* (1979), reported research showing that good schools can make a difference to the life chances of all learners. Rutter suggested that 'good' schools were those which were well organised and had clear rules and expectations of their learners. More recent research from Tim Morris and his colleagues (2021) found a positive correlation between children's enjoyment of school when they were six years old and their achievement in examinations when they were 16 – regardless of their social-class background, gender or ethnicity. These findings and other similar research suggest that lower achievement by learners from more disadvantaged backgrounds may be related to the standard of schooling they receive. It is argued that schools which serve poorer communities provide education of a lower standard, because they have less funding, more social problems to deal with, poor behavioural standards and low academic expectations.

Another in-school factor is the peer groups learners belong to. Middle-class children often have a positive attitude towards school and education; their socialisation and background lead them to value education, so they work hard to succeed in school. Groups of learners with these attitudes will support each other in their education. This is a **pro-school sub-culture** – a learner sub-culture which shares the school's values and norms of studying hard for success and working with teachers.

> ### KEY TERM
>
> **pro-school sub-culture:** a group of learners whose norms and values agree with those of the school

Figure 5.12: A pro-school sub-culture.

Middle-class children who have a positive attitude towards education usually conform to the school's requirements and expectations. Some working-class children, however, rebel against the school, because they find it difficult to achieve and fit in with the school's middle-class rules. They may develop an alternative set of values, attitudes and behaviours in opposition to the academic aims of the school. This is an **anti-school sub-culture** (also known as a counter-school sub-culture). Anti-school sub-cultures enable students to improve their own self-esteem by giving them status in the eyes of their peer group. These sub-cultures may involve:

- truanting – missing lessons or even whole school days, without permission
- avoiding school work
- cheating in their homework and in tests
- being insolent and aggressive towards teachers
- disliking and sometimes bullying students who work hard at school (such as members of pro-school sub-cultures)
- being involved in delinquency and sometimes serious crime outside school.

TIP

Make sure you can distinguish between anti-school and pro-school sub-cultures and explain the links with social class. You might wonder why working-class children would form an anti-school sub-culture, since it seems to be against their best interests. But some sociologists argue that it is understandable because these learners are unlikely to succeed in education anyway, due to the other factors discussed in this section. Therefore, forming an anti-school sub-culture is a way for working-class students to take control of their school experience.

Members of anti-school sub-cultures disrupt the smooth running of the school as a way of getting back at the system which has labelled them as failures and denied them status.

KEY TERM

anti-school sub-culture: a group of learners whose norms and values reject those of the school

Because working-class learners are more often labelled as failures, they are more likely to belong to these sub-cultures.

Selective and private education

Children from different backgrounds are likely to go to different types of school. Middle- and upper-class children are more likely to attend private, fee-paying schools and selective schools. This is another factor which can explain why working-class learners generally underachieve in comparison to middle- and upper-class learners.

Going to a private school helps achievement in the following ways:

- Classes are smaller, so learners get more individual help and attention.
- Private schools usually have better facilities and resources because they have more funds.
- Parents are fee-paying customers, so the school tries to provide a high-quality education to satisfy them and attract more customers.
- Many private schools have good reputations and a network of previous students, or alumni, who continue to support the school and its current students. This may help learners get better jobs when they leave the school.

Selective schools help achievement in the following ways:

- Learners who are selected by the school have already shown their academic potential, so teachers at the school will have high expectations.
- Student sub-cultures are likely to be pro-school, so learners are likely to behave well in lessons and encourage each other to study hard.
- All learners have a certain level of academic ability, so teachers do not need to slow down or spend extra time helping learners who need extra support.

Labelling theory

Research suggests that social patterns of underachievement in education are affected by the meanings constructed in school classrooms: learner progress is affected by the ways in which teachers and learners see each other. For example, evidence showing a link between social class and achievement may lead teachers to *expect* working-class learners to perform poorly. These low expectations may then contribute to the failure of working-class learners.

CASE STUDY 5.3

The lads

One of the classic studies of an anti-school sub-culture was by Paul Willis, who followed a group of working-class boys in a secondary school in a city in England. The 'lads', as they were known, did not come to school to learn. Instead, they came to 'have a laugh', they enjoyed breaking school rules and misbehaving in and out of lessons to annoy teachers. They did not need qualifications for the work they would do in local factories, so they saw no point in learning at school. The lads looked down on other students who did not rebel against the school, including a group of boys they called 'ear 'oles' (because they always listened to the teacher).

Task

1   What kind of sub-culture did the 'ear 'oles' have?

2   Willis argued that the anti-school sub-culture formed by the 'lads' was good preparation for their future as unskilled workers in local factories.

In what ways might their behaviour and attitude as factory workers be similar to their behaviour at school?

3   Why might this kind of sub-culture be more common among boys than girls?

Figure 5.13: A boy breaking classroom rules.

Much of the research in this area is based on **labelling** theory. Labelling theory is a view associated with interactionism (a sociological perspective which takes a micro approach). Students are not seen as passive victims of structural, material or cultural forces outside the school that cause them to underachieve, as Marxists tend to argue. Instead, interactionism focuses on interactions between individuals. In a school context, teachers are in a position of power; the ways in which they interpret the behaviour and potential of learners will affect their interactions with them.

Teachers judge and classify learners in various ways, such as high or low achieving, troublemakers, ideal learners, hardworking or lazy. This process of labelling by teachers has been shown to affect learners' performance. An early judgement about a learner made by a teacher can influence all future interactions with the learner.

KEY TERM

labelling: defining a person or group in a particular way

According to the interactionist Howard Becker, teachers judge learners on non-academic factors, such as speech, dress, personality (how cooperative, enthusiastic and polite they are), conduct and appearance. Becker argues that these factors make up a stereotype of the 'ideal student' and influence teachers' assessments of a learner's ability. The social class of the learner has an important influence on this evaluation. Teachers often assume that learners from working-class homes are poorly motivated, lack family support and will be disruptive in the classroom. They might also assume that working-class learners lack ability, regardless of their actual potential. In contrast, learners from middle-class backgrounds most closely fit the teacher's stereotype of the 'ideal student'. These learners are more likely to enter school as confident children who are already fluent and familiar with learning. As a result, teachers may assume that they have greater potential and encourage them to achieve accordingly.

Teachers' assessments and evaluation affect achievement levels. Over time, learners may adapt their own self-image to match the one the teacher holds of them. For example, they might think, 'What's the point in trying?'

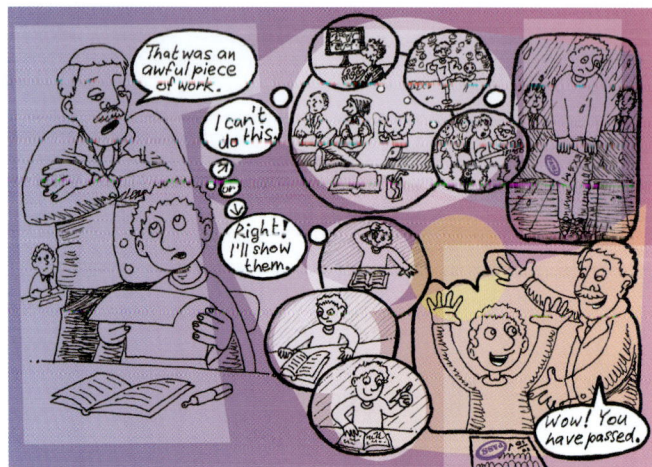

Figure 5.14: The self-fulfilling prophecy and the self-negating prophecy.

ACTIVITY: DISCUSSION 5.3

In a small group, discuss your experiences of labelling in school or college. Consider the following questions in your discussion:

1   What kinds of labels do teachers place on learners?

2   Are you aware of any of your teachers having labelled you or other learners?

3   Do you think labels are placed due to the social-class background of learners, or for other reasons (for example, their gender, their ethnicity or something else)?

4   If you have been labelled by a teacher, what impact did this have on your achievement and effort? Did you show a self-fulfilling prophecy or a self-negating prophecy?

The teacher thinks I can't do it.' Those labelled as 'bright' are more likely to perform well, meeting the teachers' expectations and predictions. Those labelled as having low ability may feel there is no point in trying. In both cases, the teachers' predictions come true. This is referred to as the self-fulfilling prophecy: learners fulfil the predictions made by the labels they are given. This suggests that differences between the attitudes and achievements of learners are created by the processes of stereotyping and labelling.

It is also possible to have a self-negating prophecy. This is when a learner is labelled by a teacher as unlikely to do well, but rejects this label and sets out to prove that it is wrong. The negative label motivates the learner to work harder and achieve success, proving the teacher wrong.

Another way of labelling learners is to put them into streams or sets, according to their predicted ability. Streaming is when learners are in one class for all lessons, with other learners of similar ability; there is a top stream for those seen as high achievers, a bottom stream for those seen as low achievers and a hierarchy of other levels in between. Setting is when learners are put in different ability groups for particular subjects. Critics say that streaming and setting involve prejudging success and failure. Learners in the top streams and sets will become confident high achievers, while those in low streams and sets will see themselves as failures. Being placed in a low stream or set may undermine learners' confidence and discourage them from trying. As a result, they might become disruptive and struggle to do well, even if they work hard.

Teachers may also be less ambitious, offering less information to lower-stream children. Streaming and setting are often linked to social class: the higher a learner's social class, the greater their chance of being placed in a top stream or set. Therefore, these practices contribute to the underachievement of working-class students.

The opposite of streaming and setting is mixed-ability classes, with no selection. In practice, many schools use setting for some subjects (such as mathematics) and mixed-ability teaching for other subjects.

Marxist explanations

Marxist views on education were considered in section 5.2. Since the Marxist view of education focuses on social class, many of the ideas discussed here would be supported by Marxists. For example, Bourdieu – who developed the idea of cultural capital – is often described as a Marxist.

Another Marxist explanation is that of class position. The French Marxist Raymond Boudon thought it essential to consider social-class background to understand the choices and achievements made by learners in education. For example, a boy from a middle-class background may see himself as a failure if he does not go to university, because his parents had assumed he would enter a profession such as medicine.

On the other hand, a learner from a working-class background might be the first person from their family to go into higher education; they might have to loosen ties with their community and move away, socially, from friends who do not go on to higher education. People from a working-class background who go into office work may have moved further up the occupational ladder than their parents. They could be seen as more successful than someone from a middle-class background who becomes a doctor or lawyer but remains at the same level as their parents. This suggests we need to consider social-class position when deciding how well learners have done in the education system.

Patterns and explanations for differences in educational achievement and experience based on ethnicity

Individual learners from all ethnic backgrounds achieve highly in education. However, in many countries, learners from some minority ethnic groups tend to do less well than the average for that country. For example, in the USA there has been concern about Hispanic and African American learners.

In the USA, statistics from 2018 show that 89.8 per cent of the whole population had graduated from high school. For learners from Hispanic backgrounds, the figure was only 71.6 per cent. The same year, 35 per cent of the whole population had graduated from college. Asian and Pacific Islanders were well above this average at 56.5 per cent, but people from Black American (25.2 per cent) and Hispanic backgrounds (18.3 per cent) were significantly below.

In some minority ethnic groups, a high proportion of people are working class. This means they suffer from material disadvantages more than the majority ethnic group. Some immigrant groups came from relatively poor backgrounds in their home country. Others had high-status positions which were lost when they moved to their new country, due to the difficulty of establishing themselves and the discrimination they faced. Therefore, the factors affecting the educational achievement and experience of children from working-class backgrounds (discussed in the previous section) combine with other more specific factors to affect the educational achievement of children from minority ethnic backgrounds.

Institutional racism

One factor that explains low achievement by some minority groups – in education and elsewhere – is **institutional racism**. Institutions in society – including the education system, the criminal justice system, the health system, the welfare system and the employment market – may operate in ways which, deliberately or unconsciously, discriminate against people from minority ethnic groups. For example, a criminal justice system can be seen as institutionally racist if the policies and practices it follows lead to people from some ethnic groups being imprisoned more than those in other ethnic groups who have acted in similar ways. The impacts of institutional racism may be felt on a daily basis by people from minority ethnic backgrounds. Learners from an ethnic minority may react against the racism they perceive in society by rebelling against the school, which represents the authority of the racist society.

Some sociologists argue that the education system itself is institutionally racist. There are differences between countries but some features – including the ethnocentric curriculum and the labelling of learners by teachers on the basis of racial stereotypes – can be seen as evidence of institutional racism within the education system as a whole.

> ## THINK LIKE A SOCIOLOGIST
>
> The term 'institutional racism' implies that racial inequality in many societies is not caused by the racist views of a few individuals. Instead, it is due to institutions themselves and the way they operate. Which institutions in your country may operate in a way which is institutionally racist? What impact might this have on the day-to-day lives and employment prospects of people from minority ethnic groups?

> ## KEY TERM
>
> **institutional racism:** when the functioning of an institution or organisation involves systems and expectations that lead to discrimination against an ethnic group

Ethnocentric curriculum

Even in multicultural societies, there is often one dominant group. Ethnocentrism occurs when the culture of this dominant group is promoted as the only or the most important one. Ethnocentrism can be unconscious, when people in the majority group assume that their cultural perspective is the only important view. Ethnocentrism can also come from the misguided belief that members of minority ethnic groups need to be assimilated into the majority culture; that is, they should give up their own culture and traditions and adopt the host culture's norms and values. In education, sociologists argue that many countries follow an ethnocentric curriculum.

An ethnocentric curriculum can be seen in:

- the teaching of language. The languages and cultures of ethnic minority learners may be seen by the school as being of lesser value.

- the teaching of literature. Poetry and books from the culture of ethnic minority learners may not be considered worth studying.

- the teaching of history. Learners from ethnic minority groups may learn nothing about their own people's experiences.

- religion, including worship at assemblies. The ethnic minority learners' beliefs may be ignored and they may even be forced to follow the practices of the majority.

- celebration of festivals based on the dominant culture. Ethnic minority learners' festivals may be ignored.

This may lead ethnic minority learners to lose interest, believing that lessons are not relevant to them. They might also come to think that their culture is inferior or unimportant, which will affect their confidence.

Ethnocentrism can also exist without the presence of a dominant group. Many countries that were once colonies still follow the education system of the colonising power. For example, Sierra Leone in West Africa was once a

British colony. In schools there, teaching is in English although this is not the native language of the learners. Lesson content may be based on British culture and resources may be UK-focused, without information about African geography and culture.

Role models

One of the outcomes of institutional racism is a lack of role models for children from minority ethnic groups, either in school (as teachers and other staff) or in wider society (in business, politics and other high status professions). As a result, learners from minority ethnic groups might limit their ambitions because they believe they do not have the same opportunities as learners from the majority ethnic group.

Linguistic factors

Minority ethnic groups may be taught in a language that is not their native language. This is the case for many children in lower-income countries, where schools use the language of former colonial country (such as English or French). The learners speak other languages at home, so they might find it difficult to understand subjects that are taught in the colonial language.

In some cases, learners' native languages are devalued and seen as inappropriate for school. For example, the kind of language spoken by some minority ethnic groups may be thought by teachers to be ungrammatical, wrong and an indication of a lack of education or intelligence. For example, African American vernacular English (AAVE) – the language used by African Americans – was widely assumed to be an ungrammatical and substandard form of English. Teachers discouraged children from using it. However, the American linguist William Labov found that AAVE had a grammatical structure and could be used to express complex and abstract ideas. Before Labov's study, African American learners who used AAVE would have been marked down, even if they had the same level of understanding and ability as learners using standard English. Their language held them back in terms of their educational achievement.

Being able to use more than one language (being bilingual, or even polylingual) can be an advantage, however, by facilitating students' ability to learn.

Cultural, material and social factors

The ethnic background of learners – including cultural, material and social factors – can influence their achievement in many ways.

KEY TERM

ethnocentrism: the belief that the people, customs and traditions of your own race or country are better than those of other races or countries

---

For example:

- A learner's culture may or may not place a high value on learning and academic success.

- If cultural values (related to religion or other views) clash with the values of the school, this can slow a learners' progress.

- A learner's dress, appearance or way of speaking may reinforce a stereotype held by teachers in relation to ethnicity, leading to a self-fulfilling prophecy. Due to a combination of ethnicity and social class, a minority ethnic learner's family may have less cultural capital; as we have seen, this may hinder their achievement in school.

- Material factors, such as lack of money to buy resources or access school trips, can disproportionately affect children from some minority ethnic backgrounds, who are more likely to be part of the working class.

Home/community factors

The British sociologist Louise Archer researched why children with Chinese backgrounds in UK schools were so successful compared with children from other ethnic groups. Parents valued education highly and invested time and money in their children's education, however wealthy they were.

Figure 5.15: Chinese parents may encourage their children to value learning from an early age.

Children were socialised to see educational success as very important. Their parents talked with them frequently about their schoolwork and about planning their career, so they had clear goals. Archer interviewed several Chinese learners. One of them explained that while white British children are told to do their best, Chinese children are told to 'be the best'.

This strong motivation from Chinese learners' cultural background was an important factor leading to their high achievement. This research suggests that the influence of culture, home background, upbringing and a learner's ethnic community can make a significant difference to educational outcomes.

In-school factors

To be meritocratic, schools need to ensure that all learners have equal opportunities to succeed. However, schools may be institutionally racist in the following ways:

- Schools may discriminate when placing learners in streams and sets. Learners from minority ethnic groups may be put in lower streams or sets as a result of assumptions based on their ethnicity, rather than their individual ability.

- Many schools have an ethnocentric curriculum.

- Teachers might assume that learners from minority ethnic groups are unable to do well, or label them 'troublemakers'. This may become a self-fulfilling prophecy.

- Schools may not deal with racism from students towards minority ethnic groups. Racism is sometimes treated as unimportant, despite the damage it can do.

Pro- and anti-school sub-cultures

As discussed in the section on social class and educational achievement, pro- or anti-school sub-cultures are an important in-school factor. These may be formed based on ethnicity as well as social class.

In a book titled *Black Masculinities and Schooling* (1997), Tony Sewell studied African Caribbean boys in a British secondary school who were part of an anti-school sub-culture. He referred to them as 'rebels'. They were so opposed to the school's rules that were sometimes violent towards other learners and staff. They were very aggressively masculine. Sewell saw their behaviour partly as a response to racist teachers and racism in the school more widely. However, Sewell also found other African Caribbean learners who responded to the school in different ways. He concluded that the rebels should not be seen as typical of all African Caribbean boys.

Anti-school sub-cultures do not always show a simple rejection of the school and academic success. They can be more complicated.

Máirtín Mac an Ghaill described a group of female learners from minority ethnic groups in UK colleges who succeeded in their education despite being strongly critical of it. The 'Black sisters' were from African Caribbean and Asian backgrounds and were in an inner-city college studying for A Levels. They did not like the college or the schools they had been to before; they criticised the way in which streaming had discriminated against them, the teachers' failure to recognise their ability and the ethnocentric curriculum. However, they decided that it was important to them to succeed in education. They worked hard – even while rejecting the college's authority – and they did well. Although their sub-culture could be described as anti-school, they were still pro-education in a more general sense.

Labelling theory

Teachers often make assumptions about learners from different groups by labelling them. This can lead to self-fulfilling prophecies. For example, learners from minority ethnic groups may be more likely to be put in low streams and sets. This may be because of language differences or teachers' stereotypes, rather than ability.

In the UK, it can be argued that many African Caribbean learners are labelled and stereotyped by schools. Compared to other ethnic groups, much higher proportions of African Caribbean boys are excluded from schools. While there may initially have been bad behaviour from some boys in this group, this has led to an expectation of poor behaviour from *all* African Caribbean boys; as a result, teachers label these boys and have low expectations of them. The boys, often from working-class backgrounds, may struggle at school. Their extroverted behaviour – which might be accepted in other contexts – leads to them being labelled as troublemakers.

It can be very difficult to reject labels like this and they can become a master status. This means the label becomes the single most important thing about the person in the eyes of others. The label is then internalised by the person who is labelled and they come to believe that it describes them correctly. For example, a boy who has been labelled a troublemaker may be suspected whenever something goes wrong, even if he is completely innocent. He may start to believe that he is 'trouble' and make choices based on this; he might feel there is no point in trying to behave well, since he will be blamed anyway. This leads to the self-fulfilling prophecy.

Labelling can work in different ways. The Chinese learners studied by Archer found that teachers had high expectations of them – but this was not necessarily a good thing. These learners received little praise or effort for doing well, because their success was only to be expected. Also, when they did have difficulties, teachers gave them little help because they assumed they could help themselves.

Archer found that many schools had few Chinese learners, so these learners were not able to form a peer group of their own. The other, non-Chinese learners often had high expectations of the Chinese learners and saw them as 'geeks'. This shows that labelling can be done by peers as well as teachers. A label like 'geek' suggests academic ability and a desire to please teachers, which is seen in a negative light. It is therefore a label that learners might try to reject. For example, some learners may stop working hard – risking failure – because they want the approval of their peers.

Patterns and explanations for differences in educational achievement and experience based on gender

In most countries, there are clear differences between the educational achievement and experience of boys and girls. These gender inequalities in education have changed over time and vary between countries. Boys have always been more likely to go to school, complete their education and get qualifications. This is because schooling for boys was seen as more important because it helped them find work, which would allow them to support a family. Schooling for girls was seen as less important. Even girls who were doing well at school might leave to help their family, or get married, without completing their education. In countries like the UK, this was the case until the late 20th century. Changes to education then led to more equal opportunities for boys and girls, with all learners staying in school until they took examinations and obtained qualifications.

> **KEY TERM**
>
> **gender inequalities:** differences in experience and outcomes for males and females, based on their gender; for example, in terms of educational achievement

It soon became clear that girls were doing better than boys in most subjects at GCSE level.

Without clear patterns (as there are with social class and ethnicity), the questions sociologists ask about gender and educational achievement are rather different. They include:

- How are girls disadvantaged in education? How were they disadvantaged in the past?
- Why are girls now doing better than boys in some countries, such as the UK?
- Why do boys now underachieve in some countries?

Differential gendered socialisation and social control

Boys and girls are socialised into gender roles. By the time they start school, children have clear ideas about the behaviour and attitudes appropriate to both sexes; they learn these ideas from the culture they are growing up in. Girls may be influenced to see their future in terms of marriage and motherhood, rather than a profession and career. Most boys will also marry and become parents but they are likely to see their future more in terms of work. Girls may be socialised into feeling that qualifications are unnecessary for them, so they do not work hard in school. They may expect to work when they leave school, but only for a few years. On the other hand, a good education can sometimes help a girl to find a high-status husband, so marriage and education cannot be regarded as two simple alternatives.

In modern industrial societies, there has been a shift away from the traditional gender roles. Today, girls are much more likely to have career aims and to be motivated to work hard in school to achieve these aims. This may explain why girls are now doing better: their socialisation has changed and having a career is now seen as more important. Girls' attitudes and motivations have changed because there are more opportunities for them, as well as more successful women who act as role models. Girls know that they do not have to become housewives and mothers; they can have a career as well or instead.

In many modern industrial countries, there are fewer traditional male manual jobs (for example, in engineering and mining) than there used to be. This has made it more important to gain educational qualifications in order to access other careers, for example in ICT, business and finance. However, in countries with a difficult economic situation and where most jobs available to males are still manual jobs, boys may feel there is little point in working hard to pass exams because they are unlikely to need qualifications for the jobs they will do in the future.

Gendered socialisation can also affect learners' subject choices. When choices are available – usually for GCSE and higher qualifications – there are clear differences in the subjects chosen by boys and girls. Socialisation is a factor here: boys and girls absorb messages about what is appropriate for each gender, which may be linked to gender roles in society and to ideas about which careers are suitable for men and women. For example, in many countries, boys are more likely to pursue technical subjects (including mathematics, physics and computing) and to go into careers such as accountancy, computer programming and engineering. Girls on the other hand, are more likely to continue with subjects such as history, sociology and literature, and to pursue careers working with people, such as teaching and nursing.

Teacher expectations

Boys and girls may be treated differently in schools. For example, teachers may believe that poor study habits and behaviour are 'normal' for boys, while similar behaviour from girls is not tolerated. This may relate to gender stereotypes and expectations, since males are traditionally expected to be more outgoing, confident and dominant than females. However, as mentioned in section 5.2, some teachers also have lower academic expectations of girls and are less likely to encourage girls to study hard.

Cultural and social factors

In terms of differences in educational achievement, material and cultural deprivation are less relevant to gender than to social class and ethnicity. However, where a family has limited resources to spend on education, girls' education may be seen as less important than boys'. As a result, the resources that are available may be used to educate sons, rather than daughters.

Research has found differences in the approach that girls and boys take to their studies. Girls seem to be better motivated and work more consistently over long periods.

> ### KEY TERM
> **gendered socialisation:** the way that males and females are taught the expectations relating to their gender roles

For example, they spend more time on homework, they concentrate better in class and they are better organised. They also seem to benefit more than boys from coursework and continuous assessment – where they can work steadily over a period   rather than examinations.

These differences could have several explanations. It has been argued that girls mature earlier than boys. Therefore, by the age of 16 (when learners in many countries take examinations) they are more likely to recognise the importance of studying hard. Differences in attitude towards education could also be related to gender socialisation and peer pressure. Girls are more likely to underestimate their ability and believe that they have to work hard to succeed. Boys, on the other hand, can be too confident. They overestimate their ability and believe they can do well without working hard. Hard work may also be seen as more acceptable by female peer groups, whereas boys are more likely to form anti-school sub-cultures. For some boys, especially those from working-class backgrounds, studying hard may not be seen as masculine; as a result, there may be social pressures on boys not to try too hard at school.

Most schoolwork is based on reading and writing. Boys tend to have different skills and interests. They would do better if more schoolwork was active and practical. Boys might also believe that reading is more appropriate for girls. It has been suggested, for example, that mothers are more likely to read to their young children than fathers and that, because of this, both boys and girls come to see reading as a female activity.

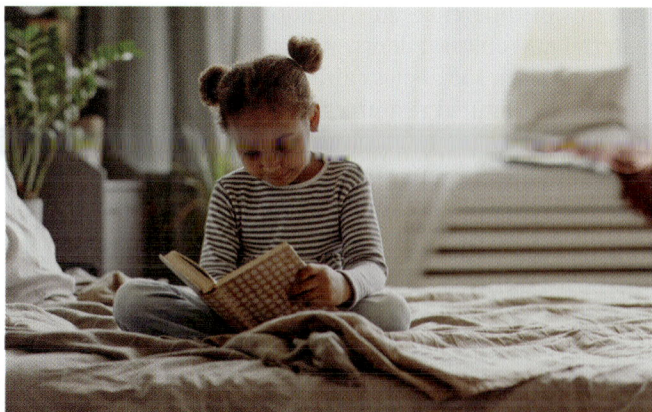

Figure 5.16: Girls are more likely to spend time reading than boys.

Access to education

In some countries, girls have less access to education than boys and often leave education at an earlier age. This may be due to financial constraints or cultural reasons. This issue is discussed in more detail in the section on global differences in education.

In-school factors

As well as the gendered curriculum and associated differences in subject choice, the organisation of schools (the hidden curriculum) may give learners the message that gender is important and that there are different expectations of boys and girls. For example, registers may be separated into boys and girls and seating plans may be based on gender. School uniforms, where they exist, are usually different for boys and girls.

Some classroom activities, such as science experiments, may be dominated by boys. Textbooks in subjects such as science and technology may show boys, rather than girls, in the illustrations, and there may be more male teachers delivering these subjects in schools. These factors can give girls the message that some subjects are not for them. For similar reasons, boys may be put off subjects such as dance and domestic science.

In most countries, schools now make an effort to ensure that girls have the same opportunities as boys to study and succeed. Similarly, advice from teachers and others is now more likely to encourage students to pursue any careers which interest them, regardless of gender. Some countries have developed programmes to encourage girls to aim higher, especially in science and technology. These schemes may provide extra resources for schools and run conferences with successful females to act as role models.

Teaching is a female-dominated profession in many countries. However, the senior levels in teaching and in education are still male-dominated. Even in primary schools, which tend to have even higher proportions of female teachers, half the head teachers in the UK are male. As a result, although boys have fewer role models among teachers, those they do have are likely to be senior staff. Girls may also get the impression that women do not go into leadership.

Peer groups in mixed schools still tend to be single sex. Both of the studies of sub-cultures discussed in the ethnicity section (by Sewell and Mac an Ghaill) are about gender as well as ethnic differences. There can be pro- and anti-school sub-cultures of either gender.

However, female peer groups are more likely to be pro-school, sharing the school's norms and values regarding learning. Girls often support each other in their studies.

Boys, on the other hand, are more likely to belong to anti-school sub-cultures and may be affected by a masculine culture which values respect from male peers above academic achievement. Some boys may think they will lose status in the eyes of their peers if they work hard or do well academically, since these qualities are now associated with girls. Instead, they try to gain respect by challenging authority, which may get them into trouble at school and stop them making progress.

A recent development in the UK, according to research by Carolyn Jackson, is that more working-class girls in British secondary schools are behaving in ways previously associated with working-class boys, such as fighting, swearing and being aggressive. This involves only a minority of girls but it shows that working hard has come to be seen by some girls as uncool. Jackson suggested that not working was a method of self-protection from the effects of failure: if learners did not do well, they could claim that it was because they did not care or try hard. This might be a response to the pressure on both boys and girls to do well, and the challenges faced by learners from working-class backgrounds in relation to these pressures.

Labelling theory

Teacher labelling can apply to gender as well as to social class and ethnicity. Teachers may make assumptions about gender, giving boys and girls different kinds of attention. Girls are praised for their appearance, good behaviour and neatness of work. In boys, however, individuality and creativity are valued more highly.

Boys are more likely to be labelled as problems, by teachers and by schools. Of the learners excluded from British schools due to bad behaviour each year, less than one in five are girls. This does not mean, of course, that girls do not have problems. Rather, girls are less likely to act out their problems in a way that demands attention. Being labelled in a negative way may lead to a self-fulfilling prophecy and can be a cause of underachievement.

Feminist explanations

As discussed in section 5.2, feminist sociologists focus on the experience and achievement of girls in what they see as a patriarchal education system within a patriarchal society.

Over the last 30 years – since girls have started to outperform boys in many countries – a lot of political attention has been paid to the reasons why boys underachieve. Feminists point out that there was far less interest in gender inequality in education when girls were underachieving. They also argue that there are continuing disadvantages for girls, which tend to gain less attention. For example, girls still face the following problems in education:

- lack of confidence in their ability
- dominance of boys in classrooms
- receiving less of teachers' time than boys
- gendered subject choices
- assumptions by teachers.

It seems likely that girls would have an improved experience in education if these problems could be overcome. Addressing these issues may also lead to related improvements in life chances for women, especially in terms of employment.

MAKING CONNECTIONS

How do gender roles and expectations in the family, reinforced through primary socialisation, affect girls' education?

Global differences in educational achievement

Availability of schools

In many countries, accessible schooling for all children is a relatively new development. For example, when many African countries achieved independence in the 1950s and 1960s, there were very few schools. The schools that did exist were for the children of the colonial administrators and other staff. Most people did not have access to a school, apart from a few faith schools. Countries such as Sierra Leone needed to build a national school system with limited resources, in terms of both money and staff; there were very few teachers or teaching materials. In some countries today, there are still not enough schools for all the children. Children in rural and remote areas might have to travel a long distance each day to get to the nearest school, and class sizes in some schools are very large, with over 50 children in one class.

The schools that are available may not be able to provide a good education. This is often because they lack basic necessities such as:

- electricity
- drinking water
- toilets
- ventilation in classrooms
- books and other teaching resources
- special equipment, such as for a science laboratory
- qualified teachers
- a secure, safe school site.

Figure 5.17: A school in Uganda, powered by one solar panel.

Poverty/wealth

Many children still do not go to school, or leave school without finishing their education, because their families are poor. Children can work, either helping with a family farm or business, or doing household tasks. This means their parents have more time to earn money to support the family. Many countries have made education free to encourage more children to go to school. However, there are still some costs, such as uniforms and books, and the time children spend in school is time they cannot spend helping their family. For some families, even if education is free, it makes more sense for the child not to go to school.

Poverty is also linked to poor health. Because of diet and living conditions, children from poor families are more likely to be ill and to miss school as a result. In parts of Africa, many children miss a lot of school because

they have malaria or other diseases; this means they fall behind in their studies. Other factors related to poverty also affect achievement. For example, children whose homes do not have electricity will find it much harder to study after dark.

At the other end of the scale, wealthy families can buy the education they want for their children. Some have a private tutor who provides one-to-one teaching outside school. This gives the children of wealthy families an advantage and makes it more likely that they will achieve in education, whatever their ability.

Access to education for girls

In the past, most schooling was reserved for boys and girls received very little education. In some developing countries, boys are still more likely to go to school than girls. This is often because parents think the education of their sons is more important. The future of a boy is seen in terms of a successful career, being able to support his own family when he is an adult and perhaps being able to support his ageing parents. A girl, however, may be expected to marry: she will join her husband's family, perhaps taking their family name, and her main responsibility will be to them. For a family with limited income, paying for a daughter's education, or losing her contribution to the family while she is at school, may seem unnecessary.

Girls can also find the experience of school difficult. For example, about one in three schools in Africa has no toilets. Where there are no toilets or they are poor quality, girls may stay away from school when they have their period, to avoid embarrassment.

The United Nations and its member governments are strongly committed to education for girls. It is seen as a human right and an essential part of a country's development. One of the UN's Global Sustainability Goals is that all young people and most adults should achieve literacy and numeracy by 2030. However, to achieve this goal, there needs to be a huge increase in education for girls: UNESCO estimates that 129 million school-aged girls worldwide do not go to school.

Where more girls go to school, there are enormous benefits for families and for society, as well as for individuals. It has been shown that educating girls has positive outcomes in improving the living standards, health and nutrition of families. For example, better educated women are more informed about nutrition and healthcare, and they can teach their families about this as well. They often marry at a later age and, if they choose to become mothers, have fewer and healthier children. They are also more likely to have formal jobs and to earn more money.

Variations in class sizes

Smaller class sizes seem to lead to higher achievement, so class size is considered important. When there are more learners in a class, it is more difficult for the teacher to pay attention to all the learners' needs and to make sure they can keep up with their studies. In most industrialised countries, a class size of around 25–30 is normal in state schools; class sizes are smaller in private schools. In many developing countries, however, class sizes are still much higher and there may be more children than chairs and desks. According to UNESCO, in 2016, the average class size in Malawi, the Central African Republic and Tanzania was more than 70 learners per class. Class sizes are highest for the youngest children, those starting school. Therefore, many children do not get a positive start to their school lives.

Norms, values and cultural differences

Going to school has only become the norm around the world fairly recently, so it is not always firmly established. In some families and communities, going to school is not seen as important. This can be based on parents' experience; if parents did not go to school, they may see little value in their children going. Other parents around the world, and their children, place a high value on school. Many people view school and qualifications as the only way out of the poverty or low standard of living they were born into.

Access to the internet/digital resources

Globally, schools vary in terms of their digital resources. Some schools have computers for learners to use, connected to the internet via a high-speed internet connection. Such resources can greatly improve education: learners develop ICT skills and they are also able to search for information related to their studies. However, some schools have limited access to computers and internet, and some even lack electricity.

The COVID-19 pandemic affected people everywhere, regardless of country, income or gender. During the pandemic, many schools around the world closed, often for months at a time. It was difficult for learners to continue their studies and there has been a global discussion about the 'Covid Generation'; people are concerned about the ways in which the pandemic affected children and young people, both socially and

educationally. However, children with access to a good internet connection at home were able to continue studying, at least partly. Many schools put lessons and resources online, so that learners could follow them at home. When examination centres had to close, some examinations were also available online. Other schools did not have the digital connections necessary to provide online learning. As a result, many children around the world received no education during lockdowns because they had no access to digital devices. There is a clear digital divide between schools and learners with digital access and those without.

MAKING CONNECTIONS

How did COVID-19 affect other areas of social life you have studied, such as identity, social stratification and the family?

Strengths and limitations of the different explanations for differences in educational achievement

As we have seen, the explanations for social class, ethnicity, gender and global differences have strengths and limitations. All these factors may have an impact on some children in some circumstances but there are no universal explanations which can fully explain the differences in educational achievement between countries, genders, social classes and ethnic groups.

It should also be remembered that social class, ethnicity and gender cannot easily be separated as factors that affect educational achievement. Each individual learner has a gender and belongs to a social class and an ethnic group, so these factors will affect their experience of education in different combinations, as will the country in which they live.

- For example, lower achieving ethnic groups are usually those from the working class.

- Girls from working-class backgrounds do less well than girls from middle-class backgrounds.

Social class may be the most important factor, since children from poorer backgrounds and poorer countries tend to have the lowest achievement in education, regardless of their ethnicity or gender. However, all societies are different and there are variations between countries.

TIP

Make sure you understand that gender, ethnicity and social class overlap and intersect with each other – this can be a useful evaluation point. For example, in some countries today, girls generally achieve better grades than boys. However, middle-class girls achieve more highly than working-class girls, and boys from higher social-class backgrounds also outperform working-class girls.

STRETCH AND CHALLENGE

Suggest reasons why social-class background and material factors might be more of an influence on a learner's educational achievement and experience than gender or ethnicity.

ACTIVITY: WRITTEN 5.3

In what ways do social class, ethnicity and gender interact as influences on educational achievement? Write around 300 words on this. Try to use examples from your own country, or a country you are familiar with, in your answer.

CHECK YOUR UNDERSTANDING 5.3

1   Work with three other learners. Each of you take one area of educational inequality: social class, gender, ethnicity and global differences.

2   List as many factors as you can which may explain educational inequality in the area you have chosen, as well as their strengths and limitations.

3   Share your answers with the other members of your group. Each learner can add any ideas that have been missed out.

KEY POINTS

- There are patterns in educational achievement and expectations relating to:
  - social class
  - ethnicity
  - gender
  - global differences.
- There are explanations of these patterns, including:
  - material factors
  - cultural factors
  - home factors
  - in-school factors.
- There are global differences in educational achievement, explained by reasons including:
  - differences in the availability of schools
  - poverty
  - access to education for girls
  - access to the internet and digital resources.

SUMMARY

- Education and schooling take different forms, including formal and informal education.
- There are different types of schools and alternative approaches.
- Education has roles and functions, which can be described using functionalist, Marxist and feminist views.
- There are patterns in educational achievement and experience, as well as differences, which can be explained by a range of material, cultural, home and in-school factors.

KEY SKILLS EXERCISES

1 Evaluation

Of the three main sociological theories – functionalist, Marxist and feminist – which do you think gives the most convincing account of the role and functions of education today? Write a 250-word justification of your choice.

2 Knowledge and understanding

Without consulting this book or any notes, write definitions of the following terms.

meritocracy; hidden curriculum; cultural capital; anti-school sub-culture; labelling; selective education; setting; vocational education; ethnocentrism; progressive schooling

You do not have to use the exact wording of the definitions in this book. It is better to show your understanding by writing a definition in your own words.

Ask your teacher or a peer to check your work.

3 Analysis and evaluation

Consider this statement: "Social class differences in educational achievement can best be explained by what happens within schools." To what extent do you agree with this view?

Write a 500-word answer to this question. Include the strengths and limitations of the view in the question and of other possible explanations. Include a short conclusion that sums up your answer.

IMPROVE THIS ANSWER

Family, education and crime

Discuss reasons why educational achievement is different in different countries.

Your answer should include:

- at least three developed points with evidence.

One reason why educational achievement is different in different countries is that there is poverty in some countries. Where standards of living are low, children will not be able to afford resources needed for school, such as pens and uniforms and their parents may not be able to afford for them to go to school at all. A second reason is access to resources such as digital devices and the internet. In some countries, more schools and learners have access to these than in others. They can be important in helping educational achievement, as shown in the COVID-19 pandemic, during which the extent to which countries were able to keep education going with online lessons and assessment varied.

Commentary and task

This answer requires one more reason why educational achievement is different in different countries. Choose either access to education for girls or variation in class sizes. Write the point in your own words and then develop it, for example by referring to a particular country or countries.

PRACTICE QUESTIONS

Family, education and crime

a   Define the terms:

   i   official curriculum   [2]

   ii   faith schools   [2]

b   Give **two** examples of alternative approaches to education.   [2]

c   Describe **three** ways education helps society to function.   [6]

d   Explain **three** aspects of the labelling theory view of education.   [6]

e   Discuss reasons why educational achievement is different in different countries.

   Your answer should include at least **three** developed points with evidence.   [8]

f   Evaluate the view that differences in educational achievement between social classes are the result of cultural and social factors.

   Your answer should include:

   •   at least **three** arguments for and **three** arguments against the view

   •   a conclusion.   [14]

SELF-EVALUATION CHECKLIST

After studying this unit, complete this table:

You should be able to:	Needs more work	Almost there	Ready to move on
5.1 What is education and schooling?			
Understand the difference between formal and informal education			
Explain the strengths and limitations of different types of schools			
Explain alternative approaches to education and their strengths and limitations			
5.2 What are the roles and functions of education?			
Explain the functionalist view and its strengths and limitations			
Explain the Marxist view and its strengths and limitations			
Explain the feminist view and its strengths and limitations			
5.3 What factors help to explain differences in educational achievement and experience?			
Explain patterns in educational achievement and experience			
Explain differences in educational achievement and experience based on social class			
Explain differences in educational achievement and experience based on ethnicity			
Explain differences in educational achievement and experience based on gender			
Explain reasons for global differences in educational achievement			
Understand the strengths and limitations of the different explanations for educational achievement based on social class, ethnicity, gender and global differences			

> Unit 6

Crime, deviance and social control

POLICE LINE DO NOT CROSS   POLICE LI

LEARNING INTENTIONS

In this unit you will learn how to:

- Understand the difference between crime and deviance and the relativity of crime and deviance

- Understand the difference between formal and informal social control

- Describe agencies of social control, how they control individuals and prevent crime and deviance

- Understand debates about the effectiveness of agencies of social control and their methods

- Describe types and examples of crime

- Understand how crime is measured

- Describe patterns of crime and victimisation

- Understand explanations for crime and deviance based on age, ethnicity, gender and social class

- Understand debates about the importance of these explanations

- Assess sociological theories on crime and deviance
- Describe the aims of punishment and the effectiveness of different types of punishment
- Assess the effectiveness of different types of policing and law enforcement.

Introduction

All societies and cultures have expectations and rules for the behaviour of their members. In a society, behaviour has to be controlled; people cannot just do what they like. When these expectations and rules are broken, the social group may punish the rule breakers. Sociologists of crime and deviance are interested in how rules and laws are made and how they are kept or broken. They are interested in who makes the laws, who breaks them and who decides what happens as a result.

Modern industrial societies have many laws. They have police forces and legal systems of courts and judges; they also have a series of punishments, including prison, for people who break the law. Governments and the media express concern about rising crime rates. For sociologists, it is interesting that most people break laws and norms at some time, without being called criminals or deviants. There are very clear patterns regarding which types of people are most likely to be labelled 'criminal' or 'deviant', and which types of people are most likely to be victims of crime. This unit explores some of the research and discussion about crime, deviance and social control.

6.1 What are crime, deviance and social control?

The difference between crime and deviance

Deviance refers to any act that does not follow the norms and expectations of a social group. **Crime** involves acts that break a law set by the government or rulers. Deviance is a wider category of behaviour than crime, because it includes acts which go against social norms but do not involve breaking a law.

The term deviance is usually used to describe behaviour that is disapproved of by others because it goes against the norms and values of society. Because countries make laws to criminalise behaviour they wish to prevent, most crimes are also deviant. However, sociologists have often studied deviance that is not necessarily criminal, such as taking a drug which is disapproved of but not illegal. For example, in most European countries today, cigarette smoking is still allowed in some public places but is generally disapproved of. Other examples of deviance which are not criminal include wearing inappropriate or shocking clothing, or behaving in a rude or offensive way. People may negatively sanction this behaviour by showing their disapproval or outrage but such behaviour is not a criminal offence in most countries.

Not all crimes are necessarily seen as deviant, either. For example, most people agree that speeding (driving faster than the speed limit) is a crime, yet a large minority of drivers in many countries break speed limits regularly. This could suggest that speeding is not 'deviant', despite being criminal, because it is part of the social norm of driving. There are also outdated criminal laws in some countries which are rarely obeyed or punished.

Deviance and crime are both relative: what is considered to be deviant or criminal varies from time to time and place to place. In Unit 2, we looked at the idea that culture is relative, meaning that norms and values vary between societies. Because deviance is behaviour which goes against society's norms, it can also be seen as relative. Different countries make their own laws, so crimes also vary in relation to culture. This means there are no acts which are criminal or deviant by their nature.

> **KEY TERMS**
>
> **deviance:** behaviour that goes against the norms or values of a group
>
> **crime:** actions that break formal written laws

For example, killing someone is not always considered a crime or even a deviant act; it is not a crime for soldiers to kill enemy soldiers in wartime, and some countries impose the death penalty on serious criminals. Another example which shows how deviance and crime are relative to time and culture is homosexuality. Same-sex relationships were illegal in many countries in the past but in much of the world today, homosexuality has been decriminalised. In many countries, same-sex relationships are no longer seen as deviant and, as discussed in Unit 4, same-sex marriage is now legal in many parts of the world. However, homosexual relationships are still criminalised in over 70 countries, including Iran, Pakistan and Bangladesh in Asia, and Chad, Nigeria, Sudan and Somalia in Africa; punishments vary from two years imprisonment and a fine in Chad, to the death penalty in several African and Asian countries.

In sociology, most early research and theory was about crime. From the 1960s onwards, there was a greater interest in deviance, especially in some deviant youth sub-cultures. Sociologists were often sympathetic to the deviant sub-cultures they studied; they wanted to understand how and why the behaviour of certain groups was *labelled* as deviant, rather than assuming that it *was* deviant or wrong. They argued that there was nothing about the actions of these sub-cultures that made them deviant; rather, it was the reactions of other people that led to them being *called* deviant.

TIP

The words deviance and deviancy are used interchangeably. There is no difference in their meaning. Be sure, however, not to confuse crime and deviance: although they may overlap, they do refer to different things.

KEY TERM

sub-culture: a group of people within a larger culture which has its own distinctive norms and values

Formal and informal social control

This section discusses formal and informal social control, as well as the agencies of social control and how these agencies control individuals and prevent crime and deviance. Ideas about informal and formal social control were introduced in Unit 2.

Social control can be informal, using various techniques of persuasion by family, friends, colleagues and the media. It can also be imposed more formally by a wide range of institutions, such as social work departments, medical authorities and the police. Some groups feel the force of social control more than others, especially young people.

Formal social control

Formal social control is enforced by governments or their agencies, such as the police and courts, or by people in other positions of authority. These agencies can impose formal sanctions (punishments), such as fines or imprisonment. Formal agencies of social control may also use more informal sanctions. For example, if a person commits a minor offence, the police may explain to them why it was wrong and warn them against doing it again, without making an official record.

KEY TERMS

formal social control: social control imposed by people or organisations who have the authority to implement rules or laws

informal social control: ways of controlling behaviour imposed by people without a formal role to do this (such as peers)

agencies of social control: people or organisations who carry out social control

The formal agencies of social control are:

- **The police.** By **policing**, they are responsible for investigating criminal acts and catching offenders.

- **The courts.** The law courts hear charges brought against people, decide whether they are guilty and impose punishments.

- **The armed forces.** In some countries and situations, the armed forces play a part in formal social control. For example, a government may use the armed forces in situations where the police are unable to cope. The armed forces often have more resources than the police for situations such as riots; for example, they may be able to use tear gas, water cannons and even guns.

- **The government.** The government is ultimately responsible for social control. It has to ensure law and order so that businesses can operate and citizens can go about their daily lives. Governments control the police, the courts, the armed forces and the penal system.

- **The penal system.** The penal system is responsible for carrying out the punishments imposed on offenders by the law courts. It includes **prisons** and other institutions such as detention centres.

Figure 6.1: A man in a prison cell.

Informal social control

Informal social control is an important way of controlling people's behaviour. Although it may be less obvious or threatening than formal control, it is very powerful. Methods of informal control include critical comments, ridicule, sarcasm and disapproving looks as negative sanctions, and words of praise as positive sanctions (rewards). Informal social control also includes **socialisation** into values which guide the individual towards socially acceptable behaviour. Through socialisation, people internalise norms and learn to control their own behaviour, conforming even when they are alone.

> **TIP**
>
> Remember from Unit 2 that the main agencies of informal social control are also the main agencies of socialisation.

The main agencies of informal social control are:

- **Family.** Close relationships between individuals give family members a sense of belonging, but these relationships also create obligations and expectations that limit what individuals can do. Disapproval by family members will affect an individual's behaviour. People learn within their families what behaviour is acceptable and what is not.

- **Education.** Through the education system, individuals are socialised into values that guide their behaviour. Within schools, a range of sanctions are used to exercise social control; for example, a teacher may stop a learner misbehaving just by looking at them or saying their name.

> **KEY TERMS**
>
> **policing:** the ways in which the police carry out their work, such as investigating crimes and arresting offenders
>
> **penal system:** the formal system responsible for enforcing punishment for crimes
>
> **prison:** a building where criminals are forced to live as a punishment
>
> **socialisation:** the process of learning the norms and values of a culture

- **Workplaces**. These usually have formal rules, such as what workers can wear and times to start and finish. There are also norms which new workers are socialised into, enforced by a range of sanctions imposed by the employer and by colleagues.

- **Peer groups**. These have powerful ways of exercising informal social control, such as making negative comments and the threat of exclusion from the group (**ostracism**).

- **Traditional and digital media.** Reporting about criminal behaviour and court cases in newspapers, on television or online informs people about which behaviour will be punished. It often reinforces shared social feelings about what behaviour is right and wrong.

- **Religions**. These have rules about behaviour for their followers. For example, holy texts such as the Koran and the Bible set out certain rules and forbid some behaviour. Some religious rules become part of the law in countries where one religion is dominant. In other countries, religious rules help to shape a general set of values on which laws are based. People who follow a religion will be influenced by the religion's attitudes to behaviour. For example, Christianity has the concept of sin and Christians may fear that God will punish them if they commit a sin. This can be a more effective form of social control than the fear of being arrested by the police.

> ### KEY TERM
>
> **ostracism:** the exclusion of someone from a community or group

Debates about the effectiveness of agencies and methods of social control in achieving conformity and preventing crime

Functionalists and Marxists tend to agree that informal social control is essential for the smooth running of capitalist societies. However, functionalists see this as a good thing which works in everyone's interests, while Marxists argue that social control

prevents the working-class from recognising and rebelling against their exploitation. Functionalists say that **conformity** is a result of a value consensus, created through socialisation and reinforced through informal social control. Marxists see informal social control as a form of indoctrination, which leads people to accept the ruling-class ideology. This means that few people challenge the system and, when they do, their effectiveness is limited. They will be labelled as criminals and punished through formal social control. For both functionalists and Marxists, formal social control occurs only when socialisation and informal social control have not worked.

> ### KEY TERM
>
> **conformity:** behaviour that follows the usual standards expected by a group or society

In most societies, informal and formal social control work together to ensure that most people conform to social expectations most of the time. They can be seen as effective in achieving the goal of a stable society, which functionalists support but Marxists do not. The extent of conformity today would shock someone from a few hundred years ago. In *Visions of Social Control* (1985), Stanley Cohen identifies several ways in which the nature of social control has changed over the last 200 years:

- The state is increasingly involved in social control. We now have institutions and systems, such as police forces, to deal with criminals and other deviants. Recently, the state has begun to hand over control to private organisations; this has led to private prisons and companies with their own security guards, which do not rely on the police.

- Society has developed detailed classification systems for criminals and deviants, with explanations for their behaviour. We use these classification systems to decide what to do with them.

- Criminals and other deviants are increasingly segregated from the rest of society. They may by physically removed from society – as in the case of criminals who are sent to prison – or socially segregated through negative media coverage, for example.

- A greater range of punishments for criminals has been developed and there has been a move away from inflicting physical pain on people in public.

Instead, sanctions today include imprisonment, rehabilitation programmes and community sentences.

- Families, schools and local communities are increasingly expected to help enforce conformity.

Cohen said that video **surveillance** had increased: public spaces were being replaced by private ones (for example, high streets replaced by arcades and malls, and natural parks replaced by theme parks) where people are watched more than they would have been in the past. The people involved in this surveillance may argue that it is designed to increase public safety. However, it does mean that our day-to-day behaviour is much more closely monitored by those in authority.

Figure 6.2: Video surveillance.

ACTIVITY: RESEARCH 6.1

Use the internet to find out how attitudes towards one or more of the following are different in different countries:

a   the use of cannabis (marijuana)

b   drinking alcohol

c   smoking tobacco cigarettes.

Are they considered deviant, criminal or neither in each country? Does this depend on the context (such as the age of the person doing it and where it is being done)? If so, how? What sanctions, if any, are imposed in each country?

KEY TERM

surveillance: observing and monitoring people's behaviour as a form of social control

Different types and examples of crimes

There are many different types of crime. The following list covers some of the most important types. Note that some crimes fit into more than one category; also, within each category, there are many more specific crimes.

Violent crime

Violent crime involves the use or threat of physical force which will harm the victim. In some violent crimes, the violence itself is the purpose of the crime; for example, murder, assault and rape. In others, the violence is used as a way to commit another crime (such as theft). Violent crimes often involve weapons, but in some cases the criminal uses their physical strength to attack the victim.

Property crime

Property crime involves a threat to private property. The most common type of property crime is stealing (theft), in which the criminal takes property from the victim. The property stolen can be money or goods. Goods that are most likely to be stolen are those with a high value, which are portable and can be concealed – for example, jewellery and mobile phones. Motor vehicle theft is also common is many countries. There are specific terms for different types of private property crime. For example, robbery is property theft with violence or the threat of violence, and burglary is property theft following the unlawful entering of a house or other building.

Another type of property crime is deliberate damage to or destruction of property, such as arson (deliberately starting a fire), criminal damage and vandalism.

KEY TERM

property crime: theft of or intentional damage to things owned by an individual, group or organisation

Figure 6.3: A burglar breaking into a building.

White-collar and corporate crime

White-collar crimes are those that middle-class people are able to commit because of their occupation. Middle-class people usually have more opportunities for occupational crime than working-class people because their jobs give them access to money, resources and information. For example, a person working in a finance department may have opportunities to defraud the company and conceal the evidence. White-collar crimes are non-violent and the motive is usually financial gain.

White-collar criminals do not fit the stereotypes of criminals. Their crimes are dealt with differently. For example, tax evasion in the UK is dealt with by His Majesty's Revenue and Customs (HMRC), rather than the police. When HMRC decided in 2011 to take stronger action on tax evasion – with the aim of recovering £15 billion in lost revenue – this was done not by arresting and charging people, but by asking middle-class professionals to pay what they owed in return for not being charged. Working-class people who falsely claim benefits are much more likely to be taken to a court, even though the amounts of money involved are much smaller than in middle-class tax evasion.

White-collar crimes may not be recorded in official statistics because companies prefer to avoid the publicity of a criminal case. For example, an employee caught stealing from their company may simply be dismissed, without involving the police. Middle-class people who are charged with a criminal offence such as white-collar crime may be more skilled at using the criminal justice system. They understand their rights and will be able to afford a good lawyer to represent them. If found guilty, they may be given a less severe punishment than

a working-class offender (for example, a community sentence rather than a prison sentence) because they do not fit the stereotype of a typical offender.

MAKING CONNECTIONS

What do you think a Marxist sociologist might say about the differences in treatment between middle-class white-collar criminals and working-class criminals?

Corporate crime is when companies and businesses break the law. It overlaps with white-collar crime, but corporate crime is usually in the interests of the company as a whole, rather than individual employees. Corporate crime includes:

- bribery and corruption
- breaking health and safety laws, or environmental protection laws, such as those controlling pollution
- false and deceptive advertising
- false accounting, such as concealing profits to avoid tax.

In a 2020 article, 'Shifting imagineries of corporate crime', Tombs and Whyte identify four categories of corporate crime: corporate theft and fraud; crimes against consumers; crimes against workers; and crimes against the environment. They argue that these crimes have become normalised.

Often, corporations do not have to break the law; instead, they can put pressure on governments and manipulate the law so it serves their interests. Groups of companies working together can make it difficult for governments to act against them. For example, tobacco companies were able to delay government efforts to control and reduce smoking.

KEY TERMS

white-collar crime: non-violent crime committed by middle-class people for financial gain; for example, fraud, embezzlement, bribery and identity theft

corporate crime: offences committed by corporations or organisations, usually in pursuit of profit for the corporation, rather than the benefit of individuals

CASE STUDY 6.1

Crimes against workers

Crimes against workers include death, injury and disease caused by working; sexual and racial discrimination; and violations of wage laws. Each year, over 2.3 million people die globally as a result of work-related injuries or diseases, according to data collected by the International Labour Organization (ILO, 2015). This is almost four per cent of global deaths every year. In 2005, the ILO stated that around 64 per cent of these deaths occur in Asia, although crimes against workers occur in all parts of the world.

It is often difficult to calculate figures for deaths of workers, because the actual cause of death may be disputed. For example, authorities in India, Pakistan, Nepal, Bangladesh and Sri Lanka have reported that over 6500 workers from their countries have died during the construction of the stadiums for the 2022 Qatar FIFA World Cup, for reasons including heatstroke, heart attacks, falling from heights and being hit by falling objects. However, Qatar's government says that between 2014 and 2020, there were only 37 deaths of workers building World Cup stadiums – and 34 of those were not work-related.

Task

1 In what ways can deaths caused by working be seen as corporate crime?

2 Look again at the statistics relating to the deaths of workers constructing the stadiums for the 2022 Qatar FIFA World Cup. Give possible reasons for the different figures given by the workers' countries and by the Qatari government.

Large multinational corporations can use their size to evade the law, for example by transferring money within their companies and departments to avoid taxes. Tombs and Whyte argue that, in many countries, governments make certain practices legal or fail to enforce laws and regulations against large corporations because these corporations are so powerful and important to the country's economy.

Prosecutions of corporate crimes are unusual. In cases that attract attention, one employee often takes the blame, while the company is not charged. For example, a manager may be blamed for not following health and safety regulations even when these regulations have been ignored throughout the company (sometimes on the orders of those in charge).

Expressive crime

Expressive crime involves emotions, such as strong anger or frustration. Such crimes are usually unplanned and they have no purpose beyond expressing the offender's emotions. Examples include domestic violence and some assaults. Expressive crime can be contrasted with instrumental crime.

Instrumental crime

Instrumental crimes have a clear aim; for example, the criminal may want to have more money or possessions, or to improve their social position. Examples of instrumental crimes include theft, burglary and fraud. Instrumental crime may involve violence. However, in contrast with expressive crime, the violence is designed to achieve a goal (such as obtaining money), rather than being an expression of anger.

KEY TERMS

expressive crime: offences involving emotions, such as strong anger or frustration, which are usually unplanned

instrumental crime: offences which have a clear goal from the point of view of the criminal

Gang crime

Gang crime refers to criminal activities carried out collectively, as a result of membership of a gang. A gang is a group of people who often have a territory and a hierarchical structure with a leader. Many gang members are young people and gangs may form for protection against other gangs. They often become involved in violent crime and other criminal activities such as drug-dealing, vandalism and theft.

Gang crime can be seen as a type of **organised crime**, but gangs are usually local rather than global and they are more likely to involve young people. However, some gangs do run criminal activities (such as drug-dealing) in an organised and businesslike way.

Green crime

Sociologists are increasingly interested in **green crime**, also called environmental crime. The victims of green crime may be people, but they can also be other living things or the natural environment itself. The offenders are often, but not always, corporations (see corporate crime). Examples of green crimes include:

- the global trade in protected species of animals, including their body parts

- poaching (illegal hunting and killing) of protected species, such as rhinos and elephants, usually to sell their body parts such as horns and tusks

- dumping of toxic waste in rivers or elsewhere, which can lead to long-term illness or death

- contamination of drinking water as a result of mining

- deforestation and illegal logging, for example in the Amazon rainforest.

Sociologists studying green crimes note that it can be particularly difficult to decide whether a law has been broken or not. For example, a company that dumps toxic waste from its factories on public land may not have broken a law in that country, although the environmental impact may be felt in other countries as well. Moreover, the normal and non-criminal actions of corporations cause environmental damage. For example, the manufacture and use of plastics is contributing to the climate crisis. Sociologists studying green crimes increasingly refer to 'harms' rather than 'crimes'; they are interested in the consequences, regardless of whether the actions are technically criminal.

Figure 6.4: Illegal ivory tusks recovered by officials.

STRETCH AND CHALLENGE

Green crime is a new way of thinking about people and the environment. To what extent do you think it is helpful to think of some harms as 'crimes', even if no law has been broken? What are some of the problems with doing this?

KEY TERMS

gang crime: criminal activities carried out by a group of (often young) people, who have a territory and a defined leadership and internal organisation.

organised crime: criminal activities which are planned and carried out by powerful groups

green crime: offences which damage the natural world, with resulting harm to humans, other living things and the environment

Global crime, e.g. organised crime

Organised crime is carried out by organisations that work like businesses, except that their activities are illegal. Organised crime involves a wide range of offences, such as drugs, smuggling, gambling, theft and protection rackets. In the past, organised crime seems to have been widespread in some countries but not in others. Examples of widespread organised crime include the Mafia in Italy (and later the USA), the Triads of Hong Kong and the Yakuza of Japan.

The activities of criminal organisations have become increasingly global. They cooperate with each other across international borders while also competing against each other, in a similar way to legitimate businesses. Globalisation transformed many areas of social life in the late 20th and early 21st centuries, and it also changed crime. Some types of crime grew and new types of crimes emerged, such as green crime and cybercrime. Other **global crimes** often carried out by criminal organisations include:

- illegal trade, for example of drugs and weapons

- people trafficking – the moving (and usually selling) of people and body parts, usually from low-income countries to wealthier ones. For example, there is an organised illegal trade in which people pay criminals to transport them across borders and seas to seek asylum or find work elsewhere

- global financial crime, in which money earned illegally is 'laundered' through legitimate businesses and banks. This involves a complicated and secret series of moves to 'clean' the money, erasing all traces of the original criminality.

Figure 6.5: Global organised crime often involves drugs, money and violence.

Cybercrime

New technologies have led to new types of crime, usually referred to as **cybercrime**. Many cybercrimes are the digital equivalents of crimes that existed before, such as fraud, scams and harassment. Some are more specific to new technologies, for example sending spam (unsolicited bulk emails), which is illegal in some countries. As with other types of crime, cybercrimes can be committed by individuals, groups or organisations, or even by the state. Some cybercrimes target victims through their devices – for example, infecting them with a virus. Others involve the use of computers as a means of carrying out the crime.

Crimes involving the internet specifically can be referred to as **internet crime**. Cybercrime includes internet crime but it is a wider term which also includes the use of other digital technology to commit crime.

> ### KEY TERMS
>
> **global crime:** offences which are worldwide, for example involving international networks
>
> **cybercrime:** crime involving use of new technologies, such as computers
>
> **internet crime:** any crime or illegal activity committed on, through or using the internet

There are many types of cybercrime. They include:

- spreading computer viruses and malware. One example of this is ransomware, which allows a cybercriminal to take over an individual or company's files. The criminal then demands a financial payment to return the files – like a ransom

- fraud and identity theft

- internet scams targeting individual users

- websites with obscene or offensive content, and the spread of obscene or offensive content by email and text messages

- cyberstalking and cyberbullying, which involve harassing individuals using social media

- trade in illegal drugs and other illegal goods (the internet makes it easier for buyers and sellers to contact each other)

- cyberterrorism, in which the internet is used for deliberate, widespread attacks on computers or computer networks. For example, an activist group may try to hack into and disable the website of a government or a corporation.

CASE STUDY 6.2

Anonymous

Figure 6.6: An anonymous hacker.

An example of global cybercrime is the semi-organised hacking carried out by a group known as 'Anonymous'. Anonymous is the collective name of a loose and decentralised group of hackers with constantly changing membership and without leaders. They see themselves as 'hacktivists', using their hacking skills as a form of activism or protest. They claim that they are defenders of internet freedom, opposing surveillance and censorship of the internet. For example, Anonymous have hacked the websites of government, financial and security organisations, to retaliate against attempts to prevent sharing of films and music online. Anonymous breaks laws in attacking these websites, but justifies the crimes as defending freedom. However, Anonymous has also acted as an online **vigilante group**; for example, they have worked to track down child pornography on the internet and expose the criminals behind it.

Some people see Anonymous hackers as cyberterrorists. Others see them as social and political activists who use their expertise for the public good. In 2022, Anonymous hacked Russian television channels to show viewers there what was happening in Ukraine following the Russian invasion. They replaced the propaganda that was being broadcast by the Russian media.

Task

1   How does this case study show how difficult it is for police and other authorities to tackle cybercrime?

2   In what ways are Anonymous hackers different from stereotypical criminals?

Hate crime

In **hate crimes**, victims are targeted because of their characteristics, such as their ethnicity, faith or sexual orientation. Hate crimes may be motivated by racism, prejudice against a religion, prejudice against people with disabilities, homophobia or transphobia (types of hatred based on sexuality or gender identity). It can be difficult to decide whether a hate crime has been committed; the police and courts will look for evidence that the offender chose the victim specifically, because of their characteristics. In most cases, the offender will be charged with another offence (such as theft or assault). However, if this offence is identified as a hate crime, it may be investigated differently by the police and the courts may impose a harsher sentence.

> ### KEY TERMS
>
> **vigilante groups:** self-appointed people with no legal authority who punish people they believe are offenders
>
> **hate crime:** offences in which the victim is targeted because of certain characteristics, related to, for example age, faith, sexuality or race

Domestic crime

Domestic crime is also referred to as domestic abuse. This is when one person tries to control and manipulate another, usually within a family. The abuse can include controlling and threatening behaviour, and often violence. It can also include neglect, especially with young children. The offender is usually, but not always, male; the victims are usually his female partner and children. Domestic offences are underreported for many reasons – for example, the victim:

- may be afraid of further abuse if they report the offender

- may see it as a private matter and not want anyone else to know (including family and friends)

- may feel they are to blame; domestic abusers often manipulate their victims into believing this

- may believe the police will not be able to help or will not believe them

- may not want the offender to be punished. For example, they may still love the offender, or have no other way to support themselves and their children

- may feel that the criminal justice system will not help them. In the past, and still in some countries, domestic crime is seen as private and there is a belief that the police should not get involved

Feminists see the causes of domestic crime in the patriarchal nature of society, and of the family.

ACTIVITY: WRITTEN 6.1

Design a large poster for wall display that shows, in a colourful and informative way, the different types of crime listed in this section. Write a description and give an example for each type of crime.

Measuring crime

This section considers the ways in which crime is measured, as well as their strengths and limitations. The three ways discussed here are official statistics, self-report studies and victim surveys.

Official statistics

Official crime statistics are one of the main sources of information about crime. The main sets of official statistics on crime are:

- **police figures** showing the total numbers of different types of offences recorded by the police in a specific time period. Government statistics, which are usually published each year, are compiled from figures submitted by police forces.

- **court records** showing the total number of convictions for different offences. There are also records showing the offenders' characteristics, such as their age, gender and ethnic group, and their previous convictions (if any).

Strengths of official statistics

- Official statistics provide information that can be used to understand the patterns and trends of crime in a country. They also show what types of people offenders and victims are.

- Official statistics are usually published online. They are freely available for the public and researchers to use in order to understand whether crime is increasing or decreasing, and which crimes are most common.

Limitations of official statistics

Official crime statistics are often taken at face value and people use them to make assumptions about the extent of crime and the characteristics of offenders.

KEY TERMS

domestic crime: offences in which the offender and the victim live in the same family home or are in a relationship

official crime statistics: official figures showing the number of crimes and offenders recorded in a country during a specific time period

These assumptions then influence governments, the police and others in deciding how to deal with crime. However, official statistics are socially constructed and need to be treated with caution; assumptions may be based on inaccurate and misleading data. Interpretivists claim that official crime statistics tell us more about the decisions made by the people who compile them than about the actual extent of crime.

Many crimes do not appear in the official figures. Police statistics only include crimes which the people are aware of and which they decide to record. Unreported and unrecorded crimes are known as the 'dark figure' of crime: they are not known and it is impossible to estimate how many there may be. Official police statistics have been shown to underrecord crime, but to different extents for different types of crime and different types of offender. There are several reasons for this:

Reporting

Most crimes that are recorded in official statistics are reported to the police, either by the victim or by a witness. Few crimes are uncovered by the police. Various factors influence whether or not victims and witnesses report crimes to the police. For example:

- People do not report crimes they regard as trivial or when they do not believe the police can do anything to help.

- Victims may only report crimes if it will benefit them. For example, if a stolen item is insured, the victim is likely to report the theft; most insurance companies require this. However, if there is no realistic chance of the stolen goods being recovered, the victim may decide there is no point reporting the theft.

- Some crimes are seen as private matters between individuals, in which the police should not be involved.

- Victims may not report a crime because they do not want the offender to be punished, or because they are embarrassed. Domestic crimes and sexual offences come into this category – both are known to be significantly underreported.

- Witnesses may not report a crime because they do not want to get involved; for example, they might not want to give a statement to the police or appear in court.

- Victims and witnesses may be concerned about their safety if they report an offence. For example,

they may be afraid of the criminal or have been threatened by them.

- Some communities distrust the police and may be reluctant to have any contact with them.

Invisible crime

Some white-collar crimes and corporate crimes are unlikely to come to the attention of the police. For example, there are some areas of work where fraud and theft are common and unlikely to be reported (see the section on white-collar and corporate crime). Credit card fraud – even when it involves large sums of money – is usually dealt with by the credit card company rather than the police. Other 'invisible' crimes include crimes with no obvious victim to report them, such as drug-taking, underage offences and speeding. Crimes where the victim is a business are also less likely to be noticed or reported; for example, a lot of shoplifting is not detected and, even when it is, the shop or store may not involve the police. Many companies simply allow for a certain amount of loss of stock.

Interpretation and application of the law

The police play a crucial role in interpreting and applying the law and deciding which incidents should be recorded as crimes. The police have discretion (a certain amount of choice) when deciding whether to arrest someone and what to charge an offender with. They might make assumptions, often based on stereotypes, about where trouble is likely to occur and focus their attention and resources in these places. As a result, they are more likely to be aware of and record offences in these areas.

There are differences between police forces depending on the priorities of senior police officers. For example, police in some areas are stricter on drugs; if they choose to 'crack down' on these types of crimes, they may uncover offences that would otherwise be unrecorded. In other areas, burglary or road traffic offences may be prioritised.

Police forces are often under pressure to achieve targets and to 'solve' a high proportion of crimes. Some use a practice known as 'cuffing' to manipulate the statistics, to create the impression that crime is less common or less serious than it actually is. Cuffing involves removing crimes from the records or recording them as less serious offences.

Recording of crime

The recording of crime is shaped by the media and political pressures. For example, police forces may be under pressure to clear up particular crimes or to act on something which is causing a moral panic. This increased police focus will lead to the statistics for that particular crime increasing, even though the actual number of offences is not changing.

Inevitably, police statistics miss out a lot of crime. Therefore, sociologists and others (including governments) use two alternative techniques of measuring crime to try to get the full picture. These methods are self-report studies and victim surveys.

ACTIVITY: RESEARCH 6.2

Find out what crime statistics are published in your country. They will probably be on an official government department or police website. You may also be able to find statistics for some crimes on websites of global organisations that collate statistics from different countries.

Write a summary of the patterns of crime (the amount of different types of crime) and the trends in crime (whether crime is going up or down) in your country.

REFLECTION

How useful were the statistics in helping you to understand the extent of crime in your country? What else would you like to know? Are there reasons why you could not find this information, or why there were no statistics available?

Self-report studies

These are confidential questionnaires or interviews asking respondents whether they have committed listed criminal acts. For the purposes of anonymous and confidential research, people may reveal crimes that are unknown to the police. Participants are informed that they cannot be identified and that no information will be passed to the police or other authorities.

Official statistics show that most crime is committed by men and by working-class people. Self-report studies, however, reveal that significant numbers of crimes and deviant acts are committed by women and by middle-class people. This calls into question the

accuracy of theories based on the official statistics (for example, those assuming that most crime is committed by working-class males).

Strengths of self-report studies

- They provide information that cannot be gathered in any other way, from the offenders themselves.

- They can uncover hidden crimes.

- They can provide information about victimless crimes, such as drug-taking.

Limitations of self-report studies

- There are concerns about the validity and accuracy of the responses. Respondents may exaggerate to impress their peers or the researcher. On the other hand, even though self-report studies are anonymous, many people who have committed an offence may not admit to it, especially if they were never charged by the police.

- Most self-report studies ask about relatively trivial criminal offences – such as travelling on public transport without paying – or about deviant acts rather than criminal ones, such as missing school without permission. This limits their usefulness in giving an overview of crime.

- Respondents are unlikely to give honest answers to questions about serious offences. If a respondent does admit to a serious crime, this raises ethical issues: should the researcher report them, despite the promise of anonymity?

- Most self-report studies have been carried out on young people, with a focus on deviance and minor crimes. It is generally accepted that adults, especially those with established careers and a lot to lose, are unlikely to answer honestly. As a result, self-report studies rarely ask about categories of crime such as white-collar crime.

- Self-report studies are carried out on individuals, so are not appropriate to investigate corporate crime.

KEY TERMS

moral panic: exaggerated social reaction to deviance, usually fuelled by the media, that creates a demand for action

self-report studies: research that asks people what crimes or deviant acts they have committed

---

Victim surveys (local and national)

Victim surveys ask a sample of people what crimes they have been victims of, usually over the previous year or several years. Most respondents are more willing to report crimes they have been victims of, rather than crimes they have committed themselves (as in self-report studies). Victim surveys uncover unreported crimes and can show new patterns. The findings of victim surveys suggest that, at the most, only about half of all crimes are reported.

Victim surveys can be carried out at a national level. A good example of this is the Crime Survey for England and Wales (CSEW), which is carried out every year. The CSEW has found there is considerable underreporting of many crimes. It has also revealed, for example, that the group thought to be the main offenders – young working-class men in inner cities – are also the most likely to be victims of crime.

Not all countries have a large-scale annual victim survey like the CSEW. However, many include victim surveys as part of other research on their populations. For example, in Mauritius, questions about victimisation and views on crime and policing are included in the Continuous Multipurpose Household Survey, which is carried out every year and also includes questions on other areas of social life, such as employment and housing. The International Crime Victims Survey collates data from victim surveys around the world.

There are also local victim surveys, carried out by sociologists or research organisations who want to understand people's experiences of crime in particular areas, often cities. An example is a victim survey carried out in Lahore, Pakistan in 2017 by IDEAS (the Institute of Development and Economic Alternatives). Despite concerns over rising crime in Lahore – based on the official statistics – the victim survey revealed that the citizens of Lahore are less likely to be victims of crime than people living in other comparable global cities. The survey also found that crime is concentrated in certain parts of the city, particularly around commercial centres.

Such information can be used to understand the reasons for crime and also to inform local governments in relation to crime prevention strategies.

Strengths of victim surveys

- They reveal crimes that have not been reported to the police or recorded elsewhere.

- They provide the most accurate estimates of total amounts of crimes that have victims.

- They can reveal trends in crime.

Limitations of victim surveys

- They cannot uncover all types of crime. For example, they do not uncover victimless crimes, such as drug use or crimes against organisations or businesses. They also do not usually include crimes against children, as children are rarely respondents in these surveys. This is a problem because children are at high risk of being victims of some types of offences.

- The data may not be valid. It is thought that some types of crime, such as sexual offences, are under-reported in victim surveys.

- Victim surveys rely on the memories of respondents, which may be faulty; for example, they may have forgotten exactly when an offence occurred. This also affects validity.

- People are not always aware that they have been a victim of a crime. For example, some victims of fraud may be unaware of it, so these crimes would not be reported.

- There is no way of checking the validity of what respondents say.

- Victim surveys are carried out on a sample of respondents, rather than the whole population. (This contrasts with police statistics, which cover the entire country.) Even if the sample is representative, the results of victim surveys may lack generalisability, especially for rare crimes.

KEY TERM

victim surveys: research that asks people what crimes they have been victims of

---

STRETCH AND CHALLENGE

To what extent do you think a self-report study is a better way of researching crime than a victim survey or official statistics? What problems would you encounter if you carried out a self-report study on your fellow learners?

CHECK YOUR UNDERSTANDING 6.1

1   Working with a partner, name three agencies of informal social control and three agencies of formal social control and explain briefly how they control behaviour.

2   Write a paragraph explaining why corporate crimes are less likely to lead to prison sentences than crimes such as robbery.

3   Identify some problems with self-report studies and victim surveys as ways of measuring crime. Discuss your answers with a partner and see if you remembered the same points.

KEY POINTS

- The terms 'crime' and 'deviance' mean different things.

- Both crime and deviance can be seen as relative in terms of time and culture.

- The formal agencies of social control include:
    - the police
    - the courts
    - the armed forces
    - government
    - the penal system.

- The informal agencies of social control include:
    - family
    - education
    - workplace
    - peer group
    - traditional and digital media
    - religion.

- Both formal and informal agencies of social control prevent crime and deviance in various ways and with varying effectiveness.

- There are different types and examples of crimes, including:
    - violent crime
    - property crime
    - white-collar/corporate crime
    - expressive crime
    - instrumental crime
    - organised crime
    - gang crime
    - green crime
    - global crime
    - cybercrime
    - hate crime
    - domestic crime.

- Crime is measured in different ways, including:
    - official statistics
    - self-report studies
    - victim surveys (local and national).

- Each method of measuring crime has strengths and limitations.

- Some crime is unreported and unrecorded.

6.2 What are the patterns and explanations of crime and deviance?

Patterns of victimisation by age, social class, gender and ethnicity

According to official statistics and victim surveys, groups that are most likely to commit crime are also most likely to be victims of crime. This includes young people, males, working-class people and some minority ethnic groups. The victim and offender of a crime often belong to the same group; for example, young working-class men are often victims of crime by other young working-class men.

Age

Children are at risk of being victims of some crimes because of have low status and little power. For example, they may be vulnerable to neglect and abuse within the family. Even if they do tell an adult what is happening, they may not be believed.

In some countries, the rights of children are abused. Child labour is against the law in many countries, because it takes away the child's right to an education. Child labour normally refers to children under 15 working for more than 14 hours a week (and usually not attending school). The International Labour Organization estimates that, in 2020, there were about 160 million child labourers (aged 5 to 17); 79 million of them were engaged in hazardous work, against international law. The great majority were in developing countries and there were far more boys than girls. Note, however, that not all of these cases would break the law in that country.

Children may also be used in wars – sometimes as soldiers but also as, for example, cooks, messengers and spies. An set of international standards called the Paris Principles state that children (under 18 years old) should be treated primarily as victims, even if they have taken part as fighters.

Teenagers and young people have a higher risk of being victims of some types of crime, especially violent crime, because they are more active and more likely to be in public places where crimes occur. Some violent crime may be related to gang membership and committed by other youths. The World Health Organization estimates that around 200,000 young people (between 10 and 29 years of age) are victims of homicide every year; this is 42 per cent of all global homicides.

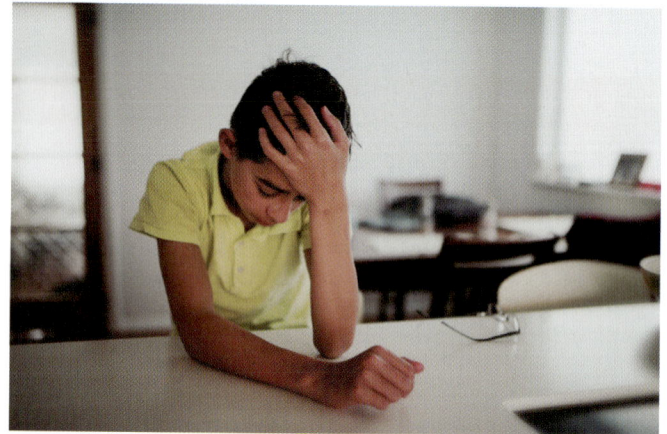

Figure 6.7: Teenagers may be victims of crime from other teenagers.

For other types of crime, older people are more at risk. For example, many older people are less familiar with digital technologies than younger people. As a result, they may be at risk of cybercrimes such as online fraud, because they are less able to detect when something looks suspicious. Older people in need of care can also be at risk of abuse, such as neglect, by their carers.

Social class

Working-class people can be victims of theft and burglary because they are unable to afford resources to protect them from these crimes. Wealthier people may have a burglar alarm or video surveillance of their property, or anti-theft devices on their cars. Some can even afford security guards or live in a gated community which outsiders cannot enter without permission. So, although middle-class people have more possessions that could be stolen, they are more able to protect themselves and their property. In addition, crimes such as theft and burglary are often quite local; criminals rarely travel far to find victims. This means that people living in the same area as potential offenders (usually working-class areas) are more at risk of victimisation.

Gender

Victim surveys show that many women are afraid of crime, especially when they are out at night, but also that their chances of being attacked are actually small. Therefore, some sociologists argue that women's fears of being attacked are exaggerated, perhaps because the media overreports crimes against women which take place outside the home. However, this can lead to a self-fulfilling prophecy if fewer women go out, those who do are more vulnerable, because there is less chance of the attack being seen by other members of the public. The risk of attack increases and the media image becomes the reality. Statistically, women are more likely to be victimised in the family home rather than outside; most assaults against women are by people known to the victim, not by strangers.

> **KEY TERM**
>
> **self-fulfilling prophecy:** when people are aware of certain expectations and so they act in ways that make those expectations come true

Women are more likely to be victims of the most underreported crimes, such as sexual assault (including rape) and domestic violence. Domestic crime is discussed in section 6.1 and domestic violence is also covered in Unit 4.

As with other crimes against women, most rapes are committed by someone who is known to the victim; these crimes often take place in the victim's home. Research suggests that many rape victims will not report it to the police, for reasons including shame and embarrassment, fear of not being believed, and the trauma of having to relive the attack in court. Feminists argue that patriarchal values reinforce these issues and that traditional attitudes about appropriate behaviour for men and women need to be challenged.

Despite these specific areas of female victimisation and women's fear of crime, young men are actually more likely than young women to be victims of violent offences, particularly those committed by strangers and gang-related violence.

Ethnicity

The extent to which ethnicity increases the risk of being a victim of crime varies between societies, according to the status of the group.

Minority groups who experience prejudice and discrimination are more likely to be at risk of crime. Members of the majority group may feel able to victimise members of the minority, believing that the police will not investigate thoroughly. There is also the risk of hate crime based on racism (discussed in section 6.1). However, in many societies *intra*-racial crime (crime *within* an ethnic or racial group) is more common than *inter*-racial crime (crime between members of *different* racial or ethnic groups). This suggests that even though members of ethnic minority groups are more likely to be victims of crime in some countries, this is not always due to racism or hate from other ethnic groups. Instead, crime may take place within a community or area between people from the same minority ethnic background, often related to gangs or poverty rather than ethnicity.

Patterns of crime (committed) by age, social class, gender and ethnicity

Age – young people

Most crimes are committed by young people. The age group most likely to commit a crime is 15 to 25, though this varies by country. Crimes by young people attract a lot of media attention and governments face increasing pressure to prevent crimes by young people.

Juvenile delinquency refers to crime committed by young people who, if they were adults, would face criminal prosecution. Many countries have separate systems for young offenders, such as juvenile courts and juvenile detention centres. These systems aim to prevent young people from coming into contact with and being influenced by older offenders, and to try to ensure that young people's futures are not damaged by having a criminal record. However, in most countries, more serious offences by juveniles are dealt with in adult courts.

Some offences by young people are status offences: they are offences only because of the age of the person committing them. Examples include smoking or drinking alcohol when underage. Most offences by juveniles, though, would also be offences if they were committed by adults, such as theft and damage to property.

High proportions of young people commit deviance and minor criminal offences. Despite media concern, these crimes are almost always non-violent and are not repeated. It has been argued that limited, small-scale offending is a normal part of growing up.

In modern industrial societies, young people have an extended period of adolescence when they feel they are neither children nor adults. Anti-social and delinquent acts can be seen as a way of testing the boundaries of this new status. However, some juveniles are persistent offenders and commit multiple offences. These young people are at high risk of becoming adult offenders.

Age – adults

Some young offenders continue committing crimes as adults; there are some 'career criminals' who spend most of their adult lives going in and out of prison. However, according to the crime statistics, more crime is associated with young people and may be explained by their tendency to experiment and test boundaries. Another explanation for these patterns is that adults commit crimes which are less visible, and they are more careful and less reckless than teenagers, planning any crimes in advance. These factors may mean they are less likely to be caught and prosecuted. Some of the crimes committed by adults – such as white-collar crime – are underreported and underrecorded and adults may be able to use their status and power to avoid detection or conviction.

Age – older people

Very little crime is committed by older people. High-profile cases are occasionally reported in the media but they are exceptional. Sometimes, the reports are about crimes committed when the person was younger; for example, people charged with war crimes at the International Criminal Court are often brought to trial many years after the events.

As modern industrial societies experience ageing populations (see Unit 4), crimes by older people may make up a growing proportion of all crimes. Japan is already experiencing more crime committed by older people: in 2007, one in seven of all crimes (including 150 murders) were committed by people aged over 65. The Japanese government has begun building special prison accommodation for elderly people. The rise in crime by older people in Japan may be linked to growing economic problems and to older people feeling less connected to their families and communities.

Social class

Official statistics suggest that most crimes are committed by members of the working class. This particularly applies to the kinds of crime which appear most in statistics, such as violent offences and robberies.

However, some sociologists suggest that this is because the law acts in the interests of higher classes. As you will see in later sections, it is possible that higher classes commit just as much crime as the working class, but that it is not recognised and recorded in the same way.

Gender

Official statistics show that men are responsible for far more crimes as women and that there are far more male than female criminals; this is the case in all countries, although the proportions vary. Men and women also commit different types of offences – although these also vary between societies. For example, males tend to commit more violent offences, including homicide. Shoplifting is one crime for which men and women commit similar numbers of offences.

Ethnicity

Official statistics for the UK show that some minority ethnic groups commit more crimes than would be expected, given their numbers in the population. However, as discussed earlier in this unit, police statistics and self-report studies should be analysed very cautiously. Sociologists question whether the different rates of arrest and imprisonment for ethnic groups reflect different levels of crime, or whether they are the result of institutional racism within crime control agencies (such as the police, the courts and the media). Institutional racism within the criminal justice system is discussed in more detail later in this section.

As we have seen, working-class people are more likely to appear in crime statistics for certain types of crime. Since certain minority ethnic groups in many countries are largely working class, the differences in crime rates between ethnic groups could be due to social class rather than ethnicity. In addition, most crime is committed by young people and minority ethnic groups tend to contain a higher proportion of young people than the majority group. As a result, age may also partially explain the higher crime rates in some minority ethnic groups.

Explanations for crime and deviance based on age

Police targeting/stop and search

The police are more likely to suspect young people of crime, especially if they are in a group and behaving in a way that attracts attention. The police may therefore **stop and search** young people, because they think they will find evidence of wrongdoing or criminal intent, such as drugs or a weapon. On a large scale, this police **targeting** of young people will inevitably find some evidence of criminal activity; this in turn will result in continued targeting. Police targeting also makes it more likely that young people will be hostile and aggressive towards the police.

Self-fulfilling prophecy

Police targeting of young people can result in a self-fulfilling prophecy: young people react badly to being targeted and these negative reactions confirm the police's suspicion of young people. This leads to a spiral, in which the police target more young people and young people react more and more defiantly. This is called **deviancy amplification**.

Stereotyping

The police actions described here are based on **stereotyping**. Stereotypes about young people may be believed throughout society. However, the powerful position of the police means that if they act on these stereotypes, there will be significant consequences in terms of targeting young people and applying practices such as stop and search in a discriminatory way.

Gang culture

Young people are more likely to belong to a gang than other age groups. The word 'gang' is used in different ways. Sometimes, a group of young people may be labelled as a gang – and seen as deviant – because of their appearance or cultural choices (such as music). At other times, a group of friends who spend time together in public places might be seen as a gang. More often, however, the term 'gang' implies an organised group which has a name, a territory and a hierarchy with leaders. Such gangs are often involved in criminal activities, such as violence and drug-dealing. Gang members are socialised into a **gang culture**, adopting a set of norms and values which are deviant in relation to wider society. These values often involve putting the gang first and being prepared to defend its members, territory and reputation in any way necessary. In some areas, especially in inner-city ones, it may be normal for young people (particularly boys) to belong to a gang. As a result, these boys run the risk of being drawn into criminal behaviour.

Figure 6.8: Police conducting stop and search.

Socialisation and social control

If a young person is brought up by criminal parents or has older siblings who are involved in crime, they are more likely to be delinquent. They are socialised into deviant or sub-cultural values: delinquent behaviour is expected and may even be approved of. Less social control is applied to teenagers than to children and adults. Children are subject to a lot of social control from their parents, and adults are subject to social control based on their commitments.

Teenagers, however, have more freedom as their parents allow them more independence. This can result in an increase in deviant behaviour at this age. Socialisation from peers and the media can also encourage teenagers into deviant behaviour.

Lack of opportunity

In some societies, opportunities for young people are limited; there may be few jobs, even for those with educational qualifications. Young people who want more money and possessions may be tempted to turn to crime.

Status frustration

The term **status frustration** was first used by the American sociologist Albert Cohen. He argued that all young males want status (respect from their peers). Middle-class boys may gain status through academic success. However, many working-class boys feel status frustration because they are failing at school and so lack this source of respect from others. As a result, working-class youths may look for an alternative source of status. They may gain respect from some of their peers by adopting deviant values and committing deviant and criminal acts, such as misbehaving in school, taking drugs and committing acts of vandalism.

KEY TERM

status frustration: when people (particularly working-class males) feel frustrated because they are unable to achieve respect from their peers due to their position in society

ACTIVITY: DISCUSSION 6.1

In a small group, discuss these two questions.

1   Is a certain amount of deviance a natural part of growing up?

2   What should society do about teenage deviance if it is a temporary phase?

Let everyone contribute and try to reach a group consensus.

REFLECTION

Did your group manage to let everyone have a say? Did one person's views seem to count for more and if so, why? What advice would you give to another group who wanted to make sure everyone had a chance to speak and to be listened to?

Explanations for crime and deviance based on ethnicity

Institutional racism

One explanation for crime and deviance based on ethnicity is that the criminal justice system is institutionally racist. This means that the police, the courts and the penal system work in ways that discriminate against one or more ethnic groups. This can happen even though the people working with the criminal justice system are not necessarily racist as individuals. For example, very few minorities are represented in the criminal justice system. As a result, there is a lack of knowledge and understanding which contributes to institutional racism.

The term **institutional racism** became widely used in the UK after the case of Stephen Lawrence. Lawrence was a young African Caribbean man who was stabbed by a gang of racist white youths in London. An inquiry into the investigation of his murder found that the police made stereotypical assumptions about Stephen and the friend he was with based on their ethnicity, failed to investigate his murder properly and did not take statements from witnesses or follow up leads. These findings demonstrated the institutional racism in the police.

KEY TERM

institutional racism: when the functioning of an institution or organisation involves systems and expectations that lead to discrimination against an ethnic group

The belief that minorities are treated differently – and considered to be of less value – contributed to the Black Lives Matter movement. This started in the USA and became a global movement during 2020.

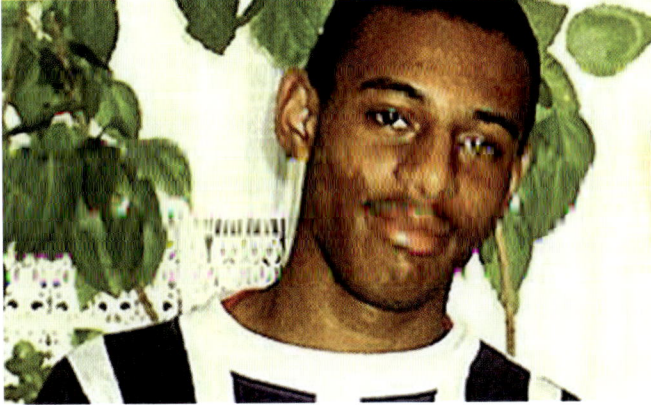

Figure 6.9: Stephen Lawrence.

Prejudice and discrimination

Individuals from minority ethnic groups may commit crime as a response to experiences of racism, **prejudice** and **discrimination**. For example, an individual may be unable to achieve good qualifications in school or find a job they are qualified for, because of discrimination. This leads to disillusionment and rejection of society and its values. People from ethnic minorities may experience institutional racism within the education system and the criminal justice system – for example, they may be labelled by teachers or the police and treated differently based on racist stereotypes. Such treatment will increase feelings of anger and disillusionment. The Black British sociologist Paul Gilroy argues that people from minority ethnic backgrounds carry the 'scars of imperialist violence', which lead to resentment and resistance against authority. Gang membership may be one response to these feelings and widespread feelings of injustice can also erupt into protests and riots.

It is important to note, however, that most people who experience prejudice or discrimination do not turn to crime. An alternative reaction may be to turn to religion, to gain a sense of belonging; for example, a person might join an evangelical Christian church or one with connections to their country of origin.

Police targeting/stop and search

Policing practices affect crime statistics. If the police stop and search people from some ethnic groups more often than others, it follows that more crime will be uncovered in these ethnic groups.

The monitoring organisation Human Rights Watch has documented racially discriminatory policing in many countries, including the USA, France and Brazil. In 2020, the unlawful killing of George Floyd by a police officer in the USA sparked global protests as part of the Black Lives Matter movement. Following this, the United Nations commissioned a global report on systemic racism and excessive use of force against people of African descent by law enforcement agencies. The report, published in 2021, identified 190 police-related deaths involving Black individuals over the previous ten years worldwide; some of these deaths occurred during the policing of minor offences, such as road traffic stops.

Material and relative deprivation

Minority groups often share the same values and aspirations as the rest of society. Where the normal routes to achieving these goals – such as success in education – are blocked, people may turn to crime in response. **Material deprivation** is when people cannot afford material goods that most others in a society would see as necessities (for example, new clothes, a car, other consumer items or even adequate housing). **Relative deprivation** is the feeling of having less than others in your society or community. This can be fuelled by the media, including social media, since many people compare their lifestyle and possessions to those they see online. Feelings of relative deprivation are especially common among young people and people from minority

> ### KEY TERMS
>
> **prejudice:** an unfair and unreasonable opinion or feeling, especially about a particular group of people, that is formed without knowledge and often based on stereotypes
>
> **discrimination:** treating a person or group of people differently to other people, often based on prejudice
>
> **material deprivation:** being unable to afford material goods which most people in a given society would see as necessities
>
> **relative deprivation:** feeling disadvantaged in comparison to others in your society

ethnic groups, who may be disadvantaged by racism within society.

Stereotyping

Racist stereotypes can lead to police targeting, resulting in more arrests and greater resentment against society. This in turn may lead to gang membership, protests and riots (as discussed previously). Victims of crime are also affected by racist stereotypes. For example, a victim of a robbery which took place in a dark street may describe their attacker as Black when reporting the robbery to the police – even if they did not clearly see their attacker – because they believe stereotypes relating to the ethnicity of violent offenders.

Gang culture

As we have seen, gang culture exists in some areas, particularly inner-cities, and young people growing up in these areas may join or form gangs. Young people from minority ethnic groups are more likely to grow up in these inner-city areas. As a result, they may be more likely to join a gang. They may also join gangs for protection from other gangs and from racist attacks, and they may carry a weapon (such as a knife) for the same reason.

Status frustration

Young people from minority ethnic groups are more likely than the majority to experience status frustration, because many of the usual routes to gain status are blocked to them. They may see crime or gang membership as the only ways in which they can gain status.

Explanations for crime and deviance based on gender

Chivalry thesis

One controversial explanation for the lower crime rate among women than men is the **chivalry thesis**. This is the idea that women are less likely to be charged or convicted of crimes because they are treated differently (compared with men) by the police and courts. The chivalry thesis suggests that women are traditionally viewed as vulnerable, delicate and innocent and that these views affect the predominantly male criminal justice system. As a result, women are underrepresented in crime statistics.

For example, the police may believe that girls are influenced by their male companions, so they might caution young

female offenders rather than bringing charges against them. It is also suggested that judges sometimes give lighter sentences to female offenders because they take into consideration the woman's family responsibilities (such as caring for children). A judge might also think that criminality is 'out of character' for a woman, so she is less likely to repeat an offence than a man.

However, the same stereotypes can lead to an alternative view. Some sociologists suggest that courts are in fact harder on women, because female offenders are seen as acting against their 'true' nature (as wives and mothers). Similar behaviour by males may be seen as wrong but not unnatural. Females convicted of serious crimes – particularly those involving violence or where the victims are children – are often given harsher sentences than their male counterparts.

The chivalry thesis has also been criticised for being racist and classist. Though middle-class white females may be treated more leniently, because they are seen as innocent and in need of protection, Black women and those from working-class backgrounds are not treated in the same way.

Culture of masculinity

Masculinity refers to the attitudes and behaviour associated with being a man in a particular culture. The dominant form of masculinity in modern industrial societies is referred to as hegemonic masculinity. This 'ideal' form involves, for example:

- controlling emotions (except anger); for example, not crying in public

- being physically strong

- being willing to use violence to resolve problems

- being competitive.

> ### KEY TERMS
>
> **chivalry thesis:** the theory that women are treated more leniently than men within the criminal justice system
>
> **masculinity:** the attitudes and behaviour associated with being a man in a particular culture

There are alternative forms of masculinity but they usually have a lower status because they do not involve being 'traditionally masculine'.

As boys grow up, they become aware – through socialisation – of what is expected of men in their society and they try to seem masculine (for example, through success at sport or by showing dominance over others by bullying). Boys who cannot show at least some aspects of hegemonic masculinity may be given negative labels by their peers. The idea of hegemonic masculinity can be applied to crime and deviance because it may be expressed through aggression, violence or rule-breaking. Many societies encourage this form of masculinity, often through the media. For example, many films feature physically strong male characters using violence to achieve their goals. This view of how to express masculinity can particularly influence teenage boys, who are trying to negotiate and create their own identities.

Girls are under equivalent pressures to acquire a feminine identity. However, the expected behaviour – such as care over clothing and appearance – is less likely to lead to deviance or crime.

Explanations of crime based on masculinity can be criticised for:

- assuming that all men are socialised into the same set of values, that stress hegemonic masculinity

- not recognising that some aspects of masculinity and the masculine role – such as acting with restraint, being brave and protecting those who need protection – are positive and do not necessarily lead to crime

- not recognising that males have choices in how they express their masculinity; for example, some reject hegemonic masculinity.

THINK LIKE A SOCIOLOGIST

Do you think there is a culture of hegemonic masculinity in your society (or in your school or college)? How might this affect the behaviour of men, for example in their occupations?

Socialisation and social control

Boys and girls are socialised into different gender roles. For example, boys may be given toys, such as toy weapons and action figures, which encourage rough and aggressive play, while girls are more likely to be given dolls and books, encouraging more nurturing and thoughtful behaviour. The masculine roles that boys are socialised into increase their chances of being involved

in crime and deviance (compared with the feminine roles which girls are socialised into). In most societies, there is also greater control over women than men. For example, women or girls are expected to spend most of their time at home. In contrast, men or boys have more freedom to move around and tend to spend more time in public spaces. As a result, they may have more opportunities to commit crime than women.

In many countries, women's lives are changing as they acquire greater independence. The rates of crime by women are going up slightly in some places, although they are still well below those for men. It has been argued that women's greater independence may lead to more crime by females. However, it may also be the case that the rise in female crime shown in the statistics is a result of chivalry becoming less common as older stereotypes fade away and females are treated more equally by the criminal justice system.

Misogyny

Misogyny is hatred of women, primarily by men, which involves seeing females as inferior or a threat to them. It is an aspect of sexism embedded in many cultures. It can be part of the socialisation of boys, related to hegemonic masculinity. Misogynists are prejudiced against women and assert their perceived dominance over women in a range of ways which are deviant and in some cases criminal. Some misogynistic men try to control women through sexist comments and insults or harassment. Other misogynists attack women, for example committing domestic violence, sexual assault, rape and even murder.

KEY TERM

misogyny: hatred of women, primarily by men

It has been argued that misogynistic crimes are a type of hate crime, although they are not treated in that way by the law or the police in many countries. In some countries, there are debates about whether to criminalise more aspects of misogynistic behaviour. These include harassment in public (such as calling out sexist comments) and posting of images online without consent. In recent years, there have been campaigns and protests – sometimes following high-profile assault and murders of women by male offenders – aiming to raise awareness of misogyny and levels of violence against women. Such campaigns call for debate about the type of masculinity that boys and men are taught.

Figure 6.10: Misogynistic attacks include domestic violence, sexual assault, rape and even murder.

Stereotyping

The idea of stereotyping based on gender has been covered in the sections on the chivalry thesis, the culture of masculinity, socialisation and social control, and misogyny. The police may act on these stereotypes by targeting males, especially groups of young males, and being more ready to stop and search them.

Gang culture

Gang culture has been discussed in relation to age and ethnicity. It is also an explanation for gender differences in crime rates because there are more boys than girls in gangs and some gangs are exclusively male. The presence of a gang culture in an area can therefore lead more males than females into gang membership and possible involvement in crime. The role of girls in gangs tends to be different to the role of boys; girls are often passed between the male gang members as if they are 'property' and they are sometimes used to carry drugs or weapons since they are less likely to be stopped by the police. There has been some research into the existence of all-female gangs but they seem to be rare in most countries.

Lack of opportunity

For males, lack of opportunity is a factor in crime: they may turn to crime if other routes to material possessions or status are blocked. This is the case, for example, when there is a lot of unemployment and males cannot earn money to support themselves and their families.

For women or girls, lower rates of crime can be explained by lack of opportunity to commit crime.

As stated earlier, women and girls are often expected to spend time at home with family and they experience more social control. This means they have fewer opportunities to commit most types of crime.

Explanations for crime and deviance based on social class

Social exclusion

Some members of the working class experience **social exclusion**, which means they do not feel accepted or valued as members of society. For example, members of the working class may feel that their views are not listened to by politicians and others in authority. People living in poverty are most likely to feel socially excluded. This exclusion can make individuals feel less bound by norms and rules, so they are more likely to break them. Additionally, if society does not provide opportunities for people from working-class backgrounds to succeed in legitimate ways – such as through education – then some of these people may turn to crime as an alternative way to gain money and status.

> ### KEY TERM
>
> **social exclusion:** when society does not provide a group with the rights and benefits available to others in the same society

Material and relative deprivation

Material deprivation – lacking resources and money – does not directly lead to crime. However, it does increase the possibility; for example, someone may steal food because they are hungry, or they might steal goods if they cannot afford to buy them.

Some sociologists use the idea of relative deprivation to explain patterns of crime in cities and among disadvantaged groups (such as the working-class). Relative deprivation is when individuals or groups see themselves as deprived compared to others. This leads to resentment and increases the likelihood of crime in the group that sees itself as deprived. This can also happen if there are no organisations or representatives to protect the interests of a disadvantaged group; if people have no outlet for their feelings of anger, they may turn to vandalism and rioting.

Inadequate socialisation

Another explanation for working-class people committing more crime than other classes is that their socialisation is different. This view is usually argued by functionalist and New Right sociologists, who suggest that inadequate socialisation leads to crime. New Right sociologists link inadequate socialisation to lone-parent families and those in poverty; they criticise these parents for failing to teach their children the right norms and values, and for not providing good role models and discipline. The views of New Right sociologists are considered later in this section.

KEY TERM

inadequate socialisation: socialisation that does not fully instil the shared norms and values of a society; individuals who are inadequately socialised are more likely to become deviant

---

Lack of opportunity

In many societies, upward social mobility (see Unit 7) is limited and most people remain in the same class. Some people are dissatisfied by the lack of opportunities to improve their lives. These feelings, combined with a sense of relative deprivation, may cause them to turn to crime.

Status frustration

Status frustration was explained in the sections about patterns of crime and deviance based on age and ethnicity. When Albert Cohen first used the term status frustration, he connected it with social class. He argued that working-class boys lacked status due to educational inequalities and that this was the main cause of their

deviance: they were trying to gain respect from their peers in other ways.

Power inequalities

The ruling class in a society (which may include the upper and middle classes) has the most power. This power can be used in various ways that affect crime and recorded rates of crime. For example, the ruling class has the power to:

- make laws, deciding which acts are crimes and which are not
- criminalise things that the working class do, such as striking or membership of trade unions; this protects the power of the ruling class
- ensure that things the ruling class does to protect its wealth and privilege (such as tax evasion or allowing big companies to mistreat their workers) are not criminalised
- decide how the criminal justice system is used. For example, the types of crimes committed by the working class (such as robberies and assaults) are policed and publicised much more than the types of crimes committed by the middle class (such as white-collar crime).

Together, this power results in higher recorded rates of crime by the working-class than by other classes.

Police targeting/stop and search

Police targeting and stop and search have been discussed in the sections about patterns of crime and deviance based on age and ethnicity. These points also apply to working-class areas and to young working-class men in particular; they also relate to stereotyping.

CASE STUDY 6.3

Juvenile delinquency

Figure 6.11: Members of a teenage gang.

The American sociologist William Chambliss studied two delinquent gangs in an American city. Chambliss called the working-class gang the 'roughnecks'. They were involved in fights, stole petrol from cars, shoplifted and had all been arrested at least once.

The other gang, the 'saints', were middle-class. They were also involved in serious delinquency such as truancy, drinking, wild driving, petty theft and vandalism. However, none of them was arrested during the two years of Chambliss's research. Their acts were seen as harmless pranks and, if the police did notice them, the 'saints' had the support of influential parents to help get them out of trouble. Chambliss said that the police did not take middle-class delinquency seriously because the middle-class youths did not conform to their image of typical delinquents.

Task

1   What differences would official statistics have shown on delinquency between the working-class and middle-class youths?

2   How does this study show the importance of police stereotyping in relation to the social class of offenders?

The strengths and limitations of each explanation for crime and deviance

Within the explanations for crime and deviance in terms of age, ethnicity, gender and social class, several strengths and limitations have been suggested.

To develop your evaluation of these explanations further, consider how the social groups and explanations intersect and overlap. You may have noticed that several ideas appeared more than once; for example, stereotyping and gang culture. This is because all individuals belong to a group in each of these categories: they belong to an age group, an ethnic group, a gender and a social class. Many sociologists, such as Albert Cohen, have focused on explaining deviance committed by young working-class males, recognising that age, social class and gender intersect to explain their behaviour.

For example, Cohen argued that status frustration affected young working-class boys in particular, rather than girls, older people or those from the middle class.

Within any group, there are people with different attributes and different experiences. For example, within your age group (teenagers), there will be girls and boys from different ethnic groups and different social classes. However, people often mix with others who are similar to them, so it is common for groups of young people from the same ethnic group, the same social class background and even the same gender to form a deviant sub-culture or a gang. This makes it difficult to evaluate the separate influences of age, gender, social class and ethnicity on the group's behaviour.

There are debates within sociology about the relative importance of the various attributes and explanations. For example, Marxists emphasise the importance of social class while feminists emphasise the importance of gender. Their explanations of crime are considered next, along with specific strengths and limitations.

ACTIVITY: WRITTEN 6.2

1   Identify the explanations that are used for more than one category (for example, police targeting/stop and search appears as an explanation related to age, ethnicity and social class). For each explanation, make a set of notes about how it applies to each category.

2   Now decide whether it would be possible to apply the explanation to a new category. For example, could police targeting/stop and search be used as an explanation related to gender? Suggest and explain ways in which each explanation could be applied to other categories.

Sociological theories on crime and deviance

This section discusses sociological theories relating to deviant and criminal behaviour: postmodernism, interactionism, functionalism, Marxism and feminism. These theories have been introduced and applied in previous units, so you should be familiar with some of their ideas.

Postmodernism

The postmodernist approach to crime tries to take account of changes to societies in the last few decades. Societies have become more fragmented, so they are less likely to be held together by a shared set of values. Postmodernists do not believe it is possible to identify the causes of crime or to develop a theory that explains crime for everyone. They reject the other explanations in this section: they feel that every crime is an individual act which cannot be universally explained.

Postmodernists argue that crime is a socially constructed idea; what counts as a crime varies enormously between societies and over time. This mean there is no point in studying why people become criminals, because certain behaviours may or may not be criminal in different cultures and at different times. Instead, we should study particular crimes or types of crime, the motivations of the individuals who commit them, and the harm that different actions might do – rather than focusing on strict legal definitions of whether something is 'criminal' or not.

When explaining individual crimes, postmodernists focus on the emotions that may lie behind a criminal act. For example, Jack Katz argues that some young people commit crime just because they can; because it is fun and exciting. As a result, postmodernists tend to reject explanations for crime which focus on the structure of society, or on factors such as social class or gender; instead, they tend to focus on individual choices and emotions.

Strengths of postmodernism

- It can be argued that postmodernists are right that different types of crime need different explanations; it is wrong to suggest there can be a single comprehensive explanation of crime.

- Postmodernism has led to some important developments in studying crime; for example, those studying green and corporate crime are now more concerned with the harms caused than whether a law has been broken.

- The recognition that crime may be related to individual feelings and emotions in a particular moment – rather than being caused by wider social factors – makes sense in today's individualist world

Limitations of postmodernism

- Most sociologists think that postmodernists go too far. It is still important to look for factors that explain crime, in the hope of reducing the harms caused by crime.

- It is difficult to find evidence for explanations of crime but that does not mean we should give up.

- The patterns of crime in relation to age, ethnicity, social class and gender suggest that some causes of crime do apply to whole social groups, rather than individuals.

Interactionism (including labelling and moral panic theory)

Interactionism was developed long before postmodernism but there are similarities. Both theories agree that crime is socially constructed and that it is important to look at the interpretation of behaviour as well as its meaning for the people involved. Interactionists say that everyone, at some time, does things that could be labelled as criminal or deviant, but only some people are labelled in this way.

Interactionists do not try to explain the initial act; instead, they look at the responses to the act that may result in a label being applied. They are interested in how individuals come to be labelled as deviant and the consequences of this for the labelled person. Interactionists are also interested in how certain acts come to be defined as deviant, when others do not. Howard Becker argued that a deviant is simply a person who has been labelled deviant, and deviant behaviour is behaviour that people label as deviant. Becker argued that there is nothing about the behaviour or the person themselves which makes them different or bad. Chambliss's research (described in Case study 6.3) is a good example of this: working-class youths were more likely to be labelled as deviants than middle-class youths, even though the acts they committed were similar.

Labelling can give someone a particular status and can even lead to the reassessment of that person's life in terms of the label. An individual's self-concept is largely formed from other people's views, so they tend to see themselves in terms of the labels they are given. This can lead to a self-fulfilling prophecy: the person becomes what the label says they are.

> **KEY TERM**
>
> **labelling:** defining a person or group in a particular way

Public labelling can lead to rejection or the loss of family and friends, encouraging further deviance. The labelled person's sense of their own identity may also change. For example, they may adopt a deviant identity and join a deviant sub-culture which shares and reinforces their new norms and values. This can lead to an increase in deviance, known as deviancy amplification. Alternatively, a labelled individual may try to reject the label; this is known as the self-negating prophecy (see Unit 5).

Labelling is most likely to have an effect when the people who give the label have power over the labelled person. Judges, teachers and parents are in positions of power and, as a result, the labels they use can stick. Labels are also more effective when the labelled individuals do not have other sources of information about themselves; for example, they have no one to reassure them that the label does not apply. A powerful person may be more able to reject a negative label, so it is less likely to affect their self-concept and lead to a self-fulfilling prophecy.

Strengths of interactionism and labelling theory

- Interactionism recognises the importance of society's reactions to an action and acknowledges that reactions depend on context.

- Interactionism recognises that individuals have some choice, for example in whether to accept a label or not. It also draws attention to the importance of power, in terms of the person labelling and the person being labelled.

- Interactionist ideas have led to some changes in the criminal justice system; for example, young offenders are often not named in media reports, so they have a chance to avoid the label and are more likely to avoid future crime.

Limitations of interactionism and labelling theory

- The interactionist definition of deviance does not take into account some behaviour which would always be seen as deviant, whatever the context or reaction. For example, acts such as murder are always deviant, whether or not there is a social reaction against them.

- Most people know they are breaking norms and laws even if their actions are not detected, so deviance is not created by the label, as interactionists imply.

- Labelling theory tends to imply that deviants are the passive victims of the labels applied to them. However, individuals can choose to be deviant, whether or not they have been labelled.

- Labelling does not fully explain why some people are labelled and others are not, or why some activities are against the law and others are not. Becker does discuss power and the idea of the 'underdog' (someone who is disadvantaged and has no power), but Marxists would argue that class structure and who benefits from labelling should be explored more fully.

- Labelling theory tends to put the sociologist on the side of the deviant or criminal, seeing them as the victim of labelling. However, the label may have been applied because of a deviant or criminal act which caused serious harm and should be condemned.

Moral panic

This idea is linked with interactionism. The term 'moral panic' was first used by the South African interactionist sociologist Stanley Cohen in his book *Folk Devils and Moral Panics*, published in 1972.

Cohen argued that the media often label certain groups or individuals, turning them into folk devils (people to be feared) and exaggerating the amount and impact of any crime or deviance they commit. This creates a stereotype, so that all members of the group are assumed to have the same characteristics. The media define the group as a threat to social values and overreact to fairly minor behaviour. In this way, the media creates a moral panic, which involves:

- **Exaggeration.** The behaviour of the group is reported as worse than it is, using exaggerated language. For example, a small fight is reported as if it had been a large-scale battle or riot.

- **Prediction.** The media claim that the deviance will happen again and will be worse, unless strong action is taken.

- **Symbolisation.** The media show how folk devils can be recognised, for example by their appearance or clothing.

The example Cohen used to develop his ideas was the media coverage of fights between mods and rockers – two youth sub-cultures in the UK in the 1960s. He argued that these clashes were fairly minor, but the media turned them into a major cause for concern among the British public. This led to calls for tougher policing and more laws to criminalise young people's behaviour. The teenagers involved were turned into folk devils.

Figure 6.12: Mods and rockers clashing in Margate, England in 1964.

Folk devils are represented by the media as being totally different from 'us', the supposed majority to which readers or viewers are made to think they belong. Media reporting and moral panic encourage a strong response by the police and courts. This has the effect of changing the group's perception of themselves, so they increasingly act in the way they have been defined. Thus, moral panic actually increases the amount of deviance. In Cohen's example, the media coverage encouraged some young people to go to places where the media predicted that fights would take place; the young people then became involved in fights with the opposing sub-culture, when they probably would not have done so otherwise. A deviancy amplification spiral can develop: the media response leads to more deviance, which leads to a stronger media response which, in turn, leads to even greater deviance and so on. Usually, however, the media interest ceases after a while and the moral panic ends.

The term moral panic is now widely used in both sociology and the media. Moral panics are often about young people and relate closely to ideas of labelling and the self-fulfilling prophecy.

Strengths of moral panic theory
- Moral panic theory draws attention to the importance of the media in applying labels.
- It also draws attention to the ways in which the media can increase deviance, through their reporting and their influence on the opinions and responses of the public, the police and the government.

Limitations of moral panic theory
- This theory does not explain the initial behaviour of groups who become folk devils.
- Opponents argue that people do not passively take in ideas from the media; instead, they think about and question what they see and read.
- New forms of media, including social media, are more interactive. This means that media portrayals of a group as folk devils can be more easily challenged. This has led to claims that moral panic theory is now outdated. There is no longer a centralised source of information, so the media does not create moral panics in the same way today.

THINK LIKE A SOCIOLOGIST

How much are you influenced by media coverage of crime? Does it make you change your behaviour or your opinion of certain types of people? Have you ever questioned whether certain crimes are exaggerated in media coverage?

Functionalism (including the New Right, sub-culturalism and strain theory)

Functionalists see crime as functional for the wider society. They argue that a limited amount of crime is socially necessary, inevitable and beneficial; there cannot be societies without crime. The functionalist Emile Durkheim imagined a 'society of saints', in which very minor lapses in behaviour would be punished. Too much crime, however, is dysfunctional and can lead to social collapse.

For functionalists, society is based on shared values and beliefs. People agree about what is right and wrong and they act accordingly due to effective socialisation. Laws provide clear boundaries and make it clear what the punishment will be for breaking the law. People can also express their opinions about a crime to further reinforce these boundaries (for example, through condemnation in the media and in conversations with other people). Sometimes, values change and this shows that a change in the law is needed. Criminals therefore perform a useful function in helping the law to reflect the shared values of society, reinforcing the boundaries of behaviour and ensuring that most people accept the value consensus.

Shared norms and values can be weakened in periods of change and stress, so people no longer feel integrated into society. Durkheim was concerned about the effects of industrialisation and urbanisation; he thought that when people no longer shared norms and values, there would be crime and disorder. He argued that a small amount of crime, which is publicly punished, is important to prevent the loss of the value consensus and the disorder this would bring. However, crime must not be allowed to go unpunished or become widespread, since this would threaten social stability.

Strengths of functionalism

- Functionalism is unusual in pointing out that crime can, in some ways, be good for society.

- Functionalism recognises the importance of socialisation and how this can reduce crime and deviance.

Limitations of functionalism

- Functionalism assumes the existence of a shared set of values across society. This is unlikely to be the case today: not everyone shares the same goals.

- The idea that crime is functional for society is questionable. It is hard to see how a crime can be good from a victim's point of view.

- Durkheim could not explain why, if everyone is socialised into the value consensus, some individuals commit crime.

- Durkheim's analysis did not attempt to explain different types of crime, although other views influenced by Durkheim have tried to do this (see the sections on strain theory and the New Right).

The ideas of Durkheim and early functionalists were developed further by the American sociologist Robert K. Merton in **strain theory**. Merton was interested in situations where there was a mismatch between goals and means:

- goals are the things societies encourage people to want (similar to values)

- means are the ways in which people can achieve these goals (similar to norms).

KEY TERM

strain theory: Merton's explanation of crime as resulting from a mismatch between society's goals and the socially approved means of achieving them

In the USA in the 1930s, there was great emphasis on the 'American Dream'. This meant achieving material success and becoming wealthy through hard work and study; it was believed that this would bring happiness. All Americans accepted this as a goal but not all were equally able to achieve it. People from wealthier backgrounds were more likely to achieve financial success; for most Americans, however, the goal was unattainable – regardless of how hard they studied and worked. The 'strain' caused by this mismatch meant that some people turned to socially unacceptable ways of getting money.

In this way, the goals of the American Dream caused deviant behaviour. Merton suggested there were five possible responses to this situation:

1   **Conformists** continued to work hard, believing they could achieve the goals. An example of a conformist is someone who works in a shop or a bank and keeps trying hard to succeed and make money from their career. They conform to society's means and the goal of success.

2   **Innovators** found new ways to achieve the goals, most of them considered to be deviant. An example of an innovator is someone who makes money from dealing in drugs or stealing from others. They accept the goal of financial success but use deviant means to achieve it.

3   **Ritualists** carried on working and conforming even though they knew they could not achieve the goal. An example of a ritualist is someone with a low-paid job who just keeps going but knows they will never be rich. They still conform to society's norms but they have given up on the goal of material success.

4   **Retreatists** rejected both the goals and the means and were resigned to failure. An example of a retreatist is someone who becomes an addict or follows another deviant lifestyle, giving up on the idea of achieving material success. They do not follow society's norms or means and they have rejected the goal of material success.

5   **Rebels** adopted different goals and also adopted their own ways to achieve their goals. An example of a rebel is someone who joins a religious sect and lives a life without money, or someone who becomes an activist or protestor about political issues. They reject the goal of success based on money and set their own goals, which they actively pursue.

Merton said that a lot of working-class crime could be explained by this theory: people struggled to achieve the goal of material success through legitimate means, so they turned to crime instead. This approach is known as strain theory because it sees crime as the outcome of strain between what people wish to achieve and what is possible.

Strengths of strain theory

- It is useful for explaining crimes committed for material gain (such as theft and fraud); it can also explain crimes such as drug-taking that result from giving up on the goals entirely.

- It has been claimed that Merton's ideas explain the rapid rises in crime in Eastern European countries after the end of communism: people in countries such as Poland knew about and wanted the consumer goods available in Western Europe, but had few ways of getting them.

- Merton was influenced by Durkheim's ideas about values, but adapted them to explain reasons for crime and different types of crime.

- Merton's approach was developed by later sociologists into various sub-cultural theories, explained in the next section.

Limitations of strain theory

- Like functionalism, strain theory assumes that almost everyone in a society shares the same values. This is disputed by other theorists such as Marxists and feminists.

- It cannot explain crimes committed by people who have already achieved their goals, such as white-collar crime.

- Many people fall into more than one of Merton's categories; for example, a conformist may also have concerns about climate change and attend protest marches at weekends.

ACTIVITY: DISCUSSION 6.2

Discuss the following questions in a group of four or five:

1   How useful is Merton's theory in explaining crime and deviance today? Think about the goals society seems to set us, and people's chances of achieving those goals in the current economic situation.

2   Can you think of any other crimes, apart from white-collar crime, which cannot be explained by any of Merton's responses?

3   In what ways are Merton's ideas similar to and different from those of functionalists like Durkheim?

New Right

New Right sociologists are also influenced by functionalism and share the same views about the importance of socialisation into a value consensus to keep society functioning effectively. The New Right argues that families are a key agent of socialisation and that changes to the structure of families have contributed to a rise in crime. They contrast the traditional nuclear family of the 1950s and earlier with modern families. They say that the older type of family provided stability and moral values but modern family types do not do this as well. They point to the following changes as evidence that the moral fabric of society is weakening:

- An increase in cohabitation (living together without being married) has undermined the idea of marriage.

- An increase in divorce has undermined the idea of marriage as a partnership for life. This has created instability and uncertainty in families and led to a rise in single-parent families.

- Greater independence of women means they no longer devote themselves to the home and family, so the socialisation of children is less effective.

- There are more families without fathers, so more boys grow up without appropriate role models. As a result, they might struggle to live as men are meant to (according to this view) – as breadwinners.

New Right sociologists argue that these developments have weakened the bonds that prevent people, especially young men, from offending.

TIP

Be aware that the New Right view is controversial and disputed by many sociologists, because it seems to blame single mothers and families living in poverty for all the problems in their life, including crime. Alternative interpretations of the same findings – for example, by Marxists – see poverty itself as the root of the problem (not family structures or inadequate socialisation). It is important to be able to contrast and evaluate all sociological explanations.

Charles Murray, an American New Right sociologist, sees the failings of modern families in the context of failing communities in the USA. Murray first developed his ideas referring to Black inner-city areas in the USA. In some inner-city areas, communities have been replaced by what he calls the underclass. According to Murray, this underclass comprises people who are unemployed and do not want to work;

people who prefer to live on welfare benefits or the proceeds of crime. In the underclass, young people have short-term relationships, so children are routinely born outside serious relationships. Fathers do not stay with mothers to look after their children because they do not see them as their responsibility. As a result, children grow up without learning the wider values of society. In areas where there is an underclass, law-abiding working-class people are driven out and local communities are destroyed. This leads to rapidly increasing crime rates in these areas.

Strengths of New Right explanations

- The New Right view tries to take account of how social changes, such as in families, might affect crime.

- These views have been influential in affecting the policies of political parties in several countries. There are also popular among some parts of the media.

Limitations of New Right explanations

- The New Right explanation is based on a misleading view of the past. The New Right assume there was a 'golden age' when things were much better than they are now. However, the traditional family was patriarchal and not at all 'golden' for women, who had to sacrifice a chance of higher education and challenging work to devote themselves to their family.

- New Right views are based on the values of those who propose them. The New Right disapprove of certain aspects of modern family life, so they look for evidence that they have negative outcomes.

- New Right views ignore crime committed by people who have grown up in nuclear families, and people from the middle class who commit crime (such as white-collar crime). They also ignore the many people who grow up in lone-parent families or in poverty that do *not* commit crime.

- The New Right are accused of 'victim-blaming': they blame those in poverty for their situation, assuming they are lazy and have the wrong norms and values. Many people living in poverty worldwide are extremely hard-working and are desperate to improve their situation. They bring up their children to accept the value of education and hard work.

Sub-culturalism

When a group is materially or culturally deprived, or experiences status frustration, a new sub-culture may emerge with its own norms or values.

This new sub-culture can provide an alternative set of norms, allowing its members to gain success, status and respect from their peers.

Several sub-cultural theories were developed in the USA in the mid to late 20th century. Some of them were influenced by the views of Merton and strain theory and so can be linked with functionalism. Sub-culturalists particularly focus on explaining youth deviance, because young people tend to form sub-cultures which then influence their norms and values.

We have already considered the sub-culturalist Albert Cohen and his ideas on status frustration. Cohen argued that young males share the value of status, but those from the working class are forced to behave in deviant ways to achieve this status from their peers.

In a similar analysis, Cloward and Ohlin suggested there were three possible types of sub-culture linked to crime and deviance:

- **A criminal sub-culture.** In some working-class communities, there were successful criminal role models and a career structure for aspiring criminals (for example, in areas where the Mafia was strong). As a result, some young men chose crime as a career. An example is the Chicago gang studied by Venkatesh (see Unit 1).

- **A conflict sub-culture.** Where there is no sub-culture with role models and opportunities to be a successful criminal, both legal and criminal ways of achieving goals are blocked. In these situations, young men might turn to violence and gang warfare against each other.

- **A retreatist sub-culture.** Where young men feel unable to succeed, either legally or by crime, they might turn to drugs or alcohol as an escape.

MAKING CONNECTIONS

Explain the similarities between Cloward and Ohlin's three deviant sub-cultures and Merton's five responses. Which of Merton's responses do Cloward and Ohlin's sub-cultures match with?

Cohen, Cloward and Ohlin assumed that everyone in society shared the same values – a desire for status or financial success. In a slightly different sub-cultural explanation, Walter Miller argued that young working-class boys had their own sub-culture, which was distinctly different from that of middle-class youths. The values of this working-class sub-culture could lead people into deviance. Miller identified the following values – or 'focal concerns' – that encouraged deviance among working-class boys in sub-cultures:

- **accepting fate** – a feeling that you have little control over your life, so you need to make the most of any chances

- **seeking autonomy** – trying to control your own life and therefore resist authority

- **views on trouble** – confrontations with authority and with others are normal and unavoidable

- **attractions of excitement** – looking for fun and enjoyment

- **virtues of smartness** – looking good and understanding the rules of the street

- **virtues of toughness** – being masculine by being aggressive.

Strengths of sub-cultural theory

- It offered an explanation for collective deviance and explained why so much youth deviance was not done for economic gain.

- It offered insights into offending by young people in particular; the search for status is almost certainly an important reason why young people commit crime.

- Cloward and Ohlin's ideas explain why some young people become involved in different kinds of deviance.

Limitations of sub-cultural theory

- These sub-cultural views are based on the USA in the 1950s and 1960s, so they could be seen as outdated and irrelevant to other countries and cultures. For example, there is limited evidence that the types of sub-culture identified by Cloward and Ohlin exist in other countries.

- Miller was simplifying in saying there was one working-class sub-culture; there are many variations and they do not all share the values he suggested.

- Sub-culturalists tend to focus on male criminality. They are criticised by feminists for ignoring girls and the possible reasons why they do not become involved in deviant sub-cultures.

Marxism

The Marxist view is that laws are made by the state and reflect ruling-class interests (because the ruling class controls the state). Laws criminalise the actions of the working class; they protect private property, which is essential to capitalism. Marxists point out that some crimes involving property are punished more severely than crimes involving violence or even death; this shows that property is valued more highly than life.

Where functionalists see a shared set of values, Marxists see an ideology that the working class is tricked into accepting: they are in a state of false consciousness. Marxists also argue that the laws that do not exist – such as those that could limit inequalities or prevent corporations from exploiting workers and consumers – are as significant as the laws which are passed. Law creation is as important as law enforcement. Marxists are interested in crimes committed by the powerful, including corporate crime, and also in the fact that many harmful acts committed by governments and corporations are *not* against the law. Marxists argue that some activities of capitalists and companies should be illegal, raising important questions about how we define crime. This idea has also been used in recent debates about green crime.

Some Marxists also argue that the values promoted by capitalism *encourage* crime. Capitalist values include making money and promoting individualism and greed. These values encourage people from all classes to make money, using deviant needs if necessary; this explains working-class crime such as robbery and also explains white-collar and corporate crime.

Marxist sociologists have often focused on crimes committed by the ruling class. Such crimes often involve considerable harms; for example, pollution affects the health of billions of people. While other sociologists focus on explaining the crimes which dominate official crime statistics – that are largely committed by the working class – Marxists also consider crimes committed by states and large-scale events such as wars and slavery.

Marxists argue that the official statistics are misleading because they only consider acts that have been defined as crimes. The ruling class makes the laws and decides who should be punished for what crimes. The actions of the working class are more likely to be criminalised, while the actions of the ruling class are less likely to be defined as criminal.

The law is also selectively enforced; for example, the penalties for white-collar crime are often lower than the penalties for crimes committed by working-class people. This is in the interests of the ruling class and supports the capitalist system for these reasons:

- By punishing and blaming individuals from the working class, it deflects attention from those who are really to blame for social problems. This reinforces the belief that individuals, not institutions, are responsible for crime.

- It neutralises potential opposition. Working-class people who challenge the system can be charged with offences and imprisoned.

For Marxists, the true criminals are those who benefit from a system based on exploitation.

Strengths of Marxism

- Marxist explanations of crime draw attention to crimes that are ignored by other explanations, such as white-collar and corporate crime. In particular, corporate crime can have devastating effects but it is rarely investigated or punished.

- Marxists draw attention to how crime comes from the nature of society. The extent of crime today can be explained by capitalist value systems that encourage greed and individualism.

- Marxism explains the high rates of working-class crime in official statistics as a result of the class system.

- Marxist explanations consider wider issues relating to harm, rather than focusing on actions that have been defined as crimes.

Limitations of Marxism

- Some laws are clearly in everyone's interests, not just the interests of the ruling class. For example, some laws give the state powers to control industry and commerce. However, Marxists argue that all laws act in the interests of the ruling class – even laws that appear to be against ruling-class interests. For example, the capitalist system needs a healthy, safe population of workers and consumers who are loyal to their workplace; this explains laws about health and safety at work.

- The Marxist view has been criticised for ignoring the reality of crimes committed by working-class offenders and the effects on other working-class people. The Marxist view does not recognise that most victims of crimes committed by the working class are also working class. Working-class crime is a very real problem for its victims and should not be explained as something invented by the ruling class to distract attention from other issues.

- The Marxist view is based on the values of those who propose it, so contradictory evidence may be ignored. For example, non-capitalist societies also have crimes, while some capitalist societies – such as Switzerland – have low crime rates.

- Marxist views place too much emphasis on social class. Feminists would say Marxists do not take account of patriarchy.

Feminism

Feminist sociologists studying crime are interested in the relationship between gender and crime, and in the impacts of crime and the criminal justice system on women in particular. They draw attention to the fact that women commit less crime and the lack of attention other sociologists give to this. Many early (male) sociologists looked for explanations of crime without considering why females are so much less deviant than males. Feminist sociologists suggest that, as well as looking for explanations for male crime, we should look for reasons why there is so much less female crime. These ideas have been considered in the earlier section on explanations for crime and deviance based on gender.

Important feminist ideas in relation to crime are:

- **Patriarchy.** Crime happens within a patriarchal society and the patriarchal nature of society – in which men expect to be in positions of power over women – leads to some crime. The criminal justice system is also patriarchal; most police, judges and so on are male and many of them hold misogynistic views.

- **Masculinity and femininity.** The gender expectations in society, and the pressure to conform to these expectations, lead to a situation where males are more likely to engage in behaviours that may lead to crime. There are strong pressures on women as well (for example, the pressure to appear and behave in feminine ways) but they are less likely to lead to crime.

- **Women as victims of crime.** Most theories of crime do not recognise the extent of domestic violence, sexual harassment and sexual violence against women. Such crimes often involve misogyny and feminists argue that they should be taken more seriously by law-makers, by the criminal justice system and by sociologists.

Strengths of feminism

- Feminism draws attention to neglected aspects of crime, including female victimisation and the fact that most offenders are male.

- Feminism shows that most crime can be linked to the patriarchal nature of society and the power relations and gender expectations associated with this. Feminists suggest that deep and far-reaching changes in values and attitudes are needed to resolve issues relating to crime.

Limitations of feminism

- The criminal justice system does not always operate in a patriarchal way. Some laws protect women and at least some offences against women are investigated and punished. There are also now senior police officers and judges who are women.

- Feminist views place too much emphasis on gender. Marxists would say that feminists do not take account of social class and capitalism; Marxists argue that powerful men – rather than all men – are the cause of crime.

CHECK YOUR UNDERSTANDING 6.2

Write down answers to the following questions:

1   Describe the 'typical victim' and the 'typical criminal' according to the official crime statistics.

2   Explain what is meant by the following terms and identify the groups each term might apply to, in relation to crime:

- gang culture
- police targeting/stop and search
- inadequate socialisation
- institutional racism
- chivalry thesis
- status frustration.

3   What is the main focus of each of these sociological explanations of crime?

- postmodernism
- interactionism/labelling theory/moral panic theory
- functionalism
- the New Right
- strain theory
- sub-culturalism
- Marxism
- feminism

4   Now swap your answers with a partner and see if they remembered anything you did not.

KEY POINTS

- The official crime statistics show patterns of victimisation and patterns of crime in terms of age, ethnicity, gender and social class.

- Explanations for patterns of crime based on age include:
  - police targeting/stop and search
  - self-fulfilling prophecy
  - stereotyping
  - gang culture
  - socialisation and social control
  - lack of opportunity
  - status frustration.

- Explanations for patterns of crime based on ethnicity include:
  - institutional racism
  - prejudice and discrimination
  - police targeting/stop and search
  - material and relative deprivation

  - stereotyping
  - gang culture
  - status frustration.

- Explanations for patterns of crime based on gender include:
  - chivalry thesis
  - culture of masculinity
  - socialisation and social control
  - misogyny
  - stereotyping
  - gang culture
  - lack of opportunity.

- Explanations for patterns of crime based on social class include:
  - social exclusion
  - material and relative deprivation
  - inadequate socialisation

CONTINUED

- lack of opportunity
- status frustration
- power inequalities
- police targeting/stop and search.
- There are debates about the importance of age, ethnicity, gender and social class in explaining crime and deviance; each explanation has strengths and limitations
- There are different sociological theories on crime and deviance:

- postmodernism
- interactionism (including labelling and moral panic theory)
- functionalism (including the New Right, sub-culturalism and strain theory)
- Marxism
- feminism.
- Each of these sociological theories has strengths and limitations.

6.3 How is crime dealt with in different societies?

Aims of punishment

When an offender has been convicted of an offence in a court, they usually face punishment. There are several aims of punishment; some overlap and some conflict with each other.

Deterrence

A **deterrent** involves making the offender or others refrain from committing the offence again. This can be done by making them aware of the consequences if they offend, such as losing their freedom. Punishing one person can be a deterrent to others; this is known as general deterrence. A punishment can also deter the offender from reoffending, known as individual deterrence.

Retribution

Retribution means revenge. This is sometimes expressed in the phrase 'making the punishment fit the crime'. For example, the punishment for murder might be execution – a life for a life. Retribution is also used in a more general sense: punishment is used to make the offender suffer for what they have done, but not necessarily in the way they made the victim of the crime suffer. This aim tends to conflict with the aim of rehabilitation (discussed later): punishments with the aim of retribution are usually harsh, but harsh punishments

are arguably less likely to lead to rehabilitation. However, retributive punishments can also achieve the aims of deterrence and incapacitation.

Incapacitation

Incapacitation means preventing the offender from committing more crimes, for example by imprisoning them or banning them from an area or activity. The death penalty is the most extreme form of incapacitation.

Rehabilitation

Rehabilitation aims to prevent the offender from committing further crimes by changing their attitudes and behaviour. For example, prisoners may be given opportunities for education and training, so they have ways of earning money when they are released. The hope is that this will prevent them from turning back to crime.

KEY TERMS

deterrent: a punishment intended to discourage offenders or others from committing an offence

retribution: punishments intended as a means of revenge for wrongdoing

incapacitation: punishments intended to physically prevent the offender from reoffending

rehabilitation: re-educating or retraining offenders to try to prevent further offending

Some rehabilitative sentences address the causes of the criminal behaviour; for example, an offender might receive treatment for addiction or go on an anger management course. The aims of rehabilitation are different to those of deterrence or incapacitation; the intention is to change offenders, not just stop them committing a crime.

Recent developments in rehabilitation include restorative justice. This involves meetings between the offender and their victim, so the offender can hear about the impact of their crime on the victim. This has proved successful in reducing reoffending, particularly for minor offences, because it helps offenders to understand the impact of their actions and see their victims as people. It also involves victims in the process of dealing with the offence, which many find helpful.

Protection of citizens

Another aim of punishment is to protect citizens, making society a safer place. This aim relates to several of the other aims mentioned above. If punishment deters people from offending or reoffending, then crime rates will be lower and the public will be safer. Incapacitation of criminals (for example, by imprisonment) also protects citizens. Rehabilitation is another way of protecting citizens, because it reduces the likelihood that offenders will reoffend.

Different types of punishment

Community sentencing

A **community sentence** is when the offender is made to do unpaid compulsory work for a set period. The punishment is often related to the offence; for example, someone convicted of vandalism may be made to repair property.

Financial penalties

Another form of punishment, usually for less serious offences, is **financial penalties**. Offenders may pay a sum of money (a fine) to the court as punishment.

Prison

Imprisonment means sending offenders to a prison, where they are deprived of some of the freedoms enjoyed by people outside prison. A prison sentence is sometimes known as a custodial sentence. Prisons in many modern industrial societies try to rehabilitate offenders; for example, prisoners may have the chance to study and

gain qualifications so it is easier for them to find work – and they are less likely to return to crime – when they are released.

In other societies, living conditions in prisons are very poor. Prisoners may spend most of their time in their cells, and cells may be crowded, with few facilities. In such prisons, riots are common as prisoners protest against the conditions.

Prisons are very expensive to run, because prisoners have to be fed, clothed and supervised by prison wardens. Global data on imprisonment or incarceration rates (the number of people in prison per 100,000 of the population) show wide variation between different countries. Recent data from the World Prison Brief shows that the USA has the highest incarceration rate, at 629 per 100,000 of the population. The rate is 132 in the UK, 200 in Mauritius and just 39 in Pakistan.

Rehabilitation programmes

Offenders may be given the chance to follow a rehabilitation programme. These programmes take different forms but they all aim to give the offender skills or knowledge that make it less likely they will reoffend. Rehabilitation programmes can run alongside other punishments, such as community or prison sentences. Alternatively, they can be separate sentences, for example courts in some countries can refer offenders to programmes to treat drug or alcohol addiction. Rehabilitation programmes that involve education and training within prison may also provide guidance and support for offenders when they are released.

Capital punishment

Capital punishment, also known as the death penalty, involves taking the offender's life. Capital punishment is much less common now than it was a hundred years ago;

KEY TERMS

community sentencing: punishments that involve non-custodial sentences (where the offender is not sent to prison); instead, the offender may have to do unpaid work for the community

financial penalties: punishments that involve paying a sum of money

capital punishment: the legally authorised killing of someone as a punishment for a crime

it has been abolished in 70 per cent of the world's countries. In 2022, 55 countries retain the death penalty as a sentence which they are prepared to carry out, including China, USA, UAE, India and Pakistan. In 2020, Amnesty International recorded a total of 483 executions across 18 countries – the lowest number of executions for ten years. However, some countries carry out their executions in secret and do not release figures, so the number could be much higher. Outside China, 88 per cent of the executions recorded in 2020 took place in Iran, Saudi Arabia, Iraq and Egypt.

In the past, much of the world used the death penalty, sometimes for quite minor offences. Executions were often carried out in public, to increase the deterrent effect. This is less important now, because the media will make people aware of what has happened. In the past, executions were also more about retribution; they were as painful as possible to make the offender suffer. Executions today are usually designed to be quick and they are usually carried out in private, although some countries allow relatives of the victim to attend.

Corporal punishment

Corporal punishment is a physical punishment intended to cause pain. It has the advantage of being over quickly, although the physical and mental pain for the person being punished may last a long time. For the criminal justice system, it can be a way of saving money compared to prison, for example. An example of corporal punishment is flogging or whipping an offender. This is still used in some Asian countries, particularly those which follow Islamic Law.

Exile and ostracism

These were common forms of punishment in the past. **Exile** involves the offender having to leave their home and community to start a new life elsewhere. People who were exiled were often told they would be killed if they returned. A version of exile can be found in modern societies in the form of an injunction or restraining order, which a court may impose as part of a punishment. An injunction may state that an offender must not visit a certain area or make contact with a certain person; if they do, they will be punished more severely. Injunctions are sometimes used in domestic violence or harassment cases and the offender can be monitored via electronic surveillance.

Ostracism involves being shunned by and excluded from a community or group: no one speaks to or

helps the offender. Someone who is ostracised is not necessarily exiled; they may continue to live among the community.

Non-custodial sentencing

Sometimes, instead of a prison sentence, an offender is given a conditional sentence. This means they have to follow certain rules – such as keeping a curfew or avoiding certain areas or people – in exchange for a lighter sentence. The offender is put under surveillance to make sure they are following these rules; for example, they might wear an electronic 'tag' that tells the authorities where they are. This can be seen as a form of rehabilitation, because it allows an offender to keep their place in the community – but with restrictions on what they can do, where and when.

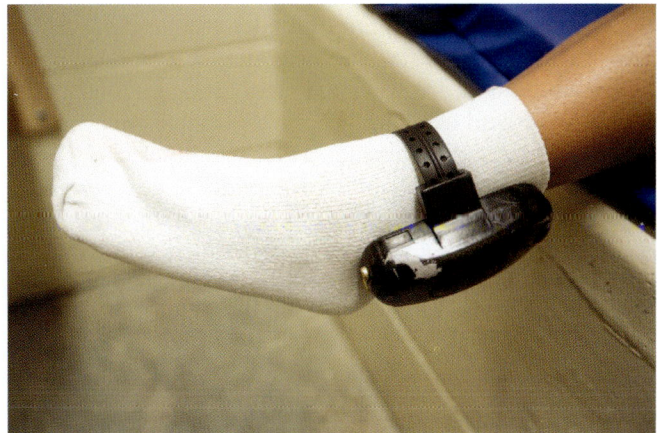

Figure 6.13: An electronic tag.

Probation

Probation is a period of time when an offender is monitored within the community. An offender may be sentenced to a period of probation (for example,

> **KEY TERMS**
>
> **corporal punishment:** physical harm inflicted on an offender as punishment, for example by whipping them
>
> **exile:** punishment in which the offender has to leave their home and community
>
> **probation:** serving a sentence, or part of it, in the community under supervision

two years) instead of a custodial sentence or when they are released from prison. Probation is often used alongside other community measures, such as unpaid work or treatment for addiction. During this time, the offender is closely monitored and attends regular meetings with a probation officer, to ensure they are following certain rules imposed by the sentencing judge. (For example, they may be subject to an injunction or a restraining order as well.) If the terms of the probation are broken, the offender may be sent (back) to prison.

Probation can be seen as a rehabilitative approach to punishment. It is a way of checking whether an offender has reformed and is safe to live within the community without reoffending. Some prisoners released on probation will have an electronic tag to monitor their movements.

Police cautions

For minor offences where the offender accepts their guilt, the police in some countries can give a **police caution** instead of arresting and prosecuting an offender. This allows them to avoid the long and expensive process of arrest, trial and sentencing, which can be seen as unnecessary for a minor offence. A police caution is a quick and proportionate way of dealing with minor offences. It involves a warning of consequences if there are further offences and it is recorded in the offender's criminal record.

> ### KEY TERM
>
> **police caution:** a warning given to an offender who admits their guilt, with no further action

Social media and vigilante groups

In some situations, individuals or groups of citizens decide to punish criminals themselves. This is usually because they believe that the police and criminal justice system are not dealing with crime or with a particular type of crime. The growth of social media means that allegations about what has happened, or who has done what, spread quickly but people are unable to check how accurate the information is. People may gather where an offence has happened and attack the alleged offender.

Vigilante groups are self-appointed groups which set out to punish perceived offences. They have no

legal authority and their actions are often illegal. Vigilante groups cannot investigate crimes using the correct procedures, as the police and other authorities do; as a result, they often target innocent people by mistake. Vigilantes sometime work online.

Recently, vigilante groups have formed on the border between the USA and Mexico. Some Americans believe that the authorities are not doing enough to prevent migrants illegally crossing the border from Mexico into the USA. They have decided to hunt migrants themselves.

> ### ACTIVITY: RESEARCH 6.3
>
> Using the internet and other sources of information, and by asking people you know, find out which types of punishment are used in your society. Which are used the most? Which are not used at all? Why do you think this is?

> ### REFLECTION
>
> Which sources of information did you use? When you visited websites, did you ask yourself whether the information was accurate? How could you check this? Which sources of information do you think were the most trustworthy and why?

> ### ACTIVITY: WRITTEN 6.3
>
> Look again at the types of punishment listed in this section. Choose one that you think is useful but could be used more in your society. Write a blog post or newspaper article (around 250 words) and make sure you:
>
> - Make the case for that type of punishment being used more often.
> - Discuss the types of crime it would be appropriate for.
> - Give your writing a title that will make people want to read it, such as 'Give prisoners the skills they need to help them go straight'.

The effectiveness of different types of punishment in dealing with crime

As you have seen, there are many different types of punishment. All have their supporters and all are more effective for some crimes and criminals than others. Governments adjust their use of punishments according to their ideology, patterns and trends in recorded crime and public opinion. For example, in recent decades, there has been a considerable increase in the number of prisoners in countries such as the UK and USA. This is not usually because of rising crime or because prisons are effective; rather, it allows governments to claim that they are tackling crime.

Figure 6.14: Prisoners often have to wear a uniform, taking away their individuality.

The most controversial types of punishment are imprisonment and capital punishment. There are prisons all over the world and imprisonment is the most common way of punishing serious offences. However, many offenders who go to prison reoffend after being released; they are recidivists. Many people argue that prisons are not effective at rehabilitation. Offenders cannot commit crimes while they are in prison, but they may learn more from other prisoners about how to be a successful criminal. Some prisoners who serve long sentences become socialised into prison life and routines; as a result, they find it difficult to adjust to everyday life when they are released. Having been a prisoner is also a form of labelling: a person who has a prison record will find it difficult to get employment.

Data on recidivism (reoffending) are difficult to compare because different countries use different ways of measuring reoffending and different timescales. However, reoffending rates are often very high. Seena Fazel and Achim Wolf researched reconviction rates – the number of criminals who were convicted of a crime after their release from prison. They found that, within two years of release from prison, the reconviction rate was 36 per cent in the USA, 40 per cent in France, 59 per cent in the UK and 61 per cent in New Zealand. These data suggest that imprisonment is ineffective in terms of deterrence or rehabilitation.

Capital punishment is now widely seen as something which should rarely, if ever, be used. Many countries have abolished the death penalty; other countries very rarely use it, even though they retain it. Capital punishment obviously prevents the offender reoffending but opinions differ on whether it works as a deterrent for others. Many murders, for example, are the result of a violent outburst of emotion; the murderer does not stop to think about the consequences of what they are doing, so no deterrent would be effective. Evidence suggests that countries that retain the death penalty for murder have similar or even higher murder rates than those that have abolished it.

Community sentences and other punishments involving rehabilitation are sometimes criticised for being too 'soft' on offenders and not achieving the aim of retribution. However, countries which focus on rehabilitation in their penal system tend to have lower crime rates than those which focus more on retribution. For example, in Sweden, prisons have comprehensive education and training programmes and provide treatment for issues which many offenders may have, including drug and alcohol addiction and mental health problems. Reoffending rates in Sweden are much lower than in many other countries, with prisoner numbers falling at a time when they are rising in other countries.

Policing and law enforcement

Police forces are organisations formed to enforce the law and to impose social control in most countries. They protect private property and the safety of individual members of society. The police are allowed to use force in some situations and, in many countries, they carry weapons such as firearms. The police forces of different societies vary considerably in their size and functions.

Most countries also have other **law enforcement agencies**; for example, the USA has the Federal Bureau of Investigation (FBI), which investigates criminal activities on a national level, as well as individual police forces for each of the 50 states.

For Marxists, police forces are part of the repressive state apparatus; that is, they are used by the ruling capitalist class to protect itself against the working class. The police are often used to control protests and demonstrations, so they have an openly political role. According to Marxists, the police are the first line of defence when ideology fails to keep the working class under control. In situations where the police cannot cope with demonstrations, the army may be called in. For riot control, the police may use weapons such as batons, rubber bullets and electroshock weapons.

Today, more crime transcends national borders. This has led to increased cooperation between police forces in different countries, especially in sharing information.

Policing strategies, e.g. targeting and stop and search

Because of the nature of policing, it is inevitable that the police will tend to focus on some types of crimes and offenders rather than others. As discussed in section 6.2, police targeting is when the police focus on a particular area or group of people, because they believe they are more likely to be involved in criminal behaviour than other groups. Examples of groups that are targeted in this way include young males, the working class and members of some minority ethnic groups. Police targeting of Black people in the USA – with several high-profile cases of Black people killed by the police – led to the Black Lives Matter protests and campaigns to defund the police. It has been argued that stop and search is an important police power, which allows the police to prevent drug-related offences and violent crimes such as stabbing. However, it is a very controversial power and is arguably used to target certain groups based on stereotyping. Targeting and stop and search have been discussed already, in relation to young people, minority ethnic groups and the working class.

Surveillance, including digital surveillance

One way in which the police can target particular groups and places is through surveillance. New technologies have led to surveillance becoming widespread. Surveillance may focus on individuals or groups who are suspected of being involved in crime. However, it can also be far more general; in modern industrial societies, everyone is under surveillance in some way.

Types of surveillance include:

- computer surveillance – by monitoring websites visited, emails and instant messaging

- telephone surveillance – by monitoring telephone calls (often called phone tapping)

- surveillance cameras

- aerial surveillance – for example, by helicopters, satellites or unmanned aerial devices (drones)

- identity card systems

- tracking use of credit or debit cards

- biometric surveillance – monitoring people to identify patterns or traits that may indicate their emotional state or likely behaviour

- use of social networking behaviour (for example, Twitter, Facebook and phone calls) to track contacts, interests and connections between individuals and groups

- electronic tagging of people, animals or goods

- undercover surveillance – in some countries, police officers monitoring protest groups or criminal gangs have joined groups under false identities and becoming deeply involved in their activities.

Crime prevention

In recent decades, interest in **crime prevention** methods has increased. This is based on the view that there are always some bad people in a society, so it is impossible to completely get rid of crime. However, there are strategies which can be used to reduce the likelihood of crime; these strategies may be used by individuals (to protect themselves and their property) and by local and national governments (to make crime more difficult to commit).

KEY TERMS

law enforcement agencies: the police and other organisations with legal powers to tackle crime

crime prevention: techniques used by governments and individuals to reduce the amount of crime which takes place

Individuals may protect themselves by installing burglar alarms and security locks on homes or cars. Alternatively, they might modify their behaviour, for example they might avoid using their mobile phone in a public place or leaving their wallet in a visible place.

The design of the environment can reduce the likelihood of crime. Designers and architects can try to minimise crime by ensuring that entrance doors are visible, well-lit and can be monitored, or by planting thorny bushes outside ground-level windows to deter burglars.

Crime prevention involves changing the calculation that a potential criminal makes when deciding whether or not to commit a crime. Examples include:

- closed circuit television cameras (CCTV). These can provide evidence that helps to catch offenders. More importantly, however, they can prevent an offence being committed in the first place, since a potential offender is less likely to commit a crime if they know they will be seen.

- cameras used for traffic control. Drivers are less likely to break the speed limit or drive through red traffic lights if they know that they will be identified by a camera.

- control of credit card fraud through a series of checks for irregular use and other patterns. These methods do not prevent all fraud but they makes it difficult for a thief to profit much before the fraud is detected and the card is cancelled. This means the effort involved in stealing the card details becomes less worthwhile.

In some cities, wealthy people protect their luxury lifestyles by segregating themselves from the urban poor. They pay for private protection, using security guards, rather than relying on the police force. Those who can afford it live in gated communities with strictly controlled access that keeps out people who do not live there. Such privileged people may rarely come into contact with people from other classes.

A sociological theory that led directly to changes in policing and policy was the 'broken windows' theory. This was based on the observation that if there were signs of neglect in an area – such as a broken window being left unrepaired – there would soon be other problems such as litter, graffiti and vandalism. If people saw small incidents going unpunished, this could lead to growing deviance and an increase in more serious criminality.

CASE STUDY 6.4

Crime prevention in New York

Figure 6.15: Zero tolerance policing was adopted in New York in the 1990s.

The broken windows theory led to the zero tolerance policing policy adopted in New York and elsewhere in the 1990s. The police and authorities acted against minor deviance and crimes such as begging, dropping litter, possession of drugs and selling goods on the street without a licence. The aim was to give a message to criminals that the law would always be enforced and that more serious crime would not be tolerated either. The policy was hailed as successful: the crime rate – including the rate for the most serious crimes – fell in cities where zero tolerance was implemented. However, the approach has been controversial:

- Homeless people were removed from the centre of New York but the underlying problem remained. These people were still homeless so the problems were just displaced (moved elsewhere).

CONTINUED

- Crime rates also fell in other cities in the 1990s, where zero tolerance policies were not brought in. The fall in crime rates at this time may have been related to other factors, such as the decline in the number of young males in the population (due to falling birth rates in the 1970s and 80s) and also to changes in the international illegal drug trade.

Task

1   How would the following groups have reacted to this policy?

a   people living in the centre of New York

b   the homeless people who were moved out.

2   Your school has decided on a zero tolerance policy in relation to behaviour. Minor offences such as walking too quickly or speaking loudly outside lessons will be punished on the grounds that this will prevent more serious misbehaviour. What is your reaction? Do you think this policy would work?

Community and military-style policing

Community and military-style policing can be thought of as two extremes of policing.

Community policing is when the police work within a community. They are very visible, patrolling streets and talking to people. They visit schools to give advice to children and young people and they try to build good relationships with community leaders. Community policing makes people feel safe, because they can see the police and know they are working to protect them. It also aims to build trust in the police, so that members of the community will report crimes and cooperate with the police, rather than regarding them with suspicion. Community policing may have a deterrent effect. However, it is unlikely that the police will happen to walk past as a crime such as a robbery is committed.

Figure 6.16: Community policing.

Military-style policing involves well-equipped and usually armed police being sent to where they are needed, to deal with particular crimes or events.

The police appear as outsiders and may have little knowledge or understanding of the area and community. In this style of policing, the police are similar to an army: they are sent in from outside, they use force, they obey commands from officers and they sometimes use military terminology such as 'the war on drugs'. They may use military-style equipment such as weapons.

Figure 6.17: Military-style policing may be used to control public protests.

KEY TERMS

community policing: a policing strategy that involves the police working with the local community and building positive relationships

military-style policing: a policing strategy that involves the use of military-style tactics by the police to crack down on behaviour which is seen as a threat to social order

The effectiveness of different types of policing and law enforcement in dealing with crime

Police and policing have changed as society changes. Police forces today are often larger and better equipped than in the past and remain one of the main ways in which societies try to tackle crime. However, crime remains a significant problem everywhere. policing may help to control crime but it does not prevent it.

Policing works best when it has the support of citizens. This support is not always there. Military-style policing can seem like an invasion, which can turn local people against the police. Some communities and groups, such as Black people in the USA, feel that the police are often hostile to them and target them more than other groups. Not everyone feels they can turn to the police if they need help or if they are a victim of crime.

One new challenge is the growth of cybercrime and global crime. It is very difficult to police cybercrime because cyberspace exists outside national boundaries. The victims of hacking or other cybercrimes may live in a different country to the offender. More and more crimes – including cybercrime – are global (see section 6.1), so policing needs to be global as well. However, different countries have different laws and they may not agree about what is a crime or how different crimes should be dealt with. There is some cooperation between police forces through Interpol (the International Criminal Police Organization), which allows police forces to share information and work together to track down offenders. Unfortunately, policing does not have the resources necessary to stop, for example, global trades in drugs and people.

ACTIVITY: DISCUSSION 6.3

In a small group, discuss the following question: If you had unlimited money and resources, how would you tackle crime in your country? Listen to each other's ideas and see if you can agree about the best way of tackling crime.

Do you think you would be able to get rid of crime completely? Discuss why or why not.

CHECK YOUR UNDERSTANDING 6.3

1   Explain the difference between community policing and military-style policing.

2   How effective is prison as a deterrent? Does it work differently depending on the type of crime? Write around 200 words on this topic. Show your work to a fellow learner and ask them for constructive comments.

KEY POINTS

- Punishment can have different aims:
  - deterrence
  - retribution
  - incapacitation
  - rehabilitation
  - protection of citizens.
- Types of punishment are:
  - community sentencing
  - financial penalties
  - prison
  - rehabilitation programmes
  - capital punishment
  - corporal punishment
  - exile and ostracism
  - non-custodial sentencing
  - probation
  - police cautions
  - social media and vigilante groups.
- Different types of policing and law enforcement include:
  - policing strategies, such as targeting and stop and search
  - surveillance
  - crime prevention
  - community policing
  - military-style policing.

SUMMARY

- Crime and deviance have different meanings but can overlap. They are seen as relative to time and culture.

- Crime and deviance are prevented by formal and informal agencies of social control.

- There are different types and examples of crime.

- There are different ways of measuring crime.

- There are different patterns of victimisation and offending, in relation to age, ethnicity, gender and social class.

- There are explanations for crime and deviance based on age, ethnicity, gender and social

- class, and debates about the importance of these explanations.

- There are various sociological theories on crime and deviance – postmodernism, interactionism, functionalism, Marxism and feminism. Each theory has strengths and limitations.

- There are several aims of punishment, which may overlap.

- Crime can be dealt with by different types of punishment.

- Crime can also be dealt with by different types of policing and law enforcement.

KEY SKILLS EXERCISES

1 Knowledge and understanding

Without consulting this book or your notes, write definitions of the following terms:

- chivalry thesis
- cybercrime
- strain theory
- moral panic
- surveillance
- status frustration
- rehabilitation
- deterrent.
- green crime

Try not to use the exact wording of the definitions in this book; it is better to show you understand the meaning by writing in your own words. When you have finished, ask your teacher or a fellow learner to check your work.

2 Evaluation

Which of these sociological views do you think gives the most convincing explanation for crime and deviance: postmodernism; interactionism; functionalism (including New Right, sub-culturalism and strain theory); Marxism; feminism? Write a 250-word justification of your choice.

3 Analysis and evaluation

Evaluate the view that prisons are the most effective way of preventing crime.

Write about 500 words. Include several points for and several points against the view. Finish with a short paragraph giving your conclusion and justifying it.

IMPROVE THIS ANSWER

Discuss the view that crime is caused by deprivation.

Your answer should include:

- at least three developed points with evidence.

Crime can be caused by relative deprivation. This is when people compare themselves to others and feel that they are missing out. For example, they may see other people with expensive and desirable clothes or goods. When a person feels relatively deprived because they cannot afford these things, they may turn to theft as a way of obtaining them.

Commentary and task

The answer so far gives only one point about how crime is caused by deprivation. Write two more paragraphs of similar length. In each paragraph, try to include one more developed point, at least one key term (a sociological concept) and an example that helps to explain your point. (In the sample answer above, the key term is 'relative deprivation' and there are examples of things that people may feel deprived of.)

PRACTICE QUESTIONS

Family, education and crime

a   Define the terms:

   i   victim surveys   [2]

   ii   surveillance.   [2]

b   Give **two** examples of agencies of formal social control.   [2]

c   Describe **three** reasons why official statistics do not include all crimes.   [6]

d   Explain **three** main points of the Marxist theory of crime.   [6]

e   Discuss the view that crime is caused by deprivation.

   Your answer should include at least **three** developed points with evidence.   [8]

f   Evaluate the view that policing and law enforcement are effective in dealing with crime.

   Your answer should include:

   - at least **three** arguments for and **three** arguments against the view

   - a conclusion.   [14]

SELF-EVALUATION CHECKLIST

After studying this unit, complete this table:

You should be able to:	Needs more work	Almost there	Ready to move on
6.1 What are crime, deviance and social control?			
Understand the difference between crime and deviance			
Explain how agencies of formal social control control individuals and prevent crime and deviance			
Explain how agencies of informal social control control individuals and prevent crime and deviance			
Understand debates about the effectiveness of agencies and methods of social control in achieving conformity and preventing crime			
Explain different types and examples of crime			
Explain measurements of crime, including the problem of unreported and unrecorded crime			
6.2 What are the patterns and explanations of crime and deviance?			
Describe patterns of crime and victimisation			
Understand explanations for crime and deviance based on age			
Understand explanations for crime and deviance based on ethnicity			
Understand explanations for crime and deviance based on gender			
Understand explanations for crime and deviance based on social class			
Understand that different explanations for crime and deviance relating to age, ethnicity, gender and social class have strengths and limitations			
Evaluate sociological explanations for crime and deviance			
6.3 How is crime dealt with in different societies?			
Explain the aims of punishment			
Explain types of punishment and their effectiveness			
Explain the effectiveness of different types of policing and law enforcement in dealing with crime			

> Preparing for assessment

The information in this section is based on the Cambridge International syllabus. You should always refer to the appropriate syllabus document for the year of examination to confirm the details and for more information. The syllabus document is available on the Cambridge International website at www.cambridgeinternational.org

The syllabus

Make sure you are familiar with the appropriate syllabus for the year you will be studying for assessment. Your teacher will be able to guide you. The syllabus will indicate the topics you will be expected to know and understand. It will also direct you to the key skills you will have covered on your course that are important to the study of sociology. These skills are in the assessment objectives (AO).

There are three assessment objectives in the Cambridge IGCSE™ and O Level Sociology syllabuses (0495/2251) for examination from 2025:

1   **AO1 Knowledge and understanding**

Demonstrate knowledge and understanding of sociological concepts, theories, evidence, views and research methods.

2   **AO2 Interpretation and application**

Apply relevant sociological concepts, theories, evidence, views and research methods to support points or develop arguments.

Explain how sociological concepts, theories, evidence, views and research methods apply to a particular issue or question.

3   **AO3 Analysis and evaluation**

Analyse and evaluate sociological theories, evidence, views and research methods:

- Explain the strengths and limitations of sociological theories, views and research methods.

- Construct, develop and discuss sociological arguments.

- Reach conclusions and make judgements based on a reasoned consideration of evidence.

Most learners find the skills within AO1 the most straightforward to learn and demonstrate. There is a lot to learn and understand but the other skills are more demanding.

The units of this book cover all the content listed in the syllabus. Within each unit, you will see key terms. These are in bold the first time they appear and there is a box defining or explaining each term. The key terms are also listed in the glossary at the back of the book.

The AO2 skills mean you have to show that you can work out what sociological evidence, theories, views, etc. to apply. You must also show that you understand different types and sources of evidence and data.

The skills within AO3 are probably the most challenging to master. Evaluation is a difficult skill and you need to practise writing answers in which you evaluate different topics. Ask your teacher to check these answers and give you feedback. Evaluation does not have to focus on criticisms in the negative sense. A good evaluation can also show what is useful or important about a topic. Practise these different ways of evaluating a topic:

- Point out a limitation or problem in a research study. For example, the sample may be too small for generalisations to be made from it.

- Point out a limitation or problem with a theoretical perspective. For example, Marxists tend to focus on class divisions, ignoring other conflicts in societies.

- Point out when a sociological research study or theory does not seem to explain something well (or perhaps at all), or where there are exceptions to the findings.

- Identify the contribution that a research study has made to sociological knowledge or that a theory has made to sociological understanding.

- Point out differences between the findings of research studies or between different theoretical perspectives.

You can use language to show that you are evaluating. For example, use words and phrases such as 'however' or 'on the other hand' to introduce different points, which contrast with ones you have already made. Your evaluation will be even stronger if you can explain why there is a difference and which point you think is stronger.

The syllabus also gives details about how you will be assessed. The Cambridge IGCSE™ and O Level Sociology assessment is made up of two papers.

Research methods, identity and inequality

In this paper, you have to answer **two** questions, each made up of several part questions. You will have two hours and you should spend the first 15 minutes reading the questions.

The first question will be on *Research methods* and is worth 40 marks. All learners must answer this question.

There will then be two further questions: one on *Identity, self and society* and one on *Social stratification and inequality*. You will have studied both of these topics because they are the basis of sociology and lay the foundations for the other topics. However, you will need to choose just **one** of the two questions to answer. The question that you choose to answer is worth 40 marks, so the total mark for **Research methods, identity and inequality** is 80.

Family, education and crime

In this paper, you will need to answer **two** questions, each made up of several part questions. You will have one hour and forty-five minutes and you should spend the first 15 minutes reading the questions. This will leave you with 45 minutes to answer each question.

The paper has **three** questions – one for each of the following topics:

- Family

- Education

- Crime, deviance and social control.

You will have to answer **two** of the three questions. Each question is worth 40 marks, so the total mark for the paper is 80. Knowledge of **Research methods, identity and inequality** will also be useful.

Preparation skills

This section offers a few general points about how you should prepare for assessment.

Timing

Make sure you are prepared for how long you will have for each question paper and plan your time wisely. Allow yourself time to read through the paper carefully and choose which questions you are going to answer. For example, if you have one hour and forty-five minutes to complete your assessment and allow 15 minutes to read and select the questions, you will then have 45 minutes to answer each question. You should divide the total time for each question according to the number of marks allocated to each question part.

Question selection

There are two possible strategies for selecting which questions to answer. Your teachers will offer guidance. You can prepare for questions on all topics and decide when you see the questions which of them you feel you can answer best. Alternatively, you might decide in advance which topics you will answer questions on; then you can focus on those topics during your revision.

Read all parts of all questions carefully – including any source material provided as part of the question – before making your selection. Do not be tempted to choose a question just because you feel confident about the topic. Look carefully at what the question is asking you to do, as well as the subject matter.

Revision

Make sure you are well prepared for assessment by revising effectively. Throughout your study of the course, create a file or notebook on the topics as you study them. Keep your notes together with any documents or other handouts your teachers give you, including work your teachers have marked. The marks or grades your teachers give you are less important than the comments they make, identifying where you have done well and where you need to improve. Pay attention to these suggestions and act on them.

To revise effectively, you need a revision plan. Your teachers may help you with this. You need to know:

- the times and dates of your sociology assessment – ask your teacher if you have not yet been told

- the times and dates of any assessments you have for other subjects around that time

- any other commitments you have, for example family occasions or other events that you are expected to go to

- times and dates when you will be in school for lessons.

On each day, you also need to allow time for sleeping, eating and relaxing. You might find it helpful to divide each day into morning, afternoon and evening; then divide each of these in two, so you have six time slots in the day (probably about an hour and a half each). Block out slots where you have other commitments. Then, in each free slot, write the name of a subject you need to revise for, giving more time to each subject as the relevant assessment approaches. You probably need roughly the same number of slots for each subject; however, you may want to vary this – for example, if you are particularly worried or confident about a subject or if there is significantly more or less to learn for a subject. When you have done all this, you will have a better idea how many time slots you have to revise sociology.

For effective revision, you will need the following resources:

- your teachers. They are experts in the subject and in revision and essential skills. Ask questions and ask for advice. They will be pleased that you are keen to do well and will offer you their full support.

- this Coursebook

- your notes from the course – in order and divided into topic areas. Card dividers can help you to organise your notes

- paper, pens, pencils and highlighter pens

- past assessment papers. Some past papers are available on the public website of Cambridge Assessment International Education; your teachers may be able to source other past papers or practice questions.

While revising, you want to be interrupted as little as possible. Talk to your family and friends and explain when you want to be left undisturbed and why. It is good to have a space where you revise (for example, a desk or table) but it can also be helpful to sit somewhere else for a change.

When you are revising, it is important to do more than just reading. Many people find that if they just read notes or a textbook, their mind wanders and they lose focus on what they are reading. People revise in different ways and you need to find out what works best for you. You may wish to try some of the following methods, which many people find effective:

- Complete practice papers. Ask your teachers to help you find past assessments and use the practice questions in this book. You can practise individual questions but you should also try a whole assessment exercise without breaks. This will help you to work out how many questions you have to answer and how long you have to do this. It will also show you how much you can write in that time. When practising, write by hand as much as possible so your fingers are less likely to get tired.

- Write definitions of key words or names of sociologists on cards or small pieces of paper. Writing them down like this will help you to remember them and you can also use the cards for future revision.

- Revise with a friend sometimes. Revision can be lonely, so work with a fellow learner. Test each other with quiz-style questions to find out how much you both know and understand.

- Rewrite your notes or turn them into diagrams, such as spider diagrams. Be inventive and use colours to make them attractive and memorable.

- If possible, put revision notes and posters on a wall or around a mirror at home so you see them regularly and you are reminded of the key points.

You will need breaks when revising. No one can work for a very long time without a break. Set yourself targets, for example, that you will revise a topic for an hour, or write 20 definitions on cards and then reward yourself by stopping for a break or having a drink or snack. You will need self-discipline! If you think you will find this difficult, ask a family member to monitor how you are doing and tell you when you succeed.

Digital revision

Access to the internet can be very useful for revision. There are some good revision sources for sociology online; your teachers should be able to advise you on which ones might be effective to use. Some sites are less helpful; for example, a search for 'gender' will return millions of websites but few of them will be relevant to Cambridge IGCSE™ and O Level Sociology. For this reason, you should avoid wide searches.

Be careful when using the internet to revise, as you may waste time. If you think you will be tempted to check emails or social networking sites, or to visit internet sites that have nothing to do with your revision, put strict limits on this type of revision. You may also find it helps to switch off your mobile phone while you are revising.

Final preparation

- Make sure you are well rested. Go to bed at your usual time – or earlier if you sometimes stay up late. A good night's sleep will help you more than last-minute revision.

- Have something to eat. You will work more effectively and you will not be distracted by your empty stomach.

- Drink plenty of water to keep hydrated. Your brain does not work at its full capacity if you are dehydrated. If you are allowed to, take a bottle of water.

- Try to stay calm but remember that it is normal to be nervous; sometimes nerves can even help you to focus.

During your assessment

Be early and be equipped. You might need to write using a black pen, and you should take a spare pen too.

There are often distractions. People move or cough, chairs creak and there may be noises outside the room. Keep focused and try to block out anything else. At the very start of your assessment clear your mind, close your eyes and breathe deeply to prepare yourself.

Everyone arrives for assessment knowing some sociology; some people know more than others but very few will have learnt everything. Use these tips to help yourself do as well as you can with the sociological knowledge you have:

- Read the questions very carefully and do exactly what they tell you to do. Try to split each question into sections, thinking about the meaning of each word and phrase. The question will not contain unnecessary words: every word or phrase will be trying to get you to do something specific and you need to work out what this is. Remember that you have to answer the question that has been set, not the question you were hoping would come up.

- Know the timings. This includes the total time overall and the time you should spend on each question. Do not rush; work steadily. If you have any time left at the end, go back and check your answers.

- If you feel you cannot answer a question, move on to one that you can answer and return to the first question later. Your brain will continue to think about the question so you may remember something useful. For the same reason, it is a good idea to read all the sources and questions before you start writing.

- How much you write is less important than what you write.

- Try to answer every question required: it is better to write something, even if you are not sure whether it is right.

- If you have to cross something out, do this with a single clear line. If you do not have enough room for your answer, you may find extra pages you can use at the back of your answer booklet. Find a way to make it clear you have done this so your extra work doesn't go unnoticed (for example, by writing 'continued at back of book').

- For questions that require longer answers, it is a good idea to plan. Above where you will write your answer, you could list the points you want to make, the theories, studies or sociologists you want to include, etc. Decide on the order, then begin writing. Look back at your plan as you write, ticking the points you have covered. You will then be able to see how much more you have to say and you can check how much time you have left for this.

- Try to leave enough time to read over your answers at the end. First, and most important, make sure you have answered all the questions that you needed to answer. Then see if there are any good, relevant points that you could have included but did not; if so, add them. You can also correct any spelling, grammatical or punctuation errors if you have time.

After you have been assessed, try not to talk about what you wrote. If your peers included something you did not, you may begin to worry about your own answers. Remember that in sociology, there are often different ways to answer a question so your answer may be just as good as – or better than – their answers. Instead, take a well-earned break or begin your preparation for any other assessments you may have coming up.

Your answers

A lot of the sociology you have learnt will have been about the USA and the UK. This is partly because a lot of sociological research has been done in these countries, as many important ideas in sociology were developed here. Other textbooks that you may have seen – for example, for GCSE Sociology – are intended to be used by learners in the UK or elsewhere, following syllabuses that are mainly about the UK.

It is not possible to have a different textbook for every country where learners study Cambridge IGCSE™ and O Level Sociology. At times, you may have thought that the examples you are learning about seem very different to the situation in your own society. This Coursebook tries to be more international and global than other textbooks; we have included examples and information from a range of countries. However, you can show you have good sociological skills and understanding by taking ideas from textbooks and applying them to your own society and culture. You need to answer the question, of course, and you need to clearly demonstrate your sociological knowledge, but do not be afraid to write about your own society.

> Glossary

achieved status: a position in society that an individual acquires through their own effort

age: a form of stratification based on how old people are; age is often looked at in stages rather than specific numbers – childhood, youth, adulthood and old age. There are particular roles and expectations associated with each age

ageism: prejudice and discrimination against people based on how old they are

agencies of social control: people or organisations who carry out social control

agencies of socialisation: the groups and institutions which carry out the process of socialisation

aims: what a researcher sets out to achieve through their research, for example, to find out why something happens

anti-school sub-culture: a group of learners whose norms and values reject those of the school

arranged marriage: a marriage in which the partners are chosen by older family members, rather than people choosing their own marriage partner

ascribed status: a position in society that is given to an individual by their society or group; people usually have little or no control over ascribed statuses

beanpole family: a vertically extended/multi-generational family with only one or two children in each generation; this creates a tall and thin family tree (rather than a 'bushy' one with lots of siblings, aunts, uncles and cousins)

benefits: money paid by governments to people who are ill, unemployed or poor

bias: when a researcher is not neutral in carrying out their research

birth rate: the number of live births per 1000 people in the population in one year

boomerang family: a family where an adult child has returned to the family home to live with their parent(s)

bourgeoisie: in the theory of Marxism, the bourgeoisie are the owners of wealth and property, sometimes referred to as the ruling class

canalisation: channelling children towards activities that are considered appropriate for them (for example, because of their gender)

capitalism: the economic system of most countries today; based on private ownership of the means of production

capital punishment: the legally authorised killing of someone as a punishment for a crime

caste: a closed stratification system in which a group's status is fixed at birth and cannot be changed

causation: when a change in one variable has a direct effect on another variable

cereal packet family: the stereotypical nuclear family of mother, father and children with traditional gender roles, often shown in advertisements

child-centredness: when a child's needs and wishes are the most important considerations

childless families: a couple who live together and have no children

chivalry thesis: the theory that women are treated more leniently than men within the criminal justice system

civil partnership: a relationship between two people, often of the same sex, that has been formally registered, giving them the same or similar rights to married couples

closed questions: questions which allow limited or set answers

closed society: a society in which individuals' social roles and statuses are fixed

co-educational schools: schools which accept both male and female learners

coercion: the use or threat of force or violence

cohabitation: when two people who are not married to each other live together in a sexual relationship

colonialism: the policy or practice in which one country controls another country, exploiting it and occupying it with settlers

community policing: a policing strategy that involves the police working with the local community and building positive relationships

community sentencing: punishments that involve non-custodial sentences (where the offender is not sent to prison); instead, the offender may have to do unpaid work for the community

compensatory education: educational policies including financial aid, additional classes and tutoring which aim to support children from disadvantaged backgrounds and close the achievement gap between working-class and middle-class learners

conflict: disagreement; this term is used to describe a perspective on society which assumes there are basic disagreements between social groups (for example, based on social class or gender differences)

conformity: behaviour that follows the usual standards expected by a group or society

conjugal roles: the roles taken by the partners within a family – usually the husband and wife – resulting from the domestic division of labour

consensus: agreement; this term is used to describe a perspective on society which assumes that people generally share values

consumption: the buying and use of goods and resources

consumption lifestyle: a lifestyle based on what people buy and consume (rather than, for example, the work they do)

consumption patterns: variations in consumption depending on time, place and group

corporal punishment: physical harm inflicted on an offender as punishment, for example by whipping them

corporate crime: offences committed by corporations or organisations, usually in pursuit of profit for the corporation, rather than the benefit of individuals

correlation: when two variables change at the same time, suggesting they are connected

covert observation: when the group being studied is unaware of the research; covert means 'hidden'

crime: actions that break formal written laws

crime prevention: techniques used by governments and individuals to reduce the amount of crime which takes place

cultural appropriation: where culturally significant practices and artefacts from one part of the world are adopted by people in another part of the world, in a way that uses them as a fashion statement and strips them of their meaning

cultural capital: the knowledge, taste and values associated with the higher classes

cultural racism: racism based on differences between ways of life, such as religion and customs, rather than supposed biological differences

culture: the way of life of a society

culture of poverty: when poor people have a different set of values to the majority, which keeps them poor

customs: norms in a particular society that are widely accepted and continue over time

cybercrime: crime involving use of new technologies, such as computers

cycle of poverty: when poor families become trapped in poverty for at least three generations because they have no access to the resources or qualifications to lift themselves out of it

death rate: the number of deaths per 1000 people in a population in one year; also called the mortality rate

demographic trends: changes in a population, such as the birth rate and death rate

dependency culture: a set of values leading people to lose the desire or ability to look after themselves, so they become dependent, for example, on welfare benefits

deterrent: a punishment intended to discourage offenders or others from committing an offence

deviance: behaviour that goes against the norms or values of a group

deviancy amplification: when the response to norm-breaking behaviour leads to more of that behaviour

digital self: the way that someone presents themselves online, and the personae they adopt in online communities, such as forums and social media. *See also* **online identities**

digital sources: the internet and other online sources

digital surveillance: the use of digital technology to observe and control behaviour

discrimination: treating a person or group of people differently to other people, often based on prejudice

distribution of wealth: the way in which the wealth and income of a society are divided among its population

diverse: variety; cultural diversity refers to the wide differences between human cultures

divorce: the formal, legal ending of a marriage

divorce rate: the number of divorces in a year per 1000 people in a population

domestic crime: offences in which the offender and the victim live in the same family home or are in a relationship

domestic division of labour: the way in which tasks in the home (such as cooking, cleaning, childcare and repairs) are divided between men and women

domestic violence: violence within the family, usually – but not always – by males against females; the term refers not only to physical violence but also to patterns of controlling behaviour that may include emotional manipulation

dual burden: people who do paid work as well as looking after the home and family are said to have a dual burden. This is often seen to apply to women

dual worker families: families in which both partners do paid work

dysfunctional family: a family that fails to carry out the expected functions; for example, where children are neglected

educational achievement: how well individuals do in the school system, usually measured by exam results

educational inequality: when different groups (based on class, gender and ethnicity) are treated or educated differently or have different levels of educational achievement

emigration: moving away from your home country and settling in another

empty-nest family: parents living at home after their adult children have moved out

empty-shell marriage: when a married couple continue to live together, but without love or affection

equal opportunities: when everyone has the same chance of succeeding

ethical issues: issues that have a moral dimension, such as when research might cause harm or distress to the participants

ethnicity: the state of belonging to a particular group with a shared culture, including language, beliefs, history and traditions

ethnocentrism: the belief that the people, customs and traditions of your own race or country are better than those of other races or countries

exile: punishment in which the offender has to leave their home and community

expressive crime: offences involving emotions, such as strong anger or frustration, which are usually unplanned

extended family: a family with parent(s) and children living with or close to other relatives, such as grandparents or aunts and uncles

faith schools: schools which are linked to a particular religion or faith and promote that faith through their ethos and curriculum

family diversity: variations in types of families

family functions: the functions of the family; the roles it plays and for whom, according to functionalist theory

family roles: the parts played by different members of a family

fatalism: an individual's belief that they cannot control what happens to them

femininity: the attitudes and behaviour associated with being a woman in a particular culture

feminism: a political movement and sociological perspective advocating equality of the sexes

feral children: 'wild' children who have not been socialised

fertility rate: the number of live births per 1000 women of child-bearing age in the population in one year

financial penalties: punishments that involve paying a sum of money

formal education: education that takes place in classrooms, with professional teachers and set content to be taught and learnt

formal social control: social control imposed by people or organisations who have the authority to implement rules or laws

friends as family: when friendships between people who are not related to each other form a support network similar to a more traditional family

functions of education: the ways in which education contributes to society

gang crime: criminal activities carried out by a group of (often young) people, who have a territory and a defined leadership and internal organisation

gang culture: the norms and values of a group of young people who reject authority and are associated with deviance and crime

gender: the roles and expectations associated with being male or female. *See also* **gender roles**

gender equality: where men and women are treated the same and have equal outcomes in all aspects of society

gender hierarchy: a system where one gender has a higher status than the other gender; in a patriarchal society, males benefit from the gender hierarchy

gender inequalities: differences in experience and outcomes for males and females, based on their gender; for example, in terms of educational achievement

gender roles: the roles and expectations associated with being male or female. *See also* **gender**

gendered curriculum: when the content of the teaching has a bias towards one gender, usually boys

gendered division of labour: the way in which societies expect women to be responsible for some tasks (such as cleaning and preparing food) and men for others

gendered socialisation: the way that males and females are taught the expectations relating to their gender roles

generalisability: when the findings about a sample can be said to apply to a larger group of people sharing the same characteristics

global crime: offences which are worldwide, for example, involving international networks

global culture: the idea that, as a result of globalisation, there is or will be a single culture shared by people all around the world

global differences in education: differences in educational provision, outcomes and experience in different countries and regions of the world

globalisation: the complex process by which different cultures around the world are increasingly aware of, interact with and influence each other

green crime: offences which damage the natural world, with resulting harm to humans, other living things and the environment

group interview: any interview in which several people are interviewed together at the same time

hate crime: offences in which the victim is targeted because of certain characteristics, related to, for example, age, faith, sexuality or race

Hawthorne effect: the unintended effects of the researcher's presence on the behaviour or responses of the people being studied. *See also* **observer effect**

hegemonic: relating to something that is widely accepted and difficult to escape from

hidden curriculum: what learners learn in school, apart from the content of lessons, such as the importance of following rules and the consequences of not doing so

historical documents: written sources from the past used as sources of information by sociologists

home factors: factors in a child's home background that affect how they do in school

homeschooling: education of school-aged children in the home, rather than at school

homogenisation of identities: when the differences between identities of people around the world disappear, so they become similar

horizontally extended family: a family with parent(s) and children living with other relatives of the same generations, such as aunts, uncles and cousins

horizontal segregation: differences in the number of people from different groups (such as the sexes) in different employment sectors

hybrid identities: when people combine and mix aspects of different cultures to create new identities

hypothesis: a prediction or statement that research is designed to test

immigration: arriving and settling in a new country

inadequate socialisation: socialisation that does not fully instil the shared norms and values of a society; individuals who are inadequately socialised are more likely to become deviant

incapacitation: punishments intended to physically prevent the offender from reoffending

industrialisation: the process in history in which societies changed from being mainly rural and based on agriculture to being urban and with more people working in industries

informal education: education that takes place outside the classroom or through daily interactions

informal social control: ways of controlling behaviour imposed by people without a formal role to do this (such as peers)

in school factors: factors at school that affect children's educational achievement

institutional racism: when the functioning of an institution or organisation involves systems and expectations that lead to discrimination against an ethnic group

instrumental crime: offences which have a clear goal from the point of view of the criminal

internet crime: any crime or illegal activity committed on, through or using the internet

interpretivism: approaches that start at the level of the individual, focusing on small-scale interactions and usually favouring qualitative methods

intersectionality: ways in which different forms of stratification and inequality interact with each other

interviewer bias: ways in which the interviewer asks questions or interprets answers that have an effect on the findings

interviewer effect: ways in which an interviewer may influence participants' responses, for example through their characteristics, appearance or verbal cues, such as facial expressions and tone of voice

joint conjugal roles: the partners in a family carry out many tasks and activities together, with no clear separation of roles; the opposite of segregated conjugal roles

labelling: defining a person or group in a particular way

law enforcement agencies: the police and other organisations with legal powers to tackle crime

laws: rules, usually formalised by government, that are used to order the way in which a society behaves

life chances: the opportunities people have to improve their lives

lifestyle: the typical way of life of an individual, group or culture

lone-parent family: one parent and their dependent children living together. *See also* **one-parent family** *and* **single-parent family**

longitudinal study: research taking place at intervals over a long period of time

love marriage: a marriage where the couple decide to get married, with or without the consent of their families

macro approaches: approaches that take a large-scale view of whole societies

marital breakdown: when a marriage breaks down so the couple are no longer living as husband and wife (or same-sex equivalents); some breakdowns lead to divorce

marriage: the formal joining of a man and a woman in a relationship with rights and responsibilities; some countries now allow same-sex marriage (involving two men or two women)

Marxism: a theoretical perspective that sees conflict between classes as the most important feature of society

masculinity: the attitudes and behaviour associated with being a man in a particular culture

master status: when a label becomes the single most important thing about a person in the eyes of others, and is then internalised by the labelled person

material deprivation: being unable to afford material goods which most people in a given society would see as necessities

media content: the content of newspapers, magazines, film, television and radio programmes and other forms of media

meritocracy: a system in which individuals reach the social positions they deserve, based on their educational achievement, talent and skills

micro approaches: approaches that take a small-scale view of social interaction between individuals and groups in society

(international) migration: moving from one place to another, to live

military-style policing: a policing strategy that involves the use of military style tactics by the police to crack down on behaviour which is seen as a threat to social order

misogyny: hatred of women, primarily by men

modern slavery: the severe exploitation of vulnerable people for personal or commercial gain

modified extended family: an extended family who have close ties but do not all live together

monogamy: being married to one person at a time

moral panic: exaggerated social reaction to deviance, usually fuelled by the media, that creates a demand for action

multicultural society: a society in which many different cultures or sub-cultures exist alongside each other

multiple-choice questions: closed questions with a number of answers from which the respondent has to choose the correct option

myth of meritocracy: the idea that equality of opportunity does not actually exist, so belief in meritocracy is false

nature: (in the nature–nurture debate) the influence of biological factors on human behaviour

non-governmental organisations (NGOs): non-government, non-profit making bodies that address social and political issues

non-official statistics: statistical data produced by other organisations, such as charities and think-tanks

non-participant observation: when a researcher studies a group but does not take part in what the group is doing

non-selective schools: schools which accept all learners, regardless of ability

norms: the behaviour that societies expect of their members in particular situations

nuclear family: made up of an adult man and an adult woman who are married, or in a relationship, and living together with dependent children

nurture: (in the nature–nurture debate) the influence of society and culture on human behaviour

objectivity: being open-minded and avoiding bias

observer effect: the unintended effects of the researcher's presence on the behaviour or responses of the people being studied. Also known as the **Hawthorne effect**

official crime statistics: official figures showing the number of crimes and offenders recorded in a country during a specific time period

official curriculum: the subjects that are taught and the content to be covered

official statistics: statistical data produced by government and official agencies

one-parent family: one parent and their dependent children living together. *See also* **lone parent family** *and* **single-parent family**

one-person household: when only one person lives in a residence. *See also* **single person household**

online identities: the way that someone presents themselves online, and the personae they adopt in online communities, such as forums and social media. *See also* **digital self**

online learning: distance education delivered electronically, via the internet, using digital technology

online sub-cultures: groups of people who connect with each other online, through social media or other websites. They share distinct norms and values, often related to a particular interest or issue

operationalisation: finding ways to ask questions about, or to measure and observe, abstract concepts so that research can be carried out

open questions: questions to which the respondent can reply freely in their own words

open society: a society in which individuals can move between social roles and change statuses

organised crime: criminal activities which are planned and carried out by powerful groups

ostracise: exclude someone from a community or group

ostracism: the exclusion of someone from a community or group

overt observation: when the group being studied is aware that research is taking place and know who the researcher is

participant observation: when a researcher studies a group by joining them and living as they do

patriarchy: a society or organisation (including the family) in which men are dominant and women are subordinate; the dominance of men over women and children in society

patterns: links between different variables, for example, gender, ethnicity or age

peer group: people of the same status (for example, people the same age)

peer pressure: the influence of a group of people of the same age and status, to force or persuade its members to conform

penal system: the formal system responsible for enforcing punishment for crimes

personal documents: documents such as letters and diaries produced by individuals for their own purposes

perspectives: ways of viewing society and social life

pick-and-mix society: in a postmodern society, people can choose from a range of options and select what suits them best

pilot study: a small-scale test of a research method before the main research is carried out

pivot generation: middle-aged adults who care for their ageing parents, as well as for their children. *See also* **sandwich generation**

police caution: a warning given to an offender who admits their guilt, with no further action

police targeting: when the police focus on a particular group of people, believing that they are more likely to be involved in criminal behaviour than others

policing: the ways in which the police carry out their work, such as investigating crimes and arresting offenders

polygamy: being married to more than one person at the same time; for example, a man with several wives or a woman with several husbands

positivism: an approach to sociology which takes a macro (large-scale) view of society and is based on studying society in a scientific manner, using quantitative methods

postmodernism: the view that we now live in a new type of society, different from the modern society that came before

poverty trap: when poor people are unable to escape from being poor

power: the ability to influence people's behaviour

prejudice: an unfair and unreasonable opinion or feeling, especially about a particular group of people, that is formed without knowledge and often based on stereotypes

primary data: information collected by the sociologist using methods such as questionnaires, interviews or observations

primary socialisation: the process by which infants and young children absorb the basic norms and values of their culture. This is the first and most important stage of socialisation, which usually takes place in the family during early childhood

prison: a building where criminals are forced to live as a punishment

private schools: schools that are funded by fees paid by the parents or guardians of learners; not run or controlled by the government

probation: serving a sentence, or part of it, in the community under supervision

progressive schooling: education which breaks away from traditional lessons and curriculum and focuses on experience

progressive taxation: when those who earn more pay a higher rate of tax on some of their earnings than those who earn less

proletariat: in the theory of Marxism, the proletariat are working-class people who must work to survive

property crime: theft of or intentional damage to things owned by an individual, group or organisation

pro-school sub-culture: a group of learners whose norms and values agree with those of the school

protest group: a group of people who protest in order to bring about a change in society

pull factors: reasons attracting people to a new country

push factors: reasons for leaving a country

qualitative data/research: information (such as attitudes or kinds of actions) that cannot be presented in numerical form. Qualitative research generates this kind of data

quantitative data/research: information and facts that take a numerical form. Quantitative research generates this kind of data

questionnaire: a standardised list of questions used in social surveys

quota sampling: when the researcher decides in advance how many people with certain characteristics to involve in the research and then identifies them

racism: prejudice or discrimination against an individual or group because of their perceived ethnicity or race

random sampling: when each person has an equal chance of being selected

reconstituted family: a new family created when someone remarries after divorce or the death of a partner

redistribution of wealth: the transfer of some of the income and wealth from richer individuals to those who are poorer, through systems such as taxation and welfare payments

rehabilitation: re-educating or retraining offenders to try to prevent further offending

relative deprivation: feeling disadvantaged in comparison to others in your society

relativity of culture: the idea that all cultures vary and change; culture is not fixed, but relative to time and place

reliability: when research can be repeated to produce similar responses

religious sub-culture: a sub-culture based on religious faith and practices which are distinct from those of the wider culture

representativeness: the degree to which research findings about one group can be applied to a larger group or similar groups

reserve army of labour: people who are employed when an economy is booming or when they are needed, but who find themselves out of work when they are not required

response rate: the proportion of people in the original sample who actually take part in the research, for example, by completing and returning the questionnaire

retribution: punishments intended as a means of revenge for wrongdoing

role: the patterns of behaviour expected of someone because of their status in society

role allocation: sorting individuals into appropriate jobs and roles based on achievement in school

role modelling: when someone acts as an example, so their behaviour is copied by others

role models: people someone looks up to and tries to be like

same-sex family: two adults of the same-sex – two males or two females – raising their own or adopted children

sample: the group of people on whom research is carried out, used to represent the target population

sampling frame: a list of all (or most) members of a target population from which the sample is chosen

sampling methods/techniques: the different ways in which samples can be chosen

sanctions: ways of rewarding or punishing acceptable or unacceptable behaviour; usually used in the sense of punishment (negative sanctions)

sandwich generation: middle-aged adults who care for their ageing parents, as well as for their children. *See also* **pivot generation**

scaled questions: closed questions where the possible answers cover a range of statements or opinions

scientific method: the way in which scientists work, by observing, formulating and testing hypotheses, analysing the results and drawing conclusions

secondary data: information collected earlier by researchers or other organisations and used later by a sociologist

secondary socialisation: later socialisation, when people learn more specific norms for particular statuses and roles

secularisation: the process by which religion has become less important in the daily lives of many people in modern industrial societies

segregated conjugal roles: the partners in a family take distinct roles (for example, the husband as breadwinner); assumed to be normal in the traditional nuclear family

selective education: when schools choose their learners, usually based on their ability

self-fulfilling prophecy: when people are aware of certain expectations and so they act in ways that make those expectations come true

self-report studies: research that asks people what crimes or deviant acts they have committed

semi-structured interview: an interview with some standardised questions, but allowing the researcher some flexibility on what is asked and in what order

serial monogamy: when someone has more than one marriage partner during their life, but only one at a time

setting: when children are taught a particular subject with other children of a similar ability

single-parent family: one parent and their dependent children living together. *See also* **lone parent family** *and* **one-parent family**

single-person household: when only one person lives in a residence. *See also* **one-person household**

single-sex schools: schools which only accept either male or female learners

slavery: a stratification system in which one group or individual is treated as the legal property of another group or individual

snowball sampling: when one respondent puts the researcher in contact with others

social class: a shared economic and social status; for example, working class, middle class or upper class

social cohesion: the sense of belonging and amount of connectedness between groups in society

social conformity: acting in accordance with norms and social expectations in order to fit in with others

social construction: the idea that social situations and events are made by societies; they do not exist in nature as independent things

social control: ways in which members of society are made to conform to norms and values

social differentiation: the assignment of different roles and statuses to groups and individuals within a society

social exclusion: when society does not provide a group with the rights and benefits available to others in the same society

social facts: laws, values, customs and other social rules over which individuals have no control

social factors: things that affect lifestyle and life chances, such as wealth, religion and occupation

social identity: an individual's perception of themselves, based partly on ideas about how others see them

socialisation: the process of learning the norms and values of a culture

social inequality: the differences between groups in a stratification system; for example, in income or wealth

social media: internet-based applications for sharing content and communicating online, such as Instagram and Weibo

social mobility: the movement of individuals or groups up or down the social hierarchy

social stratification: a hierarchy in which groups have different statuses and different levels of privilege

standardised testing: when all learners take the same assessments, which are marked in the same way

state schools: schools that are funded and run, directly or indirectly, by the government

status: a position that someone has in a society; status can be ascribed (fixed by others) or achieved

status frustration: when people (particularly working-class males) feel frustrated because they are unable to achieve respect from their peers due to their position in society

stereotype: an oversimplified set of ideas about a particular type of person or social group

stereotyping: applying and acting upon an oversimplified set of ideas about a particular type of person or social group

stop and search: a tactic used by the police when they stop and search a person they identify as suspicious, to look for evidence of wrongdoing

strain theory: Merton's explanation of crime as resulting from a mismatch between society's goals and the socially approved means of achieving them

stratified sampling: when the sampling frame is divided, for example by gender or age

streaming: when children are taught all subjects in classes with other children of a similar ability

structured interview: an interview in which the questions are standardised (the same questions are asked in the same order) and the responses organised to produce quantitative data

sub-culture: a group of people within a larger culture which has its own distinctive norms and values

subjectivity: allowing a personal point of view to influence understanding and interpretation

surveillance: observing and monitoring people's behaviour as a form of social control

surveys: large-scale pieces of research which tend to generate quantitative data through methods such as questionnaires or structured interviews

symmetrical family: a family in which the roles of the partners are equal

systematic sampling: when there is a regular pattern in selecting from the sampling frame, for example, every tenth name on a list

targeting: when the police focus on a particular group of people, because they believe they are more likely to be involved in criminal behaviour than others

target population: the whole group that the research relates to and to whom the findings of the research will be applied

trends: changes over time in a particular direction

triangulation: use of two or more methods in the same research project

triple shift: in addition to paid work and housework, women take on emotional work in the family, supporting other family members with their worries and concerns

underclass: a group below the working class that is effectively cut off from the rest of society

universal basic income: when the government pays everyone a fixed amount of money as a regular income

universal education: schooling provided for all children, regardless of their background

unschooling: informal learning without lessons or a curriculum, in which the learner chooses what and how to learn

unstructured interview: an interview without set questions that usually involves exploration of emotions and attitudes, leading to qualitative data

urbanisation: the growth of cities; when a higher proportion of the population live in cities

validity: the extent to which research findings reflect reality and give a true picture

value consensus: widespread agreement on values

values: standards shared by members of a culture and used to judge whether behaviour is right or wrong

verstehen: a German word used to mean identifying with another person or group and seeing things from their point of view

vertically extended family: a family with parent(s) and children living with relatives from one or more other generations (for example, grandparents)

vertical segregation: differences in the number of people from different groups (such as the sexes) occupying different levels within an employment hierarchy

victim surveys: research that asks people what crimes they have been victims of

vigilante groups: self-appointed people with no legal authority who punish people they believe are offenders

virtual community: an online group of individuals who share interests, personal opinions or backgrounds

vocationalism: vocational education that prepares people for work or trains them for particular jobs or careers

'warm bath' theory: the functionalist theory that the family can act like a 'warm bath' for its members, especially men; for example, by soothing away the pressures of their day at work and making them feel relaxed and happy

wealth: money, savings and property that can be bought and sold to generate income

welfare state: a system in which the government of a country provides services (such as free education and healthcare) and gives financial support to those who need it (such as the unemployed and the long-term sick), paid for by taxes

white-collar crime: non-violent crime committed by middle-class people for financial gain; for example, fraud, embezzlement, bribery and identity theft

youth sub-culture: a sub-culture of adolescents or young adults who are usually distinguishable by their style, dress and/or musical preferences

> Acknowledgements

Reference: Henrich, J. (2021) *The weirdest people in the world: how the West became psychologically peculiar and particularly prosperous*, Harmondsworth: Penguin.

The authors and publishers acknowledge the following sources of copyright material and are grateful for the permissions granted. While every effort has been made, it has not always been possible to identify the sources of all the material used, or to trace all copyright holders. If any omissions are brought to our notice, we will be happy to include the appropriate acknowledgements on reprinting.

Figure 1.7 Homicide rate per 100,000 population from https://www.unodc.org/unodc/en/data-and-analysis/global-study-on-homicide.html; *Figure 1.8* Major source countries of refugees 2014-2015, UNHCR; *Figure 1.9* Life expectancy graph Data Source: Riley (2005), Clio Infra (2015), and UN Population Division (2019), OurWorldinData.org/life-expectancy

Thanks to the following for permission to reproduce images:

Cover Don Farrall/Getty Images; *Inside* **Unit 1** C.J. Burton/GI; Bettmann/GI; Everett Collection Inc/Alamy Stock Photo; Andrew Burton/GI; Sorbetto/GI; We Are/GI; Mutlu Kurtbas/GI; Salvador-Aznar/GI; Maki Nakamura/GI; Thomas Barwick/GI; Hinterhaus Productions/GI; Stephen Lovekin/GI; Kasayizgi/GI; **Unit 2** Peterpencil/GI; Kei Uesugi/GI; Brothers91/GI; Brandon Bell/GI; Manan Vatsyayana/GI; Svetikd/GI; Constantinis/GI; Hugh Sitton/GI; Hispanolistic/GI; Daniel Allan/GI; Hill Street Studios/GI; Paul Linse/GI; SDI Productions/GI; Track5/GI; Peopleimages/GI; South_Agency/GI; Cindy Ord/GI; Morsa Images/GI; 10'000 Hours/GI; Anand Purohit/GI; Peter Dazeley/GI; The Good Brigade/GI; Rawpixel/GI; Virojt Changyencham/GI; David Malan/GI; **Unit 3** Didier Marti/GI; Mickywiswedel/GI; Powerofforever/GI; Bloomberg/GI; Fadel Senna/GI; Hadynyah/GI; Omer Messinger/GI; markhanna/GI; Catherine Delahaye/GI; Ashley Cooper/GI; Keystone/GI; S0ulsurfing - Jason Swain/GI; Aerialperspective Images/GI; AGF/GI; **Unit 4** Compassionate Eye Foundation/Gary Burchell/GI; Maskot/GI; Kypros/GI; Maskot/GI; Xinhua/Alamy Stock Photo; Granger-Historical Picture Archive/Alamy Stock Photo; Smile/GI; Wavebreakmedia/GI; Eternity In An Instant/GI; Imagebroker/Doukdouk/GI; Anvr/GI; Skynesher/GI; Andersen Ross/GI; Thanasis Zovoilis/GI; **Unit 5** Bartosz Hadyniak/GI; Klaus Vedfelt/GI; SolStock/GI; Hill Street Studios/GI; Tim Graham/Alamy Stock Photo; Giuseppe Cacace/GI; Future Publishing/GI; Johnnygreig/GI; Mediaphotos/GI; John Slater/GI; David Leahy/GI; Will & Deni Mcintyre/GI; Westend61/GI; Peter Cade/GI; Pondsaksit/GI; Seventyfour/GI; Philippe Lissac/GI; kali9/GI; **Unit 6** Kali9/GI; Ipggutenbergukltd/GI; Peter Cade/GI; Liubomyr Vorona/GI; Stockbyte/GI; Undefined Undefined/GI; Boonchai Wedmakawand/GI; Donald Iain Smith/GI; Newstreetphoto/GI; Handout/GI; Gajus/GI; Ashley Cooper/GI; Mirrorpix/GI; Richard Ross/GI; Thinkstock Images/GI; Tim Drivas Photography/GI; Kali9/GI; Tiro83/GI

Key: GI = Getty Images

> Index